Bereavement

Its Psychosocial Aspects

Bereavement

Its Psychosocial Aspects

Edited by
Bernard Schoenberg
Irwin Gerber
Alfred Wiener
Austin H. Kutscher
David Peretz
Arthur C. Carr

with the editorial assistance of
Lillian G. Kutscher

Columbia University Press
New York and London 1975

All royalties from the sale of this book are assigned to the Foundation of Thanatology, a tax exempt, not for profit, public research and educational foundation dedicated to education and research efforts in studying the psychosocial problems inherent in dying, death, loss, grief, and recovery from bereavement.

Library of Congress Cataloging in Publication Data
Main entry under title:

Bereavement, its psychosocial aspects.

    Includes bibliographies.
    1. Bereavement—Psychological aspects.
I. Schoenberg, Bernard. [DNLM: 1. Attitude to
death. 2. Grief. BF798.D4 B487]
BF575.G7B47   155.9'37   75-16422
ISBN 0-231-03974-3

Acknowledgment

The editors wish to acknowledge the support and encouragement of the Foundation of Thanatology in the preparation of this volume.

Thanatology, as a new subspecialty of medicine, is involved in scientific and humanistic inquiries and the application of the knowledge derived therefrom to the subjects of the psychological aspects of dying; reactions to loss, death and grief; and recovery from bereavement.

The Foundation of Thanatology, a tax exempt public foundation, is dedicated to advancing the cause of enlightened health care for the terminally ill patient and his family. The Foundation's orientation is a positive one based on the philosophy of fostering a more mature acceptance and understanding of death and the problems of grief and the more effective and humane management and treatment of the dying patient and his bereaved family members.

Foreword

Services for the Bereaved:
A Social-Medicine Perspective

Victor W. Sidel

Every person looks at issues from the point of view of his special interests, and therefore it will come as no surprise that my thoughts lie at the interface between the issues of bereavement and those of social medicine and community health. I shall address three points of this interface: health-services planning, community organization, and the training and role of health workers.

With regard to health-services planning, some of the work that those who study bereavement are doing seems to demonstrate the value of some form of intervention with the family at the time of bereavement. This evidence of effectiveness should be taken into account by health-care workers in their planning of services. But the planners will also need "incidence" data in order to determine how great a need exists for such services. For example, they will need to know the age distribution of people in the community and the age-specific death rate.

To illustrate this very briefly, let us consider the Bronx. In some areas of the South Bronx less than five percent of the population is over 65; in some areas of the North Bronx, more than 20 percent of the population is over 65. In the South Bronx the population profile is very similar to profiles of South Asia, Africa, and Latin America—what the Chinese call a "pagoda" of age distribution, in which there are many young people and very few people of older age. In the northern part of the borough, however, such as the area

Adapted, as a Foreword, from a manuscript containing numerous illustrations which are not reproduced here.

which surrounds Montefiore Hospital, the pyramid almost stands on its head, with very few people of young age and many people of older age. In 1950, approximately eight percent of the people in this area—as in the United States as a whole—were over 65. By 1970, at a time that approximately 10 percent of the U.S. population was 65 and over, the figure for this area of the North Bronx had reached 22 percent. The reason for this, of course, is that younger people have moved to the suburbs, leaving their parents and grandparents behind.

Closely related to change in age distribution is change in the leading causes of death. In 1900, the leading causes of death in the U.S. were influenza, pneumonia, tuberculosis, and gastroenteritis; now they are heart disease, cancer, and stroke. If bereavement researchers or health planners are to be appropriately responsive to the service implications of bereavement studies for their community, they will also have to keep in mind issues of age distribution, numbers of deaths, and causes of death.

In short, the planning, delivery, and evaluation of services for the bereaved is yet another example of how those who are concerned with the provision of services on a one-to-one basis to the individual seeking help can join forces with those concerned with the patterns of illness and of death in the community and with the provision of services to all its members. In this way the sometimes seemingly conflicting goals of providing optimal service to the individual and of providing optimal service to the community—the latter including such problems as recognizing and meeting the changing needs and demands for service and finding ways to allocate resources so as to minimize inequities in the provision of services and to maximize efficiency and effectiveness—can best be brought together and used to strengthen rather than to weaken each other.

The second point I want to make deals with community organization. It is my view that human services should not only be responsive to immediate needs, such as those of people who are bereaved, but that the organization of such services should serve two additional purposes: they can be used as ways to bring out the best "helping" abilities of those who live in a community and therefore as tools to bring communities together. As an illustration, the People's Republic of China offers such models of organization of human services. Human services are decentralized to the most local level at which they possibly can be given. The kind of support and service that are required in bereavement would be given in China at the group level.

In the typical courtyard of a Chinese city, people of different families and of all ages live together, in a tightly knit group. Within this kind of a group, there is a network of support systems, including health workers recruited from the neighborhood and trained for brief periods of time—a pattern that simply does not exist in communities in the United States. There is a sense of togetherness and common purpose, unlike the fragmentation and alienation that is all too common here.

It is important that, as techniques are developed to help with bereavement, they be translated not just into more work for highly trained professionals but also into tools for putting underused and undersatisfied people into the role of serving their neighbors, thereby helping to bring communities back together.

Finally, we must consider the relationship of the need for help with bereavement and its problems to the training and the role of the "professional" health worker, and particularly that of the physician. An image of the physician at an earlier, less technological time depicted him seated, figuratively and often literally, at the bedside of the sick or dying patient, and sharing the patient's and the family's concern. Today the image has largely changed. An advertisement in a medical journal shows "a modern coronary arteriography laboratory." The patient is surrounded by the most complex equipment, but not a single other human being is shown; no one explains what is happening, or comforts the patient. Those who study bereavement and its problems may also help find ways to lead medicine back out of the technological morass in which it finds itself increasingly entrapped and back to its tradition of caring.

A study of bereavement, its problems, and the techniques of effective intervention is certainly vital to meet the needs of the bereaved. Equally vital is the need for all that is learned to be viewed in a larger social context and to be integrated into health services planning, community organization, and the roles and training of health workers.

Preface

Austin H. Kutscher and Lillian G. Kutscher

As clinical impressions concerning the psychosocial and physical changes experienced by the dying patient have gradually been supported by more objectively accumulated data, a number of potential mechanisms for making beneficial changes in his psychosocial environment have been conceptualized. Studies have been instituted to evaluate approaches to improved patient care. Due recognition has gradually been given to the extraordinarily complicated and virtually uncontrollable physical deterioration and to the frequently inadequate support provided by caregivers who have been educated in a tradition that has accented disease and not person, cure and not care. In studying these aspects of dying, more progressive investigators and caregivers are striving to work within the concept of studying a living patient in the dying process, whenever possible. Yet it has become painfully apparent that intensive concentration on the problems of the dying, however much it has included some emphasis on the problems of the living, has probably distracted workers from a parallel concentration on the needs of survivors. Caring for the dying is a response to a necessary professional commitment; but there is also a more dimly recognized but not necessarily less urgent call for attention to the problems of those who are being exposed to anticipatory grief, acute grief, and bereavement. Although one individual dies, a family and a community of other individuals are left bereaved. Compounding this discrepancy in number, the literature, to date, seems to indicate that for every dozen professionals involved with the dying patient, only a few are involved in the continuing problems of the bereaved-to-be and the bereaved.

Unquestionably, the dynamics of bereavement demand the deepest exploration. Bereavement is a psychosocial process for individuals; extending beyond a circumscribed boundary, it is a cultural and social issue for the community and the public. Some survivors need direct physical care; others require crisis intervention or, if pathologic bereavement ensues after a prolonged period of unresolved grief, psychiatric care; many more need practical solutions for practical problems; but all, whether from within their own emotional resources or with the assistance of concerned caregivers, must develop coping mechanisms to facilitate healthy resolution of grief, acceptance of the loss without the repression of normal emotions, reinforcement of the fact that life must go on, and even vision that reveals that tragedies may be transformed into positive growth experiences.

When dysfunction occurs following a significant loss, therapeutic measures must often be taken that are supportive to the bereaved individual and, thereby, productive for the community to which he belongs, to which he must contribute, and in which he must survive. If such dysfunction can be predicted, as a result of research studies directed at identifying "high risk" survivors, perhaps some or all of the most threatening and damaging aspects of bereavement can be avoided. Since bereavement is fertile ground for the development of illness, both emotional and physical, therapeutic measures may often be indicated and, without any doubt, these measures must be conceptualized on a base of highly sophisticated scientific principles.

Yet care must be taken lest the humanitarian dimensions of psychosocial concepts be diminished by intellectual detachment. Although the approaches to studying bereavement must be objective and advanced from a perspective of scientific criteria, research designs must give appropriate consideration to the concept that highly subjective and tumultuous human sensitivities are being delved into, touched on, and examined. The gut emotion of bereavement is one of the most compelling experiences of life and can neither be quantified nor qualified by totally objective standards. As pioneers searching for objective measurements in the field of thanatology, we must also consider with humility life's experiential lessons.

In this collection of essays, the multidisciplinary approach (always implicit in our endeavors) has been taken. The contributors have examined the psychosocial aspects of bereavement and have formed insights from sociological research; clinical studies based on psychiatric, psychological, and physiological determinations; and theoretical designs that have been augmented by anecdotal information. The value of interdisciplinary health support systems, the usefulness of self-help groups, and the prospects of methods of crisis intervention with all age groups are a few among the significant topics considered. The contributors and editors have attempted to bring scientific rigor and as much emphasis on research as was possible to their investigations without doing disservice to the complexities of bereavement.

AUSTIN H. KUTSCHER
LILLIAN G. KUTSCHER

Contents

Part Three. The Bereaved Family

Part Four. The Health Professional

Part Five. Therapeutic Intervention

Index

List of Tables

Part One

Fundamental Concepts

1

Bereavement as a Relative Experience

Arthur C. Carr

As a response to the loss of a loved person, grief is a universal reaction experienced by all individuals at some time in life. As one's interdependence on others grows, particularly through familial ties, the likelihood increases that one must also face separation, loss, and death, which elicit intense feelings of grief and mourning. The capacity that makes one capable of warm, satisfying relationships also leaves one vulnerable to sadness, despair, and grief when such relationships are disrupted.

Intense grief is easily recognized through signs of sadness and depression, which bear a temporal relationship to major separation or loss of some kind, frequently that caused by death of a loved person. During such an experience, the sympathy and attention of others are important supports which make the loss more tolerable and continued living more viable.

Generally not recognized, however, is the degree to which we are continually subjected to separations and losses which are so subtle or so well disguised that they may never be recognized or acknowledged. To a surprising degree, we are confronted with and tested by loss and separation throughout life. In many instances, such experiences or the reaction to them may be barely apparent even to the person himself. In other instances, they may be keenly experienced but custom or pride may preclude the possibility of the person sharing or expressing his sadness.

As ordinarily described, growth and development are pictured in positive terms. In the change from childhood to adulthood, from helpless depen-

An earlier version of this chapter appeared under the title, "A Lifetime of Preparation for Bereavement," in *But Not to Lose,* ed. A. H. Kutscher (New York: Fell, 1969), pp. 132–37.

dency to maturity, from childish naiveté to wisdom, from physical smallness to full development (changes which are normal and taken for granted), growth is ordinarily conceived of as *becoming,* in the sense of something developing or being added, something more or other than existed previously. Very seldom does one consider that loss, whether of a possession, a function, a value, an ideal, or a relationship, also is part of development and contributes to it.

From the time of birth, the growing child has constant experiences with loss. Perhaps the most significant one, which is generally emphasized by authorities, is that represented by the experience of weaning when the mother is no longer automatically available to gratify the infant's needs. At a time when the child has not developed full awareness of the distinction between what is his and what is not, what is subject to his control and what is not, weaning can be an experience of great consequence. How this separation and loss, a positive growth step, are integrated by the child determines his future capacity for coping with frustration and deprivation. This experience establishes the model for the way in which all later losses are handled: such significant attitudes as his basic optimism or despair, his passive resignation or the angry unwillingness to "let go," his assumed benevolence or malevolence of "fate," may stem from this early loss.

Authorities believe that the child's separation from the mother is facilitated by use of "transitional phenomena" (objects such as a doll, toy, or "security blanket") which serve as a link to the mother when she is out of the child's sight. The texture and odor of the chosen object are often important in representing its meaning as a security symbol, compensating for loss of the mother's presence.

But loss and separation are the recurring themes of human existence and development, quite apart from such major events as weaning. The first haircut, even when responded to with anticipation and pride by the child and the family, is an early experience of a separation from the body of a part that is one's own. At a time when the child's growth and development command interest and attention in the family, the child is also losing teeth, hair, and baby possessions—dolls, toys, dress, the cradle, and even the license to behave as a child. All of these are viewed by others as no longer appropriate for the "big" boy or girl. The child's increased motility, which opens new avenues for exploration, at the same time deprives him of the continuities and sameness that were previously available. Bowel training, while adding to his sense of independence, focuses on possessions that were in and of the body but that are now removed and disparaged as objects to be rejected. With each step forward, there is an experience of loss accompanying the change.

In the course of growing up, there is a continued experience with separation and loss. Important values, real and symbolic, are associated with the body. The child's conception of and perception of his body—the "body-image"—become important aspects of how he feels about himself and how he relates to others. Changes in the body occur throughout life and must be integrated into this image, both in regard to the reality of the change and in regard to the feelings about it.

Since the body is an important mediator between the external environment and the self as a psychological entity, it is natural that one would experience mourning and depression when an individual body part is removed through accident or surgery. The loss of an arm or leg, for example, presents a difficult problem of adjustment in which actual mourning for the removed limb may be experienced. Hence, doctors have learned that to prevent unnecessarily painful reactions and to facilitate recovery from and adjustment to such a loss, it is beneficial to prepare the patient and to help him understand that the loved part of the body will be handled with respect and dignity.

But in contrast to such obviously traumatic separations as those that occur with loss of a limb are less dramatic occurrences, ones that are assumed to be happy experiences but that, in reality, are as real a loss and as real a disruption to one's body-image as the loss of a limb. Childbirth, for example, represents a loss of a part of oneself that to the pregnant woman may have symbolic or real values which predetermine a mourning reaction when the child is delivered. In the elation that may surround the birth, the separation and loss, not only of the baby but also of the position of importance and attention that must be relinquished to it, may be denied. Postpartum depressions, commonly seen several days after the birth and referred to as "the blues," are much more frequent than hospital records suggest.

Old age confronts us with increasing losses concerning the body and its functions. With a rapidity of change similar to that occurring in childhood, the aged person experiences changes in function, if not actual loss, of body parts. Changes occurring in the texture of the skin, in the quality and quantity of the hair, in energy level, and in sexual prowess are all examples of loss which are real and commonplace. "Change of life," involving loss of ability to have children, may be a particularly painful experience. For reasons of pride, "good taste," or "custom," many of these losses are not to be reacted to openly in our culture. The individual is not given the opportunity to express sadness, for there is a stress on everlasting youth and beauty which makes the realities of aging difficult to accept. "Maturity" may have positive connotations, but "growing old" is usually viewed as a misfortune.

As in the changes occurring in the body, the history of one's relationship with people is replete with experiences of loss and separation. Aside from the dramatic separations brought about through death, most people are constantly experiencing partings and separations, both temporary and permanent. As one passes from childhood into adulthood, friends, lovers, and often family members are separated. Changes in residence, occupation, or place of business often entail separation from associates with whom one has developed strong ties of affection. Even important successes in life—promotion, graduation, marriage—at the same time confront one with separation and loss. Crying at weddings and sentimentality about leaving "the old school" are common expressions of the reality of loss.

Many losses take on importance because of their symbolic meaning, thereby making the reactions to them appear out of proportion to reality. Even the loss of a symptom can be mourned, necessitating as it does the change of self-image which now no longer holds. Not generally recognized is our experience of loss in regard to fantasies and hopes. Loss of a *hope* may constitute a more significant loss than that of much more tangible possessions. As one becomes older, the awareness of "what could be" or "what might have been" frequently confronts one with the feeling of loss around which there may be unrecognized sadness and grief.

It is natural and normal for individuals who lose a loved one to experience feelings of sadness, loneliness, grief, and perhaps despair. Sometimes the depression may be partially masked by complaints of feelings of weakness, lethargy, poor appetite, inability to sleep, weight loss, physical discomfort, and irritability.

It takes time for the mourner to accept and integrate a significant loss and to achieve renewed feelings of optimism, interest, and vitality. Such "working through" often includes efforts to retain a link to the lost person through fond memories and recollections. Symbolic representations of the dead person in the form of preserved possessions may serve as painful or happy reminders of that person, which the mourner uses in a manner similar to how the child used "transitional phenomena" to represent the mother in the process of separating from her. In the course of normal mourning, the mourner may adopt certain mannerisms or characteristics of the dead person, in an unconscious effort to perpetuate the loved one. Such "identification" serves a useful function in adjusting to a profound loss.

However, if feelings of guilt or loss of self-esteem become too prominent in reacting to a loss, there is the possibility that something has interfered with the normal mourning process. This may happen if the mourner is unable to recognize that in the relationship with the lost person there were negative feelings, as well as those of love. Most relationships are characterized by both love and hate (ambivalence), although these feelings may be particularly difficult to accept. When such awareness cannot be tolerated by the mourner, normal adjustment to the loss is more difficult. In the reparative efforts which then occur, the "identification" may be with the loved one's illness rather than with the person's loving characteristics. The frequency with which certain physical disorders develop after the individual has experienced a loss or separation has been explained on this basis by many investigators. Also, when the mourning process goes awry, unusual reactions (anniversary reactions) may be experienced on the anniversary of an event important in relation to the deceased. At such a time, the person is not consciously aware of the temporal relationship between the past event and the present reaction.

Regardless of how effective the mourning process is, adjustment can be made only through the passage of time. Often such events as birthdays, anniversaries, and holidays must be experienced at least once after the loss before adjustment can occur. One by one, once-shared occasions or celebrations are experienced without him or her and, in time, permit the gradual withdrawal of emotional investment in the past. The expressions "it will take time" or "time heals all wounds" thus have intrinsic wisdom. Inherent in such expressions is the recognition that a period of mourning is a normal reaction to loss or separation.

If mourning is accepted as an understandable, normal response to loss or separation, it suggests that to some degree we are always in mourning, although not necessarily clinically depressed. Losses, specific and nonspecific, are constantly presenting themselves and must be dealt with, if only on the periphery of our awareness. Because we are constantly experiencing losses, we are routinely struggling with the task of integrating them. Mourning is thus a relative and continuous process associated with all events which entail some type of loss, separation, or withdrawal of emotional investment.

What, then, are the implications of this thesis? It would seem that we bring to any major crisis a backlog of experience which helps prepare us for integrating a present tragedy. Awareness of the success demonstrated in the past should help us recognize the strength and resiliency dormant within us. Likewise, a present reaction may sometimes seem more bearable when it is made explicit that the person who is reacting to recent loss is behaving as in previous separations. Frequently, the intensity of such a reaction becomes meaningful only when we understand our earlier losses and separations. Present reactions which may seem unusually intense even to the person involved become more understandable with the realization that the reaction is not only to the present loss but to earlier losses as well. Increased awareness of the mourning processes which are ever-present within us can also greatly expand our capacity for sympathy and compassion for people who are in the more extreme stages of the continuum of bereavement.

Loss, then, is a continual experience; bereavement, as a matter of degree, is an unceasing state. Its ubiquity, its diversity in expression, and its sometimes unrecognized yet other times intolerable effects make bereavement one of the greatest challenges facing students of human behavior and particularly health personnel involved in the management of its acute states. The understanding a culture can bring to the bereavement process may well be a measure of its basic humanity.

Bereavement as Indispensable for Growth

Ned H. Cassem

Loss is by definition negative, the deprivation of a cherished object; at best it is regarded as a necessary evil. Bereavement may, in spite of itself, prove to be a good teacher for some, but few of us seek it out. Those who do are called masochists, a term we seldom apply to ourselves. Growth is by definition positive, is sought after (at least consciously) by all, and when labeled as "personal growth" or "maturity" is usually claimed as a possession by most of us to some degree (usually to a greater degree than those who know us will concede). What does bereavement or loss have to do with personal growth? Granted, the ability to sustain, integrate, and recover from loss is instantly accepted as a mark of personal maturity. Tragedy and adversity have often challenged, activated, or highlighted the loftiest sentiments and behavior in human history, so much so that systematic psychologies, such as those of Frankl or Adler, have been organized around behavioral responses to loss. Yet here the person grows in spite of the loss or disaster that has befallen him or her. Can the concept of loss be viewed as more, as somehow integral to the growth process itself?

Parkes (1972) in his extensive analysis of bereavement follows Bowlby's characterization of loss as the rupture of an attachment. The strength of the attachment determines the intensity of the trauma inflicted when it is broken. In matters of personal growth it is important to recall that the first love object is the self. The attachments to this love object are multiple and varied and include comfort, pleasure, activity, knowing, independence, roles, certain "styles of life" which we cherish ourselves living out. Summed up, these attachments can be viewed as defining the extent and limits of one's narcissism. All loss is narcissistic bereavement because all loss is personal, and loss viewed as narcissistic trauma is therefore our focus here. What is the relationship, then, between ruptured attachments to self (narcissistic injury) and personal growth? There are five conditions under which loss can be viewed as indispensable to personal growth.

Conditions Where Loss and Growth Are Identical

Few attachments are as powerfully felt as the attachment to one's mother. The narcissistic perspective of this attachment is the security experienced by the child in the mother's presence and the intense anxiety at the anticipation of separation. Development of autonomy in the child depends on the mutual success of mother and child in breaking the hold of this attachment. If the intensity remains unbroken, emotional growth is retarded. In such an instance the narcissistic loss is merely the mirror image of the gain in personal maturity.

Psychotherapy of dependency conflicts often involves an extension of this basic paradigm. The vice president of an organization who criticizes company policies and decisions outside of executive staff meetings and complains that no one listens to him, yet takes little initiative to implement or promote his ideas within the meetings, may feel too threatened to do otherwise. He maintains a position of relatively greater narcissistic comfort because maneuvering out of his hostile dependent position is more threatening and less gratifying than holding to it. Moreover, any effort to change would demand the painful loss of his cherished position as a brilliant but unappreciated (and therefore untested) inferior. For those who accept such growth challenges, the price can be a traumatic temporary upheaval which reciprocally recedes with the emergence of narcissistic relief and then gratification ("Look, Ma, no hands!") with success. For others the trauma may be too much. (Many a gifted person has been done in by a promotion.)

Sharing Others' Losses: Empathy as Narcissistic Insult and Transformation

Empathy and compassion are extolled as virtues of highest priority in interpersonal relations, particularly among the helping professions and religious or charitable organizations. Although many wonder why there is not more empathy around, perhaps insufficient attention has been given to the threatening or destructive components associated with its exercise. Kohut (1966) likens the instantaneous recognition of complex psychological states in empathy to the ability to recognize a face in a single perception. Regarding empathic understanding as part of innate human psychic equipment, he locates its origin in the primary empathy of the child with the mother, whose feelings and actions were, in the mental organization of the child, simply included in the child's self. In this experience the child is prepared for the discovery that the basic inner experiences of others are similar to his or her own. Kohut points out, therefore, that the comprehension of another's state given in empathic understanding comes through "the perception of experiential identities" (p. 263). I believe that this also accounts for the shortage of empathy, particularly for the most difficult cases where it is most needed.

Marvin was a ten-year-old boy dying of a widely spread lymphosarcoma. It was painful to look at him. He was bald from chemotherapy and his face was distorted by swollen lips and proptotic eyes that had recently become sightless. Because of the meningeal spread of his malignancy, he tended to remain motionless to reduce the occasional excruciating pains. Completely lucid, he was irritable, but when he tried to speak his swollen lips made his speech hard to understand, which only made him more irritable. On his last hospital admission, when it became clear that no further remissions would be coming, the staff and his parents made plans to have him cared for at home. When his parents arrived on the designated day, they found the boy in a deserted waiting area outside the ward, alone, miserable, crying softly. A shopping bag with his clothes and belongings stood next to him.

At home Marvin's bed was placed downstairs, close to all household traffic. He asked to talk to all visitors, including his own schoolmates and those of his three brothers. On learning of this situation a family relative took the child's father aside and sharply criticized the move home. It was cruel to the child, he said, to have him exposed to all the visitors at such a time. The advice was ignored, of course, and Marvin died at home two weeks later.

The vignette illustrates two examples of empathic failure, where empathic comprehension was avoided or repressed. Compassion is difficult because it demands what the word says: to *suffer with* the other person. By depositing the boy outside the ward in isolation, the staff members, who were generally very good throughout the course of his illness, were saying "Get him out of here, we cannot stand him. His presence is unbearable." The narcissistic identification with the child, which was intolerable and led to the blockade of a compassionate response, is clearer in the second instance. When the relative stated that Marvin's homecoming was cruel to the child, the child he was really talking about was that inner child within himself, whom he wished to shield from the cruel realities of disfigurement, pain, and death.

Kohut (1966) lists empathy as one of the ways in which narcissistic drives can be redirected with resultant personal (ego) growth. But if empathy is to be exercised with persons who are suffering, it cannot be achieved without some sacrifice of the grandiose fantasies of power, greatness, and invulnerability attributed to the self. As a consequence, some degree of loss—some fracture of the narcissistic attachments to the grandiose self (or at least to grandiose wishes)—is a requisite for this type of personal achievement.

Loss As a Developmental Showdown: To Grow or Else

Nobody welcomes loss. Yet the ability to integrate misfortune with restoration of equilibrium is a mark of maturity. Always unwelcome and usually unexpected, loss has a way of putting a person's maturity to the test. Some persons fail this most stringent of life's examinations, while others appear to achieve new levels of growth. At times the latter can be unexpected as the following example illustrates.

A 51-year-old man, left quadriplegic when his Volkswagen was crushed between a truck and a bus, was transferred after one month in a general hospital to a chronic rehabilitation center. Given little hope for recovery of even limited function, he cursed the futility of the transfer and openly regretted that his accident had not been fatal.

His history revealed that when he was two, his father left home because of his mother's marital infidelities. His mother, described by the patient as openly promiscuous after this time, abandoned him at age 12, leaving him with a deep mistrust of people, especially women. He also believed that although he could maintain a friendship for a certain time, he was not sufficiently appealing a person for anyone to develop a permanent investment in him. He married at age 19, aware of doubting whether his wife really loved him. When their only son was 10, she began to see another man during the patient's protracted absences from home. These absences appeared strategically placed so as to encourage, if not to insure, these actions on her part. During the summer his son turned 12, the patient took the boy on a long trip without the wife, but returned home several days earlier than his announced arrival date. Finding the other man living in the house, he denounced his wife's infidelity, took his son and left, bitterly convinced that no woman could love him faithfully. Eight years later he remarried, "this time to a good woman," but he was aware of his fear that one day she would leave him. Working two jobs to provide a comfortable income, he described their 12 years of marriage prior to the accident as happy, but once he had been stricken by the accident, he became convinced she would leave him ("and I couldn't blame her"). Instead, for the next nine months she daily traveled the 40 miles to the hospital. To his surprise he gradually recovered a good deal of function in both upper extremities. As discharge neared, he reviewed his past and his own anticipation of abandonment, weighing them against his wife's fidelity and the remarkable devotion of the staff (almost all women) who cared for him, undaunted by his initial negativity. "You know," he said, "this will sound crazy, but this experience, even with all I've lost, may be the best thing that ever happened to me. For the first time in my life, I think I really know what love means."

In the face of overwhelming loss, such as that visited on the man in the example, such ego transformations are probably rare. Certainly no one would prescribe personal disaster as a tonic to guarantee growth. In *Hour of Gold, Hour of Lead,* Ann Morrow Lindbergh (1973) observed: "I do not believe that sheer suffering teaches. If suffering alone taught, then all the world would be wise, since everyone suffers. To suffering must be added mourning, understanding, patience, love, openness and the willingness to remain vulnerable" (p. 212). Prior maturity is probably the best predictor of who can negotiate bereavement processes so as to grow. From the example of the quadriplegic, however, it is clear—not to mention reassuring—that the personal maturity of his wife and the hospital staff also had a great deal to do with the growth he achieved in the face of his injury. Psychologically he had to face himself as one no longer able to guarantee esteem by keeping two jobs going at once. In so doing he encountered his wife's deeper fidelity and feeling for him. By abandoning the more infantile position he could accept and return her love at a more mature level of integration.

The Bereavements of Growing Old

Despite the spas, silicone rejuvenation, and wonders of nose, face, and gluteus lifting, our protoplasmic limitations have a way of increasing relentlessly with age. The more juvenile of us continue to insist that we are swifter of foot than our sons or more flawless in complexion than our daughters. Such delusions are natural enough, but may block development of more acceptable traits which help the maintenance of self esteem, such as ability to listen, understanding, compassion, and other capacities that depend more on the central nervous system and less on skeletal muscle or integument for their function.

But how much loss can a person take and remain functional? No one considers senility a gift. In fact, discussion of such topics as senility, loss of speech, and paralysis evokes discussion of (positive) euthanasia. Almost every person envisions some limit to the degree of personal deterioration he would be willing to accept. When this is reached, death seems preferable to life. As one woman said, "I don't want to be a vegetable. If that time comes, I hope someone will have enough sense to let me die in peace."

Living wills are written to prevent heroics at times when persons cannot be sure they can speak for themselves. What is often forgotten is that dispositions may change. It does seem that a number of older persons expand the limits of deterioration they are willing to tolerate as they grow older. In an interview in 1971, one month before he died, Igor Stravinsky discussed his own criteria or limits for tolerable losses with age.

Deterioration . . . is insidious, [but] . . . the lines shift or become indistinct. . . . I once thought that my own criterion for a proper time to pull the plug would be the moment when my more and more furtive memory had retreated to a point where I could no longer recollect which of my coevals was alive and which dead. But I have long since passed beyond that, and now simply, and on the whole correctly, assume that they are *all* dead. (p. 3)

The older person who can make such changes in his loss tolerance appears to have the advantage over the one who cannot.

Can this be equated with emotional growth? It is interesting to speculate that growth stops without such an adjustment. In fact, Semrad has said that the inability to integrate loss is the royal road to dementia. Such a viewpoint regards the refusal to face deterioration as itself a major contributor to it. Again, what seems to be necessary for growth is that the person allow some (more) of his cherished delusions of power and greatness to be diminished.

Facing Death

Encounters with death and the dying, although often involving sorrow and tragedy, frequently serve as reminders of the preciousness of life. Reflection on death may often serve to italicize the value of time and of life itself. Weisman once said that if Freud had begun with a death principle instead of a life principle, he would have had to postulate a life principle to account for all the positive associations evoked by thoughts of death—or, more precisely, those associations evoked by the process of coping with death. St. Augustine once said "Let death be thy teacher," emphasizing the actual use of a conceptualized personal death as a measuring rod to evaluate the eternal worth of a present act. For dying patients there can be a certain heightening of perception once they know that they have an incurable illness. A 25-year-old poet with Hodgkins disease said that after he knew about his illness many sensory experiences changed. When he walked in the woods or examined flowers he felt as though he had never really looked carefully at them or appreciated them before. In another instance, a priest described his repeated visits to a 58-year-old woman dying of burns over 65 percent of her body. Once, uncertain at what he might do for her, he read her a passage from Mark. When he finished, she said, "You know, that passage has been read by or to me many times, but I never really *heard* it before." He continued to read to her and her feeling persisted that she was finding a great deal of previously overlooked meaning in the scriptural passages. Perhaps the most eloquent expression of the manner in which coping with dying can emphasize the positive values of living came from a letter written by the 27-year-old wife of a man who, five months after it was diagnosed, died of a lymphosarcoma. About a week after he died, she wrote the following words to several of her friends:

One real cause for celebration for Mark during these last few months was not so much the knowledge that he would be mourned after he died, but the very real knowledge that he was loved while he lived. The time between January and May was for us a grace period, a gift—a chance to live deeply and openly with the knowledge of death, and to have made real to us the love and caring support of those around us. . . .

To all of you, I would say (as I'm sure Mark would wish me to)—live out your love for one another now. Don't assume the future; don't assume all kinds of healing time for the bruised places in your relationships with others. Don't be afraid to touch and share deeply and openly all the tragic and joyful dimensions of life.

In this example one gets a clear picture of how the rupture of an attachment can sharpen a person's appreciation for the object of the attachment. For some, facing death (whether it be one's own or the experiential identity aroused by another's) can focus attention on the positive aspects of living and the value of the time one has to be alive.

Kohut (1966) lists facing death among the transformations of narcissism in the healthy productive sense. Some persons are able to develop a sense of their lives as being part of a larger whole. Investment in this larger scheme gives them the sense of living *sub specie aeternitatis,* so to speak, but enlarges the scope of their self-preoccupation. Kohut sees this as a sort of "cosmic" narcissism and regards it as a healthy transformation of the ego. Achievement of such a state is clearly not possible without some violence being done to the more purely self-centered aspects of one's narcissism. Moreover, it does not seem that this sort of ego transformation or growth in maturity occurs in spite of the damage done to our narcissistic illusions of greatness, but actually because of it.

Summary

Five conditions have been presented in which loss seems indispensable for growth. In these cases the bereavement process was viewed as all but synonymous with ego development, i.e., personal growth. In all cases the losses involved inflicted narcissistic injuries of greater or lesser magnitude. To pretend that such injuries can be sustained without danger to ego function would be to forget that narcissistic injury, as Bibring (1953) has pointed out, is the basic mechanism of depression. There are innumerable cardiac cripples and nonfunctioning elderly persons to remind us of the ravages of depression in our time. Nevertheless, in order to grow personally, we must surrender some part of our grandiose, infantile delusions of omnipotence, greatness and invulnerability. Reality (adversity, losses, aging) guarantees an assault on these delusions. The extent to which they can be altered without devastation of self-esteem probably determines the degree of successful ego development. It is perhaps unorthodox, or at least paradoxical, to label this process bereavement. But there is need to mourn the infant within all of us, despite his reluctance to die. The more comfortably he is laid to rest, the less he will impair the mature, appreciative enjoyment of life that is left and the tranquil negotiation of adversities that remain. Bereaving and growing continue to the end.

REFERENCES

Bibring, E. 1953. "The Mechanism of Depression." In *Affective Disorders: Psychoanalytic Contribution to Their Study,* ed. P. Greenacre. New York: International Universities Press.

Kohut, H. 1966. "Forms and Transformations of Narcissism." *Journal of the American Psychoanalytic Association* 14:243–72.

Lindbergh, A. M. 1973. *Hour of Gold, Hour of Lead.* New York: Harcourt.

Parkes, C. M. 1972. *Bereavement: Studies of Grief in Adult Life.* New York: International Universities Press.

Stravinsky, I. 1971. "Stravinsky: The Last Interview." *New York Review of Books* 16:3–5.

On the Work of Mourning

Joseph H. Smith

Adult grief in response to major loss is historical in two senses. First, a dominant aspect of the work of mourning repeats in memory the world that included the lost object. Second, the mourning process itself has a history in the individual's characteristic ways of responding to loss in successive stages of life. However, this is no ordinary sequence on a par with responses to other repetitive events. The full history of response to loss must ultimately include response to all change; from the primitive "automatic" change in answer to fetal or infantile loss of equilibrium on through to the adult's complex modes of comprehending and responding to the manifold forms of transience.

Adults may respond to major loss with either a capacity to grieve or a particular inability to grieve known as depression. At first glance, the grieving person and the depressed person seem indistinguishable. Both are in despair, whether agitated or withdrawn. For the most part, both are unable to be interested in anything other than that which further increases their pain. Either can scarcely believe that pain and emptiness will ever cease; either can feel his or her life to be over or wish it to be. For both, time stands still. For both, the usual cycles of life may become meaningless, while world events may pass unnoticed.

However, in close acquaintanceship, and especially over time, crucial differences between the grieving and the depressed person become apparent. Although the interests of both tend toward that which increases their pain, for the mourner this means paying attention to whatever might be connected in any way with the person he mourns; everything noticed is connected or is brought into connection with the loss. While the pain is thus heightened, nevertheless there is in this way steadfast contact both with the object of mourning and also with the fact of irretrievable loss. The pain is not experienced as useless or meaningless. On the contrary, it is itself an acknowledgment of the loss, in comparison with which all else is without significance.

Depression might best be understood not primarily as an illness but as an effort of healing—an effort to grieve—that still only partially breaks through a set of all too prevalent defenses. The defenses, in part, are those which deny loss, separation, and separateness. For every person overtly depressed, there are a hundred others—fugitives from grief—often frantically immersed in everydayness as a way of covering their sorrow. The particular constellation of defenses that characterizes such denial may be especially sanctioned by elements of our own culture. But I must here forego further discussion of the depressive character—the person of basically depressive makeup, but without the symptom of depression itself.

In overt depression, the affective response we associate with major loss breaks through, but with a continuing denial of or inability on the part of the person to know for what or for whom there is a need to mourn, or even that a need to mourn exists. It is thus abortive grieving. In depression pain consciously seems useless and meaningless. Unconsciously, there is a hope to be magically rewarded for suffering by the restoration of consciously unacknowledged losses. At some level, the person is thus aware of a wish for the impossible. For this reason hopelessness is real in a different sense from the hopelessness of grief, where loss can be overtly acknowledged.

Depression is humiliating; grief may be acknowledged in humility or in angry protest or in a variety of other ways—even in humor—but it is not humiliating. In grief, one's actual guilt in relation to the lost object can be confessed. Depression, by reason of the continuing core denial of the actual loss, is a morass of unattached guilt, anger, and despair that tends to focus in an exaggerated protestation of one's own unworthiness, but that protestation is not so much an honest confession as an effort to enforce forgiveness. In depression, nothing works. The depressive seems painfully aware of this, yet often seems able only to redouble vain efforts. No form of human misery is more acutely demoralizing.

The task, of course, is to help the depressed person to mourn. This means helping the person to know what has been lost, that his pain is worthy of his own respect, and that real hope lies in acknowledging rather than denying loss.

I have elsewhere (Smith, 1973) contrasted bereavement and depression in terms of the nature of the identifications in each. Identification—the internalization of elements of one's world and making them a part of one-self—is crucial both in coping with loss and as a means of development (Loewald, 1962; 1973). Identification can thus function either as a defense, or for purposes of healing and growth (Hartmann, Kris and Loewenstein, 1946, p. 29; Stierlin, 1973); the former is likely in situations of threat or trauma, the latter in situations of trust.

In general, the identificatory style of the depressive person is of the defensive type. (An extreme example of identification as a defense is to identify with one's enemy.) This would imply a greater than average anxiety about separation in the family and a consequent tendency to use identification primarily in the service of denying loss, rather than as a means of mourning and growth. Identifications that occur in this context tend to be generally of a more ''in toto'' type (Ritvo and Solnit, 1959, pp. 81–82, 84), and they are more likely to incline toward the more threatening or hated aspects of the object than toward the loved and admired aspects. Such imperative identifications are simultaneously difficult to relinquish, and difficult to fully integrate.

Identifications for purposes of growth are not imperative, emergency, ''in toto'' internalizations. The various aspects of the objects can be experienced and specific ones can be relinquished or coordinated as enduring aspects of the self. The difference is between relatively enforced and relatively optional identifications. The latter tend to be with the loved and admired traits of the object.

The capacity to mourn, not fully possible until adolescence or beyond, is the achievement of the capacity to identify for purposes of growth, even though a major loss initiates the process, which is one of moving away from defense in the sense of repression or denial and toward the integration of experience in the service of growth.

Weigert (1961) wrote, ''Every creative process of sublimation is initiated by some labor of mourning.'' Casually, we understand healing to mean the process of recovering or being made whole from some disease, ailment, or wound. Psychological growth, on the other hand, we ordinarily understand as the achievement of higher levels of integration without the connotation of recovering from any defect. However, in essence, the distinction between the concepts of healing and growth is not so clear. It is likely that every step in growth—every new integration—is preceded by some degree of being undone or being at a loss.

In ordinary development, the significance of such small degrees of imbalance goes largely unnoted. Indeed it is likely that consciousness in the infant begins not in awareness of the need that has evoked it, but simply in focusing on percepts at hand, certain of which become constituted as objects of need through experience. Need can then be experienced as a wish for the object (Freud, 1900, p. 565; Ricoeur, 1970, p. 370). Primary ideation, feeling, and action are thus constituted and take their bearings in terms of the presence or absence of the object.

To stress the developmental significance of the absence of the object is of course at one level only to assert in terms of its negative—the crucial importance of the object's presence. Obviously, without the physical and psychological presence of the mother, the infant would not survive. Nevertheless, it is the absence of the object, with the accompanying inevitable delay in the gratification of need, that opens up a void in which physical need can become psychological need in the form of a wish for the object; this is the first step in psychological development. In the absence of the object, needs or drives become imperative, just as does the necessity of defenses against them.

I have moved radically from the emptiness we know in adult grieving or depression (with only a mention of a prior emptiness presupposed by all creative action), to the void in which the development of mind begins. We can hardly use the same words in comparing experience of such disparate levels. "Object," for instance, ordinarily implies the differentiation of self and object, which only begins with the first wish for what might better be termed a pre-object—presumably some fragment of a remembered prior experience of satisfaction.

Similar differences would have to be acknowledged in the meaning of emptiness, need, absence, deprivation, and gratification. However, notwithstanding the importance of such differences, there are also elements of identity that unite the primitive and advanced modes of these aspects of response to an absent object. It is important that these elements also be acknowledged—especially so in the effort to see the primitive experiences as stages in the gradual development of the adult capacity to mourn.

I shall here dwell briefly on the relationship of some of these early phenomena with their advanced counterparts. We infer two kinds of primitive response to the object's absence. One is simply a heightening of the need threshold. As primitive defense it is prototypical of adult repression. The second response (which we infer from dreams and from certain psychotic phenomena understood as regressive) is that of wish-fulfillment; this is seen when the object is hallucinated in the form of some perceptual fragment remembered from a prior experience of gratification—an event I referred to earlier as a first step in psychological development. This hallucination or "perceptual identity" is prototypical of adult forms of internalization.

While repression and internalization conceptualize a useful polarity in adult response (Loewald, 1973), the distinction could not be so clear in primitive function; advanced and more complex modes of response derive from simpler phenomena. This assumption's corollary is that concepts which can be clearly differentiated and assigned to a definite set of referents in adult behavior tend to lose that clarity and become fused when applied to primitive function (Bridgman, 1927, pp. 24 *passim*). I have suggested, for example, that primitive hallucination is a prototypical manifestation of internalization of the object. We assume that, in the infant, need evokes an image of the remembered object, which is thus brought into awareness and experienced as present. The object had been internalized to the extent of memory traces in the perceptual experience of a prior actual encounter. That internalization is manifested and also brought to a higher level in the act of imaging the object in its absence. However, this would not only be prototypical recall of the object, but also prototypical anticipation of the needed object. It is not only an introjection or internalization of the object, but also projection or externalization—a first step toward experiencing the object as other. The point is that we cannot speak of internalization or externalization before the differentiation of self and object and before the opening up of temporal dimensions; nor can we speak of recall or anticipation in the properly differentiated sense of those concepts. With this limitation in mind we can speak of such primitive behavior as internalization from one point of

view and externalization from another. Loewald (1962, p. 493) has characterized such primary forms of internalization and externalization as
boundary-establishing experience, the latter a presupposition of internalization or externalization proper.

As another polarity, repression and internalization might seem—even at
the primitive level—to be opposite responses to the absence of the object.
The raising of a need threshold is primal repression. It is the tendency to
shut out both the need and its object and thereby to shut out the development
of a coherent ego that such aliment and conflict foster. In primitive internalization, on the other hand, the image hallucinated represents both the
need and the absent object. However, there is also an internalizing aspect to
repression. The hallucinated image manifests the internalization of the absent object, with the emphasis on object and with the absent crossed out—
the object is experienced as present. In primal repression the absence of the
object is internalized with the emphasis on absence and with object crossed
out. What is internalized is the pure no-saying of the world. Both repression
and internalization would be necessary phases constituting self and object.
Both are involved in the internalization of delay and the change from passive
to active experience. The no-saying of the world becomes one's own no-
saying to the need, the world, and even a no-saying by the ego to the ego.
But the internalization of the capacity to "say" no in this primitive fashion
would be a presupposition of the capacity to say yes—to know and affirm
self and object at a higher level. Denial, in other words, is a stage not only
in the acceptance of reality, but also, primitively, in the actual constitution
of the reality of self and object in the mind of the infant.

As I have indicated, my purpose is to highlight both the continuity and the
differences between the extremes of primitive and advanced response to object loss. The earlier description of adult depression and grief reflects, I
believe, a gradient toward repression or denial in the development of the
depressive and a gradient toward internalization in the capacity to mourn. It
is a matter of the gradient and not a matter of either/or in the sense of *only*
repression or *only* internalization. Both have a continuing role in the development of psychic structure. Both are involved in some degree in every
change, in every step in learning, and in every phase of development.

Summary

I have attempted to show the central place of response to loss in human experience. Mourning is, of course, not to be understood only as the painful affect but also as the totality of the individual's response to a major loss; mourning manifests not only the wound but also the healing process. The healing process, in turn, is itself the integrative function of the human mind—the capacity for psychological growth as the latter is called forth in an emergency situation.

Agreement on even this brief outline of the complexity and full history of mourning would be sufficient to compel the conclusion that any project to eliminate mourning would require a different animal. Yet, obvious as these points are, it is important to emphasize them. With the proliferation of behavioral modification programs using conditioning techniques, simplistic formulations of behavior threaten to become the norm.

But suppose there were to appear, to use a phrase of Gardner Murphy's, a relatively redeemed behaviorist—one redeemed enough to see the significance and importance of mourning in human development, but behaviorist enough to think the pain itself an unnecessary part of the process. After all, we all would do whatever we could to ease the pain of the mourner. We might *like* to think that the spirit in which such intervention is made—e.g., whether it is a free act of sympathy or a calculated act of manipulation—is of immeasurable importance. But, since the effects of such difference apparently are immeasurable, why not approach the task more systematically, perhaps even on a scale that might modify the typical response to loss in a whole society?

As a matter of fact, with sufficient control over or the collaboration of the citizenry, I believe the elimination of the *conscious* pain of both mourning and depression could largely be accomplished by behaviorist methods. The effects of such a change we can reasonably predict only in part. It would not amount to the elimination of mourning as outlined above. However, it would modify and to some extent abort or stunt the full mourning process itself. Unconsciously the wound would be there and would evoke at least partial reparative processes. Identifications, for instance, would be established, but how this identification might differ from those of normal mourning we cannot know.

In the physiological realm, we assume the survival value of pain as a signal that evokes care of physical injury and need—i.e., the actual or threatened disruption of bodily functioning. To my knowledge, we know of no reason to doubt the analogous though more complex function of psychological pain, as one mode in which a remembered, present, or anticipated disruption of one's world announces itself. Surely, the impulse to go beyond a caring response to pain, which then confuses attending to the causes of pain with eliminating the possibility of experiencing pain, is an impulse in danger of going wildly wrong. The absurd thread that runs through all Utopian schemes presupposes this confusion, as does the specifically demonic aspect of psychosurgery and conditioning therapies. As for the Utopian schemes, we must leave them to heaven. Brain surgery for psychological disorders and most conditioning projects might best be consigned to heaven's counterpart.

REFERENCES

Bridgman, P. 1927. *The Logic of Modern Physics.* New York: The Macmillan Company.

Freud, S. 1900. "The Interpretation of Dreams. In *The Standard Edition of the Complete Psychological Works of Sigmund Freud,* vol. 20, ed. J. Strachey. London: Hogarth Press, 1959.

Hartmann, H., E. Kris, and R. Loewenstein. 1946. "Comments on the Formation of Psychic Structure." *The Psychoanalytic Study of the Child* 2:11. New York: International Universities Press.

Loewald, H. 1962. "Internalization, Separation, Mourning and the Superego." *Psychoanalytic Quarterly* 31:483.

—— 1973. "On Internalization." *International Journal of Psychoanalysis* 54:9.

Ricoeur, R. 1970. *Freud and Philosophy.* New Haven and London: Yale University Press.

Ritvo, S., and A. Solnit. 1958. "Influences of Early Mother–Child Interaction on Identification Processes." *The Psychoanalytic Study of the Child* 13:64, New York: International Universities Press.

Smith, J. 1973. "Identification Styles in Depression and Grief." *International Journal of Psychoanalysis* 52:259.

Stierlin, H. 1973. "Interpersonal Aspects of Internalizations." *International Journal of Psychoanalysis* 54:203.

Weigert, E. 1961. "The Psychotherapy of the Affective Psychoses." In *Psychotherapy of the Psychoses,* ed. A. Burton. New York: Basic Books.

Conjugal Bereavement and the Social Network

David Maddison and Beverley Raphael

Conjugal bereavement, like any other crisis-inducing event, occurs within a social network. To say this is in no sense an attempt to minimize the significance of the intrapsychic processes set off by major loss—indeed, one of our major purposes is to emphasize the unique importance of the interaction between psychological processes and social network, and to indicate the extent to which the individual's mourning and its outcome can be modified by social process. Moreover, we do not imply that the forces at work are purely one-directional: persons within the social network may be either distanced or moved to provide greater support, depending at least in part on how grief is expressed.

We would add that much of the research on bereavement and its consequences seems to us to be vitiated by a failure to take social-network factors into account. Nowhere is this more true than in the case of bereavement in childhood, where relatively vast studies of an epidemiological type keep contradicting each other because so little heed is paid to the social context in which (say) the death of a child's mother occurs. In addition, there is little or no evaluation of the availability and quality of substitute "mothering" (see for example Brown, 1966).

We shall tackle this problem under three broad headings: (1) some relatively brief comments about the social consequences of bereavement, with particular emphasis on the role transition problems confronting the widow; (2) the interactions between the grieving individual and her environment that take place during the immediate crisis period and the ways these may affect the outcome of the mourning process; (3) some suggestions about the role of crisis intervention in the modification of this process.

The Social Consequences of Conjugal Bereavement

We shall take "as read" the by now abundant documentation of the morbidity and mortality following conjugal bereavement. Some of the earlier papers by Parkes (1964, 1970), and the very early work of Lindemann (1944) and later Marris (1958) provide the background, and in general terms there is a quite striking consistency between their reports of morbidity following bereavement and the findings of our own group who studied an unselected group of widows in Boston and Sydney (Maddison and Viola, 1968). Kraus and Lilienfeld (1959) and Rees and Lutkins (1967) have been prominent among those who have demonstrated the effect of bereavement on the death rate of the survivors. We continue to use an appraisal of physical and mental health, thirteen months post-bereavement, as a measure of the effectiveness or otherwise of the crisis resolution; this particular variable is of critical significance in all our research studies. But physical symptomatology, psychiatric and psychosomatic complaints are of importance here only insofar as they are in our view a valid reflection of much more fundamental problems.

It has often been remarked that widows tend to experience a great deal of painful social isolation and that they frequently encounter major problems in their attempts to reintegrate themselves into society. Obviously, the major social relationships for many of the women have previously involved married couples, and the more multi-dimensional the involvement of a woman in her husband's life, the more disorganized will be her social relationships after his death. Older widows, in particular, lack the ability to replace past relationships with ones that possess an equally satisfying intimacy. The increased complexity of urban, industrialized society certainly maximizes this problem, and of course Western culture contrasts very unfavorably with many other types of social organization in the relative absence of formal ritual or structured support for the widow, as has been demonstrated for example in papers by Mathison (1970) and by Krupp and Kligfeld (1962).

Lopata (1971), studying a large number of widows in metropolitan Chicago, has convincingly documented the fact that in contemporary Western society widows tend to constitute a minority group facing discrimination, poverty, and exclusion from full participation in society. They are passive females lacking a defined function in a male-dominated, function-oriented culture, tending all too frequently to be downwardly mobile in a society that idealizes upward mobility. Sometimes the widow's social interactions are reduced to what has been called a "society of widows."

Central to this problem is commonly a change in the widow's identity, especially as we have said where a great deal of this identity has been derived from her interactions with her husband, his ties with the outside world and its political and economic institutions. The women in Lopata's study who reported marked change were likely to have been socially active and integrated, to have had a higher education, and to have had husbands of higher occupational status. Of course some of these changes might well be in a positive direction, with the widow ultimately feeling more competent and more independent, developing aspects of her identity that had previously been undernourished because of her extreme dependence on her husband. But the finding that this type of antecedent lifestyle necessitates the greatest shift in role and identity may explain the fact that, with few exceptions, research studies have failed to find any correlation between bad outcome following bereavement and lower socioeconomic status, despite the obviously greater prevalence of financial difficulties in the low-income group. (It may even be that the extent of the drop in financial status following bereavement, rather than the absolute level of income, is an important variable here, but we know of no data to support this statement.)

We know less than we would like about the remarriage of widows, although there is some evidence produced by McKain (1969) and Schlesinger and Macrae (1971) that such remarriages are quite likely to be successful, particularly if the first marriage had been a good one, if the remarriage were motivated by needs for love and companionship rather than by material factors, if the children approved and relationships with both families were good. However, the available data tend to refer more often to the remarriage of widowers, who obviously have greater chances in this area because there are more available women than men.

The Social Network During The Bereavement Crisis

None of our work has done anything to destroy our conviction that the widow's perception of her social network is an extremely important determinant of the outcome of her bereavement crisis, as assessed thirteen months following the death. If details are required of our approach to this problem, and the techniques we have employed, reference should be made to some of our earlier papers (in particular Maddison and Walker, 1967 and Maddison et al., 1969). Briefly, our findings were as follows: the great majority of widows, both those who resolve their crisis without subsequent health impairment and those whose health deteriorated in the post-bereavement year, perceived a great deal of helpfulness during their early interactions with the environment. The difference between bad-outcome and good-outcome groups was determined in these studies by the greater number of nonhelpful interchanges reported by the former subjects; the bad-outcome women perceived their social environment as overtly or covertly hostile, nonsupportive, and failing to meet their needs. More specifically, widows who subsequently proceeded to a bad outcome tended to express the feeling that there were some people in the environment who had overtly or covertly opposed the free expression of affects, particularly those of grief and anger. There was recurrent mention by subjects in this group of their perception that other people seemed to be shocked by their feelings; one such widow saw herself as being told to control herself and pull herself together, or felt that attempts were being made to minimize her grief by a process of generalization. People would point out to her the sufferings of other widows, or try to lay down just how much grief was appropriate for a widow to feel. In other instances, a bad-outcome widow would consider that important people in her environment were themselves upset to an extent she believed was inappropriate or even competitive, or that they were being incongruously cheerful, or that they claimed to share her grief and understand exactly how she was feeling when this seemed patently untrue.

Another important finding was that the bad-outcome widows considered that some people were actively attempting to focus their attention on the present and the future, and such exchanges were seen as actively unhelpful.

They reacted with hostility to attempts to arouse their interest in new activities, the development of new friendships, or the resumption of old hobbies and occupations. They reacted particularly negatively to any premature introduction of the subject of remarriage. Many bad-outcome subjects felt that they lacked an empathic person with whom they could discuss their past life, their relationship with their husband, and the events surrounding his death— although it should be noted that some subjects felt that interchanges of this kind were actually unhelpful.

Clearly, there is a very real possibility that the widow's own long-standing modes of interpersonal relationship may in some instances have contributed, perhaps very markedly, to the nonsupportiveness she then perceives around her; her own behavior—perhaps lifelong, perhaps manifested most intensely during the terminal stages of her husband's life—may succeed in driving away from her those people who might potentially have been available as supportive figures in the social network. Projection of her own unrecognized hostile feelings may also play a part. It might be argued by critics of our approach that we are simply identifying a group whose own personality characteristics are such that they perceive hostility where none is intended, or who feel perpetually ungratified despite the attempts of others to meet their needs. This superficially attractive approach, which would throw us back to consider personality factors in the bereaved as the only issues of real importance, completely disregards, however, our convincing documentation of the objective importance of insensitivity, overt or covert hostility, absence of empathy, and ignorance of a widow's needs—all of which recur in the statements made to widows by significant others. For us, there is abundant evidence that the behavior of many people in the environment of the recently bereaved widow, including some members of the so-called "helping professions," is in active opposition to those psychological processes required for the satisfactory resolution of object loss.

Now statistical evaluation of the data from our earlier studies made it clear that the variance attributable to these interpersonal transactions, while impressive in itself, could not provide a complete differentiation of bad- and good-outcome groups. In later prospective studies, as yet unreported, we have been able to formulate additional criteria that, when applied in certain combinations to an unselected population of recently bereaved widows by independent raters of proven reliability, furnish a group of subjects of whom 80 percent will proceed to a bad outcome. These are *additional criteria,* adding to and certainly not replacing the predictive value of interpersonal transactions.

1. The presence of *additional concurrent crisis situations,* so that the individual in crisis is facing such an overwhelming mass of problems demanding solution that the coping requirements are likely to be beyond the adaptive capacities of most people. A woman who is still in the stage of acute grief following the death of her husband when she hears that her elderly mother, ten thousand miles away, is terminally ill, will be at a high risk of health deterioration, most particularly when this concatenation of events is linked with other of our predictive factors.

2. The *mode of death* may have been such as to maximize anger, guilt, or self-reproach. We not infrequently see widows whose perception of the death, rightly or wrongly, is that it was induced or hastened by the husband's failure to comply with appropriate medical instructions, or even to seek medical advice, or where he had persisted with seriously self-destructive habits in spite of medical warnings. This problem is compounded when the widow considers that his lack of forward planning has left her with less adequate insurance than would have been justified by their previous economic circumstances.

3. A *preexisting pathological marital relationship,* characterized by extreme dependence or ambivalence in the relationship between the survivor and the deceased.

In using these criteria operationally, in our current and prospective studies of the feasibility of preventive intervention during the bereavement crisis we are able to select likely bad-outcome widows with a high degree of confidence, and we are intervening with a randomly selected half of this population to determine whether we can lower the expected prevalence of health deterioration. But it is to be noted that three groups of predictive factors, out of the four groups we find helpful, are unmodifiable in the sense that they represent "past history" or factual situations we are powerless to alter, even though successful intervention may enable the widow to reevaluate some of these occurrences in ways that provide less stress on her coping mechanisms. But it is in relation to the "here and now" network of interactions, and the pathogenic influence we know them to have in their own right, that we are able to exert a maximum leverage, and it is therefore now appropriate to consider these networks in a little more detail.

In our type of society, we tend to think of the family as the first line of defense in the provision of resources to support an individual in crisis. It may well be that the present-day nuclear family, shorn of so many of its helpful extensions in an increasingly mobile world, is ill-adapted to meet this task (Maddison, 1973), though the myth tends to live on, perilously unsupported by findings such as those derived from our own bereavement studies. Open internal communication systems within the family will certainly be of assistance, as has been emphasized by Vollman et al. (1971), but preexisting roles and relationships within a specific family will nearly always be decisive. Reanalyzing some of our earlier data from a previously unexplored angle, we have shown within our widowed population that the widow's own mother, involved in 6.1 percent of all interchanges, is nevertheless responsible for 7.9 percent of the unhelpful ones. The position is even more striking with members of the husband's family, involved in 10.3 percent of the total interchanges, but 18.2 percent of the unhelpful ones. (On the other hand, friends provide almost half of all unhelpful interactions, and would appear to represent a source of powerfully pathogenic influence.) The widow perceived her interactions with her children, however, as containing a relatively low proportion of unhelpful items.

Problems with the husband's family have been commented on by others, notably Marris (1958) and Lopata (1971). Even observers more cynical than ourselves might have been surprised by the frequency with which we heard of mothers-in-law who said to the actively grieving widow: "I know that you have lost a husband, my dear, but *I* have lost my son!" Quarrels may develop over the disposition of the husband's possessions, there may be disagreements about funeral arrangements, and in particular the widow may consider that there is a failure to keep promises concerning attention to the children. In some instances the widow reported statements attributed to members of the husband's family, which we could certainly not ascribe to projection, which made it clear that they believed that she had failed to take adequate care of him, or had not really appreciated his good qualities.

Within her own family she may be able to derive great comfort from the mother-daughter relationship, ties Halbertsma (1968) has suggested are particularly important for this purpose in working-class districts. Nevertheless, there is a tendency for attention to flow both upward and downward from the middle generation, so that the recently bereaved woman in her forties feels a continuing obligation to provide care both for her young married daughter and her own elderly mother, without being able to expect that much comfort will flow in the reverse directions. Sons may offer instrumental support, but there is little reciprocation of services such as is likely to occur within the female kinship line; sisters and nieces may turn out to be more helpful.

If the widow has young children, then a new set of problems is posed. The altered patterns of family interaction following the husband's death may create serious role strains for her; not only is she required to fill both parental roles, but she is also expected to be both bereaved and comforter. If she is prevented from responding appropriately to her children's needs, she may produce for them a double deprivation. Mothers all too frequently feel that they must hide their grief in their children's presence, which thereby inhibits their own mourning (Langer, 1957). Somewhat older children may be placed in new roles, which may be very threatening to them; the family adjustment will perhaps be distorted and lacking in role gratifications for many years thereafter.

Ultimately, the widow is required to make a decision about where she is going to live. If she moves in with one of her married children, her role is likely to be far from clearly defined in this three-generational household, and problems between herself and her children, which had been regarded as "closed" many years before, may be reactivated. It is hardly surprising that widows who are able to support themselves in their own home, both financially and emotionally, state that they experience greater peace and independence. Perhaps the ideal situation is one of "intimacy at a distance," with the widow living near to but not actually in the household of her children, but with appropriate contact and support readily available. Dubourg and Mandelbrote's (1966) findings on mentally ill widows support this proposition.

But all this has really taken us too far ahead, well beyond the crisis period during which, it is clear, our maximum attention must be focused if we are to achieve any sort of effectiveness in the prevention of serious consequences. We must now return to analyze some of the implications of what has been said up to this point, and add some additional findings from social psychological research.

Intervention in the Social Network

Kurt Lewin pointed out many years ago that human behavior is always a function of two sets of variables, those involving the person and those involving the situation in which that person is functioning; Blackman and Goldstein (1968) have recently demonstrated, using their own empirical data, that one crucial aspect of the environment is an interaction of close, face-to-face members of the community with "the exchange of emotional support and services." They have advanced the concept of a "credit network," by means of which a person may receive emotional support and temporary services when in a state of crisis; their observations suggest that individuals who have fewer available supports manifest more psychological symptomatology, and this position has been further elaborated by Weiss and Bergen (1968). Cumming (1968) suggests that "anyone bound to a small group by common goals and shared values, in which there is a certain minimum specialization of roles, may be provided with one element of protection against mental illness, no matter what kinds of stresses he must endure." This is echoed by Blackman and Goldstein: "failure to be involved in such a network of credits . . . increases the probability that disability will result from a given amount of stress because no support will be available" (p. 85).

It is thus clearly important that we should give a good deal of attention to how the widow's social network might be strengthened, in these detribalized times, in ways that will lock her more securely into a situation in which spontaneous help of a nonprofessional kind will be more readily forthcoming. Organizations for widows and widowers clearly have an important potential role to play here, and we have regarded it as a legitimate part of our own undertaking to give some time to consultation with these agencies, although in our society it certainly turns out to be a harder task than it looks. Widows have frequently suggested to us that there is a particular value in sensing an empathic understanding of their plight, which they feel can most readily come from someone who has worked through an identical loss, giving them that special understanding only another widow can provide. Phyllis Silverman's "widow-to-widow" program, based at the Laboratory of Community Psychiatry at Harvard Medical School, represents a very interesting development along these lines. She notes (1971): "the offer of help should come from someone the recipient recognizes as having a legitimate right to intrude himself into his life." (p. 161). But even with the use of other widows as case aides her program has only been able to develop a significant relationship with approximately 60 percent of those who could be contacted; moreover, as in virtually all generic approaches of this type, we have to accept as an act of faith that involvement in the program has proved to be of benefit to the recipient, for we are given no criterion of successful intervention, no measure of outcome, and no control group with which comparisons can be made.

But much of the material we have already detailed emphasizes the limitations of the generic approach, the limitations indeed of using untrained intervenors, however empathic they may be. For those who lack any understanding of depth psychology or the normal processes of grief and mourning, and who are unsupported by any form of mental health consultation, this is certainly an area in which it is easy to do more harm than good, as our own data clearly demonstrate. (We are also aware, from our agency consultations, that when the untrained intervenor is male he may become extremely anxious because of his perception, accurate or not, that the widow is a sexual threat to him; indeed the folk-myth of the sexually insatiable widow is almost certainly one factor hindering her social integration into any group containing males.) Consider the following brief history of a recently bereaved woman, who is adequately representative of those we would predict as likely to proceed to a bad outcome, and who had not made contact with any clinical or therapeutic social agency:

Mrs. K. was rated as having several of our predictors of bad outcome on the basis of her initial assessment interview. She perceived her environment as grossly unsupportive, in particular in its failure to permit the expression of anger and guilt and in the absence of empathic encouragement and ego support. She was rated as having experienced a multiple crisis, in that five weeks before his death she had initiated an extremely traumatic separation from her husband, the final precipitant (after years of provocation) being her awareness that this highly disturbed man had been deliberately feeding aspirin to her twelve-year-old daughter to the point of inducing acute peptic ulceration requiring hospital treatment. Her husband's death resulted from suicide, following many threats, thus terminating a marriage which had been pathological by any standards.

During five intervention interviews many aspects of her past life and marital interaction were clarified. Serious problems had arisen during their honeymoon, fourteen years earlier, when she realized that he was seeing another woman, and his behavior became increasingly deviant over the years, showing itself in a number of sexual aberrations as well as in gross violence directed toward her. As she reviewed many memories of their life together the sadomasochistic nature of their relationship became increasingly apparent, and she was able to express considerable anger about many aspects of his behavior. She was able to discuss a very close relationship he had developed with a male friend, which she plausibly suspected might have had homosexual components, and expressed bitterness about her husband's failure to believe his daughter's allegations that this man had interfered with her sexually. In the months before his death he had become increasingly bizarre, attempting to teach his son scientology and leaving highly pornographic material around the house in the belief that his children should read it. Though she could come to terms with much of her ambivalent feeling about her husband, and face her sadness and sense of loss, she was initially troubled by severe guilt feelings that seemed responsible for an initial massive denial of the reality of his death. As she gained confidence in the intervenor, she revealed that she had on many occasions wished him dead and had said to him, not long before his death: "Why don't you go off in your car and kill yourself?" She had some awareness, though largely at an intellectual level, that she might have contributed to some of the difficulties in their marriage, and agonized over the thought that her husband "might have been different with another woman." Her guilt feeling was magnified at those times when she permitted herself to feel a sense of relief because her numerous persecutions had ended.

To add to her burdens, she was the target of a good deal of hostility from her husband's family, particularly her mother-in-law. This lady asked her at the funeral if she were "glad," and made repeated attempts to communicate with the children to try to induce them to leave their mother and come to her.

Though virtually all our predictors pointed strongly to an unfavorable outcome, she had resolved her bereavement crisis very adequately when she was followed up thirteen months after the death. From the frequency with which this sequence of events has occurred in our present study, we have good reason to believe that the intervention itself was the critically important variable.

The point here is that a general strengthening of the bereaved person's social network, including such programs as that developed by Silverman, might be postulated to be helpful for those women who are not too burdened by their own longstanding psychopathology, or who are relatively or completely lacking in those particular characteristics we have found to be so strongly associated with bad outcome. But the adequate appraisal of many of these widows, and thus an adequate appreciation of their needs, will require the services of persons whose level of psychodynamic understanding, and whose own freedom from countertransference-derived prejudices, will enable them to identify without undue delay those subjects who have complex, potentially resolvable intrapsychic and psychosocial problems related to the crisis situation. A widow, for example, who is virtually frozen by her own unexpressed rage, linked perhaps with previous experiences of loss, is unlikely to gain adequate help from a mere increase in the quality and quantity of social network supports available to her (Maddison, 1969). Some of these problems may be resolved at the community level by a community agent who is either unusually experienced and sophisticated or who has a particularly vital relationship with a skilled consultant. As reported previously by us (Maddison and Raphael, 1973), there is precious little evidence to suggest that drug treatment is helpful in these circumstances; indeed in our own studies those who do badly use significantly more psychotropic medications than those who do well (although we do not suggest that these findings are necessarily causally related).

We have to recognize, then, that if the social network during the bereavement crisis is an important variable in determining subsequent outcome, intervention in that network requires a variety of forms. It may well be true that for the majority of widows—those who show few if any of our risk factors—social welfare programs directed toward more effective support services, an empathic linkage with other widows, and an educational program directed toward bringing a greater understanding of grief and mourning to the community at large will be helpful and effective. But there will remain a large and vitally important minority for whom this will not be adequate, and even the identification of this minority may escape notice until it is virtually too late, when the thick impervious scum of neurotic and maladaptive defenses has settled on top of their unexpressed affects and unresolved bitterness. Intervention in the social network when the problem is of this kind and magnitude, therefore, must involve the introduction of a sophisticated professional or paraprofessional. His or her highly skilled tasks will be, among others, the promotion of mourning where this has been suppressed, assistance in dealing with denial when this is gross, protracted, and dysfunctional, support in reviewing the lost relationship, promotion of free discussion about the widow's reaction to certain events and interactions within her social network, and possibly some reexamination of earlier losses which may be important factors in hindering her current expression of grief, rage, and self-reproach. Altered family relationships may also require some type of intervention, and work may be required, directly or indirectly, with the widow's children or with other members of the family. Much can be gained, we have discovered, at the termination of such crisis intervention sessions, by some gentle interpretation of the transference mourning and loss, which may be expressed, in disguised form, during the last few contacts. Our own studies are providing us with good evidence that such crisis interventions will reduce the frequency of bad outcome in high-risk widows, when compared with a matched group, also at high risk, who do not receive such intervention.

But how can contacts with widows be facilitated so that such interventions can be brought about? Silverman (1971) has made the point that "the nature of bereavement is such that the grieving person finds it very difficult to ask for help, let alone find the energy to seek out a resource" (p. 170). Weiss and Bergen (1968) have commented in a wider context that one of the major problems confronting health delivery systems is to devise ways in which help can be brought to psychologically vulnerable persons without at the same time undermining their own feelings of competence, and without creating undue dependence and producing a sense of helpless inadequacy. If we are to deal effectively with the problems of the bereaved, therefore, we need to look again at the provision of health care for populations truly in need, instead of following what Hart (1971) has called the inverse care law, by means of which "the availability of good medical care tends to vary inversely with the need of the population served." But that, as Rudyard Kipling said, is another story.

REFERENCES

Blackman, S., and K. M. Goldstein. 1968. "Some Aspects of a Theory of Community Mental Health." *Community Mental Health Journal* 4:85 ff.

Brown, F. 1966. "Childhood Bereavement and Subsequent Psychiatric Disorder." *British Journal of Psychiatry* 112:1035 ff.

Cumming, E. 1968. "Unsolved Problems of Prevention," *Canada's Mental Health,* Suppl. No. 56.

Dubourg, G. O., and B. M. Mandelbrote. 1970. "Mentally Ill Widows." *International Journal of Social Psychiatry* 12:63 ff.

Halbertsma, H. A. 1970. "Working-Class Systems of Mutual Assistance in Case of Childbirth, Illness and Death." *Social Science and Medicine* 3:321 ff.

Hart, J. T. 1971. "The Inverse Care Law." *Lancet* 1:405 ff.

Kraus, A. S., and A. M. Lilienfeld. 1959. "Some Epidemiological Aspects of the High Mortality Rate in the Young Widowed Group." *Journal of Chronic Diseases* 10:207 ff.

Krupp, G., and B. Kligfeld. 1962. "The Bereavement Reaction—A Cross-Cultural Evaluation." *Journal of Religion and Health* 1:222 ff.

Langer, M. 1957. *Learning to Live as a Widow.* New York: Messner.

Lindemann, E. 1944. "Symptomatology and Management of Acute Grief." *American Journal of Psychiatry* 101:141 ff.

Lopata, H. Z. 1971. "The Social Involvement of American Widows." *American Behavioral Scientist* 14:41 ff.

McKain, W. C. 1969. *Retirement Marriages,* Agriculture Experiment Station Monograph 3, University of Connecticut.

Maddison, D. C. 1969. "Epidemiology and After: The Implications of Crisis Studies." In *Psychiatry and the Community,* eds. I. Pilowsky and D. C. Maddison, Sydney: Sydney University Press.

—— 1973. "Crisis in the Family—The Family in Crisis," *Mental Health in Australia* 5:4 ff.

Maddison, D. C., and B. Raphael. 1973. "Normal Bereavement as an Illness Requiring Care: Psychopharmacological Approaches." In *Psychopharmacologic Agents for the Terminally Ill and Bereaved,* eds. I. K. Goldberg, S. Malitz, and A. H. Kitscher, pp. 235–48, New York: Columbia University Press.

Maddison, D. C., and A. Viola. 1968. "The Health of Widows in the Year Following Bereavement." *Journal of Psychosomatic Research* 12:297 ff.

Maddison, D. C., A. Viola, and W. L. Walker. 1969. "Further Studies in Conjugal Bereavement." *Australia and New Zealand Journal of Psychiatry* 3:63 ff.

Maddison, D. C., and W. L. Walker. 1967. "Factors Affecting the Outcome of Conjugal Bereavement." *British Journal of Psychiatry* 113:1057 ff.

Marris, P. 1958. *Widows and Their Families.* London: Routledge and Kegan Paul.

Mathison, J. 1970. "A Cross-Cultural View of Widowhood." *Omega* 1:201 ff.

Parkes, C. M. 1964. "Effects of Bereavement on Physical and Mental Health: A Study of the Medical Records of Widows." *British Medical Journal* 2:274 ff.

—— 1970. "The First Year of Bereavement." *Psychiatry* 33:444 ff.

Rees, W. D., and S. G. Lutkins. 1967. "Mortality of Bereavement." *British Medical Journal* 4:13 ff.

Schlesinger, B., and A. Macrae. 1971. "The Widow and Widower and Remarriage: Selected Findings." *Omega* 2:10 ff.

Silverman, P. R. 1971. "Factors Involved in Accepting an Offer of Help." *Archives of the Foundation of Thanatology* 3:161 ff.

Vollman, R. R., A. Ganzert, L. Picher, and W. V. Williams. 1971. "The Reactions of Family Systems to Sudden and Unexpected Death." *Omega* 2:101 ff.

Weiss, R. J., and B. J. Bergen. 1968. "Social Supports and the Reduction of Psychiatric Disability." *Psychiatry* 31:107 ff.

Uses of Ethnography
in Understanding Grief and Mourning

Paul C. Rosenblatt

Data from other cultures are essential for those who are interested in thanatology. First of all, the literature on grief and mourning is short on empirical data. Compared to other areas of the behavioral sciences, this area seems to be under relatively great pressure to provide answers to questions of vital concern to people, while attempting answers to questions from a relatively small empirical base. Moreover, no matter how much interest professionals have in the topic and no matter how many pages are written about it and no matter how much it *seems* that death is no longer or never was a taboo topic, many research methodologies still seem taboo in the study of grief and mourning.

If we compare studies of reactions to a death with studies of such common topics of social science research as interpersonal attraction or voter behavior, it is evident that many research methods are not utilized in thanatology. For example, as far as I know, nobody is doing kinesic or other microanalyses of behavior of recently bereaved people. The area has seen little use of survey research or of physiological measurement. It appears that thanatology is too sensitive a field in which to do systematic research on samples of people early in bereavement, or to push typical bereaved people

This article has benefited from comments by R. Patricia Walsh and reports research supported by the National Institute of Mental Health and the University of Minnesota Agricultural Experiment Station. R. Patricia Walsh and Douglas A. Jackson assisted in the research.

to reveal embarrassing data. If these are not taboos, they are norms of propriety. As long as such taboos or norms exist, every effort to develop and exploit other potentially fruitful sources of data must be explored. Ethnographic descriptions of other cultures are one such source of data.

A second reason for attending to data from other cultures is that the norms of our society and the norms that may develop as a result of work by thanatological professionals blind us to unmet needs and alternative solutions. This problem may be especially serious in the area of bereavement because of the possibility that in their writing, counseling, and teaching, professionals who deal with reactions to death may be creating self-fulfilling prophecies. People worried about death may use things said or written about dying and death as a source of prescriptions. To the extent that any prescription may reduce anxiety for people or may give people who do not know what to do something to do, thanatologists may in the long run be creating norms for a society. From this process of self-fulfilling prophecy two problems may emerge. First, thanatologists may be blinded to alternative conceptualizations and problem solutions in the area of bereavement. Second, the means of coping that people adopt from thanatological writing, counseling, and teaching may not be optimal or may be optimal only for a few people. Therefore, thanatologists must be as informed as possible. They must know what human needs there commonly are in bereavement and what satisfies these needs. They must be able to see death reactions without the blinders provided by conventional wisdom or by conceptual developments in thanatology. They must know what the consequences of various behaviors are, and if the consequences vary in different situations or for people with different backgrounds, that too should be known.

Ethnographic data can help in this task, by increasing the general information base, telling what is typically human, and giving information on how grief and mourning are affected by various death customs. Further, data can provide ideas about alternative ways for Americans to deal with bereavement. Although the work of many people, including Bendann (1930), Habenstein and Lamers (1963), Gorer (1965), Hertz (1960), and Mandelbaum (1954), provides a tradition in the study of reactions to death that makes use of ethnographic data, there has not been much progress in exploiting this tradition and building on the work that has been done.

My associates and I have been working for several years on an extensive cross-cultural study of death customs. In our study we applied content analytic research methods to ethnographic descriptions of 78 societies from around the world. These societies vary enormously, from the Copper Eskimo to Chinese peasants, from the Basques of Spain to the Jivaro of the Amazon jungle. A major problem in the study has been that descriptions of societies differ considerably in the amount of information provided about death, grief, and mourning. But still there are many interesting generalizations to be made. I can only touch a few here.

Normal Human Reactions to a Death

From society to society there is notable consistency in reactions to a death. Some of it is not surprising; some of it is. Among the nonsurprising consistencies foremost of all is emotionality. The emotional behavior of people who were closest to the deceased may or may not include crying, anger, self-mutilation, or some other form of emotion, but we do not often find people reacting unemotionally. The form of emotional expression shows interesting patterns cross-culturally. These patterns provide a perspective on bereavement behavior of Americans.

One example of cross-cultural patterning is that women are much more likely to cry when a death occurs than men, though men often cry. Only among the Thonga of South Africa does our sample show a society in which men may cry more than women at a death. Knowledge of the sex difference puts the crying behavior of Americans into perspective. For example, the finding tempers our concern that many American men may be pathologically restraining tears during bereavement.

Another example of a cross-cultural regularity in emotional behavior is that overt expression of anger and overt aggression are less common in societies in which ritual specialists have an important role in dealing with a death up to and during initial disposal of the body. Knowledge of this provides an interesting view of the effects on bereaved Americans of clergy, funeral directors, and other ritual specialists. Apparently, certain actions of ritual specialists help to reduce or control anger and aggression.

Among the surprising consistencies cross-culturally is belief in ghosts, which occurs in almost all societies in our sample. Of 66 societies in which we could measure ghost beliefs only the Masai, the second most poorly described society in our sample, appeared to lack them. We can look at an American who admits that he believes he has had contact with the ghost of a departed loved one from the perspective of our findings about ghost beliefs. He is behaving in a way that is like most humans in the world. Rather than dealing with him as though the ghost belief is a pathology, we may profitably work with him as though he were a typical human. Pointing out to him that he is experiencing what is normal for humans to experience may provide considerable assurance to him.

Death Customs

Judging from the data, it is rare for the death of an adult not to be dealt with ceremonially. One gain from ceremony and from customs surrounding ceremony is that bereaved people do not have to make difficult decisions. To the extent that behavior promoting adjustment to death is required by custom, people are spared the anxiety of deciding whether to engage in the behavior and do not risk foregoing behavior that facilitates adjustment.

As an illustration of the value of cross-culturally common customary acts, we have data indicating that the remarriage and resumption of apparently normal married lives by widows is facilitated by what we call tie-breaking customs. One category of these customs is the elimination of reminders of the deceased. This includes practicing a taboo on the name of the deceased, destruction or disposal or giving away of property of the deceased, and changing residence. Cross-culturally these customs may usually be embedded in a set of beliefs that has nothing explicitly to do with the promotion of adjustment of widows. Instead, the beliefs may have to do with fear of ghosts, fear of contamination by disease, fear of contagious sorcery, or desire to honor the deceased. But whatever the belief system, the customs should, in theory, operate in the same way for Americans. By removing reminders of the deceased, the customs can reduce psychological barriers to constructing a new marital relationship and can reduce stimulus to experiencing grief.

As things stand now in the United States, some bereaved spouses dispose of the deceased's personal property, some move, some eliminate other reminders of the deceased. But since such behavior is not required by custom, it is difficult for many to engage in it. If it does indeed occur, it may not take place until much later after the death than it typically does cross-culturally, thereby delaying remarriage, and many Americans may not be able to engage in it at all. The cross-cultural perspective not only gives us some ideas about specific behaviors to promote adjustment, it also suggests that prescriptions through customs may be more effective than prescription for individual cases who happen to encounter professional advice. It is useful for the counselor or educator to know about cross-cultural associations of tie-breaking customs with widow remarriage, but reforms at the level of religious custom or the custom of burial societies would have far more impact.

Societies as Experiments

The societies of the world have tried in countless different ways to deal with the common human problems of bereavement and of adjustment to death. They have experienced over the centuries a degree of variation and a persistence far beyond the capabilities of any professional researcher or practitioner. From the myriad natural experiments, a small number of beliefs and customs have recurrently emerged. We may assume that these represent an optimal combination of effectiveness and ease of performance. Even though these customs and beliefs may serve a variety of societal and individual needs, one can look to the ethnographic literature for advice. There, for example, one may find answers to such questions as the ways in which people have felt about cadavers. The literature shows enormous variations in feelings, beliefs about, and treatment of corpses. By studying the literature one may determine the consequences of any particular belief about corpses that one may hold or advocate, and whether or not that belief will make it easier for people to deal with death. Will a bereaved person who fears the corpse of a loved one return more quickly to a normal life, or more slowly, than if he did not fear the corpse?

Similarly, one may find information about whether or not institutionalized aggression catharsis for a bereaved person helps him or her to build or maintain close ties with others and reduces the likelihood that he or she will anger easily; whether or not cremation is preferable to burial; whether or not the keeping of mementos of the deceased is to be encouraged; whether or not reincarnation beliefs aid or hamper adjustment to death.

Problems in Using the Ethnographic Literature

The first problem in using the ethnographic literature is information retrieval. Published descriptions exist for thousands of past and contemporary human societies. To exploit those descriptions thoroughly we shall need someone or some agency to winnow tens of thousands of ethnographic papers and monographs to identify those in which the various death beliefs and customs receive some coverage. Can we find a librarian or bibliographer to perform this important service and a grant-giving foundation or agency to support it?

A second problem in using ethnographic descriptions is that it is often hard to know what to make of nonreport of a custom or belief. Nonreport may mean that the custom or belief is absent, that the ethnographer did not observe it, though it is present, or that he did observe it but did not bother to report it. In the cross-cultural study we engaged in, perhaps the most distressing deficiency in the ethnographic reports was the almost total lack of any mention of grief pathologies or of bereavement behavior atypical of people in the society described. Whether or not that is because there are no instances of such behavior we cannot tell.

A third problem is that death has been an under-described topic in the ethnographic literature. The reasons for this are many. Some ethnographers consider it tactless, rude, or inappropriate to delve into this area. Other ethnographers have had no opportunity to observe death-related behavior. In some societies ordinary reactions to a death may make study difficult. People may be very quick to anger and attack when a death occurs, or name taboos and fear of evocation of the spirits of the dead itself may make it very difficult to discuss a death or the general topic of death with people. In addition, anthropology, like every other field, has had its fashions. It has never been particularly fashionable in anthropology to deal with death, though an interest in death-related topics, such as kinship and technology, has produced some information on it from a large number of societies. Recently, however, there have been published several excellent ethnographic monographs about death—for example, Douglass on the Basques (1969) and Goody on the Lo Dagaa of Ghana (1962). This trend can be promoted in one way through the provision of publication outlets. Anthropologists, like many other social scientists, are experiencing a contraction in publication outlets relative to the number of manuscripts prepared for publication. Editors and publishers could increase the publication of ethnographic reports dealing with death simply by providing and advertising publication outlets for anthropologists.

The trend toward rich ethnographic description of death-related activities and beliefs can also be promoted by grant support. If support were provided for ethnographic fieldwork focused on death, the study of death and reactions to it would gain considerably.

Even with published descriptions of death customs identified through competent bibliographic work and even with the encouragement of further, more detailed ethnographic work there is a fourth problem that makes ethnography of less use to people interested in thanatology than it might be. Many ethnographers obscure their data sources. It still is not common for ethnographers to report either the precise source of bits of information or to report quantitative data—frequency statistics, exceptions, and covariations. In our extensive cross-cultural study, we tried many times to determine whether we were reading descriptions of norms, descriptions of modal behaviors, descriptions of behaviors typical of contemporary adults in a society, or descriptions of specific, atypical events an ethnographer had observed, or something else. Across the cases we studied, we were never able to distinguish among these reliably. At various times it was like trying to understand death in America by reading a book of etiquette, an autobiography, or a description of one funeral in a small town in Arkansas written as though it were a description of all American funerals.

A fifth problem in exploiting ethnographic reports is that it is uncommon for ethnographers to report psychological data on the people studied. Data on dreams, anxieties, needs, ego defenses, details of social interactions, attitudes, and other types of psychological dispositions are not commonly reported. Yet such data can augment our understanding of death reactions.

Anthropology of the Thanatological Movement

From an anthropological perspective there are things to be said about the thanatological movement. The customs of thanatologists, like the customs of other groups, are channeled. The channels provide cohesion, facilitate communications, and maximize rewards. Yet the channels also limit. I have suggested that one such limit that may have been developing in thanatology is the under-exploitation of ethnography. This article is intended to counter that possible development. Two other limits I pointed out seem to be a reluctance to recruit recently bereaved people as research subjects and an unwillingness to experiment with bereaved persons as research subjects.

New social movements are often messianic. It is particularly easy for thanatology to move in that direction because so many people turn to others for help when a death occurs. Thus, through death education and death counseling the word may be quickly spread. What is the word? It is possible, as I suggested in my introduction, that the word could be almost anything and still have an effect, that self-fulfilling prophecy mechanisms will operate to make any of a wide range of death-education content and death counseling effective. For education and counseling dealing with any problem area in our society, the demand for answers outstrips the available solutions. For counseling, the problem may not be so serious, since counseling technique may carry a client a long way without the counselor having a great deal of problem-specific content to draw from. Nonetheless, all professionals who work in the area of death should be aware of the possibility that self-fulfilling prophecy may lead to the adoption of suboptimal practices. What are the consequences of the various beliefs and practices recommended or more subtly promoted? The ethnographic data tell us there are consequences to reducing fear of the dead, to ghost and reincarnation beliefs, to promoting the cathartic expression of anger in bereavement, to destroying the personal property of the deceased, to practicing a taboo on the name of the deceased, to moving from a residence that was shared with a person who has died. The professional owes it to clients, students, readers, and others to be aware of these consequences.

REFERENCES

Bendann, E. 1930. *Death Customs: An Analytical Study of Burial Rites.* New York: Knopf.

Douglass, W. A. 1969. *Death in Murelaga: Funeral Rite in a Spanish Basque Village.* Seattle: University of Washington Press.

Goody, J. 1962. *Death, Property and the Ancestors: A Study of the Mortuary Customs of the Lo Dagaa of West Africa.* Palo Alto, California: Stanford University Press.

Gorer, G. 1965. *Death, Grief, and Mourning.* New York: Doubleday.

Habenstein, R. W., and W. Lamers. 1963. *Funeral Customs the World Over.* Milwaukee: Bulfin.

Hertz, R. 1960. *Death and the Right Hand.* Glencoe, Illinois: The Free Press.

Mandelbaum, D. G. 1954. "Form, Variation and Meaning of a Ceremony," in *Method and Perspective in Anthropology: Papers in Honor of Wilson D. Wallis.* Minneapolis: University of Minnesota Press.

Part Two

The Bereavement Process

The Process and Phenomenology of Bereavement

Alfred Wiener, Irwin Gerber, Delia Battin, and Arthur M. Arkin

Bereavement is the single most important and universal emotional crisis to which our patients will be exposed. Through the ages writers have waxed poetic about the consequences of bereavement, but psychiatrists have only recently begun to study the phenomenology of bereavement, some of which remains unknown; so much so that Paula Clayton in her review article on the clinical morbidity of bereavement stated that "final answers will only be obtained from a randomly selected non-patient population of widows and widowers, studied prospectively and with adequate controls" (Clayton, 1973).

It was with a view to providing such a controlled prospective study that we began our work on bereavement at Montefiore Hospital and Medical Center five years ago.

The subjects of our study were selected from a hospital-based medical group that looks after approximately 25,000 people, giving them comprehensive and prophylactic medical care from birth on—at home, in the office, and in the hospital. Over 42 physicians, representing the various specialties

The data for this paper are from an investigation entitled, "The Aged in Crisis: A Study of Bereavement." This program was supported in part by U.S.P.H.S. Grant MH–14490 and Grant 93–P–57454/2 from the Administration on Aging, Social and Rehabilitation Service, D.H.E.W. The authors wish to thank Roslyn Rusalem, M.S., and Natalie Hannon for their dedicated work on the program and their critical suggestions during the preparation of this paper.

of medicine, are currently engaged in providing these medical services, and there are another 50 nonmedical personnel working with them in the unit. Each family unit is assigned for comprehensive medical care to an internist and, when children under 15 are present, to a pediatrician. Most of these doctors are full-time, salaried, and certified by their respective boards. The medical group's usual panel consists of 1,200 patients per internist and 900 patients per pediatrician. Most of the families have, over a period of years, developed a close relationship with their "family physicians"; where appropriate, the internist and pediatrician for a given family discuss the problems of the family as a unit.

It will be readily evident that most of the clients belonging to this group have been known to the physicians for many years, their individual records were readily available, and a fair amount of information about their psychological and social setting could be obtained.

The Population Studied

All subjects were members of families whose medical care is received from physicians in the Montefiore Hospital Medical Group. Families who experienced bereavement were randomly assigned either to a treatment group receiving psychotherapy and designated as the *T*-group or to a nontreatment group designated as the *NT*-group. The remaining families in the program were those in which *no* death in the immediate family had occurred during the previous three years. This second control (nonbereaved or *NB*-group) was drawn from the clinic's population, based on certain sociocultural characteristics, and matched to those of the *T* and *NT* bereaved groups. The *NB* subjects provided data from which estimates of "spontaneous" incidence of major morbidity and maladjustment occurred independently of bereavement.

INDICES (INDEPENDENT VARIABLES) OF COMPARISON BETWEEN GROUPS STUDIED

The chief measures employed were to have as far as possible the following characteristics: discreteness; easy availability; macroscopic scale (i.e., variables capable of reflecting and indicating finer, more subtle and elusive variables); socioeconomic as well as psychomedical importance.

The variables for measurement were selected in accordance with these characteristics. The major interest for analysis were variables for which gross counts of morbidity and maladjustment were computed.

    A. *Psychological indices*
        1. Number of referrals to the psychiatrist, clinical psychologist, and number of psychiatric outpatients contacts.
        2. Psychological mood states
    B. *Medical indices*
        1. Number of visits to the doctor. (Special note was made as to whether visit was for a major or minor illness.)
        2. Number of major illnesses, accidents, operations, hospitalizations and deaths. Although data were collected for all types of illnesses, major illness (e.g., coronary thrombosis) was separated from minor illness (e.g., flu).
    C. *Social indices:* Social activities, contacts with family members and friends, future hopes, and so forth.

INDEPENDENT VARIABLES FOR ANALYSIS

Inherent in any demonstration and evaluative program is a multitude of independent variables that can be employed. If one's major concern is the analysis and consideration of all possible variables, a situation will arise where "there are more variables than subjects." For this investigation, then, the researchers selected variables they considered to be strategic for the major proposed problem. The prime independent variable is, of course, brief psychotherapy and its relationship to major morbidity and maladjustment. However, several other variables were also explored within the overall analytical framework.

    A. *Variables related to the deceased*

The question here is, in what psychological, medical, and social ways are survivors differentially affected by the following variables:

        1. Degree of chronicity of the illness of the deceased. (The importance of this variable is that in a death following chronic illness, measured

by days in hospital or days under a physician's care, survivors may have anticipated their grief and, therefore, would differ in their bereaved reactions from survivors of an acute illness death.)
2. Nature of illness of the deceased, i.e., cardiovascular vs. malignancy.
3. Sex of deceased.
4. Age of deceased.
5. Family position of the deceased.

All families who were bereaved because of a death from a malignant or cardiovascular disease were randomly assigned to treatment or nontreatment based on a 2 to 1 ratio. Nonbereaved were matched on characteristics such as age, sex of survivor, number, and age of offspring.

It should be clearly evident that this study is dealing for the most part with an aged population in crisis. As the study progressed, we became increasingly aware that over 70 percent of this population was over 60.

The recent census has demonstrated that the rate of increase in population is highest in the geriatric (65 and over) age group. This segment constitutes approximately 10 percent of our total population, or in absolute figures over 20 million people. It is estimated that by the year 2000 the geriatric population in this country will be more than 29 million. The disturbing aspect is not the number of older people but that the aged have a disproportionately high amount of medical, social, psychological, and economic problems which, in the main, have been left unresolved. It is well known, as evidenced in the literature, that the incidence and prevalence of medical, social, and psychological problems in the geriatric population are significantly higher than in the younger age groupings. Over 75 percent of elderly people suffer from at least one chronic condition, and almost half have two or more. Hearing and visual problems are the most prevalent impairments for the aged. Some 20 percent of those who are 65 to 75 suffer from hearing loss and about 10 percent report visual problems. For the over-75 group, the figures are 25 percent and 15 percent. In the aged group, the most prevalent chronic diseases are arthritis and rheumatism (suffered by about 30 percent), heart disease (15 percent), and high blood pressure (approximately 15 percent). Patients over 65 occupy over 50 percent of beds in general hospitals. It is estimated that approximately 10 percent of the geriatric population suffers from organic brain disease, from 15 to 25 percent are significantly psychiatrically impaired, with 7 percent having psychotic illnesses. Although the aged represent 10 percent of the total population, 25 percent of reported suicides occur in this group. The economic plight of the geriatric population is well known and nearly 40 percent have an income below subsistence values. Retirement, comparative distances from close family members, continuous loss of relatives and friends because of death, the assuming of the single role of "consumer," as opposed to the previous "producer" and "participant" roles, and certain fears related to deviant conditions in the community are only a few of the problems the aged have to overcome.

The above overview of the condition of the aged, while certainly not exhaustive, appears to be sufficient to support the thesis that a large number of questions remain to be answered if the community is to deal effectively with the geriatric problems of the 1970s. A sample of some general questions would include: Who among the aged are vulnerable to medical, social, and psychological impairment of disability? What factors, especially medical and social, in the previous and existing history of the elderly render them vulnerable or immune to the stresses accompanying the aging period? What prophylactic primary interventions, if any, can reduce the impact of such stresses?

In an attempt to answer some of these questions in a scientific manner, we undertook to study the aged in a period of stress which one has to assume is the most critical in terms of social and medical functioning of all life-cycle changes. Our overall objective was to study comprehensively, within an experimental prospective design, those aged who had recently been bereaved.

Results

To our knowledge this is the first controlled prospective study into the process and phenomenology of bereavement as it affects the aged. We have shown conclusively that this process is not so muted in the elderly as has been previously believed. We are reporting in this preliminary communication on only the medical consequences of bereavement; the social and psychological consequences will be reported in subsequent papers. It is clear that a fair amount of suffering is associated with bereavement, as is evidenced from both the increased use of office visits for major illnesses and our clinical evaluation of patients receiving psychotherapy in the first six months following bereavement. It is also apparent that the deleterious effects of bereavement in the elderly may be delayed and begin to manifest themselves only after the first six months following the loss. Preliminary unpublished results in our longer follow-up show that some of these findings will bear up even in the two-to-four year period following bereavement. Table 6.1 shows conclusively that by the fifth and eighth months after the loss, the bereaved visited their physicians significantly more frequently than the nonbereaved. Table 6.2 documents the most significant finding so far to come up in our investigation. It shows that the bereaved with a poor prior

TABLE 6.1. FREQUENCY OF OFFICE VISITS TO PHYSICIANS BY NONTREATMENT BEREAVED (NT) AND NONBEREAVED (NB) BY PREDICTOR VARIABLES AT DIFFERENT TIME PERIODS [a]

	T–1 From Loss to 2 Months				T–2 Over 2 to 5 Months				T–3 Over 5 to 8 Months				T–4 Over 8 to 15 Months			
	NT		NB		NT		NB		NT		NB		NT		NB	
	%	N	%	N	%	N	%	N	%	N	%	N	%	N	%	N
Research Group	68.9	(31)	69.0	(40)	66.0	(33)	62.6	(27)	66.7	(32)[b]	64.4	(38)	62.2	(28)	69.4	(41
Male	64.4	(9)[b]	72.2	(13)	60.0	(9)	61.1	(11)	61.5	(8)	61.1	(11)	72.7	(9)	66.7	(12
Female	70.9	(22)	67.5	(27)	68.5	(24)	63.4	(26)	68.5	(24)	65.9	(27)	58.8	(20)	70.7	(29
Under 60	53.9	(7)	84.6	(11)	57.1	(8)	61.6	(8)	46.2	(6)	76.9	(10)	33.3	(4)[b]	69.3	(9
Over 60	75.0	(24)	64.5	(29)	69.4	(25)	63.0	(29)	74.2	(26)	60.8	(28)	72.8	(24)	69.5	(32
Catholic	63.2	(12)	59.2	(16)[b]	63.2	(12)	51.8	(14)	66.7	(12)	59.2	(16)	64.7	(11)	62.9	(17
Jewish	70.8	(17)	75.0	(21)	68.1	(15)	75.0	(21)	66.7	(14)	67.8	(19)	57.9	(11)	75.0	(21
Other	50.0	(1)	100.0	(3)	100.0	(2)	33.3	(1)	100.0	(2)	66.7	(2)	50.0	(1)	66.7	(2
Social Class: I	72.8	(8)	69.2	(18)	70.0	(7)	61.5	(16)[c]	80.0	(12)	61.5	(16)	46.6	(7)	76.9	(20
II	73.4	(22)	80.0	(12)	67.9	(19)	86.6	(13)	56.3	(9)	66.7	(10)	71.4	(10)	66.7	(10
III	65.2	(15)	61.5	(8)	59.1	(13)	46.0	(6)	71.4	(5)	69.2	(9)	57.1	(4)	61.6	(8
Prior Medical History: Good	53.9	(7)	60.0	(12)	53.3	(8)	60.0	(12)	46.0	(7)	55.0	(11)	35.7	(5)	70.0	(14
Fair	70.9	(17)	72.7	(24)	69.2	(18)	61.8	(21)	75.0	(18)	70.5	(24)	72.7	(16)	70.6	(24
Poor	80.0	(4)	80.0	(4)	87.5	(7)	80.0	(4)	75.0	(16)	60.0	(3)	87.5	(7)	60.0	(3

[a] Only affirmative responses reflected. History of death related illness is not applicable for nonbereaved subjects and will be eliminated for this table and others involving the nonbereaved.
[b] Chi-square significant at .05 level.
[c] Chi-square significant at .01 level.

TABLE 6.2. FREQUENCY OF OFFICE VISITS TO PHYSICIANS FOR MAJOR ILLNESSES BY NONTREATMENT BEREAVED AND NONBEREAVED, BY PRIOR MEDICAL HISTORY AT DIFFERENT TIME PERIODS [a]

Prior Medical History	T-1 From Loss to 2 Months				T-2 Over 2 to 5 Months				T-3 Over 5 to 8 Months				T-4 Over 8 to 15 Months			
	NT		NB		NT		NB		NT		NB		NT		NB	
	%	N	%	N	%	N	%	N	%	N	%	N	%	N	%	N
Good	7.7	(1)[c]	15.0	(3)	13.3	(2)[c]	15.0	(3)	0.0	(0)[b]	15.0	(3)	7.1	(1)[c]	35.0	(7)
Fair	0.0	(0)	0.0	(0)	7.7	(2)	14.7	(5)	12.5	(3)	17.6	(6)	18.2	(4)	17.6	(6)
Poor	40.0	(2)	20.0	(1)	75.0	(6)	20.0	(1)	37.5	(3)	00.0	(0)	62.5	(5)	40.0	(2)

[a] Only affirmative responses are reflected.
[b] Chi-square significant at .05 level.
[c] Chi-square significant at .01 level.
[1] Chi-square significant at .001 level.

TABLE 6.3. FREQUENCY OF OFFICE VISITS TO PHYSICIANS FOR MINOR ILLNESSES BY NONTREATMENT BEREAVED AND NONBEREAVED BY PREDICTOR VARIABLES AT DIFFERENT TIME PERIODS [a]

	T-1 From Loss to 2 Months				T-2 Over 2 to 5 Months				T-3 Over 5 to 8 Months				T-4 Over 8 to 15 Months			
	NT		NB		NT		NB		NT		NB		NT		NB	
	%	N	%	N	%	N	%	N	%	N	%	N	%	N	%	N
Research Group	62.2	(28)	62.1	(36)	64.0	(60)	64.0	(32)	62.5	(30)	55.9	(33)	62.2	(28)	59.3	(35)
Male	57.1	(8)	60.0	(24)	60.0	(9)	50.0	(9)	53.8	(7)	44.4	(8)	72.7	(8)	44.4	(8)
Female	64.5	(20)	40.0	(16)	65.7	(23)	61.0	(25)	65.7	(23)	61.0	(25)	58.8	(20)	65.8	(27)
Under 60	53.8	(7)	76.9	(10)	50.0	(7)	53.8	(7)	46.2	(6)	76.9	(10)	33.3	(4)[b]	69.2	(9)
Over 60	65.6	(21)	57.8	(26)	69.4	(25)	58.7	(27)	68.6	(24)	50.0	(23)	72.7	(24)	56.5	(26)
Catholic	47.4	(9)	51.8	(14)	63.2	(12)	48.1	(13)[b]	61.1	(11)	48.1	(13)	64.7	(11)	44.4	(12)
Jewish	70.8	(17)	67.9	(19)	68.2	(15)	71.4	(20)	61.9	(13)	60.7	(17)	57.9	(11)	71.4	(20)
Other	100.0	(2)	100.0	(3)	100.0	(2)	00.0	(0)	100.0	(2)	66.7	(2)	50.0	(1)	66.7	(2)
Social Class: I	50.0	(8)	61.5	(16)	66.7	(10)	57.7	(15)	73.3	(11)	53.8	(14)	46.7	(7)	65.4	(17)
II	72.2	(13)	66.7	(10)	58.8	(10)	80.0	(12)	50.0	(8)	53.3	(8)	71.4	(10)	66.7	(10)
III	66.7	(6)	61.5	(8)	87.5	(7)	38.5	(5)	71.4	(5)	61.5	(8)	57.1	(14)	38.5	(5)
Prior Medical History: Good	53.8	(7)	45.0	(9)	53.3	(8)	60.0	(12)	46.7	(7)	50.0	(10)	35.7	(15)[b]	55.0	(11)
Fair	66.7	(16)	72.7	(24)	69.2	(18)	52.9	(18)	70.8	(17)	58.8	(20)	72.7	(16)	64.7	(22)
Poor	60.0	(3)	60.0	(3)	75.0	(6)	80.0	(4)	62.5	(5)	60.0	(3)	87.5	(7)	40.0	(2)

[a] Only affirmative responses are reflected.
[b] Chi-square significant at .05 level.

medical history visit their physicians significantly more frequently than the nonbereaved in the first 15 months following bereavement. This finding might be interpreted in many ways. It may indicate an actual deterioration in their medical condition; on the other hand, it may be that bereaved with poor prior medical health neglected themselves before the death of their spouses and are now paying the penalty for their neglect. Or it may indicate merely that a physical illness with concomitant severe symptomatology may be the ticket of admission to receive support from their physicians, with the severity of their symptoms "legitimizing" their need. We shall need to look at these findings more carefully to try to extract the various possibilities.

Table 6.4 documents another aspect of the phenomenon demonstrated in

TABLE 6.4. FREQUENCY OF USE OF MEDICATIONS BY NONTREATMENT BEREAVED AND NONBEREAVED BY PREDICTOR VARIABLES AT DIFFERENT TIME PERIODS [a]

	T–1 From Loss to 2 Months				T–2 Over 2 to 5 Months				T–3 Over 5 to 8 Months				T–4 Over 8 to 15 Months			
	NT		NB		NT		NB		NT		NB		NT		NB	
	%	N	%	N	%	N	%	N	%	N	%	N	%	N	%	N
Research Group	80.0	(36)	80.7	(46)	42.0	(37)	22.0	(13)	43.8	(21)[c]	16.9	(10)	33.3	(15)	33.9	(20
Male	64.3	(9)	66.7	(12)	40.0	(6)	16.7	(3)	30.8	(4)	11.1	(2)	36.3	(4)	27.8	(5
Female	87.1	(27)	87.2	(34)	42.8	(15)	24.4	(10)	48.6	(17)	19.5	(8)	32.3	(11)	35.6	(15
Under 60	77.0	(10)	76.9	(10)	42.8	(6)	23.0	(3)	30.8	(4)[b]	15.4	(2)	16.6	(2)	38.4	(5
Over 60	81.3	(26)	81.8	(36)	41.6	(15)	21.7	(10)	48.6	(17)	17.4	(8)	39.4	(13)	32.6	(15
Catholic	73.7	(14)	85.2	(33)[b]	47.4	(9)	22.0	(6)	38.9	(7)	11.1	(3)	29.4	(5)	40.7	(1
Jewish	83.3	(20)	71.4	(22)	40.9	(9)	21.4	(6)	42.8	(9)	21.4	(6)	31.6	(6)	32.1	(
Other	100.0	(2)	33.3	(1)	50.0	(1)	33.3	(1)	50.0	(1)	00.0	(0)	00.0	(0)	00.0	(
Social Class: I	81.2	(13)	80.0	(20)	33.3	(5)	19.2	(5)	26.6	(4)	11.5	(3)	20.0	(3)	26.9	(
II	83.3	(15)	80.0	(12)	47.0	(8)	33.3	(5)	56.2	(9)	20.0	(3)	28.5	(4)	53.3	(
III	77.8	(7)	84.6	(11)	50.0	(4)	23.1	(3)	42.8	(3)	15.4	(2)	28.6	(2)	38.4	(
Prior Medical History: Good	69.2	(9)	90.0	(18)	13.3	(2)[b]	20.0	(4)[b]	26.6	(4)	20.2	(4)	14.3	(2)	35.0	(
Fair	79.1	(19)	71.9	(23)	53.9	(14)	20.5	(7)	50.0	(12)	11.8	(4)	36.3	(8)	29.4	(1
Poor	100.0	(5)	100.0	(5)	62.5	(5)	40.0	(2)	50.0	(4)	40.0	(2)	62.5	(5)	60.0	(

[a] Only affirmative responses are reflected.
[b] Chi-square significant at .05 level.
[c] Chi-square significant at .01 level.

Process of Bereavement

Table 6.1. It shows that the frequency of use of all medications is significantly greater for the bereaved than the nonbereaved between the fifth and eighth months following the loss of the spouse. This finding remains significant for the use of tranquilizers and antidepressants as shown in Table 6.5

TABLE 6.5. FREQUENCY OF USE OF TRANQUILIZERS AND ANTIDEPRESSANTS BY NONTREATMENT BEREAVED AND NONBEREAVED BY PREDICTOR VARIABLES AT DIFFERENT TIME PERIODS [a]

	T–1 From Loss to 2 Months				T–2 Over 2 to 5 Months				T–3 Over 5 to 8 Months				T–4 Over 8 to 15 Months			
	NT		NB		NT		NB		NT		NB		NT		NB	
	%	N	%	N	%	N	%	N	%	N	%	N	%	N	%	N
Research Group	35.6	(16)	29.3	(17)	22.0	(11)[b]	5.1	(3)	10.4	(5)	5.1	(3)	13.3	(6)	17.0	(10)
Male	28.6	(4)	11.1	(2)[b]	6.7	(1)	0.0	(0)	00.0	(0)	00.0	(0)	00.0	(0)	00.0	(0)[b]
Female	38.7	(12)	37.5	(15)	28.6	(10)	7.3	(3)	14.3	(5)	7.3	(3)	17.6	(6)	24.4	(10)
Under 60	30.8	(4)	30.8	(4)	35.7	(5)	7.7	(1)	7.7	(1)	0.0	(0)	00.0	(0)	15.4	(2)
Over 60	37.5	(12)	28.9	(13)	16.7	(6)	4.3	(2)	11.4	(4)	6.5	(3)	18.2	(6)	17.4	(8)
Catholic	21.1	(4)	22.2	(6)	21.1	(4)	7.4	(2)	00.0	(0)	7.4	(2)	11.8	(2)	14.8	(4)
Jewish	45.8	(11)	39.3	(11)	27.3	(6)	3.6	(1)	23.8	(5)	3.6	(1)	18.8	(3)	21.4	(6)
Other	50.0	(1)	00.0	(0)	00.0	(0)	0.0	(0)	00.0	(0)	0.0	(0)	00.0	(0)	00.0	(0)
Social Class: I	25.0	(4)	23.1	(6)	20.0	(3)	3.8	(1)	13.3	(2)	0.0	(0)	13.3	(2)	15.4	(4)
II	33.3	(6)	40.0	(6)	23.5	(4)	0.0	(0)	18.8	(3)	6.7	(1)	7.1	(1)	26.7	(4)
III	55.6	(5)	38.5	(5)	25.0	(2)	15.4	(2)	00.0	(0)	7.7	(1)	14.3	(1)	15.4	(2)
Prior Medical History: Good	15.4	(2)	20.0	(4)[b]	13.3	(2)	5.0	(1)	00.0	(0)	00.0	(0)	100.0	(14)	10.0	(2)
Fair	41.7	(10)	27.3	(9)	26.9	(7)	2.9	(1)	12.5	(3)	5.9	(2)	13.6	(3)	20.6	(7)
Poor	40.0	(2)	80.0	(4)	25.0	(2)	20.0	(1)	25.0	(2)	20.0	(1)	37.5	(3)	20.0	(1)

[a] Only affirmative responses are reflected.
[b] Chi-square significant at .05 level.

and for the use of general medications as shown in Table 6.6. Finally, in Table 6.7, subjective findings of ill health are significantly more frequently demonstrated among the bereaved than the nonbereaved, in the 5- to 8-months period, especially among the Jewish population.

TABLE 6.6. FREQUENCY OF USE OF GENERAL MEDICATIONS BY NONTREATMENT BEREAVED AND NONBEREAVED BY PREDICTOR VARIABLES AT DIFFERENT TIME PERIODS [a]

	T-1 From Loss to 2 Months				T-2 Over 2 to 5 Months				T-3 Over 5 to 8 Months				T-4 Over 8 to 15 Months			
	NT		NB		NT		NB		NT		NB		NT		NB	
Research Group	%	N	%	N	%	N	%	N	%	N	%	N	%	N	%	N
	60.0	(27)[b]	63.8	(37)	24.0	(12)	20.3	(12)	41.7	(20)[c]	8.5	(5)	24.4	(11)	22.0	(13)
Male	42.9	(6)	61.1	(11)	26.7	(4)	16.7	(3)	30.8	(4)	11.1	(2)	27.3	(3)	27.8	(5)
Female	67.7	(21)	65.0	(26)	21.6	(8)	22.0	(9)	45.7	(16)	7.3	(3)	23.5	(8)	19.5	(8)
Under 60	53.8	(7)	53.8	(7)	14.3	(2)	15.4	(2)	23.1	(3)	7.7	(1)	16.7	(2)	30.8	(4)
Over 60	62.5	(20)	66.7	(30)	27.8	(10)	21.7	(10)	48.6	(7)	8.7	(4)	27.3	(9)	19.6	(9)
Catholic	57.9	(11)	63.0	(17)	31.6	(6)	18.5	(5)	38.9	(7)	0.0	(0)	11.8	(2)	33.3	(9)
Jewish	62.5	(15)	67.9	(19)	18.2	(4)	21.4	(6)	38.1	(8)	17.8	(5)	26.3	(5)	14.3	(4)
Other	50.0	(1)	100.0	(3)	50.0	(1)	33.3	(1)	50.0	(1)	0.0	(0)	00.0	(0)	00.0	(0)
Social Class: I	62.5	(10)	65.4	(17)	20.0	(3)	15.4	(4)	20.0	(3)	7.7	(2)	13.3	(2)	15.4	(4)
II	61.1	(11)	60.0	(9)	29.4	(5)	33.3	(5)	56.3	(9)	13.3	(2)	21.4	(3)	33.3	(5)
III	55.6	(5)	61.5	(8)	25.0	(2)	23.1	(3)	42.9	(3)	00.0	(0)	14.3	(1)	30.8	(4)
Prior Medical History:																
Good	61.5	(8)	75.0	(15)	6.7	(1)	20.0	(4)	26.7	(4)	15.0	(3)	14.3	(2)	30.0	(6)[b]
Fair	58.3	(14)	60.6	(20)	30.8	(8)	17.6	(6)	45.8	(11)	5.9	(2)	22.7	(5)	11.8	(4)
Poor	60.0	(3)	40.0	(2)	37.5	(3)	40.0	(2)	50.0	(4)	0.0	(0)	50.0	(4)	60.0	(3)

[a] Only affirmative responses are reflected.
[b] Chi-square significant at .05 level.
[c] Chi-square significant at .01 level.

The Process of Bereavement

The process of normal bereavement in the aged has not previously been adequately documented. Our data were obtained from our more extensive clinical studies of the treated bereaved and they represent our assessment of these patients during the six months following bereavement. Certain feelings about the deceased as well as about oneself are so frequent as to be practically universal during the first three months following bereavement. These include feelings of emptiness without the deceased, both sad and happy memories of the deceased, fears, feelings of worthlessness, worries, sadness, loneliness, discontent, crying, suspiciousness, and anger directed at self, deceased, or others. By the end of the second three months following

TABLE 6.7. FREQUENCY OF FEELING ILL WITHOUT PHYSICIAN CONTACT BY NONTREATMENT BEREAVED AND NONBEREAVED BY PREDICTOR VARIABLES AT DIFFERENT TIME PERIODS [a]

	T-1 From Loss to 2 Months				T-2 Over 2 to 5 Months				T-3 Over 5 to 8 Months				T-4 Over 8 to 15 Months			
	NT		NB		NT		NB		NT		NB		NT		NB	
	%	N	%	N	%	N	%	N	%	N	%	N	%	N	%	N
Research Group	48.9	(22)	33.3	(19)	66.7	(16)	42.4	(14)	64.3	(18)[b]	33.3	(11)	44.4	(16)	45.5	(20)
Male	28.6	(4)	22.2	(4)	66.7	(4)	30.0	(3)	42.9	(3)	18.2	(2)	27.3	(3)	33.3	(4)
Female	58.1	(18)	38.5	(15)	66.7	(12)	47.8	(11)	71.4	(15)	40.9	(9)	52.0	(13)	50.0	(16)
Under 60	46.2	(6)	15.4	(2)	33.3	(3)[c]	40.0	(4)	54.5	(6)	10.0	(1)	45.5	(5)	36.4	(4)
Over 60	50.0	(16)	38.6	(17)	86.7	(13)	43.5	(10)	70.6	(12)	43.5	(10)	44.0	(11)	48.5	(16)
Catholic	47.4	(9)	26.9	(7)	45.5	(5)	38.9	(7)	41.7	(5)	11.8	(2)[c]	40.0	(6)	45.5	(10)
Jewish	50.0	(12)	42.9	(12)	81.8	(9)	53.8	(7)	78.6	(11)	64.3	(9)	44.4	(8)	47.4	(9)
Other	50.0	(1)	00.0	(0)	100.0	(2)	00.0	(0)	100.0	(2)	00.0	(0)	100.0	(2)	33.3	(1)
Social Class: I	43.8	(7)	50.0	(13)[b]	50.0	(3)	54.5	(6)	50.0	(6)	57.1	(8)[b]	50.0	(6)	50.0	(9)
II	55.6	(10)	13.3	(2)	55.6	(5)	50.0	(5)	77.8	(7)	20.0	(2)	46.2	(6)	53.8	(7)
III	44.4	(4)	16.7	(2)	42.9	(4)	50.0	(4)	66.7	(4)	00.0	(0)	37.5	(3)	36.4	(4)
Prior Medical History: Good	53.8	(7)	40.0	(8)	50.0	(3)	33.3	(3)	50.0	(4)	27.3	(3)	41.7	(5)	50.0	(6)
Fair	50.0	(12)	30.3	(10)	66.7	(10)	42.9	(9)	62.5	(10)	36.8	(7)	47.4	(9)	42.8	(12)
Poor	40.0	(2)	25.0	(1)	100.0	(2)	66.7	(2)	100.0	(3)	33.3	(1)	25.0	(1)	50.0	(2)

[a] Only affirmative responses are reflected.
[b] Chi-square significant at .05 level.
[c] Chi-square significant at .01 level.

bereavement, most of these feelings and attitudes have substantially changed toward the normal.

Clayton speaks of a "depressive complex" (Clayton, 1968) in some of her bereaved subjects. This complex consists of loss of appetite, sleep difficulties, fatigue, agitation, retardation, loss of interest, difficulty in concentrating, feelings of guilt and wishing to be dead. Suffering is, however, difficult to measure. The longer one spends listening to bereaved subjects, the more impressed one is how universal these manifestations are in the first three to six months following bereavement. We are therefore wary of evaluating symptoms at one specific time to determine the presence or absence of various symptoms.

The more carefully bereaved patients are investigated, the more frequently they are interviewed and their clinical progress evaluated; and the more common it is to find the whole gamut of symptoms, listed by Clayton and others, as being part and parcel of normal bereavement, rather than manifestations of "depression," "pathological mourning," "unresolved grief," and so forth. These clinical findings apply only to the first six months following bereavement. We cannot, at this stage, be certain how often any of these symptoms and signs will be prevalent, however transiently, over the years following bereavement. We have some preliminary evidence that some of these symptoms tend to recur at various times, precipitated by anniversaries, memories, meetings, geographical locale, etc., remain a few days, and have no permanent pathological meaning since the bereaved then continue their normal functioning.

Discussion

The findings reported in this paper are preliminary and deal only with medical morbidity and mortality and leave out the crucial psychological and social data that are still being analyzed. These findings are also the result of the first 15 months follow-up subsequent to bereavement. Even so, at this early stage of data analysis we are only beginning to rephrase some of the original questions asked when our investigation began.

The question, is there morbidity and maladjustment following bereavement and should the bereaved receive help, is too simplistic. We have to ask very specific questions: Who is vulnerable? In what way are they vulnerable? What does morbidity and maladjustment consist of? Who should receive help? By whom should the help be given? We are beginning to obtain some preliminary answers to these questions; our results seem to indicate that women over 60, especially if Jewish, suffer excessive medical morbidity. Parkes (1970) suggests that widows under 45 are especially vulnerable as well. Our most striking finding has been the clear-cut evidence that bereaved with a poor prior medical history will suffer significant need to attend their physicians for the first year following bereavement for major medical illness, as compared with the nonbereaved group with the same poor prior medical history. There are a number of possible reasons for these findings, which have been detailed above. It is clear that the physician treating a dying patient whose spouse has a major medical illness—e.g., heart disease, high blood pressure, diabetes—would do well to treat such a spouse in medical prophylaxis during bereavement to diminish, if possible, severe medical deterioration.

We have not found an increase in the number of deaths, major hospitalizations, and psychiatric decompensations in our bereaved population in the first 15 months following bereavement. We have found an increase in the number of doctor visits, intake of medications, and subjective feelings of being unwell. We want to stress again that the outstanding finding so far has been the increased incidence of office visits for major illness among the bereaved with a poor prior medical history. We believe that this finding is of crucial importance in preventive medicine and should be made known to the medical profession.

REFERENCES

Clayton, P. J., *et al.* 1968. "A Study of Normal Bereavement." *American Journal of Psychiatry* 125:168–78.

—— 1973. "The Clinical Morbidity of the First Year of Bereavement: A Review," *Comprehensive Psychiatry* 14:151–57.

Parkes, C. M. 1970. "The First Year of Bereavement: A Longitudinal Study of the Reaction of London Widows to the Death of their Husbands." *Psychiatry* 33:444–67.

7

The Bereaved and Their Hallucinations

W. Dewi Rees

The extent to which widowed people experience hallucinations of their dead spouse has rarely been investigated (Rees, 1971a; 1971b). For the sake of simplicity, the term "hallucination" is used to include "a sense of the presence of the dead person," in addition to visual, auditory, and tactile hallucinations.

METHOD

In a defined area of mid-Wales, 227 widows and 66 widowers were interviewed to determine the extent to which they had hallucinatory experiences of the dead spouse. The people interviewed formed 80.7 percent of all widowed people resident within the defined area and 94.2 percent of those suitable, through the absence of incapacitating illness, for interview. The refusal rate was 0.6 percent.

THE INTERVIEW

Each person was interviewed separately and, with four exceptions, no other person was present during the interview. The interviews were conducted in a semi-rigid manner. Each person was encouraged to talk freely about the deceased spouse, but enough direction was given to ensure that all items listed on a standardized form were covered. Particular care was taken in assessing the statements of those who reported hallucinatory experiences. Only those who did not rationalize the experience—for instance, by saying they

had seen the deceased in their "mind's eye"—were listed as being hallucinated. If there was any doubt about the reality of the experience, a nil
response was recorded. Experiences occurring in bed at night, other than
those occurring immediately after retiring, were discounted and recorded as
dreams.

STATISTICAL ANALYSIS AND RESULTS

The recorded data were transcribed onto punch cards and analyzed mechani-
cally. The statistical tests were carried out mainly with an Elliott 4130 computer programmed to test the difference between the two proportions. The
results showed that 46.7 percent of the 293 people interviewed had post-
bereavement hallucinations. These hallucinations often lasted many years,
and at the time of interview 36.1 percent still had hallucinations. Thus, almost half the widowed people had had an hallucinatory experience of the
dead spouse and over one-third still had these hallucinations when interviewed.

No difference was found between the proportion of men and women affected; 50 percent of the men and 45.8 percent of widows had hallucinations.

The most common finding was a "sense of the presence" of the dead
spouse, which was reported by 39.2 percent of widowed people; 14 percent
reported visual hallucinations, 13.3 percent auditory hallucinations, 2.7 percent tactile hallucinations, and 11.6 percent stated that they themselves had
spoken to the dead spouse.

Further statistical analysis showed that people widowed below the age of
40 were less likely to be hallucinated than those widowed after the age of
40. This finding was of particular interest because of the close association
reported by Kraus and Lilienfeld (1959) between a high post-bereavement
mortality and youthfulness of widowhood.

People widowed for under 10 years reported a higher incidence of hallucinations than those widowed for a longer period. A possible explanation for
this difference is that people widowed for over 20 or 30 years may have
forgotten hallucinations they had in fact experienced.

People whose marriages were happy were more likely to have had hallucinations than the surviving spouses of unhappy marriages. The incidence of
hallucination was decreased significantly if the marriage had been childless.

Contrary to expectation, members of the professional and managerial group were more likely to have had post-bereavement hallucinations than were other occupational groups.

Another factor associated with a significantly increased incidence of hallucination was duration of marriage. It was anticipated that in longer-lasting marriages there would be an increase in the incidence of hallucination. This expected increase was found to occur.

FACTORS NOT AFFECTING INCIDENCE OF HALLUCINATION SIGNIFICANTLY

A large number of factors were found not to affect the incidence of hallucination. These included sex and the age when interviewed. There was no variation with suddenness of death; neither was the incidence of hallucination affected by the presence of relatives at the death, or their expectation of it.

No variation occurred with cultural background as assessed by an ability to speak Welsh as well as English, with sectarian allegiance within the Christian faith, or with regularity of church attendance.

No variation occurred with residence when bereaved, whether in towns, villages, or rural areas. Residence when bereaved—whether within the Llanidloes area, Wales outside Llanidloes, or outside Wales—did not affect the incidence of hallucination; neither did subsequent change of residence.

Social isolation—assessed as feeling lonely, living alone, having relatives living nearby, or having a regular job—made no difference in the incidence of hallucination. There was no variation with the recorded history of depression requiring medical treatment, whether this occurred before or after bereavement.

PREVIOUS DISCLOSURE OF HALLUCINATIONS

Most widowed people do not disclose their hallucinations and only 27.7 percent had done so. Widows were more likely to do so than widowers. No doctor had been informed and only one person had confided in a clergyman.

Of the 91 people who had not previously disclosed their hallucinations, 51 could give no reason for not having done so. Of those who offered an explanation the most common—fear of ridicule—was mentioned by 14 people. Other reasons given were that it was too personal (7), no previous inquiry

(6), people would not be interested (6), would upset relatives if they knew (6), unlucky to talk about it (2), and various other reasons (7). Social isolation did not affect the frequency with which the information had been previously disclosed.

HELP FROM HALLUCINATIONS

Most percipients were helped by their hallucinations. Altogether 78 percent of the visually hallucinated, 66.7 percent of the auditorily hallucinated, 73 percent with a sense of the deceased person's presence, and 82.4 percent of those who spoke to the dead person found it helpful.

In contrast to the 68.8 percent of all people who were helped, 5.9 percent found the experiences unpleasant, while 25.5 percent found them neither helpful nor unpleasant.

VERBATIM REPORTS

People's reactions are best described in their own words, expressed by a variety of grammatical form and idiom. This section sets out to show in this manner the range of response elicited by the hallucinations. The reactions vary from a sense of protection and companionship to, less frequently, one of fearfulness.

"He's always with me" (widowed 2 years).

"He seems so close" (widowed 7 years).

"Very often he is by my side. It is a funny thing, I've never dreamt of him" (widowed 4 years).

"I was wondering whether I was going a little bit mental at the time" (widowed 20 years).

"Once he came to the door when I was preparing lunch and I saw him. It was an awful shock" (widowed 5 years).

"I heard, how shall I put it, sounds of consolation for the first three months" (widowed 26 years).

"I think she got me my present house. I find hearing her breathing disturbing, but I like the feeling she is in the house" (widowed 16 years).

"I feel him guiding me" (widowed 15 years).

"I fancy if I left here, I would be running away from him. Lots of people wanted me to go, but I just couldn't. I often hear him walking about. He speaks quite plainly. He looks younger, just as he was when he was all right, never as he was ill" (widowed 9 months).

DISCUSSION

The findings of this study are that hallucinatory experiences of the dead spouse are common among widowed people. Supportive evidence for this comes from the report of Marris (1958). While pursuing a socioeconomic survey, he interviewed 72 young widows in London. He found that 50 percent had hallucinations of the dead spouse, which is very similar to the Llanidloes figure of 46.7 percent. Yamamoto (1969) interviewed 20 widows living in Tokyo and found that 90 percent reported feeling the presence of the dead spouse, though none reported cultivation of the idea of the presence of the deceased. None of the Tokyo widows worried about their sanity because of their experience, and Yamamoto considered that religion helped this aspect of grieving.

CONCLUSION

It seems reasonable to conclude from these studies that hallucinations are normal experiences after widowhood, providing helpful psychological phenomena to those experiencing them. Evidence supporting this statement is as follows: hallucinations are common experiences after widowhood; they occur irrespective of sex, race, creed or domicile; they do not affect overt behavior; they tend to disappear with time; there is no evidence of associated illness or abnormality to suggest they are abnormal features; they are more common in people whose marriages were happy and who had children; people are able to integrate the experience and keep it secret. Evidence supporting the claim that these experiences are helpful is twofold. Most people feel they are helped by their hallucinations. Among those least likely to be hallucinated are those widowed below the age of 40, who, according to the evidence of Kraus and Lilienfeld (1959), are in an age group particularly likely to die soon after being widowed.

REFERENCES

Kraus, A. S., and A. M. Lilienfeld. 1959. "Some Epidemiological Aspects of the High Mortality Rate in the Young Widowed Group." *Journal of Chronic Disease* 10:207 ff.

Marris, P. 1958. *Widows and their Families*. London: Routledge and Kegan Paul.

Rees, W. D. 1971a. *Hallucinations of Widowhood*. (M.D. thesis), University of London Library.

Rees, W. D. 1971b. "The Hallucinations of Widowhood." *British Medical Journal* 4:37 ff.

Yamamoto, J., K. Okonogi, T. Iwasaki, and S. Yoshimura. 1969. "Mourning in Japan." *American Journal of Psychiatry* 125:1661 ff.

8

Weight Loss and Sleep Disturbance in Bereavement

Paula J. Clayton

Clinicians and researchers have long been searching for symptoms to differentiate reactive (or neurotic) depression from endogenous depression. Kiloh and Garside (1963), using factor analysis on clinical features recorded in hospitalized patients suffering from neurotic and endogenous depression, found that along with other clinical features, early-morning awakening and weight loss of seven pounds or more were correlated positively with endogenous depression. In fact, early-morning awakening was the symptom that most significantly correlated with the endogenous depression.

We have systematically and prospectively studied the response of a group of recent widows and widowers to the deaths of their spouses. Bereavement may be considered a well circumscribed model for grief and the response to death may be a circumscribed model for a reactive depression. Because we have a group of people who responded to the stress of bereavement with depressive symptoms, with some of them having a more numerous and serious collection of depressive symptoms, it seemed worthwhile to look at the symptoms of early-morning awakening and weight loss in this group at one month and 13 months. This article presents the results.

Method

The methods of this study have been described elsewhere (Clayton et al., 1971, 1972; Bornstein et al., 1973). In summary, 109 randomly selected white widows and widowers were interviewed within one month of the death of their spouses and again at 13 months. Of the original group of subjects, four died (4 percent) within 13 months. Of the remaining 105, one was never located although he was known to be alive, 12 refused to be interviewed, and 92 were reinterviewed at 13 months. This paper will deal only with those 92 seen at both interviews. Of the 92, 65 were women and 27 were men. The mean age of the group, similar in both sexes, was 61 years. At each interview a complete list of depressive symptoms was systematically inquired about and recorded. If a positive answer was recorded, additional information was gathered. For instance, when subjects reported weight loss they were then asked about how much weight had been lost, when the weight loss had begun, and when it had ended. With sleep disturbance we recorded whether or not the subject had experienced trouble getting to sleep, early-morning awakening, poor-quality sleep, or sleeping too much. The statistical method used was a chi-square test with Yates's correction.

Results

Table 8.1 indicates the sleep disturbance that these subjects experienced at one month and at 13 months. As the table shows, 78 percent of our population experienced sleep disturbance at one month and 49 percent were still experiencing sleep difficulty at 13 months. As can be seen, the largest number of people complained of early-morning awakening alone or with

TABLE 8.1. SLEEP DISTURBANCE IN THE FIRST YEAR
OF WIDOWHOOD

	Time Since Death	
	1 Month *(N = 92)* %	*13 Months* *(N = 91)* %
Type of Sleep Problem		
None	21	50
Sleep too much	1	1
Initial insomnia, poor sleep	36	18
Early morning awakening alone or in combination	42	31

other sleep problems, both at one and 13 months. Of the 39 people who reported early-morning awakening at one month, 29 still had some sleep problem at 13 months whereas of the 33 people who reported initial insomnia or poor-quality sleep, only 15 were still experiencing some sleep problem at one year. This difference is significant at the .025 level. Thus, if one experiences terminal insomnia (synonymous with early-morning awakening) at one month, the chance of continuing to have sleep difficulty is greater than if one has initial insomnia at one month. In addition, no one reported sleep difficulty for the first time at one year, so those 22 percent with no sleep difficulty at one month (and others like them who may be seen in a doctor's office) will continue to experience no sleep problem. It was also found that the 22 percent without sleep difficulty at one month never showed the serious depressive syndrome seen in nearly one-half of the widowed at some point during the year, so no sleep difficulty at one month predicts a good outcome (Clayton et al., 1973). There is no association between sleep difficulty (at either one month or 13 months) and age. Significantly more females than males report sleep disturbance at one month (88 percent of the women and 56 percent of the men ($p < .005$) but not at one year.

TABLE 8.2. WEIGHT LOSS IN THE FIRST YEAR OF WIDOWHOOD

	Time Since Death	
	1 Month (N = 91) %	13 Months (N = 91) %
Amount		
None	52	37
Weight gain only	8	12
Weight loss 1–5 pounds	21	14
6–10 pounds	14	16
11–15 pounds	3	7
16–20 pounds	1	2
21 or > pounds	1	12

Table 8.2 shows the weight problems that the bereaved experience. By one month, 40 percent of these people reported a weight loss (this excludes the weight loss the survivors experienced during the terminal illness of the

deceased). In 5 percent the weight loss at one month was already more than 10 pounds. By 13 months, 52 percent reported a history of weight loss, although in this case it was the total amount of weight lost despite the fact that some of it may have been regained. Of interest, though, is that 21 percent reported weight loss of 11 or more pounds and 12 percent of the entire population had lost 21 or more pounds by the end of the 13-month period. Of the 47 people who reported any weight loss, 8 were men and 39 women. Of the 44 with no weight loss or weight gain only, 19 were men and 25 women. This difference is significant at the .025 level, indicating that women report weight loss significantly more often than men. Of the 21 percent who lost more than 10 pounds only one was a man (an alcoholic). Again this is a significant difference ($p < .025$) between men and women. Because of the way it was coded, using information from both interviews, it is impossible to say anything additional about those who reported no weight loss at one month. Unlike sleep disturbance, some moved from the no weight loss to some weight loss during the year, and the percent reporting weight loss increased by one year. The 5 percent ($N = 5$) who reported weight loss of 11 or more pounds by one month were continuing to lose weight to an even greater extent by 13 months. In only one of these five cases could the weight loss be due partially to a physician's order to diet (a diabetic lady with many physical problems). In these five patients and in the larger number of 19 who reported weight loss of 11 or more pounds at 13 months there is no obvious correlation with the age of the subjects (their average age is 59, only slightly younger than the sample), whether they were working or not working, or the length of the deceased's illness. Only one additional patient reported that she had lost weight because of dieting. Although the majority of those with great weight loss had what could be called a depressive syndrome at some point, only 42 percent had a relatively long period of depression.

Weight loss and sleep disturbance do not necessarily occur in the same patients. But almost all of those who lost 11 or more pounds reported sleep disturbance (mainly terminal insomnia) at one month and at 13 months.

At one month, 27 percent of the subjects took hypnotics and 40 percent took tranquilizers. By one year, 29 percent reported taking hypnotics at some time since the death and 32 percent used tranquilizers during the same period. Although most of those who reported drug use at one year were the same as those who reported it at one month, 11 percent of the entire population began to use hypnotics for the first time *after* the first-month interview and 9 percent used tranquilizers in this same time period. At one month, approximately one-half of the population were not using any drugs, one-fourth of them were using tranquilizers only, one-eighth were using hypnotics only, and one-eighth were using both. At one year, again one-half of the population were using no drugs, one-sixth each were using tranquilizers only, hypnotics only, or both. Equal percents of men and women used hypnotics at one month and one year. This means there was a trend (not a significant difference) for more men than women to use drugs for sleeping problems, since there were more women reporting sleeping difficulty both at one month and one year.

Discussion

Many authors, as Parkes summarizes, report sleep disturbance and weight loss in the widowed in early bereavement (Parkes, 1972). Most authors deal only with widows. The finding here that these two symptoms occur much more frequently in women makes comparisons with other authors more valid. In fact, finding that 79 percent of the bereaved experience sleep difficulty in the first month is very similar to the figures reported by other authors in Parkes's book. Parkes himself mentions that in the first month of bereavement 15 of 22 widows he studied prospectively had recognizable weight loss and describes insomnia in 17, and severe insomnia in 13, with difficulty in getting to sleep and a tendency to wake up early or during the night. To my knowledge this is the only description of the sleep problem.

Early-morning awakening and great weight loss are thus not uncommon in the bereavement period and in this reactive depression. It must be said that these two symptoms are not pathognomonic of the endogenous depression. This seems important to remember, as it must be supposed that there are numerous other less-well-defined stresses that produce similar symptoms.

REFERENCES

Bornstein, P. E., P. J. Clayton, J. A. Halikas, and W. L. Maurice. 1973. "The Depression of Widowhood After Thirteen Months." *British Journal of Psychiatry* 122:561 ff.

Clayton, P. J., J. A. Halikas, and W. L. Maurice. 1971. "The Bereavement of the Widowed." *Diseases of the Nervous System* 32:597 ff.

—— 1972. "The Depression of Widowhood." *British Journal of Psychiatry* 120:71 ff.

Clayton, P. J., M. Herjanic, G. E. Murphy, and R. A. Woodruff Jr. 1973. "Mourning and Depression: Their Similarities and Differences." Paper presented at the Annual Meeting of the Canadian Psychiatric Association, Vancouver, B.C.

Kiloh, L. G., and R. F. Garside. 1963. "The Independence of Neurotic Depression and Endogenous Depression." *British Journal of Psychiatry* 109:451 ff.

Parkes, C. M. 1972. *Bereavement.* New York: International Universities Press.

9

Studies in Grief: A Preliminary Report

John J. Schwab, Jean M. Chalmers, Shirley J. Conroy, Patricia B. Farris, and Robert E. Markush

As one part of a series of comprehensive studies on mortality and grief in Alachua County, Florida, we have interviewed 45 relatives of decedents who had participated in a large-scale social-psychiatric study of the county in 1970 (Schwab and Warheit, 1972). The purpose of this preliminary report is to assess these relatives' grief reactions, examine in more detail those whose grief was unresolved after one year, and describe the interviewers' emotional responses.

Background

Our studies have two major purposes: (1) to evaluate the Associated Mortality Rate, a statistic developed by Markush and Siegel (1968) that reflects possible relationships between mental illness and mortality and (2) to carry out a comprehensive investigation of the frequency and character of grief reactions. Alachua County was selected for this investigation because the information, which had been gathered from 1,645 randomly selected respon-

This research was funded by NIH Contract No. HSM-42-72-206 (ER).

dents (The Florida Health Study), can be used to ascertain possible relationships between psychosocial factors, mortality, and grief.

The county has been in the throes of social change; the population has almost doubled since 1950 and urbanization is a prominent feature. Of the 105,000 persons, 75,000 live in or near the one centrally located city which is now an educational, medical and technological center for the region; the remainder live in small towns and scattered rural settlements. Despite the rapid rate of social change in the county, there have been no major changes in mortality patterns since 1950; death rates have been much higher for blacks than whites. The relative rank order by race and sex has been slightly different in the county than in the state and the nation; in the county blacks of both sexes had the highest death rates, while in the state and nation males of both races had the highest rates (See Table 9.1).

TABLE 9.1. OVERALL DEATH RATES PER 1,000 POPULATION BY RACE AND SEX FOR ALACHUA COUNTY, FLORIDA, AND THE UNITED STATES: 1950 AND 1970

	Alachua County	*Florida*	*United States*
Non-White Male			
1950	14.4	13.5	12.5
1970	13.4	12.2	11.6
Non-White Female			
1950	11.2	9.7	9.9
1970	9.7	8.1	8.3
White Male			
1950	6.9	10.8	10.9
1970	6.7	13.6	11.1
White Female			
1950	6.3	6.9	8.0
1970	5.0	8.7	8.2

From the Florida Health Study data, an age-controlled comparison of decedents' and survivors' scores on eight scales measuring psychopathology showed that the decedents in the 45–64 age group had higher mean scores than the survivors on all of the scales, significantly higher on five. In the 65 plus age group, the decedents had higher scores than the survivors on seven of the eight scales, significantly higher on three. These preliminary findings, particularly the decedents' higher depression and mood scores, indicate associations between emotional distress and mortality, which we are investigating further by interviewing 200 relatives of adult decedents in the county in 1973 (Schwab et al., in preparation).

Method

The interviews, which were conducted in the homes of the 45 relatives, lasted approximately one hour. Only two persons refused to be interviewed; each declined because of illness and referred us to another relative. The respondent group consisted of 20 spouses, 12 children, 6 siblings, 3 parents, 2 other relatives, and 2 friends.

The interview schedule contained 265 items, many of which are directly comparable to items in the Florida Health Study. It covered six major areas: (1) demographic information on decedent and respondent, (2) physical and mental health of decedent and respondent, (3) social functioning of decedent, (4) life events of decedent, (5) health care and death-related facts, and (6) grief reactions. The interview focused primarily on details of the decedent's life during the last three years.

To assess grief reactions, for each interview we systematically prepared individual profiles consisting of 22 items (e.g., cause of death, relationship, temporal measures). Each respondent's reaction was impressionistically rated as intense, moderate, or minimal. We then compared these three levels of grief with: (1) relationship of respondent to decedent, (2) sociodemographic data on the respondent, (3) time interval between death and interview, (4) length of illness, (5) time interval between the respondent's awareness of impending death and the death, and (6) satisfaction with decedent's medical care.

We examined in more detail the data on those respondents who manifested unresolved grief one year after bereavement. The interviewers also rated their own emotional responses to each interview as high, moderate, or minimal.

Grief Reaction

Of the 45 respondents, 22 were rated as having intense grief reactions, 7 as moderate, and 16 as minimal.

RELATIONSHIP

As shown in Table 9.2, significantly more spouses and parents than other respondents were rated as grieving intensely ($p < .001$); 90 percent of the 20 spouses and all of the three parents received intense or moderate ratings, while only one-third of the children and siblings exhibited intense grief. The one "other" relative whose grief was intense was an aunt who had acted as a surrogate mother to the decedent.

TABLE 9.2. RELATIONSHIP OF RESPONDENT TO DECEDENT BY LEVEL OF GRIEF REACTION [a]

| | Type of Relationship | | | | | | | | |
| | Spouse (N =20) | | Parent (N =3) | | Child (N =12) | | Sibling (N =6) | | Other (N =4) | |
Level	N	%	N	%	N	%	N	%	N	%
Intense	12	60	3	100	4	33	2	33	1	25
Moderate	6	30	—	—	1	8	—	—	—	—
Minimal	2	10	—	—	7	58	4	67	3	75
Total	20	100	3	100	12	100	6	100	4	100

[a] $X^2 = 13.68$, $df = 1$, $p < .001$. The X^2 was obtained using the Bhapkar (1968) method. The categories were collapsed into spouse-parent and all others to calculate the statistic.

SOCIODEMOGRAPHIC DATA ON THE RESPONDENTS

The respondents' demographic characteristics were not differentially associated with ratings of intense grief (See Table 9.3). About one-half of blacks and whites, of males and females, and of those under and those over the age of 65 were rated as having intense grief reactions.

TIME INTERVAL BETWEEN DEATH AND INTERVIEW

We thought that the interval between death and the interview might have a bearing on the ratings for intensity of grief. However, we found no statistically significant differences: of those interviewed one to six months after bereavement, 54 percent were rated as grieving intensely; in the group interviewed 7 to 11 months after bereavement, 38 percent were rated as intense;

TABLE 9.3. SOCIODEMOGRAPHIC CHARACTERISTICS OF RESPONDENTS
BY LEVEL OF GRIEF REACTION [a]

| | Level | | | | | | | |
| | Intense | | Moderate | | Minimal | | Total | |
Characteristics	N	%	N	%	N	%	N	%
Race								
Black	10	48	3	14	8	38	21	100
White	12	50	4	17	8	33	24	100
Sex								
Male	5	42	0	0	7	58	12	100
Female	17	52	7	21	9	27	33	100
Age								
Under 65	8	50	1	6	7	44	16	100
65 +	14	48	6	21	9	31	29	100

[a] None of the above comparisons were significant. The chi-square used is the variation presented by Bhapkar, 1968.

and of those interviewed more than 12 months after bereavement 50 percent were rated as intense. As shown in Table 9.4, 12 of the 24 interviewed one year after bereavement had intense grief reactions, a proportion strikingly similar to the 10 of the 21 with intense grief interviewed within the year.

TABLE 9.4. TIME INTERVAL BETWEEN DEATH AND INTERVIEW
BY LEVEL OF GRIEF REACTION [a]

| | Time Interval (mos.) | | | | | | | |
| Level | 1–6 | | 7–11 | | 12 + | | Total | |
	N	%	N	%	N	%	N	%
Intense	7	54	3	38	12	50	22	49
Moderate	4	31	0	0	3	12	7	16
Minimal	2	15	5	62	9	38	16	36
Total	13	100	8	100	24	100	45	100

[a] X^2 = N.S. Categories were collapsed into less than one year and more than one year to calculate the statistic using the Bhapkar method.

LENGTH OF ILLNESS

Comparing the level of the respondents' grief reactions with the length of the decedents' terminal illnesses showed that extended illnesses were significantly associated with higher percentages of intense grief reactions. As shown in Table 9.5, 68 percent of those whose decedents' illnesses were longer than one year had intense grief reactions in contrast to about 30 percent of those reporting either illnesses of less than one year's duration or death not preceded by illness ($p < .001$).

TABLE 9.5. LENGTH OF ILLNESS BY LEVEL OF GRIEF REACTION [a]

| | Time Interval | | | | | |
| | Death not Preceded by Illness | | Illness of Less than One Year | | Illness of More Than One Year | |
Level	N	%	N	%	N	%
Intense	4	31	3	30	15	68
Moderate	0	—	2	20	5	23
Minimal	9	69	5	50	2	9
Total	13	100	10	100	22	100

[a] $X^2 = 14.59$, $df = 1$, $p < .001$. The X^2 was obtained using the Bhapkar (1968) method. The categories were collapsed into illness of less than or more than one year to calculate the statistic.

TIME INTERVAL BETWEEN AWARENESS AND DEATH

There were 13 sudden deaths. For the remaining 32 respondents, we classified the length of time that they were aware of a possible death in the family into three categories: none (less than a day or two), less than 12 months, or more than 12 months. As shown in Table 9.6, the respondent's length of awareness that the relative would die was not associated with the level of the grief reaction. From 54 to 60 percent of those in the three different length-of-awareness categories were rated as intense.

SATISFACTION WITH MEDICAL CARE

Dissatisfaction with medical care seemed to be related to feelings of guilt or frustration, possibly influencing the intensity of grief. Thirteen of the 45 respondents expressed such dissatisfaction; of these, 8 were rated as intense, 2 as moderate, and 3 as minimal.

TABLE 9.6. LENGTH OF AWARENESS BY LEVEL OF GRIEF REACTION ($N = 32$) [a]

| | Length of Awareness | | | | | |
| Level | None | | -12 mos. | | $+12$ mos. | |
	N	%	N	%	N	%
Intense	5	55	7	54	6	60
Moderate	1	11	2	15	4	40
Minimal	3	33	4	31	0	0
Total	9	100	13	100	10	100

[a] $X^2 = $ N.S. Using the Bhapkar method (1968), categories were collapsed into length of awareness of less than one year and greater than one year to calculate the statistic. Categories were also collapsed into no awareness compared to awareness of under and over one year.

UNRESOLVED GRIEF

Our culture traditionally allows one year for grieving, a period formally defined by some religions and by social patterns. Of the 24 respondents interviewed more than one year after the decedents' deaths, 12 were rated as grieving intensely, 3 as moderately, and 9 as minimally. We are labeling intense reactions persisting one year or more after bereavement as unresolved grief.

The 12 with unresolved grief consisted of 5 spouses, 4 children, 1 parent, 1 sibling, and 1 aunt. In an attempt to examine more closely the unusually large number with unresolved grief, we looked at the relationship between respondent and decedent, the length of illness, and the relative's length of awareness of impending death as possible factors.

Of the five spouses with unresolved grief, three had nursed their husbands or wives through terminal illnesses lasting longer than one year, yet only one of them indicated awareness for one year that the illness would be fatal; the other two admitted being aware of the impending death for only a few days. One respondent whose spouse had been ill for two months had not believed he was going to die. The fifth respondent's spouse had died suddenly.

The deceased parents of the four children with unresolved grief had had illnesses lasting longer than one year. Length of awareness of the serious nature of the illness was not associated with grief; one had no awareness, two were aware for less than one year, and one was aware for more than one year.

One parent and an aunt with unresolved grief had nursed their relatives through long terminal illnesses and were aware of impending death for more than one year. One sibling, who was still grieving intensely after one year, was an elderly black man whose main function in life had been caring for his older sister; he was not aware that her short illness would lead to death.

Interviewers' Emotional Responses

The three interviewers have been surprised by the eagerness of most respondents to talk with them. Many respondents reported that family and friends were reluctant to "talk about" the deceased. The interviewers were also surprised by the respondents' willingness to describe intimate details of their lives.

Since most human beings have limited experience with death, we were concerned about the interviewers' emotional responses to dealing with bereavement on a continuing and regular basis and to leading the bereaved through the details of the decedent's life during the three years before death. The interviewers' most common reaction was sadness. Many of the respondents were aged widows or widowers whose marriages, whether good or bad, had lasted a long time. Following the loss they felt, and often were, very much alone with few economic or social resources and little possibility of improvement in their situations. All of the interviewers sympathized with these respondents and felt sad following the interviews.

The interviewers also felt a sense of anger and frustration. This was provoked by seeing a respondent's pathetic mode of life, by hearing about poor medical management, or by feeling helpless as a member of a research group when confronted with real social needs. This latter point has raised questions about the social responsibility of researchers on a project of this sort. In many instances, respondents had been individuals living in dire poverty with inadequate food or medicine and little care.

There were five instances in which the interviewers became upset. One case involved a spouse who seemed concerned primarily about his sexual prowess as he described a marriage that had been filled with tension and threatened violence for years. Two interviews were upsetting because of the description of the apparently poor medical treatment the deceased had received. One interview was disturbing because the death seemed so tragic; a young veteran hanged himself in jail a few hours after he had been incarcerated for a misdemeanor. The fifth was a young girl whose mother's lengthy terminal illness produced a deterioration of their previously close relationship.

The interviewers encountered some unanticipated responses from individuals who, despite dire circumstances, had shown exceptionally great dignity and strength—who demonstrated the ability of human beings to deal with catastrophe after catastrophe and maintain a sense of personal worth and concern.

Conclusions

This preliminary study showed the following distribution of grief reactions: one-half of the respondents had intense reactions to their loss, one-sixth had moderate reactions, and slightly more than one-third had only minimal reactions. A close relationship between the respondent and the decedent appeared to be the most consistent factor associated with intensity of grief; more spouses and parents tended to have intense reactions than did other relatives. The respondents' sociodemographic characteristics—race, sex, and age—were not associated with the level of grief. Surprisingly, we found that 50 percent of the respondents *interviewed more than one year after their loss* displayed intense grief reactions.

An analysis of the data reveals that grief is a complex, highly personal reaction and that its intensity is associated with a number of incongruities. For example, we found numerous discrepancies regarding the reported length of the decedents' illnesses and the respondents' awareness of the outcome.

Many of the respondents, particularly the poor and those without personal physicians, maintained that they had not been informed about the serious nature of the illness. Of course, we know from clinical experience that some relatives deny obvious facts about diagnosis and prognosis even when informed. We do not have data in this study to assess the extent of denial, but it appears that lack of information and communication difficulties as well as denial interfere with anticipatory grief processes.

The large percentage displaying unresolved grief points to the magnitude of this problem. The apparent lack of social supports we observed seems to be contributory. Furthermore, many respondents reported that their friends and relatives showed concern and willingness to talk about the loss for only a few weeks. Thus it seems‹ that many did not have an opportunity to express their sorrow or ventilate their feelings over a period of time.

This preliminary study indicates that it is possible to carry out a more comprehensive, epidemiologic investigation of grief. Almost all of these respondents were eager to cooperate with the interviewers. In many instances the relatives expressed gratitude openly, thanking the interviewers or occasionally inviting them to visit again. We think that the respondents' willingness to discuss the details of death in the family and bereavement with a stranger indicates that they have not had sufficient opportunities to talk about their loss and their feelings and thus resolve their grief. To us it also appears that they regarded the interview as evidence that someone "in the system" cared.

REFERENCES

Bhapkar, V. P. 1968. "On the Analysis of Contingency Tables with a Quantitative Response." *Biometrics* 24, no. 2 (June).

Markush, E., and D. G. Siegel. 1968. "Prevalence at Death. 1. A New Method for Deriving Death Rates for Specific Diseases." *American Journal of Public Health* 58, no. 3: 544–77.

Schwab, J. J., and G. J. Warheit. 1972. "Evaluating Southern Mental Health Needs and Services." *Florida Medical Journal* 59, no. 1.

Schwab, J. J., et al. In preparation. "Studies in Mortality 1: Psychosocial Variables."

Part Three

The Bereaved Family

10

Changes in Attitudes Toward Death: The Widow in Great Britain in the Early Twentieth Century

Jeffrey C. Lerner

Death is a topic we normally avoid. Our own death and that of others provoke such extreme anxiety that we go to great lengths to avoid the idea or to construct elaborate rationalizations that help us to understand and deal with the unacceptable biological reality. The rationalizations may change, but the underlying need for them remains the same. Yet death is a biological necessity, and it behooves us to attempt to manage our anxiety and to use what tools we have to understand death as a social and psychological phenomenon. Historical research is one such tool. By using it, we can look at the ways man has attempted to rationalize death in the past, in order to advance our understanding of particular historical periods, and provide a perspective for the evaluation of present customs and attitudes, with a view to their possible modification.

Periods of transition or national stress are particularly fruitful for conducting such historical inquiry. World War I marks a meaningful watershed in British history, a division noted by historians in many areas of social, economic, and political life. It has not been considered that this division may also hold true in respect to attitudes toward the bereaved. Because the topic is so broad, it is best looked at in the context of a specific case study. This article focuses on society's social, economic, and psychological support of widows in the prewar and war periods.

It is well to first establish a general framework. Actually, two frameworks are needed, one generally psychological and the other generally historical. Psychologically, we must differentiate and understand two quite different processes, that of coming to terms with one's own death and that of dealing with the deaths of loved ones. The fundamental paradox in thinking about our own death is that it is impossible. The thought that "I will no longer exist; I will no longer act in this world" requires an animate subject or agent who thinks this thought, and who can this agent be but the self? Freud (1918) has expressed the idea succinctly:

Our own death is indeed unimaginable, and whenever we make the attempt to imagine it we can perceive that we really survive as spectators. Hence the psychoanalytic school could venture on the assertion that at bottom no one believes in his own death, or to put the same thing in another way, in the unconscious every one of us is convinced of his own immortality (p. 14).

However, the inability to conceive of our own death may render us unable, or at least unwilling, to sympathize with the deaths of others. It may obscure our perceptions of the problems of bereavement—problems that seem remote from us. (It is also this paradox which leads to the idea of an afterlife.)

The process of mourning, the process of adjusting to bereavement, is in some ways more complex. A woman who loses her husband, to take our particular case, must deal with two problems: her own grief and the financial constriction caused by the loss of her husband's income. She has conflicting impulses: to remember and to forget, to grieve and to seek a new life, to blame herself or others or the dead person (Marris, 1958, p. ix). Paradoxes appear here, too: the mourner may deny the fact of death, even going to the extent of imagining a voice or a key in the door, or fantasizing about the imminent return of the deceased. Another common reaction is to dwell in great detail on memories of the dead person—in Freudian terms, to "hypercathect" his image. This is an attempt to resurrect him, to make him live in one's own consciousness, since he has been lost in physical reality. It is perhaps well known that physical complaints such as rheumatism, insomnia, and chest pains are common; and so stressful is bereavement that widows and widowers themselves are more likely to die in the years immediately after bereavement than are married people of similar age and class (Hendin, 1973, p. 170). Social supports for the bereaved may come from various sources and in various forms, and important changes in the sources of support occur in the period we have here selected for study.

For our historical framework, we should indicate in general terms the social and intellectual trends important for understanding developing attitudes toward death in early-twentieth-century Britain. Very broadly, two processes should be considered: secularization and the combined impact of industrialization and urbanization. Secularization implies the decline of the importance of religion in attitudes toward death, and the rise of secular ideologies for the rationalization of death and the characterization of the afterlife. Darwinism was in part responsible for this process and represents a new formulation of the viewpoint that death is a biological necessity and an undeniable scientific fact, not requiring or even admitting further philosophical speculation. Industrialization and urbanization led to the breakdown of the extended family network that had formerly cushioned the fact of death, and to the breakdown of many regional customs that had formerly ritualized burial and mourning. Indeed, as cities became ever more densely populated, even the most basic customs broke down; there was no longer room to bury the dead in churchyards, for example, and it became a practical necessity to operate cemeteries (Wilson and Levy, 1938). Cremation was even proposed as a solution, but was too radical a challenge to the doctrine of resurrection of the body to be accepted, even by the law, until 1903.

Along with religious and familial shifts taking place before the war, there were changes in the economic lives of the bereaved. In contrast to private provision for widows, the state was increasingly obliged to take a hand in supporting them. We shall consider this in detail, because it is significant of broad social change.

An introductory section on death and the war presents some material relevant to understanding the problem of widows, but is in no sense exhaustive. It is intended to place our study into the broader social context.

Death and the War

The first public expressions about death and the war were poems. Poetry was the traditional medium for discussing death, so that it is hardly unusual to find it employed at the beginning of the war. One poet, Xanthus (1914), published "The Dead Volunteer" only four days after war was declared. The poem is about a clerk who leaves his tedious, unheroic job to go to war. He is killed but he "goes to join the men of Agincourt." Poems such as this one were written largely for their patriotic implications and purpose, and they used death as a rather vague image devoid of appreciation of its nature. *The New Age* (a Guild-Socialist journal with an antiwar tone) was quick to comment on the banality of the spate of war poems. It singled out for special comment William Watson's "The Funeral March for Kaiser Wilhelm II," a 59-stanza work. It is a hate poem, which imagines the Kaiser's death and his funeral in which the earth itself will not accept the Kaiser's body but rather "vomit[s] him back" (Hood, 1914).

Romantic poems that did not treat death seriously were perhaps a natural expression of attitudes toward death at the beginning of the war, but by the autumn of 1914 it became obvious that the soldiers would not be home for Christmas. Britons were, against their will, facing a long war and death on a scale heretofore inconceivable. By September 1914 everyone Kipling knew had lost a relative in action (Ausubel, 1960). By the new year, poems by the bereaved began to appear. Cloudesley Brereton (1915) wrote "In Memoriam C.A." to voice his sorrow at the death of his friend. (A brief time later the casualty list included Brereton's brother, J.N.B.).

Brereton's poetry represented real change in expressing attitudes toward death. Brereton's predecessors wrote of bravery; he writes about his sense of loss. Had the war ended by Christmas, as everyone expected, there would have been little change in attitudes toward death. The sentiments would have been only of heroic death and private loss. But such was not the case. "As 1914 drew to its close," says A. J. P. Taylor (1963), "the pattern had been drawn for the First World War, a pattern not foreseen by anyone in a responsible position before the war started: not a short war of quick decisions, but a war of deadlock and prolonged battering which seemed as if it might go on indefinitely. No one had prepared for this; no one knew how to handle it" (p. 367).

In 1915, the British were learning to live with the constant threat of death. In May, a writer for the *New Statesman* (a Fabian journal) wrote (in an article entitled "Fear Not Them That Kill the Body") that

One of the most noticeable results of the war has been the general diminution of the fear of death. . . . we are sure that in hundreds of thousands of cases men and women regard death with less fear to-day than they regarded some little fleeting pain in tooth or chest or stomach only ten months ago.

This "group-emotion" of "group-fearlessness" did not only apply to soldiers.

The civilian too—we do not mean every civilian, but an immense number of civilians—finds himself trampling his terrors under foot with a strange unconcern.

Londoners did not lose their sleep for fear of air raids; they still went on holiday to Deal and Folkestone (on the south coast) where the danger from air raids was greatest, and they "would be far more nervous of an outbreak of chickenpox than all this vomiting of death from the skies" (*The New Statesman,* 1915).

By June 1915 (*The Lancet,* p. 1265), 10,955 officers and 247,114 noncommissioned officers and men had been killed and wounded or were missing. "We live under a constant sense of gloom, for every day brings news of the death of the son or brother of one of our friends," historian James Bryce (Ausubel, 1960) wrote, and the journalist Henry Lucy noted:

The very multitude of names of killed, wounded or missing does something to blunt the sharpness of sympathy. Death on the battlefield has become so much a matter of course as to deprive it of some of its terrors (quoted in Marwick, 1968, p. 133).

After the Battle of the Somme (July through November 1916), in which the British had some 420,000 casualties, 20,000 on the first day alone, enthusiasm for the war faded. "Idealism perished on the Somme," says A. J. P. Taylor (1965). Indeed the fiasco reinforced the growing sense of the interminable war. Today we know that the war ended in 1918, but contemporaries lived from day to day in the hope that somehow tomorrow would be the last day of war. The Somme was a great disappointment.

The pre-Somme spirit was perhaps best characterized in the poems of Rupert Brooke. Brooke was quoted in sermons to comfort the bereaved, while the post-Somme poets would no longer serve this purpose. Wilfred Owen wrote *Anthem For Doomed Youth,* which stands in contrast to Brooke's spirit.

After the Somme the trend of feeling was away from glorious death, dying for a reason and a cause, and toward a feeling of bitterness at loss of life. Those who now faced death wanted revenge on those who sent them to war while they themselves remained safe at home (Graves and Hodge, 1963, p. 15). It was a question of fairness; the unanimity of the struggle had broken down. Are the brave boys of the Great War, asked Dr. R. W. MacKenna (1917, p. 188), author of *The Adventure of Death,*

to be penalized for their bravery in defense of right, while the self-indulgent gourmand, who hides behind his fatty heart—the result of his own vices—which protects him from being called upon for service, extracts out of life every ounce of enjoyment it can offer? It is quite impossible to believe that such obvious unfairness can satisfy the demands of ordinary justice. But, unless there is a life beyond the grave, there is no assize which can readjust the inequality.

It was only after the reason for dying came into question that the general public began to take a fresh look at the phenomenon of death.

Freud's *Thoughts for the Times on War and Death* was translated into English in 1918. It was now acceptable to write that the war was not a holy crusade against some evil demon, but rather that the responsibility for the slaughter lay upon many shoulders. Said Freud (1918, p. 5),

It cannot be a matter for astonishment, therefore, that this relaxation of all moral ties between the greater units of mankind should have had a seducing influence on the morality of individuals; for our conscience is not the inflexible judge that ethical teachers are wont to declare it, but in its origin is "dread of the community" and nothing else. When the community has no rebuke to make, there is an end to all suppression of the baser passions, and men perpetuate deeds of cruelty, fraud, treachery and barbarity so incompatible with their civilization that one would have held them impossible. . . .

In criticism of this disillusionment, certain things must be said. Strictly speaking it is not justified, for it consists in the destruction of—an illusion! We welcome illusions because they spare us emotional distress, and enable us instead to indulge in gratification. We must not then complain if now and again they come into conflict with some portion of reality, and are shattered against it.

The wisdom of repressing the morbid fears resulting from the war experience came into question. W. H. R. Rivers (1918), the British psychologist, endeavored to show that in some cases more harm than good resulted from following the "usual advice" to avoid and repress or suppress the vivid recollections of terrifying war experiences. In some such cases, he wrote, if the patient succeeded in banishing his painful memories during most of the day, the memories in question, and the depressing thoughts associated with them, were apt to emerge with redoubled force during the night or on various occasions when the resistance of the brain was temporarily at its minimum. It sometimes seemed preferable, he reported, for the patient boldly to face the memory of his fearful experiences during the day, when his reasoning faculties were at their best, and endeavor to search out and associate more or less consolatory reflections with such recollections. By these means sudden, overpowering attacks of depression (involving possible danger of suicide) might be avoided. This frankness was not confined to the pages of psychological journals. Rivers was quoted and reinforced by Dr. F. P. Weber (1918) in his very popular *Aspects of Death and Correlated Aspects of Life in Art, Epigram, and Poetry.* Weber said that civilians with a pathological fear of death would do well to face their anxiety.

Books dealing with death, including nonmilitary death, became increasingly frequent. The war had increased consciousness of death as an important part of life. MacKenna (1917, p. x) wrote, "In the far-off days that preceded the war few of us gave much thought to the ultimate ending of our lives, for, to every healthy man his own Death seems a remote contingency."

This was no longer the case. Doctors' studies of dying patients, such as those of Sir J. F. Goodhart and Sir William Osler (Weber, 1918, pp. 122, 125), which had once been obscure, were now of public interest, as were such questions as "Is it the doctor's responsibility to prolong the life of a dying patient with drugs?" and "How does one care for the patient who knows he is dying?" (These are questions modern thanatologists still ask.)

With this background in mind, we can look at the specific case of the widow. Widows constitute a social group whose situation has not been treated systematically by historians. We shall look at some interesting developments in the social supports available to widows, and in the mourning process, which occurred in this period. The war accelerated some trends, while it revealed contradictions and weaknesses in previous attitudes and practices.

Victorian Customs

During the Victorian period, it was the custom for a widow to wear mourning for about two and a half years. John Morley (1971) described mourning dress:

For the first twelve months, she should wear a paramatta dress and mantle, with crepe applied to the skirt, in one piece, to within an inch of the waist. Her sleeves should be tight to the arm, with lawn cuffs and collar; her body should be covered entirely with crepe. Her bonnet also should be covered entirely with crepe; inside should be a widow's cap with a crepe veil with a deep hem. . . . A year after the death "widow's silk" could replace paramatta; it should be still heavily trimmed with crepe; after six months of this the crepe could, during the next three months be lightened, and jet [jewelry] and fringe be introduced. Twenty-one months after bereavement crepe could be left off entirely—this was known as "slighting" the mourning—and plain black be worn; two years after the bereavement the widow could go into half mourning for six months. The colours worn in half mourning were grey, lavender, mauve, violet, or black, grey and white stripes; the change should be gradual. (p. 68)

Mourning was worn in different degrees and for various time periods after the deaths of other members of the family. Thus one mourned a child for 12 months, a grandparent for nine months and a sibling for six months. It was worn only for relatives—and the Sovereign, the vicar, etc.—which indicated that the rules of mourning were based on the institution of the family, that sacred focus of Victorian life.

Mourning clothes were a great inconvenience to the wearer, but at the same time of great value. Mourning was a badge that identified a bereaved person and showed that person's stage of bereavement. Thus it served two general purposes; it was a public acknowledgment of the death, and it helped the widow reorient herself after the shock of her husband's death.

The latter purpose is very important because it expresses the central conflict of bereavement. On the one hand it allows the widow formally to recognize the death, which is the first step in the revision of social relationships (e.g., relationships with her children, her deceased husband's relatives, her married friends with whom she no longer has equal status, etc.). On the other hand, wearing mourning allows her to assert the surviving importance of her deceased husband, which makes death less absolute since until the mourning period is complete he is considered to have living needs. In performing this latter function, it also sets a definitive time limit on the mourning process. When the time limit expires, society obligates the widow to return to normal life.

The psychological process of mourning is slow and painful. Yet it must be experienced completely if the widow is to emerge from her bereavement in a healthy rather than in a melancholic state. It was, and of course still is, important for the individual widow, for her children, and for society at large that she recover. Widows who do not recover suffer from physical deterioration (loss of weight, rheumatism, asthma, bronchitis and cramping chest pains, ulcers, skin irritation, loss of sleep, etc.), from apathy (which adversely affects their care of their home, their children, and their job performance) and of course, from their personal psychic distress (Marris, 1958, p. 13). Mourning customs help to achieve a successful emergence from bereavement and are necessary to avoid the otherwise harmful effects. The Victorian widow had the advantages of the support afforded by strict mourning customs. She also had the disadvantages.

The disadvantages of mourning customs were many and became increasingly burdensome as the century drew to a close. Mourning clothes were expensive (and the expense came at a time when the woman could least afford it), physically too constricting in an age when women's clothes were becoming less constricting, and, perhaps most important, symbolic of the repression of women. It was on women that the burden of mourning fell. A wife had to mourn for the deceased relatives of her husband while the reverse was not true. In addition, men made only slight alterations in their dress during mourning (for example, donning an arm band and a black tie) and still went to parties and other social events. By 1889, *Woman's World* (Morley, 1971, p. 63) said that mourning was "a survival of the outward expression of the inferiority of women." In addition to these reasons, it appears that the elaborate style of mourning simply collapsed under its own weight. It underwent modifications according to fashions in dress and became increasingly obsessive and morbid as it came less to reflect its original purpose.

Excessive mourning clothes, like the other obsessive customs practiced by the Victorians—including elaborate funeral processions, the sending of black-bordered memorial cards, wearing of jewelry made from the hair of the dead person, epitaph samplers stitched by children, the hiring of mourners—waned as fashion changed and as better material and social conditions made life easier for more people and increased the lifespan (Morley, 1971; Parliamentary Papers, Volume 37).

Formal mourning became increasingly less strict as regards the time it was worn for and the steps in "slighting," but it remained a general practice to wear it among all social classes until the First World War. So important was the custom that even the poor would spend every penny they had upon the funeral and the mourning dress. Mrs. Bernard Bosanquet, in her 1898 study of the poor in the East End of London, noted that "the greatest festival of all is perhaps the funeral." She reported that the women bought mourning dresses and had a feast regardless of whether or not they could afford it. One widow, she wrote, hired a hearse and four horses and a mourning carriage and pair of horses, and as a result of this extravagance had to apply to the Poor Law Guardians for financial assistance within two weeks. Mrs. Bosanquet did not speculate on what motivated a poor widow to spend her meager funds on this "greatest festival of all": she failed to sympathize with the dilemma, the desire to save money for one's self (to be practical) and the desire to see one's husband honored.

The War Widow and Death Customs

While death and widowhood were not the topics of daily conversation before the war, at least they could be discussed on appropriate occasions with some degree of real emotion. For example, "The Widow in Bye Street," a narrative poem by John Masefield (1912), tells the story of a poor widow who devoted her life to bringing up an only son who was later hanged for murder. The treatment of the widow, though romantic, contains many realistic emotional elements. For example, the widow spends her burial club money to move into a room near the prison. It was no small sacrifice to give up one's burial money and accept a pauper's burial from the parish. After the hanging the widow goes home and draws the blinds (an indication of a death in the household), muses about her dead husband and waits for her (dead) son to come home. Months later she is still thinking about his favorite foods, taking walks she once took with him and absent-mindedly singing songs she once sang to him. These are phenomena observed in widows of today; the emotions of grief were understood and articulated then.

After the war broke out, emotions of grief eventually came to be sublimated. In August 1914, correspondents still wrote to fashion magazines for advice on mourning clothes. The rules of mourning were elaborate, but not so strict as they had been in Victorian times, and we can see this in *The Queen's* (1914) advice:

For evening dress, one of the heavier qualities of crepe de Chine is more generally adopted than anything else. . . . As to style, a plain, well-cut skirt, slightly trained, is in the best taste and a bodice either moderately decollete back and front only, when perhaps a little more elaborate white relief would be permissible. For ordinary days wear a quite plain coat, a skirt, of dull cloth. . . . And for afternoons, and etc., a gown of crepe cloth . . . or silk . . . , supplemented by a mantle. I gather from the fact you are wearing a hat and not a bonnet, that you are not going to any great extreme. And all you get now should last so far as expression goes, the decreed year and a day for the first year's mourning. (p. 296)

In August, London's magasins de deuil, department stores devoted exclusively to the sale of mourning clothes, were still advertising in the newspapers. (Pound, 1964).

After the battle of Mons on August 22, 1914, in which 1,600 British soldiers died, letters were sent to the *Times* expressing the "strong and widespread feeling" that the customary mourning used in civilian life not be worn for soldiers. The soldiers had fallen in "a sacred cause," and, said the Duchess of Devonshire, Lady Landsdowne, and other ladies who had near relatives serving in the war, they "will not show their sorrow as for those who came to a less glorious end." The *Times* (1914) was all in favor of the idea.

The stricken must determine for themselves how they may best meet their own longing to honour their cherished dead, but as the wishes entertained in the highest quarters rightly count for very much in matters of convention, we feel sure that a few words of timely approbation uttered from them would bring success to a movement that seems to us in many ways worthy and becoming the chastened grief of English hearts.

The idea did not catch on immediately. In November 1914 *Sketch* magazine printed a photograph of wounded men and of women attending the funeral of a comrade. The caption notes "the ubiquitous wearing of mourning."

At the beginning of the war, individual deaths were still distinctive. The *Sketch* praises General Allenby, who wrote a condolence letter to a lady whose son he had seen die.

The comfort of such a letter is incalculable to those at home: the marvel of them is that soldiers in the battle remember the needs of bereaved relatives in England and find time to frame their condolences in such comforting and noble terms.

As the casualty lists grew longer and the deaths lost their uniqueness, the carry-on spirit made the wearing of mourning "taboo" (Playne, 1931). Women should work, not mourn. " 'Are we downhearted? No!' is their battle cry, too, and they 'carry on' as bravely as any warrior of them all" (Bell, 1917). Patriotic work replaced grief. People had less energy to give toward helping friends and they felt constrained by their own or their friends' grief. Nobody wanted to be dependent on friends if a "cruel fate forced dependence on us" (Ignota, 1915, p. 501).

During the first months of the war it was still possible to exhume the bodies of dead soldiers and send them home. This soon had to be stopped because of its impracticality. It was possible to bring back a few bodies—the body of a grandson of W. E. Gladstone was disinterred under fire at Poperinghe and sent home "in obedience to pressure from a very high quarter"— but the practice was ended in recognition of the egalitarian spirit of the war, the result of the comradeship bred by the life of hardship and horror in the trenches (Longworth, 1967, pp. 4, 14).

There was of course a great deal of concern over the establishment of war cemeteries and the marking and recording of the individual graves. Bereaved relatives at home were assured that each grave was marked. J. Esslemont, a chaplain in the army, wrote a pamphlet in which the bereaved were told this (1915).

In spite of assurances, many graves were not marked or recorded. A letter to *Times* written on behalf of a woman who lost her brother expressed the growing public demand for better methods. Comrades in his regiment had given the lady particulars of the exact locality and even described the temporary wooden cross and its inscription erected over the grave. She found the place, where quite a number of victims had been interred, but every trace of the identifying crosses had disappeared. "I will not dwell on the distress of our friend," wrote the correspondent, "and my sole object in approaching you is to point out that there must be thousands of similar painful cases." The demand for reform led to the creation of the Graves Registration Commission (later Imperial War Graves Commission) in March 1915 (Longworth, 1967, p. 6). The Commission was headed by Fabian Ware, and his personal influence brought about a number of innovations, among which was the making of photographs of the graves. Some 2,000 of these photographs were sent out by August 1915 (Longworth, 1967, p. 6).[1]

[1] By April 1917, according to Longworth, 12,000 photographs had been sent.

The directions must have been useful for the bereaved who went on tours of the "Devastated Regions" in the first summer after the war (Graves and Hodge, 1963, p. 34). However, tours made by the bereaved during and after the war were privately arranged or made with groups, such as the British Legion. There was no financial provision made for widows to visit the graves (Rigby, 1973).

It must have been a hardship for the many widows, unable to afford the fare to France, not to see the graves of their loved ones. Graves were perhaps of greater importance to Victorians and Edwardians than they are today. One Victorian commentator said cemeteries were visited by "every individual more frequently than any other scene, except that of his daily oc-cupation" (Morley, 1971, p. 48). Some sense of the importance of graves during the war can be gained from the numerous letters and articles written on the subject by dead soldiers' relatives. An even greater indication of the importance of graves is that in one 1915 article, "The German Idea of Death," the author overcame the strong taboo against saying anything in praise of Germans and concludes that "by looking at German cemeteries, one can tell that Death is to him [the German] a little less wasteful and a little more glorious than to us" (Bunston, 1915).

The same controversy raised over graves also raged over war memorials (Graves and Hodges, 1963, p. 30). Should they be plaques or obelisks, or should the money be used to build memorial parks or gardens? Graves and memorials were important for bereaved persons. They are a physical tribute to the dead, and being physical objects they assert the reality that indeed the lost husband or other relative is really dead and not just missing. Tending the grave can help the bereaved alleviate his responsibility (and guilt).

Unlike the soldiers at the front, the women did not become disillusioned with the war or turn their anger on the government. One mother addressed her anger to the disillusioned common soldier of post-Somme days (Graves, 1957).

> To the man who pathetically calls himself a "common soldier," may I say that we women, who demand to be heard, will tolerate no such cry as "Peace! Peace!" where there is no peace. The corn that will wave over land watered by the blood of our brave lads shall testify to the future that their blood was not spilt in vain. (p. 229)

Rebecca West (1916) deplored the widow who sat home alone in a house that "has grown horrible." She lauded a widow who while nursing in Serbia died of enteric fever, because she had taken part in "the ritual of honorable death."

Those widows who did not turn their grief into patriotism might have sought comfort in a type of romantic avoidance. Here are two examples. The first is from a pocket-sized book of consolation, *Brave Words About Death from the Works of R. L. Stevenson* (1916). The preface to the book tells us that Stevenson faced death with a "gay courage" and with "buoyancy of spirit." An excerpt reads

So long as men do their duty . . . they will be leading pattern lives; and whether or not they come to lie beside a martyr's monument, we may be sure they will find a safe haven somewhere in the providence of God. It is not well to think of death, unless we temper the thought with that of heroes who despised it. (p. 24)

We do not know if the widows also turned to religion as a source of consolation in any greater proportion than before the war. It is tempting to believe that some did experience a renewed faith in God. MacKenna wrote "What they once hoped for weakly, they now know and believe with the full strength of their love" (1917, p. 190). No doubt many participated in the huge popularity of spiritualism enjoyed during the war (Graves and Hodges, 1963, p. 23). The bereaved, particularly widows, are likely to have vivid dreams about the dead and hear voices as a result of their inability to realize their loss (Gorer, 1967, p. 54).

A small proportion of widows—about 15 percent each year of the war—if we take London statistics as roughly representative of the country at large—remarried, which was of course the best consolation in bereavement. The 1921 census lists the total population of widows in Britain at 1,428,093. Of these, 228,342 were war widows although veterans continued to die from war injuries, and by 1926 there were 251,462 war widows.

Prewar Financial Circumstances

Aside from her grief, the widow had to adjust to new financial circumstances caused by the loss of the breadwinner. This could be a rather drastic change. A rich widow *might* suffer little or no financial loss. The middle-class widow of Victorian times, unless her husband had been insured, found herself in a very difficult position. Opportunities for middle-class women were few, and they were apt often to be tinged with social disapproval (Reader, 1966, p. 167). Teaching was a possibility, if she were skilled; keeping a shop was also possible if she had some surplus money. Writing, as Anthony Trollope's mother did, was not particularly respectable. The only other possibility was to become a governess.

This situation gradually changed in late Victorian and Edwardian times, as more women became teachers (after the Education Act of 1870), nurses (50,000 of them in 1891), and clerks (5,989 in 1881, 117,000 in 1911). If all else failed, there was private charity to fall back on. Organizations such as the Society for the Relief of Necessitous Widows and Children of Protestant Ministers and the Society for Relief of Widows and Orphans of Medical Men existed to help the widow in need. However, it is likely that most middle-class widows received financial support from their families.

Unfortunately, it is hard to assess the emotions of the middle-class widow during her period of adjustment to her new way of life. Did she willingly accept money from relatives? Did she sacrifice her autonomy by moving in with her parents? How did she treat her children? What was her state of health? These and other questions, to which we have some answers for modern widows, remain unanswered for Victorian times. Aside from the historical merit of knowing answers to these questions, they might aid us in judging how useful mourning customs and the nature of the financial support available were in aiding the widow to recover from her bereavement.

Our clearest picture of widowhood before World War I is that of the poor widow in Edwardian times. At that time the state markedly increased its participation in affairs that were once family and church matters. Naturally the effect of Edwardian social legislation was greatest for the poor; naturally the government kept a closer eye on the poor at whom the legislation was directed.

The Balfour Government remained reluctant to authorize increased expenditure upon social welfare—other than education (Education Act of 1902)—until 1905, when it took three further initiatives. It recommended the appointment of a Royal Commission on the Poor Law and the Relief of Distress, which dealt in part with widows. It promoted the Unemployed Workmen Act, which was a last attempt to deal with unemployment by relief work, and it issued an order permitting the Poor Law Guardians to give relief in the form of meals to undernourished school children. When the Liberals came into office in 1906 they continued to usher in what we now recognize as a new beginning in British social legislation. The local authorities were authorized to undertake school medical inspections, and the state took responsibility for old people in the form of pensions (1909) rather than relief work. Finally, in 1911, the enactment of health and unemployment insurance recognized that the welfare of individuals of working age was also the concern of the state (Read, 1972, p. 19). The state was now intervening in family matters, and the legislation reflected an anxious recognition of the relation between urban environment, working conditions, social stability, and morality. The difference between Victorian and Edwardian legislation was largely a difference between harshly correcting the poor's shortcomings and offering state services to the poor.

This change, beginning in the Edwardian period, also affected widows. Before the Poor Law was revised in 1909, the widow could draw on four sources for financial aid. The first of these was her own family. A 1957 study of kinship in East London showed that the extended family networks in existence before government-built housing projects had not been weakened by the move into these projects (Young and Willmott, 1964). For example, over half of the women interviewed had seen their mother within the previous 24 hours (Young and Willmott, p. 29). In fact the mother proved to be the focus of family life, especially for the daughter (Young and Willmott, p. 29). She was of great material help to the daughter; for example, at the time of the daughter's confinement, 25 of 28 mothers gave substantial assistance to the daughters (Young and Willmott, p. 35). It is reasonable to assume that kin networks of this type existed in Edwardian East London. (It would be interesting to check this by surveying people alive at the time.)

It must be borne in mind, however, that kin networks are often less useful than they might be in the event of bereavement. Marris's 1958 (pp. 68–85) study of widows in the same area of East London showed that, if anything, contacts between the widow and her "extended family" became less rather than more frequent. This was caused by both practical and emotional difficulties (less spare time, less money for entertainment and fares, as well as feelings of resentment at being pitied, apathy, and pride in independence). If this condition were true in Edwardian times, then family help, qualified by the shift occasioned by bereavement, may be assumed to have aided the widow, but only to a limited extent. On an absolute scale, though, the widow's relationship with her extended family, and consequently her social and economic status, was worse after bereavement than before. The kinship study also showed that the problem is one of relatively large dimensions. For the proportion of people who had lost a parent by the age of fifteen was 26 percent to 29 percent in the Edwardian period (Young and Willmott, 1964, p. 7).

The widow's second resource was the friendly society. Unlike the middle-classes, whose lives might be insured with reputable companies, the poor held their insurance with friendly societies.[2] These societies were only partially regulated by the government (Friendly Societies Act 1896); they were often local clubs and were often corrupt. Some sense of this corruption can be gained by looking at the practices of the collectors for the societies. Books containing the names of dues-paying members were their personal property rather than the property of the societies. These books could be offered for sale and they fetched large sums. Even the general secretaries did well; in one scandal it was revealed that they received £5,000–£6,000 a year (£300 sufficed to sustain a middle-class London family including such extras as a maid and expensive clothes and food) (Peel, 1929, pp. 181, 186; Brabrook, 1898, p. 77). Even when the societies were well-administered, the benefits were not large, typically ranging up to £20 (Brown and Taylor, 1933). Presumably some of this was spent on the funeral in order to avoid the "humiliation and indignity of having to leave to the parish the duty of burying the remains of those to whom they were attached in life" (Brabrook, 1898, p. 75). A funeral might cost between £3 5s and £53, and a cremation, made legal in 1903 but not very popular during this period, about £5 5s in London (Noble, 1914, p. 10).

A third source of funds was provided by private charity. Unfortunately these funds were distributed haphazardly and under moralistic supervision, and they were usually inadequate to prevent destitution. The Charity Organization Society was careful not to make the widow materially better off than before her husband's death or even to put her on a par with her previous sit-

---

[2] The Prudential Assurance Company had one-third of the British population on its books (or 13 million policies) (Brabook, 1898, p. 79).

uation. The *Charity Organization Review,* in a 1906 article (pp. 48–49), responded to criticism of its philosophy by citing this example:

A man, a skilled workman, in regular employ, earning £3 to £4 a week, died leaving his widow and children unprovided for. Would it be really equitable to tax a large number of people to whom £3 a week would be luxury in order to make that widow as well off as before her husband's death, and in order to encourage—for that is the main point—all other husbands earning high and regular wages to spend them all in full assurance their widows and children would be amply provided for?

The Society did not want to encourage extravagance. On the other hand, it did not address itself to problems of other widows,—those, say, whose husbands earned £1 a week and were only occasionally employed; were their husbands, one might have asked, also irresponsible? Questions like this were asked but not answered.

The fourth and last resource of the poor widow was the Poor Law. The Poor Law reflected government attitudes, and the government from late Victorian times onward played the chief role in helping poor widows.

The Poor Law and its workhouses were hated institutions throughout the nineteenth century. The harsh "principles of 1834" had been modified over the course of time by lenient administration. By the Edwardian period officials of the Poor Law felt it necessary to rationalize the system, which during the last 70 years had been administered unevenly throughout the country.

On top of merely rationalizing the existing procedures, there was another reason for doing something about the Poor Law. Industrialism had brought with it "cyclical unemployment," a phenomenon that appeared in the depressions of 1879 and 1886–87 and that meant that thousands of able-bodied men were temporarily destitute through no fault of their own. There was a human need to have the state provide for those who suffered under the industrial system. There was also a political motive for revamping the Poor Laws. Even temporarily destitute men were voters. They had helped the Liberals win their stunning victory over the Conservatives at the end of 1905. Over the years the poor and their champions were increasingly insisting that the state take responsibility for the welfare of its people in a new way. They wanted the state to prevent destitution and genuinely to relieve it, not simply enter upon inquests as to how that destitution came about. So when the Royal Commission was set up in 1905, it split into two camps, those who wanted to tidy up the Poor Laws, authors of the Majority Report, and those who wanted to abolish the Poor Law and bring in a system to prevent destitution, authors of the Minority Report (Cole, 1946, pp. 101–3). Both factions agreed that the most scandalous cases of inadequate Outdoor Relief (meaning relief given to those living at home, outside of Poor Law institutions) revealed by the Commission were those of widows with children (S. and B. Webb, 1963, p. 741).[3]

The Commission investigated whether or not widows were used as sweated labor and what effects their employment had on the wages of other workers. In so doing, it produced a good deal of general information about widows. The Report gives some figures about the numbers of widows on relief. In the year ending September 30, 1907, 70,000 widows with children were relieved. The numbers given indoor relief on any one day seem to have averaged about 35,000, of which only 5,000 were classified as "able-bodied." In 1907 and 1908 the numbers of "able-bodied" widows on out-relief hovered around 33,000. This was a decrease from 1884, when the number was 41,486, and reflects a decrease in the general population of the proportion of widows to women aged 20 and upward. The information provided in the report is not sufficient to determine trends in the policies of the Poor Law Guardians—that is, policies regarding whether or not money would be dispensed to the able-bodied widow or to the widow with only a small number of children.

A number of interesting attitudes can be discerned in the Majority Report. First of all, the Commissioners did not believe that an experimental scheme, tried in Glasgow, for granting complete maintenance to widows had been successful. They did not feel that the granting of out-relief had a deleterious effect on general wages and conditions of employment. They admitted that sweated labor was a reality, but saw out-relief to widows at most as an indirect and incidental cause. Like modern critics of welfare, they believed that relief often had detrimental effects on character, because those capable of self-support often preferred not to work. They concluded by suggesting that "every case seems to call for special and individual attention. . . . Outdoor

---

[3] In practical terms the difference between indoor and outdoor relief was that the latter entailed the dissolution of the family unit, as widows were relieved in separate institutions from their children.

relief administered on a fixed scale regardless of other resources or of home conditions stands condemned by its results" (p. 157).

By contrast, the authors of the Minority Report (who were the Fabian Socialists Beatrice and Sidney Webb) were convinced that widows were forced to work in sweatshops, that their employment led to poorer working conditions for the working class as a whole, and that the maintenance of the family unit at a decent standard of living must be enforced by the government.

The recommendations of the Royal Commission were not systematically adopted by the Guardians in the prewar period. This is evident from a 1913 report on the conditions of widows in Liverpool. This highly detailed study, severely critical of the Guardians' slowness in implementing the Commission's recommendations, gave details of a number of individual cases. One example was the case of Mrs. Y, who had three dependent children and a blind mother and worked as a rag collector. Her weekly income including relief for the five of them was 6s.6d. when 13s.11d. was estimated for their subsistence (Rathbone, 1913). The author of the report, Eleanor Rathbone, wrote "The astonishing thing to us is not that so many women fail to grapple with the problem successfully, but that any succeed" (p. 29). One of the interesting suggestions she made was that day care be provided for working widows (p. 25). Rathbone had a sensitive understanding of the physical, psychological, and financial problems of widowhood. She believed that widows were ignored because women were not eligible to vote.

Finally, just after the outbreak of the war, the Local Government Board presented an important circular to the Guardians. Its two most salient points were that a normal standard of income should be provided, not necessarily according to the 1834 principle of insisting on rates lower than the wages of the lowest-paid independent laborer, and that relief could be given before the family resources were depleted (i.e., prevent destitution and not wait until it occurs before relieving it). Unfortunately, the circular's recommendations were not implemented, supposedly due to the outbreak of war.

Financial Provisions for War Widows

The problem of dealing with widows became radically different with the advent of war. It soon became apparent that there would be a great increase in the number of widows; furthermore, the government was held more directly responsible for war widows and would have to provide for them if it expected large numbers of men to enlist willingly. Another factor that increased pressure on the government to act was that for the first time the problem became acute for the middle classes. (It is interesting to note that, just before the outbreak of war, in May, June, and July of 1914, several questions were asked in Parliament about proposed legislation on widows' relief, and as late as July 14, the reply by the President of the Local Government Board, Herbert Samuel, was "I am not in a position to make any promise of legislation on the subject.")

Although it was incumbent on the government to ensure assistance to war widows, plans for doing so were the subject of controversy throughout the war. Government proposals were criticized both for being inequitable in principle and confusing in actual administration. The first Parliamentary debate on widow's pensions occurred November 11–27, 1914. There was unanimity on the proposition that pensions must be paid, but disagreement as to the scale of payment. Conservative and Liberal members wanted a sliding scale, based on the husband's civilian income, and emphasized the problems of the middle-class widow who had been accustomed to an income of £3, £4 or £5 a week. Prime Minister Asquith and Hayes Fisher, M.P., chairman of the Royal Patriotic Fund for 14 years and commissioner of Chelsea Hospital for three years during the Boer War (both pension-granting organizations), both made this point. Labour members demanded a flat rate of £1 a week minimum, an idea that had been passed as a resolution by numerous town councils, unions, friendly societies, local authorities, and churches. Mr. Brace, a Labour M.P. with close connections to the Miner's Federation, rested this proposal on the argument that the home was the important social unit and that £1 weekly was necessary to maintain it.

A sliding scale based on the soldier's rank was, in fact, implemented. The actual amounts paid changed fairly often during the course of the war. In August 1914, a private's widow under 45 got 5s. weekly if she had no children and 8s. if she had two children. By November 1918, she would have gotten 16s.6d. if she had no children and 30s.6d. if she had two children (Peel, 1929, p. 217). (However, we must remember that the cost of living had almost doubled during the course of the war.)

The actual calculation and payment of pensions seems never to have been clear or equitable, even in terms of the principles guiding the plan. But problems and confusions in administration were especially prevalent in the opening months of the war, when the idea of a short war still prevailed. Four different sets of regulations appeared between August 1914 and February 1915 (Harris, 1915, pp. 97–105). Complaints, suggestions, and attempts at clarification continued to appear throughout the war, according to reports in contemporary periodicals. (See "The Coordination of War Pensions," 1916.) A Pensions Ministry was set up on December 22, 1916, to coordinate the payment of war pensions by local committees (Sherran, 1917, p. 22).

Private charities also attempted to help war widows. The Soldiers' and Sailors' Families' Association made weekly allowances, and, like the government, used a rising scale of payment according to the rank of the dead husband (Barrington, 1915, pp. 582–99). Lady Beatty set up an admirable aid plan for the widows of sailors after the battle of Jutland. This fund sent out monthly letters and checks, without requiring queues, waiting lists, or long delays and humiliating circumstances (MacDonald, 1917).

In sum, more attention was paid to the widow's problems than before the war, and the aid given them was not given grudgingly or conceived as charity. This was rather natural, considering the circumstances under which these women had been widowed, but the effect was to change attitudes toward women widowed in other circumstances.

No actual change in policies toward the civilian widow was made during the war, however, perhaps because the entire population was employed (Webb, 1963, pp. 889–910). Articles published in 1919 claimed that the principle of providing for war widows had been fully accepted and that no new principle would be involved in extending pensions to all widows (Scurfield, 1919, pp. 140–43). In 1920, the Ministry of Health issued a report inquiring into the implementation of the 1914 circular on civilian widows. It showed that the recommendations of the circular had for the most part been ignored by the Guardians, and that widows were still living under deplorable conditions. This 1920 report was prefaced by an extract from the "Introduction to the Local Government Report (1918) on Mothers' Pensions in the United States of America," which described the American system of giving pensions to widows. Presumably this was a hint to the Guardians that, were action not taken on the circular, a pension system might be useful in Britain too. In fact, pensions for widows over the age of 65 were instituted in 1925, although the scheme, interestingly enough, was criticized for requiring workers' contributions: the Women's Co-operative Guild argued that a pension was a matter of right and hence should be noncontributory (Breckinridge, 1927, pp. 249–57).

Another factor in the extension of pensions to civilian widows was that women over 30 had been given the right to vote in 1919, in large part because of their instrumental role in war work. In the postwar period they actually constituted the majority of the British population, so that M.P.'s were obligated to pay attention to women's concerns (the 1919 Sex Disqualification [Removal] Bill gave women full citizenship rights, the 1920 Unemployment Insurance Act included women as well as men, etc.) (Cuddeford, 1967, pp. 82–83). However, the pension system was the result more of the human need than of partisan political maneuvering (Breckinridge, 1927).

The effect of the Widows, Orphans and Old Age Contributory Pensions Act was nearly to halve the numbers of widows with children in receipt of Outdoor Relief. The number dropped by 29,946 to 30,671 (Webb and Webb, 1963, pp. 742–43). The widow's financial problems were not solved, and they are not solved as yet; but the war made the concept of a pension acceptable, which was a crucial step in the direction of the state taking responsibility for the widow.

Conclusion

Attitudinal changes are difficult phenomena to characterize and catalog. This is particularly true when the subject is "taboo," when it is obscured because it is unsettling rather than because it is not of interest. Society's attitudes toward death, the dying, and the bereaved were different before and after the war. In 1926, historian C. S. Peel wrote, "There is less talk of death—more of 'passing on' " (p. 43). In speech and in custom some people tried to take the harshness out of death. Nonreligious burial services were written that showed a preference for quoting Shakespeare or Grey rather than St. Paul (Godfrey, 1919). Books such as F. W. Barbellion's, which described the author's last years of torment while dying of multiple sclerosis, were popular (Barbellion, 1919). The heritage of these responses to death is still with us. (Barbellion wrote under the name of "B. F. Cummings.")

But perhaps the greatest changes, those which affected the greatest number of people intimately, were in areas such as the ones we have discussed in this essay. There are over 600,000 widows in Britain today. The Marris study (1958), although only a small sampling, reported that 90 percent of those aged 40 or more at widowhood wore mourning for over three months and 64 percent of the younger widows did so. Marris also notes, however, that widows had a tendency to dismiss formal mourning as a waste of money and an ostentatious display of grief irrelevant to its sincerity (Marris, 1958, pp. 35–36). A good custom is an asset that should not be cast aside lightly. Originally it was practiced because it proved useful; now it is practiced because it formerly proved useful. What we have seen is that before the war the emotional aspects of bereavement were recognized by society through its requirement that the widow perform rather strict mourning duties. Prewar society provided outlets for the grief of widowhood. During the war grief was forbidden. Psychic energy that was formerly channelled into the bereavement was now diverted elsewhere, often into a rather neurotic sense of patriotism and romanticism. The loss of the formal mourning ritual has made it difficult for the modern widow to know, by society's standards, when and by what means she has fulfilled her duty to her husband. She has lost the cushioning and support that could facilitate her recovery from bereavement, and she is likely to become melancholic. Geoffrey Gorer (1967), whose book *Death, Grief and Mourning* is an excellent study of bereavement, concludes that a secular mourning ritual should be developed.

Whereas the prewar widow was more likely to be better off emotionally than the postwar widow, she more likely was worse off financially. The development of pensions for widows was an important change. Although only the rudiments of the present system were established as a result of the war, the idea was accepted because of a change in public consciousness. Its acceptance helped mitigate the loss of social and economic status caused by the husband's death. The poor widow was, and naturally still is, most likely to suffer crippling economic disability because of her bereavement. When she was joined in her plight by large numbers of middle-class widows, the financial aspects of widowhood were recognized as a serious problem necessitating and deserving compensation, not stigmatized charity, from the state. Thus largely as a result of the war, both the social and the economic positions of the widow shifted as though they were components in a hydraulic ratio. The social position worsened while the financial position improved.

This study has helped us trace and understand not only the customs and economics of bereavement but through them some attitudes toward death as a social and psychological phenomenon. The historical approach provides the factual background for understanding our present-day attitudes, pointing to the modifications that have brought us thus far.

REFERENCES

Ausubel, H. 1960. *In Hard Times*. New York: Columbia University Press (quotation: R. Kipling to B. Matthews, March 4, 1919 and September 20, 1914).

Barbellion, W. N. P. [B. F. Cummings] 1919. *The Journal of a Disappointed Man*. London: Chatto and Windus.

—— 1920. *A Last Diary*. London: Chatto and Windus.

Barrington, C. 1915. "Soldiers' and Sailors' Families." *The Nineteenth Century*, September, pp. 582–99.

Bell, H. 1917. *British Women in the War*. New York: G. A. Shaw.

Bosanquet, Mrs. B. 1898. *Rich and Poor*. London: Macmillan and Company.

Brabrook, E. W. 1898. *Provident Societies and Industrial Welfare*. London: Blackie and Son.

Breckinridge, S. P. 1927. "Widows' and Orphans' Pensions in Great Britain." In *Social Science Review*. Chicago: University of Chicago Press.

Brereton, C. 1914–15. "In Memoriam C. A." *The Quest*, October–January, pp. 367–68.

Brooke, R. "The Dead." (Quoted in E. Blunden. 1958. *War Poets 1914–18*. London: Longmans, Green and Company).

Brown, C. H. L., and J. A. G. Taylor. 1933. *Friendly Societies*. Cambridge: Cambridge University Press.

Bunston, A. 1915. "The German Idea of Death," *The British Review*, July, p. 107.

Charity Organization Review, 1906, pp. 48–49.

Cole, M. 1946. *Beatrice Webb*. New York: Longmans, Green and Company.

"The Coordination of War Pensions." 1916. *The Contemporary Review*, October, pp. 482–86, and *The Times* (London), July 20, 1916, p. 9.

Cuddeford, G. M. 1967. *Women and Society*. London: Hamish Hamilton.

Esslemont, J. 1915. *The Chaplain and the War*. Edinburgh: T. and T. Clark.

"Fear Not Them That Kill the Body." 1915. *The New Statesman*, May 15, p. 126.

Freud, S. 1918. "Thoughts for the Times on War and Death," *Psycho-analytical Epitomes No. 4*, p. 14.

Godfrey, W. S. 1919. *A Burial Service for the Use of People Who Do Not Subscribe to Any Orthodox Creed, Who Worship No Gods and Who Cherish No Expectation of Life After Death.* London: Grant Richards, Ltd.

Gorer, G. 1967. *Death, Grief and Mourning.* Garden City, New York: Doubleday.

Graves, R. 1957. *Good-bye to All That.* Garden City, New York: Doubleday.

Graves, R., and A. Hodge. 1963. *The Long Week-End.* New York: Norton.

Harris, H. W. 1915. "The Soldier's Wife—A Liberal View," *The Englishwoman,* February, pp. 97–105.

Hendin, D. 1973. *Death as a Fact of Life.* New York: Norton.

Hood, A. 1914. "The Kaiser's Funeral March." *The New Age,* November 26, p. 91.

Ignota. 1915. "Friendship and the War." *The Spectator,* April 10, p. 501.

The Lancet, June 1915, p. 1265.

Longworth, P. 1967. *The Unending Vigil.* London: Constable and Company.

MacDonald, H. R. 1917. *Our Children.* London: St. Clements Press.

MacKenna, R. W. 1917. *The Adventure of Death.* New York: G. P. Putnam's Sons.

Marris, P. 1958. *Widows and Their Families.* London: Routledge and Kegan Paul.

Marwick, A. 1968. *The Deluge.* Boston: Little, Brown.

Masefield, J. 1912. "The Widow in Bye Street." *The English Review,* February, pp. 377–424.

Morley, J. 1971. *Death, Heaven and the Victorians.* Pittsburgh: University of Pittsburgh Press.

Noble, G. A. 1914. *Cremation, Its History and Modern Practice.* Uxbridge: The Hillingdon Press.

Owen, W., "Anthem for Doomed Youth." (Quoted in E. Blunden. 1958. *War Poets 1914–18.* London: Longmans, Green and Company.)

Peel, C. S. 1926. *A Hundred Wonderful Years 1820–1920.* London: John Lane The Bodley Head.

—— 1929. *How We Lived Then 1914–1918.* London: John Lane The Bodley Head.

Playne, C. 1931. *Society at War.* London: Houghton Mifflin Company.

Pound, R. 1964. *The Lost Generation.* London: Constable.

The Queen, August 14, 1914, p. 296.

Rathbone, E. 1913. *Report on the Conditions of Widows Under the Poor Law in Liverpool.* Liverpool: Lee.

Read, D. 1972. *Edwardian England,* Historical Association Pamphlet No. 79. London: Cox and Wyman.

Reader, W. J. 1966. *Professional Men.* London: Weidenfeld and Nicolson.

Rigby, V., (Imperial War Museum), to J. C. Lerner, February 6, 1973, (Personal correspondence).

Rivers, W. H. R. 1917. "Repression of War Experiences," *Journal of the Royal Society of Medicine, Section for Psychiatry,* December 4. (Cited in F. P. Weber. 1918. *Aspects of Death and Correlated Aspects of Life in Art, Epigram, and Poetry.* London: T. Fisher Unwin, Third Edition.)

Scurfield, H. 1919. "Mother's Pensions." *Journal of the Royal Sanitary Institute,* November, pp. 140–43.

Sherran, W. 1917. "War Pensions." *The Englishwoman,* October-December, p. 22.

The Sketch, November 18, 1914, p. 137.

Stevenson, R. L. 1916. *Brave Words About Death from the Works of.* London: Chatto and Windus.

Taylor, A. J. P. 1963. *The First World War—An Illustrated History.* London: Hamish Hamilton.

—— 1965. *English History 1914–1945.* New York: Oxford University Press.

Webb, S., and B. Webb. 1963. *English Poor Law History: The Last Hundred Years.* London: F. Cass.

Weber, F. P. 1918. *Aspects of Death and Correlated Aspects of Life in Art, Epigram, and Poetry.* London: T. Fisher Unwin, Third Edition.

West, R. 1916. "Women of England," *Atlantic Monthly,* January, pp. 1–11.

Wilson, A., and H. Levy. 1938. *Burial Reform and Funeral Costs.* London: Oxford University Press.

Woman's World, 1889. (Quoted in J. Morley. 1971. *Death, Heaven and the Victorians.* Pittsburgh: University of Pittsburgh Press).

Xanthus. 1914. "The Dead Volunteer," *The Spectator,* August 8, p. 202.

Young, M., and P. Willmott. 1964. *Kinship in East London.* Baltimore: Penguin Books.

ADDITIONAL BIBLIOGRAPHY

I. Public Documents

Great Britain, *Parliamentary Debates* 4th series, Commons, vol. 41 (1896).

Great Britain. *Parliamentary Debates,* 5th series, Commons, vol. 62 (1914).

Great Britain. *Parliamentary Debates* 5th series, Commons, vol. 68 (1914).

Great Britain. *Parliamentary Debates* 5th series, Commons, vol. 182 (1925).

Great Britain. *Parliamentary Papers.* Vol. 37 (*Accounts and Papers*). Cmd. 744. 1920.

Great Britain. *Parliamentary Papers.* Vol. 37 (*Reports*). Cd. 4499. 1909.

Great Britain. *London County Council* (*London Statistics*). Vol. 25. 1914–15.

Great Britain, *Pensions Ministry* (*Annual Reports*). 1918–1926.

II. Books

Carrington, H. and J. R. Meader. 1913. *Death, Its Causes and Phenomena with Special Reference to Immortality.* London: William Rider and Son.

Davey, R. n. d. *A History of Mourning.* London: McCorquodale and Co.

Playne, C. E. 1928. *The Pre-War Mind in Britain.* London: George Allen and Unwin.

Puckle, B. 1926. *Funeral Customs, Their Origin and Development.* London: T. W. Laurie.

Yudkin, S. and A. Holme. 1963. *Working Mothers and Their Children.* London: Michael Joseph.

III. Periodicals (for the periods 1914–18).

The Atheneum.

The Charity Organization Review.

The Fortnightly Review.

The Englishwoman.

The Lancet.

The New Age.

The New Statesman.

The Nineteenth Century.

The Quest.

The Queen.

The Sketch.

The Spectator.

The Times (London).

V. Miscellaneous Sources

Marrin, Albert. 1968. *The Church of England in The First World War.* Columbia University Doctoral Dissertation.

What Happens After Death? 1916. A symposium by leading writers and thinkers. London: Cassell and Co.

Unexpected and Untimely Bereavement: A Statistical Study of Young Boston Widows and Widowers

C. Murray Parkes

In this paper I shall present evidence to support my contention that untimely and unexpected bereavements constitute a special risk to psychological and social adjustment, I shall describe the special features of the reaction to such bereavements, and I shall discuss some of the theoretical problems we must face if we are to explain these reactions.

Reactions to unexpected bereavement are an important topic for research for both theoretical and practical reasons. They are important for the light they may throw on the pathogenesis of abnormal grief and the causation of reactive illnesses, for their practical implications for prevention, and for the light they shed on the ways people need to be prepared for the losses likely to occur in their lives.

It has often been asserted that sudden unexpected bereavements are a likely cause of pathological grief (Shand, 1914). Volkan (1970) claims to have found that *all* the 23 psychiatric patients with "pathological grief" whom he studied had experienced a sudden bereavement. Unfortunately, he does not distinguish between those cases where the death was sudden and those where it should have been expected but was not. Unexpected bereavements were much less common among the psychiatric patients studied by Parkes (1965), and a paper by Bornstein, Clayton, and others (1973) raises serious doubts concerning the pathogenic influence of unexpected bereavements.

The research to be described was carried out at Professor Gerald Caplan's Laboratory of Community Psychiatry at Harvard Medical School. Cooperation was obtained from 50 widows and 20 widowers under the age of 45 who were living in Boston and its vicinity at the time of their spouses' deaths. We chose a young age group because other studies had shown that the untimely death of a husband or wife gives rise to a more severe and protracted reaction to bereavement than does a similar bereavement in old age (Maddison and Walker, 1967; Stern, et al., 1951; Parkes, 1972). In Maddison's study, for instance, age was so strong a determinant of outcome that it outweighed all other factors. By holding age constant and at the same time choosing an age group at special risk, we hoped to discover why some people at risk come through the experience of bereavement to make a good adjustment while others have lasting problems in coping.

Our research ran into the usual snag that arises when one attempts to obtain the collaboration for research purposes of an unselected sample of newly bereaved, and therefore emotionally disturbed, subjects. Half of those whom we approached after locating them from the death registration records preferred not to be interviewed and another sixth dropped out in the course of the following year. We did not think it right to intrude upon private grief when people were reluctant but we did contact a group of the "refusers" by telephone a year later and found them neither better nor worse adjusted than the rest, so we think that our sample is probably fairly typical of young Boston widows and widowers.

The selection of the sample is not crucial for our purposes here. Suffice it to say that we ended with 68 bereaved men and women from the Boston area. They came from varied races, social classes, and religious groupings although the majority were white, Catholic, and native American, with one or more children at home and relatives living nearby.

Each one was interviewed at home by an experienced interviewer at three weeks, six weeks, and 13 months after bereavement; most were reinterviewed one, two, or three years after that. Interviews were semi-structured: respondents were encouraged to talk freely and only toward the end of the interview were a number of fixed questions asked. In this way, each interviewer was able to make a good empathic relationship with the widow or widower and obtain information about emotional issues that might otherwise have been concealed.

All interviews were tape recorded and the data coded for statistical analysis independently by two coders, who listened to the tapes and made a series of assessments. Only those ratings which were reliably coded by both coders were used in the analysis of the data.

It is not my intention to give a full account of the results of this major study, many of which have been or will be reported elsewhere, but one or two of the findings are of particular interest and provide background to the more detailed considerations that follow.

We did, for instance, find evidence that the physical health and psychosocial adjustment of many of our widows and widowers had been affected by their bereavement. By comparison with a control group of married men and women, our bereaved respondents had three times as many hospital admissions during their first year of bereavement and they spent significantly more time sick in bed than the control group. A third of them consulted a professional person for help with an emotional problem during the year and similar proportions had problems with sleeping, appetite, and consumption of tobacco, alcohol, and tranquilizers—all of which distinguished them from the control group. Widowers in particular reported more acute physical symptoms than the control group, and these were mostly autonomic symptoms such as sweating, trembling, or dizziness. There was also evidence that bereaved subjects were more likely than controls to complain of problems of restlessness, difficulty in remembering things and making decisions, life being a strain, and feelings of loneliness. The bereaved group were naturally more depressed than the control group, and among those who were followed up this depression did not improve until well into the second year. Further details of this part of the study have been published by Parkes and Brown (1972).

We were, of course, interested in the question of what distinguishes those who make a good adjustment to bereavement from those who do not, and for this purpose we devised a number of rather complex "outcome" measures, details of which will be published in a forthcoming book co-authored by Ira Glick, Robert Weiss and myself. These "outcome" measures enabled us to identify subgroups with extreme good and extreme bad outcomes, and we then carried out a discriminant functions analysis to discover which of 18 key measures, derived from the three-week and six-week interviews, successfully distinguished the two groups.

TABLE 11.1. SCALE FOR THE PREDICTION OF OUTCOME AFTER BEREAVEMENT

Predictive Variables	Vector	Eta	p
Coder's Prediction of Outcome	0.42	0.49	0.0004
Yearning (3–4 weeks after bereavement)	0.41	0.46	0.001
Attitude to Own Death	0.04	0.45	0.0015
Duration of Terminal Illness	0.16	0.44	0.0016
Socioeconomic Status	0.19	0.30	0.034
Anger (3–4 weeks after loss)	0.44	0.20	0.071
Self-reproach (3–4 weeks after loss)	0.32	0.25	0.074

Results of this analysis are shown in Table 11.1 in which the seven variables that made the greatest contribution to predicting good or bad outcome are listed. The best single indicator was the "Coder's Prediction of Outcome." This was a general assessment made by the coders after they had listened to the first two interviews. It was not a blind guess, because the investigators had listed the features that previous research and clinical studies had pointed to as probably determinants of outcome. But the coders were free to weight these factors as they wished when making their predictions.

The second two features, "yearning" and "attitude to own death," both reflected the respondents' state of mind after bereavement. Respondents who seemed to the coders to be pining intensely and continuously for the dead person and those who said they would welcome death were more likely to be found in the "bad outcome" group a year later.

The fourth item is of particular importance to this article. This indicates that "bad outcome" was associated with a brief terminal illness in the person who had died. It was derived from a 5-point scale whose points were labeled "6 months or more," "2–5 months," "3–30 days," "1–2 days," and "instantaneous." Thus, those who had a high score on this scale had had very short illnesses indeed or had died from an accidental cause (homicides and suicides were excluded from the study).

Item five is an assessment of socioeconomic status based on the occupation of the principal wage earner. It indicates that people of low social class were more likely to be found in the "bad outcome" group.

Finally there were two features whose association with "bad outcome" only reached borderline significance but which are included here because of their prominence in the psychiatric literature on grief and mourning. Both anger and guilt, as assessed by the coders, were more common in the "bad outcome" group.

This was a multivariate analysis in which the interaction between the variables was taken into account. For instance, the high incidence of sudden deaths in the "bad outcome" group was not explained by a high incidence of accidents in people of low social class. Nor was "anger" a predictor of outcome simply because widows and widowers who have undergone a sudden bereavement are more likely to be angry.

Indices not significantly associated with poor outcome included the sex of the respondent, race, number of children, duration of marriage, size of household, sleep pattern, alcohol consumption, severity of "numbness" in the immediate post-bereavement reaction, and an overall measure of emotional reaction. Several of these were associated with "bad outcome" on bivariate analysis but the association ceased to be predictive when other variables were taken into account. Thus Negro race predicted "bad outcome" when considered alone but ceased to be predictive when the social class factor was controlled. It was the absence of any correlation between outcome and the sex of the respondent that allowed us to include widows and widowers together for the purposes of our statistical analysis, but this does not mean that there were no differences in response between the sexes.

(Since this study was carried out, a questionnaire derived from these items has been in regular use at St. Christopher's Hospice in London as a means of identifying bereaved people who may be in special need of help. Research is still in progress but I can report a significant association between a high score on this questionnaire and "depression" as measured 18 months after bereavement in this British study.)

Table 11.2 shows the certified causes of death in our sample. A third of the spouses had died from cancer, usually a chronic condition that gives long notice of the coming death, but there were many among those with heart failure, strokes, and accident or injury who had little or no warning of their coming demise and whose wives or husbands were similarly ignorant.

Probably the best of our "outcome scores" was one that was reached by combining assessments on a number of psychological, social, and physical

TABLE 11.2. CAUSES OF DEATH

	n	%
Neoplastic Disease (Cancer, Tumor, Leukemia, etc.)	24	34
Disease of the Circulatory System (Heart Failure, Arteriosclerosis)	18	26
Disease of the Nervous System (Stroke, Cerebral Hemorrhage, etc.)	9	13
Injury or Accident (excluding suicide or homicide)	7	10
Diseases of Respiratory System (Pneumonia, Bronchitis)	3	4
Diseases of the Digestive System (Liver Failure, Appendicitis, etc.)	3	4
Diseases of the Genito-Urinary System (Nephritis, Kidney Failure, etc.)	3	4
Other Diseases	3	4

health measures. We called this "combined outcome." Table 11.3 shows the correlations between various antecedent factors relating to the mode of death and "combined outcome" 13 months after bereavement. From these it appears that it is not so much the nature of communication with the dying spouse or the presence or absence of the respondent at the moment of death that determined outcome 13 months later, but the length of time during which the survivor had an opportunity to prepare himself or herself for the coming bereavement. Further confirmation comes from the finding of bad outcome in 7 out of the 11 respondents whose spouses died outside home or hospital (e.g., in the street).

From this it would seem that sudden death occurring in the course of a chronic illness that is not expected to be fatal would be just as traumatic as deaths from brief illnesses that were not known to exist beforehand. In other words, both duration of illness and duration of termination need to be taken into account. For purposes of further analysis, therefore, we identified a

TABLE 11.3. CORRELATIONS BETWEEN MODE OF DEATH AND "COMBINED OUTCOME" SCORE 13 MONTHS AFTER BEREAVEMENT

	r	p
Cause of death *not* cancer	0.27	<0.05
Short duration of terminal illness	0.29	<0.05
Respondent not present at death	0.17	N.S.
Preceding death, survivor and partner discussed eventuality of death realistically (plans, wishes, etc.)	−0.16	N.S.
Survivor says he deliberately avoided talk of possibility of death with partner	−0.10	N.S.
No opportunity to discuss death with partner	0.25	0.05

subgroup of 24 respondents who all said that they had had less than two weeks' warning that their spouse's condition was likely to prove fatal and/or less than three days warning that death was imminent. We called this subgroup the "Short Preparation Group," and compared them with the remaining 46 respondents, who had had a longer preparation for bereavement, and whom we called the "Long Preparation Group." Eighteen of the Short Preparation Group and 41 of the Long Preparation Group were reinterviewed two to four years after bereavement, so we are able to follow the progress of these groups beyond the first year of bereavement (see Table 11.4).

TABLE 11.4. SOME INDICES OF "OUTCOME" 2–4 YEARS AFTER BEREAVEMENT IN SHORT AND LONG PREPARATION

	Short Preparation Group (18)		Long Preparation Group (41)		p
	N	%	N	%	
Coder's Overall Outcome					
Good or Very Good	1	6	26	63	<.001
Combined Outcome Score					
<19	3	17	15	37	<.05
Remarried	1	6	11	26	<.07 [a]
Problems Some Concern—					
Role Functioning	13	72	14	34	<.02
Financial Affairs	14	81	12	29	<.01
Coder's Assessments:					
Acceptance Good or					
Very Good	9	50	35	85	<.05
Attitude to the Future					
Good or Very Good	5	28	28	68	<.01

[a] One-tailed Chi-squared test. Others are two-tailed.

Thirteen months after bereavement, only 13 percent of the Short Preparation Group were rated as having a "good" outcome and two to four years later the proportion had dropped to 6 percent. Comparable figures for the Long Preparation Group were 60 percent and 65 percent. At the two- to four-year followup, only one of the respondents in the Short Preparation Group, a widower, had remarried compared with 11 (7 widowers and 4 widows) in the Long Preparation Group,[1] 72 percent of the Short Prepara-

[1] This difference just misses the 5 percent significance level but is supported by other figures indicating that dating is more common in the Long Preparation Group (see Table 11.9).

tion Group were having difficulty in performing their jobs, and no less than 81 percent had financial problems (compared with 34 percent and 29 percent of the Long Preparation Group). On the coders' assessment a quarter of the Short and two-thirds of the Long Preparation Group had by that time taken a positive attitude to the future.

These persisting differences between the two groups are very striking— some of the most striking that I have come across in any psychological research—and they raise some important questions. What happens at the time of an unexpected bereavement to set the bereaved person off on so disastrous a course? What are the other psychological consequences of unexpected bereavement? How could such a course be prevented or modified? We can give only partial answers to some of these questions.

TABLE 11.5. DEMOGRAPHIC FACTORS × LENGTH OF PREPARATION FOR BEREAVEMENT

		Short Preparation Group (24)		Long Preparation Group (46)		p
		N	%	N	%	
Sex—Male		7	29.17	13	28.26	N/S
			30		28	
Mean Age of Respondent		37		36		N/S
Race—Negro		8	33	8	17	N/S
Socioeconomic Status	I	2	9	5	11	N/S
	II	4	17	8	18	
			26		29	
	III	2	9	11	24.5	
	IV	3	13	11	24.5	
			22		49	
	V	6	26	6	13	
	VI	6	26	4	9	
			52		22	

Before doing this, one other complicating factor must be discussed. When we came to examine the differences between the Short and Long Preparation Groups, we found certain demographic differences between them. These are shown in Table 11.5. From this it is apparent that the Short Preparation Group contains a larger proportion of respondents of low social class (semiskilled and unskilled manual occupations) than the Long Preparation Group and a slightly larger proportion of black respondents. As I have already explained, this bias was corrected in the discriminant functions analysis in which the variance due to race and social class was taken into account, but it needs to be borne in mind in some of the analysis that follows and that could not be so easily corrected.

Why this association between unexpected deaths and low social class or between expected deaths (which in this study usually means cancer) and higher social class exists is not clear. Such association as has been demonstrated between cancers and social class usually favors those of higher status, but it may well be that men and women in manual occupations are at greater risk of accidental death.

TABLE 11.6. EARLY REACTION AT 3–4 WEEKS AFTER BEREAVEMENT × LENGTH OF PREPARATION

	Short Preparation Group (24)		Long Preparation Group (46)		p
	N	%	N	%	
Immediate Reaction of Disbelief	15	63	11	24	<.01
Overall Anxiety at interview					
moderate to severe	10	43	8	18	<.05
Overall Affective upset at interview					
moderate to severe	10	43	9	20	<.05
Emotional Disturbance Score >10	14	67	10	14	<.01
Self-reproach at interview (some)	16	69	17	37	<.05
Coder asserts respondent would welcome					
own death or doesn't care	11	46	7	16	<.02
Respondent agrees: "I wouldn't care					
if I died tomorrow."	7	30	3	7	<.05
"How could he/she leave me?"	7	33 [a]	3	7	<.02

[a] Percentage corrected for missing data.

Leaving aside this problem, we can now look at how our two groups reacted to the bereavement itself. The early reaction is shown in Table 11.6, which gives the significant differences between the two groups as assessed at the time of the first interview three weeks after bereavement. Two-thirds of the Short Preparation Group reported an immediate reaction of disbelief to the bereavement. This type of reaction was reported by only a quarter of the

Long Preparation Group. Brief episodes of extreme distress often seemed to precede it. Mrs. H., a woman of 45, had refused to look at the possibility that her husband might die after he had his first coronary attack. "You know," she said, "you don't believe these things." He had made a good recovery but died suddenly at work some months later. His brother came to give her the news. At first she misunderstood. "I thought, well they took him to the hospital and I must, I must go." But when he insisted that her husband was dead, "I just put my hands to my head and started to scream. Very loudly, screaming and screaming. I think I even hit my brother-in-law," she said. Then, seeing the fear on the face of her ten-year-old son, she forced herself to stop screaming. Thereafter, she exerted a rigid control over the expression of feelings and went about the practical tasks of arranging the funeral and caring for the children in a competent and effective way. But when seen by our interviewer 17 days after bereavement she said, "I don't even believe it now, now that it's happened."

The process of grieving took a very different course in the Short Preparation Group from the course taken in those who had been able to anticipate the death. The Short Preparation Group became much more emotionally disturbed and more anxious, and two-thirds of them expressed feelings of guilt or self-reproach. A third said they would not care if they died tomorrow and a similar proportion expressed feelings of resentment toward the dead person in such terms as "How could he/she leave me?" Reactions of this type were exceptional in the Long Preparation Group.

The overall picture is of an intense shock reaction rapidly followed by severe separation anxiety and confused feelings of anger and guilt similar to those so often found to be associated with pathological reactions to bereavement (see, for instance, Parkes's 1965 study of bereaved psychiatric patients in whom reactions of guilt, anger and disbelief were usually reported). "Damn you, A—, damn you for doing this to me," said Mrs. H., confessing her anger with her husband for dying. "Actually those days were very confused, very confused. . . . People, people all day long. . . . I remember nobody wanted me to do anything and that made me very angry and very nervous. . . . I don't think I got more than about four hours sleep in a whole week." Asked how she felt about people visiting, she vigorously expressed a wish to avoid such painful reminders, then tried to take back her anger: "I, I sound like a bitch, I really do," she said, "but it's so confusing." Inside she felt dead, "It's a terrible feeling. . . . Nothing, nothing inside you at all. . . . I am completely dead inside."

By contrast, the members of the Long Preparation Group were less confused and had much less difficulty in accepting the reality of what had happened; their grief, although severe, was by no means so extreme as that of the Short Preparation Group. In addition, they showed hardly any evidence of guilt or anger, and their reaction was thus qualitatively different from the early reaction of the Short Preparation Group as well as being less severe.

It seems reasonable to guess that two factors played a part in accounting for this difference, though it is not now possible for us to assess the relative importance of each. One factor is the opportunity anticipation provides to the about-to-be-bereaved to make restitution for any deficiencies in the relationship with the dead person. Anyone who has treated patients with terminal conditions is aware of the devotion and self-sacrifice with which family members care for the patient. Long-standing quarrels are patched up, personal plans are set aside, and every effort is made to provide love and security at a time when it is greatly needed. In this way, those who are to survive seem to justify their survival and, in a sense, to pay with their devotion a debt to the one who must die. When death occurs, they may reproach themselves for their failure to do more; but they have at least done something, and most are reassured by their friends that in fact they "did everything possible."

The unexpectedly bereaved have no such opportunity. "If only I had realized . . ." they say, and all the harsh words, unfulfilled intentions, and angry feelings that passed between them and the dead person in the final weeks are recalled bitterly to mind. It is, perhaps, the unpaid debt to the dead, the guilty feeling that one has no right to survive, no right to enjoy life when the one whom one cursed is dead, that faces the survivor with an insoluble problem.

The other factor undoubtedly playing a part is the sheer magnitude of the change with which the bereaved person is suddenly faced. When death is gradual, realization is gradual. The full implication of the coming situation does not dawn all at once, but is spread out in time so that "he is very ill" becomes "he may die one day," which in turn becomes "he is about to die," eventually "he is dead." Each step in the progress toward bereavement allows the survivor to begin to come to terms with reality. By this I mean that he or she begins to realize that the assumptive world, the set of assumptions about the self that must relate to that world, must all change. Little by little, contingency plans are made—"If he should die, then I shall do such-and-such." These plans are limited in extent. It is emotionally wrong to make detailed plans for one's own widowhood while one's husband is still alive; plans and wishes are too closely allied for that. But that does not prevent some anticipation—"If the worst comes to worst, then I could always stay with my sister for a while." These half-formed emergency plans do at least enable the possibility of the spouse's death to become rather more real; they begin the process of realization that is what grief is about.

When death is unexpected, the bereaved person is abruptly expelled from a familiar world into a strange one without purpose or meaning. A great many of the assumptions that guided thought and behavior up to now have been invalidated—so many that it is hard to know which ones remain valid. Habits that have been established over many years, all the "we" thoughts and other-related actions, now lead to a painful series of blind alleys. It is the sheer magnitude of the change that seems so overwhelming to the unexpectedly bereaved, hence, it seems, the immediate reaction of disbelief that was reported by two-thirds of our Short Preparation Group. As one widow described it at this time: "I'm in a dream world waiting for the day when I know and realize with every cell that he's gone and then I think something horrible will happen."

Table 11.7 shows the significant differences between the two groups as they were disclosed at the second interview, six to eight weeks after bereavement. Anxiety and depression continue, but there is no longer a significant difference between the amount of anger and guilt expressed by the two groups. This, however, may be a fallacy resulting from the way the information was obtained. The second interview was never intended to replicate the first, and our interviewers—having elicited information about discreditable feelings of anger and/or guilt in the first interview—may well have felt there was no need to raise such issues again at the second.

By the second interview, two-thirds of the Long Preparation Group were already socializing with others outside the home, and in 85 percent the coders were predicting a good outcome; the Short Preparation Group tended to remain shut up at home and coders were rather less likely to be optimistic

TABLE   11.7.   LATER   REACTION   6–8   WEEKS   AFTER   BEREAVEMENT × LENGTH OF PREPARATION

	Short Preparation Group (24)		*Long Preparation Group (46)*		*p*
	N	%	N	%	
Overall Anxiety at interview moderate to severe	13	54	13	28	<.05 [b]
Coder asserts would welcome own death or doesn't care	10	52 [a]	9	18	<.05 [b]
Respondent agrees: "I don't seem to laugh any more."	8	42 [a]	6	14	<.05 [b]
Has visited grave by 6–8 weeks interview	10	43	32	70	<.05 [c]
Initiates and accepts more invitations to be with others	9	38	30	65	<.05 [c]
Coder predicts good outcome	14	59	39	85	<.05 [c]

[a] Percentage corrected for missing data.
[b] One-tailed Chi-squared test.
[c] Two-tailed Chi-squared test.

about their prospects. An interesting point was the failure of many of the Short Preparation Group to visit the grave. Far from being a sign of grief, visiting the grave often seems to represent a willingness to come to terms with the reality of the loss, to signify acceptance of the fact that the lost person is dead and buried. Many of the Short Preparation Group were certainly not ready to look at that fact six to eight weeks after bereavement. "I do not want to go to the grave," said Mrs. H., "I don't see any point to this really. I don't know what I can do at the grave." Of her grief she said, "It's getting worse, because I'm giving it so much more all the time every day, in every way. . . . It doesn't get better." Feelings of anger persisted: "I'm very bitter," she said, "very resentful, I really am." She felt ashamed at the way she had screamed and sworn at the children for no good reason. She expected to mourn for the rest of her life. "I'll never get over it," she said.

A year later, the Short Preparation Group had changed very little. They were still more depressed than the Long Preparation Group, and 42 percent continued to express feelings of guilt or self-reproach (compared with 18 percent of the Long Preparation Group, $p < .05$). They were still much less likely than the Long Preparation Group to be rated as "more sociable" than they had been (23 percent and 59 percent, $p < .02$) and half of them were not working outside the home (compared with only a fifth of the Long Preparation Group, $<.05$). Their reluctance to engage in formal mourning was reflected in the fact that whereas three-quarters of the Long Preparation Group had visited the grave three or more times in the course of the year, this was the case in only a third of the Short Preparation Group ($p < .01$).

Our findings at this time definitely conflict with those reported in a study by Bornstein, Clayton, Halikas, Maurice and Robins (1973), who found no evidence that widows and widowers who had a "depressive symptom complex" a year after bereavement were more likely to have had a sudden bereavement than those who had no such symptoms. Their study was carefully conducted and deserves to be taken seriously.

When Bornstein's study was brought to our notice, we attempted to replicate it by rescoring the respondents in our series using the same criteria of "depressive symptom complex" as Bornstein. These were that the respondent should report a depressive mood and, in addition, four or more of the following symptoms: loss of appetite, sleep difficulties, fatigue, agitation, retardation, loss of interest, difficulty in concentration, feelings of guilt, and wishing to be dead. Thirteen months after bereavement, three-quarters of our Short Preparation Group still had a "depressive symptom complex" compared with 42 percent of the Long Preparation Group ($p \leq .05$). (See Table 11.8.)

TABLE 11.8. "DEPRESSIVE SYMPTOM COMPLEX" 13 MONTHS AFTER BEREAVEMENT × LENGTH OF PREPARATION

	Short Preparation Group		Long Preparation Group	
	N	%	N	%
"Depressive Symptom Complex"	17	74	19	42
No "Depressive Symptom Complex"	6	26	26	58

$p < 0.05$ (with Yates's correction).

Why do our results differ from Bornstein's? Our samples differ from theirs on two minor points and a major one. The first minor point is our method of assigning patients to the Short Preparation and Long Preparation Groups. We included in the Short Preparation Group the spouses of patients who had died in a brief termination after a long illness as well as those who had a short total illness; Bornstein included only those who had been ill for less than five days. Second, our study was carried out in Boston, whereas Bornstein's was in St. Louis. Finally, the major point, our study was confined to the under-45 age group while Bornstein's covered the whole age range. We know of no reason why St. Louis should differ from Boston in the reactions to bereavement but suspect that it is the last fact that explains the difference in our findings. Nearly half of the St. Louis patients were over the age of 60 so that however sudden the bereavement may have been it can hardly be regarded as untimely. Other studies have indicated that conjugal bereavements in the over-60 age group give rise to a much less pronounced affective reaction than those which occur in the young. (Indeed one newspaper editor has pointed out that you can tell the age of a person who has died by the tone of voice of the person who phones the newspaper to insert the obituary notice.)

It seems, then, that in order to bring about the reaction we have described, a death must be both sudden and untimely.

"It doesn't seem to be much better," said Mrs. H., 13 months after her bereavement. She was still irritable, lonely, and insecure, easily tired and depressed. "I could never feel like myself again," she said. She had tried to avoid thinking about her husband throughout the year but memories would break through despite her attempts to avoid them and then she would feel very frightened. "Sometimes I wake up in the morning . . . and I see him. You know I see his face, or a gesture he might have made, or in the casket, and then I get very unnerved and I just get up and start doing something. There's no other way (sobbing), it isn't any better—no better than it ever will be." Asked what thoughts kept recurring she said, "Oh, how I miss him really and how much I loved him and what a terrible thing it was for him to die so young."

For the followup, 59 respondents were located, 18 from the Short Preparation Group and 41 from the Long. Some of the differences between the two groups are shown in Table 11.4, where it is demonstrated that the Short Preparation Group had more problems with role functioning and financial affairs and were less likely to be remarried than the Long Preparation Group. Table 11.9 shows some other significant findings, which go some way to explain these differences.

It is soon apparent from reading these statements that many of the

TABLE 11.9. FEATURES AT FOLLOWUP 2–4 YEARS AFTER BEREAVEMENT ×
LENGTH OF PREPARATION

	Short Preparation Group (18)		Long Preparation Group (41)		p
	N	%	N	%	
Sense of Presence of the Dead Person (occasional to always)	11	61	8	19	<.01
Feels: "I try to behave as he/she would want me to."	15	83	18	44	<.02
Feels: "As if I could have done something to prevent his/her death."	8	44	6	15	<.05
Feels: "I still ask myself why it happened."	11	61	12	29	<.05
Feels: "It's not real; I'll wake up and it won't be true."	8	44	6	15	<.05
Feels: "Down deep I wouldn't care if I died tomorrow."	8	44	6	15	<.05
Loneliness (often to always)	8	44	6	15	<.05
Overall Anxiety (moderate to severe)	13	72	13	32	<.02
Socializing (fair to poor)	9	50	8	19	<.05
Will not yet consider dating	8	44	4	10	<.01

members of the Short Preparation Group are still, two to four years after bereavement, unable to throw off their ties to their dead spouse; 83 percent say they try to model themselves on him, 61 percent still ask themselves why the death had to happen, and as many have a sense of his presence near at hand, although this does not seem to prevent them from being lonely. Respondents are still unable to put aside the feeling that they could have done something to prevent the death. So strong are the memories of the world now passed that the present world seems unreal by comparison.

This preoccupation with the past—fixation, to use the psychoanalytic term—is constantly being challenged by reality. Hence the level of anxiety reported by nearly three-quarters of the Short Preparation Group.

Mrs. H., whose feelings had changed very little, was aware that her failure to cope was leading to trouble. "I feel helpless, I feel useless," she said, "I feel as if I can't even earn my money and I know I should be able to try." Asked if she was in financial difficulties she admitted, "I will be—eventually," but she had little intention of doing anything about the situation. Lacking confidence in her own ability, she was constantly wondering what her husband would have done in her situation and resenting her dependence on him, "Oh, oh, I curse him, I do." She said, "I curse him for rendering me hopeless and helpless and useless and I blame him for things I know aren't entirely his fault." At the same time, she felt that he watched over her, "and sometimes I think he even helps me even though he's dead, I think he helps me make decisions."

Tied to the past, the widow or widower is coping poorly in the present and without plans for the future. Small wonder that social relationships are few and prospects of remarriage negligible. Robert Weiss, who has made a particular study of the social relationships of the widows in this group, found that although some were going out with members of the opposite sex, not one was oriented toward remarriage. They continued to see themselves as tied to their husbands and had no hope or wish for a lasting relationship with anyone else. "I'm very definite about that," said Mrs. H., "I'll never marry again. And it isn't that my children don't want me to. . . . I don't think I'm ever going to like anybody as much as I liked him" (in Glick et al., 1974).

Weiss has suggested that these women are afraid to remarry for fear of again losing the person they love and suffering as they have suffered this time, and many of our widows agreed that "it's safer not to fall in love."

We do not know how long these reactions to bereavement continued. Other studies suggest that they may last for many years, but as our own study did not continue beyond the fourth year, we can set no limit to the duration.

Nor have we found any unique features of these reactions to bereavement that enable them to be distinguished from other pathological reactions. In Parkes's (1965) study of bereaved psychiatric patients, it was reported that the symptoms characterizing pathological reactions to bereavement are not qualitatively different from those characterizing "normal" or "typical" grief—only certain aspects may be prolonged or exaggerated. The same applies to the reaction to sudden, unexpected bereavement. The typical reaction we have described corresponds to the "Chronic Grief" syndrome first reported by Anderson in 1949, but there is no reason to believe that it is caused only by sudden, unexpected bereavements. Other factors—such as a passive clinging type of relationship with the former spouse—have also been shown to predispose to reactions of this type.

What does appear most clearly from this study is the logical interrelationship of the sequence of features that makes up the reaction, and it may well be that similar sequences may arise after other forms of sudden change. The immediate reaction of disbelief reflects the fact that although a person's life space may be radically altered in a moment of time, his internal models of the world take very much longer to change. Awareness of the discrepancy between the world that is and the world that up to now we have assumed to exist, the Assumptive World, is responsible for the intense affective reaction that follows. As in all forms of grief, the initial reaction seems to reflect a deep-seated need to search and, if need be, fight to recover what is lost. What is different from typical grief is the intensity and duration of this reaction. Whereas the widow or widower who is prepared for bereavement soon gives up the struggle to recover the past, the unexpectedly bereaved is still struggling two to four years later.

Clearly, something has happened to prevent the normal process of extinction by which redundant models of the world are given up. Somehow the lack of preparation for a massive loss has prevented a normal process of unlearning from taking place. Instead of the repeated frustration of the search leading to its gradual abandonment, it seems almost as if grieving has become a normal part of life. Why should this be? Part of the answer may be the development of certain patterns of thought and behavior, which enable the bereaved person to continue to feel as if the bereavement had not occurred. These are defensive mechanisms that can be switched on whenever the anxiety becomes intolerable and that enable that anxiety to be avoided or at least mitigated. The defense mechanisms are of two kinds—those enabling the individual to avoid reminders of the real situation and those producing an illusory feeling of reunion. Typical avoidance mechanisms are the refusals to visit the grave or other reminders of death and the derealization that places a screen between the self and the real world so that the latter seems to assume a dreamlike quality—"I'll wake up and it won't be true." Illusions of reunion with the dead person are apparent in the illusion of his presence near at hand and in continued attempts to relate to him by fulfilling his presumed wishes and devising ways to prevent his death as if that had not already occurred.

All of these defense mechanisms were evident in the majority of our Short Preparation Group two to four years after bereavement, and it may be that their success in enabling the bereaved person to avoid changing the assumptions on which he or she had based his or her conduct and thought for so long was self-perpetuating. On the other hand, that success was far from complete. Most of the widows and widowers in this group admitted to experiencing a great deal of anxiety and to being dissatisfied with their lives. This dissatisfaction gives us hope that further change in the direction of a greater commitment to the present and future world and a gradual loosening of the ties to the dead person will occur.

The extent to which we should regard the reactions of these unexpectedly bereaved people as pathological is debatable. The relative scarcity of eligible men means that—for many of the widows at least—an orientation toward remarriage would have been unrealistic. But the failure of so many of the widows to find and retain a steady job and the financial difficulties that resulted do seem to justify us in regarding their reactions as unhealthy.

Two important implications arise from this study. First, members of the care-giving profession must do all in their power to find ways to prepare people for bereavement so that reactions of this type are prevented. Second, we must recognize that those unexpected and untimely bereavements which do occur are likely to give rise to special problems in adjustment; we should therefore develop means of mitigating these consequences.

REFERENCES

Anderson, C. 1949. "Aspects of Pathological Grief and Mourning." *International Journal of Psychoanalysis* 30:48 ff.

Bornstein, P. E., P. J. Clayton, J. A. Halikas, W. L. Maurice, and E. Robins. 1973. "The Depression of Widowhood After 13 Months." *British Journal of Psychiatry* 122:561 ff.

Glick, I. D., R. S. Weiss, and C. Murray Parkes. 1974. *The First Year of Bereavement.* New York: Wiley, Intersciences.

Maddison, D. C., and W. L. Walker. 1967. "Factors Affecting the Outcome of Conjugal Bereavement." *British Journal of Psychiatry* 113:1057 ff.

Parkes, C. M. 1964. "The Effects of Bereavement on Physical and Mental Health: A Study of the Case Records of Widows." *British Medical Journal,* 2:274 ff.

—— 1965. "Bereavement and Mental Illness," *British Journal of Medical Psychology* 38:1 ff.

—— 1972. *Bereavement: Studies of Grief in Adult Life*. New York: Tavistock, London and International Universities Press (Paperback, Harmondsworth, England: Penguin Books).

Parkes, C. M., and R. J. Brown. 1972. "Health after Bereavement: A Controlled Study of Young Boston Widows and Widowers." *Psychosomatic Medicine,* 34:449 ff.

Shand, A. F. 1914. *The Foundations of Character*. Book 2, Chapter 10, "The Laws of Sorrow." London: Macmillan Company.

Stern, K., G. M. Williams, and M. Prados. 1951. "Grief Reactions in Later Life." *American Journal of Psychiatry* 108:289 ff.

Volkan, V. 1970. "Typical Findings in Pathological Grief." *Psychiatric Quarterly* 44:231 ff.

Pathological Bereavement:
A Plan For Its Prevention

Thomas C. Welu

After being virtually ignored for past decades, the plight of the person left behind by a suicide (the survivor-victim, to use Shneidman's neologism) is finally being intellectually evaluated and researched by members of the helping professions. This embryonic focus is justifiably concerned with the potential pathological dangers of an unresolved bereavement process.

Shneidman (1973) succinctly pleads for an all-out therapeutic effort to provide help and comfort to the survivor-victims of a suicide when he states that:

In the case of suicide the largest public health problem is neither the prevention of suicide nor the management of suicide attempts but the alleviation of the effects of stress in the survivor-victims of suicidal deaths, whose lives are forever changed and who, over a period of years, number in the millions.

The above statement does indicate the magnitude of this almost ignored public health problem, but it is also true that the prevention of suicide and the management of suicide attempts are inextricably bound with the plight of the survivor of a suicide. To alleviate the "effects of stress in the survivor-victims of suicidal deaths," we must approach this public health problem with a philosophy of intervention based on a program of prevention whose ultimate goal would be the prevention of suicide. In the final analysis, the magnitude of the survivor-victim population is the direct result of our current inability to prevent suicide.

The past battle against the endemic problem of suicide has been piecemeal at best. The past and present efforts of Suicide Prevention Centers to effectively prevent suicide have been quite parochial. In examining the primary and secondary prevention activities of Suicide Prevention Centers I found that they were actively involved with only one small segment of various possible secondary prevention efforts while primary prevention activities were effectively nonexistent (Welu, 1972).

These deficiencies resulted from a plan of suicide prevention that was not systematically formulated but that instead had come into existence because stopgap measures were needed and immediate government moneys were available. Hindsight allows us to see that this nonsystem of prevention has had no significant effect on the suicide rate although undoubtedly some lives have been saved.

It is time to reevaluate our past efforts at suicide prevention and formulate a new, well-thought-out plan of attack based on the public-health levels of prevention model (Welu, 1972), which would have the benefit of an organizing scheme to help identify areas where intervention can take place. Within the public-health model's primary and secondary prevention plan there is a definite place for intervention efforts aimed at the survivor-victim population. However, it is a grave error to concentrate exclusively on survivor-victims while ignoring such areas as prevention of suicide and management of suicide attempts. We must realize that our ultimate goal should be the prevention of suicide, which will lead to a lower number of survivor-victims. Currently, there is little indication that such preventive efforts will succeed. Therefore, we shall continue to be faced with a multitude of individuals who have been emotionally and psychologically touched by a suicide. Thus, the need to concentrate our therapeutic efforts upon this population of survivors will continue to exist. There is no question that, from a purely humane point of view, the survivors of a suicide are a population whose psychological hurts demand an immediate response from those individuals with a professional commitment to the betterment of mankind.

We have finally recognized the problem and now we must begin to try to alleviate its potentially devastating effects using the therapeutic armaments currently at our disposal. There is much we don't know, but this lack of knowledge should not deter us from seeking new solutions.

We shall now examine the effects of a suicide on the survivor-victims.

This glimpse into their psychological world will be gleaned from their personal experience and the narratives of others. We shall attempt to determine whether the lives of survivor-victims are psychologically and emotionally disrupted by a suicide in their family, and shall collect evidence to reinforce the need for therapeutic intervention with this population. After this brief examination a special followup program for the survivor-victim of a suicide will be constructed with an emphasis on the need for immediate followup and continuity of care. Finally, the necessity of evaluating programs designed to provide therapeutic relief for survivors of a suicide will be stressed and a method to evaluate the proposed followup program will be illustrated and explained.

With the above objectives in mind let us delve into the actual world of those individuals who have been touched by the suicide of someone close to them.

Aftermath of a Suicide

Only recently has a concerted effort been made to substantiate the negative psychological, sociological, and physical effects a suicide has on those left behind.

In a recent publication (Cain, 1972), one finds a host of collected data and cases that at the very least make an intellectual plea for immediate support and therapeutic concern for the survivor-victim. Also documented is the fact that a suicide often contains within its aftermath potentially damaging repercussions on the family members left behind.

To add to the abovementioned documentation of the seriousness of a suicide's aftermath and its impact on the survivors I should like to present in detail the post-suicide bereavement processes of two individuals whose sons committed suicide and left them with many guilt-producing, unanswered questions.

Obviously, the documentation of two persons' lives being psychologically and emotionally disrupted by a suicide should not be interpreted as an inevitable consequence experienced by every survivor-victim. But it does illustrate that in some cases a suicide can certainly contribute to post-suicide, self-destructive behavior exhibited by the survivor.

Mrs. A., a 40-year-old, divorced, unemployed, black woman, was first contacted when she arrived in the emergency room for medical treatment after she had attempted suicide by ingesting 18 tablets of Prednisone (a medication used for the treatment of rheumatoid arthritis). Her medical chart revealed that she had a history of pericarditis and was currently under a physician's care for that condition.

Mrs. A. was interviewed; she related that her only son was currently in jail on a robbery-murder charge and that she felt quite lonely and had no one except her son to rely on. During her early years, Mrs. A. lived in a foster home and she hoped her son would have a better life than she had. Unfortunately, following her suicide attempt the patient was sent home without a psychiatric consultation.

Seventeen days after this attempt Mrs. A. was informed by prison authorities that her son had hanged himself in his cell. The effect of her son's death manifested itself in many ways for four months after his suicide. At a four-month followup interview, Mrs. A. stated that her general health was poor and that she was suffering from a chronic "blood disease," stomach trouble, "nerves," and a "disposition towards pneumonia." As a result of her poor physical state she wasn't permitted to work and was on welfare. Mrs. A. related that she had moved three times since her son's death.

She appeared lethargic and depressed and stated that she continued to think about killing herself. Mrs. A. emphasized her loneliness and related that she couldn't "deal with this isolation." Along with this sense of loneliness existed an overwhelming sense of guilt about her failures in raising her son. She questioned the reported cause of her son's death and believed that someone else might have killed him.

Mrs. A. cried frequently, did not sleep well, felt depressed, got tired for no apparent reason, and spent all of her time alone.

After the followup interview, an effort was made to initiate a treatment regimen for Mrs. A. by referring her to a local Community Mental Health Center. Despite a promise given to provide treatment, followup care was never carried out by the Center. Within a year Mrs. A. attempted suicide twice more.

In summary, we can say that the suicide of Mrs. A.'s son had a negative effect on the psychosocial-physiological functioning of Mrs. A. One could speculate with relative accuracy that the ensuing self-destructive behavior was one of the aftermaths of an unresolved, pathological bereavement process whose potential healthy resolution was left unaided by a totally inadequate followup and treatment system.

At the time of her suicide attempt, Mrs. B. a 49-year-old, black woman, divorced for 25 years, was employed by a homemaker service and lived with her 80-year-old aunt.

Six months before Mrs. B.'s suicide attempt her only son (31) had committed suicide by shooting himself in the head. The shooting had occurred while her son was visiting his father. After a brief conversation, the son told his father good-bye, went upstairs, and shot himself with a pistol he frequently carried.

Mrs. B. went to the funeral and afterward recalled, "I wanted to kiss my son's body good-bye but they wouldn't let me at first because the side of his head was all bandaged. Finally, after much insistence, I did kiss him."

Mrs. B. also said that at the time of her son's death she "took the whole ordeal quietly and didn't scream."

One week before her suicide attempt Mrs. B.'s fiancé (they were to be married in a week) died of a heart attack. Mrs. B. related that when she received this news she "just went to bed and didn't go to the funeral or anything." Since his death she had been very depressed and withdrawn and just sat in her room all the time. "Everything seemed to hit me at once," she said.

A week after her fiancé's death Mrs. B. went out drinking, came home, and took "about nine or ten prescription pills." Later that same evening Mrs. B. went to her room, took some more pills, and fell asleep. She awakened groggy the next day, became drunk, and called the police—telling them she had taken an overdose. Mrs. B. was brought to the emergency room and was evaluated medically. When seen in the emergency room the patient kept repeating that she "needed help and needed to be loved." A psychiatrist was not immediately available, and Mrs. B. refused to wait one-half hour for one to arrive. Finally, she was discharged in the care of a friend. An interview was held the next day at Mrs. B.'s apartment. During the course of the interview Mrs. B. attributed her suicide attempt to the fact that she was still depressed over the death of her son. She spent the whole interview time talking about her son's death, how it happened, and what it meant to her. Also, during the course of the conversation Mrs. B. said that she was going to get a "hot" gun next week from a friend and "kill herself like her son did."

Because of the seriousness of Mrs. B.'s situation she was referred to the Community Mental Health Center. The Center agreed to contact Mrs. B. and set up a treatment program. (Mrs. B. was agreeable to this.) However, contact was never made with the patient and she received no followup attention from the Center.

Here again, we see from the above account that the suicide of a family member plays havoc with the survivor's emotional life and, in the case of Mrs. B., it was a significant factor in triggering off a suicide attempt. Also, the lack of followup concern by the referred treatment agency is deplorable.

In a Darkness, by James Wechsler (1972), vividly describes parents' efforts to obtain psychiatric treatment for their son, who ultimately killed himself. For over a period of nine years, eight therapists diagnosed and "treated" their son, Michael. The residual psychological pain and guilt prompted Mr. Wechsler to write a moving account of his son's life and death, which ends with the following haunting question:

We are no wiser now than before about whether Michael's affliction, in the present state of medical knowledge, was hopeless or whether he was ultimately a victim of a fatal blindness on the part of parents and therapists alike. One psychiatrist whom we respect told us afterward that suicide occurred most frequently among patients "just when they had begun to get better," but this only confirms our sense that the final warning we received from Phil [their son's friend] was inexcusably minimized by both ourselves and the two therapists to whom it was transmitted.

We have seen that survivor-victims of a suicide are often emotionally and psychologically disrupted to such an extent that immediate supportive intervention should be initiated. Now we shall outline and discuss a special followup program to provide immediate and continuous supportive intervention.

Special Followup Program

One of the first prerequisites of any successful followup program for the survivor-victims of a suicide is the identification of a group of caregivers who would be able to contact the bereaved within 48 hours and begin a therapeutic relationship.

Quick contact is important because it not only provides needed support at a time when the survivor-victim's world has fallen apart but also establishes a relationship that has a greater chance of enduring throughout the period of bereavement.

Clergymen have immediate access to the survivor-victims because society has always accepted them as a group whose role was to provide comfort and consolation at times of crisis. Stone (1972) also recommends clergymen as the ideal caregivers:

Most people, both churched and unchurched, actually expect the minister to be present after a death. Since he is the one designated by society to deal with the deceased and their survivors, he can involve himself and the church immediately, and can continue his contact with the family long after the death. These unique advantages make him the ideal person to work therapeutically with the bereaved.

If clergymen are employed as caregivers, a new group of professionals or paraprofessionals would not have to be created; furthermore, there would be almost no expense involved in recruiting the clergy to perform a service they have already dedicated themselves to.

However, before becoming actively involved in a therapeutic relationship with the bereaved, each clergyman should attend a special training program whose goal would be to provide the basic fundamentals necessary to lead the bereaved through the maze of a "normal bereavement period."

The special followup program should be put into operation whenever a suicide occurs. A clergyman would immediately be notified and he, in turn, would contact the survivor-victims, attend the funeral services if able, and visit the home of the survivors, where they would have the opportunity to begin talking about the suicide and their feelings about this sudden loss.

Therapeutic contact between the clergyman and survivor-victims should be quite frequent during the first few months and should continue on a less intense basis until the bereavement process was worked through in a healthy manner.

The specific therapeutic techniques and methods to be used in promoting a healthy bereavement process have been sufficiently explained and outlined in a number of books and articles (Kutscher, 1969; Lindemann, 1944; Stone, 1972). It should be mentioned here, however, that the type of followup program I have proposed is similar to the one devised by Silverman (1969), where the primary caregivers were widows who contacted the widows of men who had suicided and provided the "kind of help a well-informed, generous neighbor could provide."

In summary, any effective followup program for the survivor-victims must include contact with the survivor as soon as possible after the suicide; a trusting and support-giving relationship; continued followup and continuity of therapeutic support, which should take place, whenever possible, within the environment of the survivor.

Evaluation of Effectiveness

Too often, programs providing a particular service are initiated because of a crisis situation that demands immediate attention. Because of this almost blind rush to provide a service the whole question of an evaluation of its effectiveness is lost sight of or not even considered in the push toward a solution.

We must not let this type of precipitousness blind us from recognizing the need for evaluating programs designed to alleviate the psychological and emotional suffering of the bereaved. Now is the time to design pilot programs with built-in evaluation components so that we can say, with some empirical conviction, that the bereaved actually benefited from the provided therapeutic intervention. The special followup program I have outlined has the following evaluative components built into its overall design.

EVALUATION DESIGN

All of the suicides (determined by the medical examiner or coroner's decision) and their respective immediate survivors in a particular city or defined location would be randomly divided into an experimental group and a comparison group.

Obviously, it is impossible to create a control group in the strict sense of the word. Even if we wanted to (and ethically this would be questionable) we could not prohibit those survivors in the control group from seeking the help of friends, relatives, and professionals. What we can do, however, is to add an additional followup component and then test its effectiveness and ability to smooth out and depathogenize the bereavement process.

In forming the experimental and comparison groups by random assignment we are able to create two "equal" groups, distinguished only by the fact that the experimental group would receive a special followup program. The essential component of such a program would be immediate identification and followup with an emphasis on continuity of care. Since we presently have no empirical evidence indicating that a followup program is better than no systematic followup at all, we would not be withholding a bona fide treatment plan from those survivor-victims constituting the comparison group.

Now let us turn to a crucial step in the evaluation process—the establishment of criteria that can be used to measure whether a program's effects have been positive, neutral, or negative. One goal of further research into the normality and pathology of the bereavement process should be the formulation of a quantifiable schedule containing those elements of bereavement which are considered normal and those which depict a pathological process. However, such a schedule is as yet nonexistent, therefore, we have to rely on our judgment as to which criteria are adequate in distinguishing a normal from a pathological bereavement process.

In a previous program evaluation study we found that observable and countable criteria are extremely useful as determiners of a program's effectiveness (Welu and Picard, 1973). The underlying assumption of using such criteria is that their presence or absence during the followup period indicates whether pathological or normal bereavement process is taking place.

The following selected criteria for judging the special followup program's effectiveness are by no means meant to be all-inclusive, and the method of quantifying, defining, and justifying them as adequate criteria will be left to the reader's judgment.

EVALUATIVE CRITERIA

A. *Self-destructive behavior.* A long- or short-range, direct or indirect injurious process or action (over which man has some actual or possible control) through which man impairs his functioning, may shorten his life and will frequently increase his pain and misery.

1. *Suicide attempts.* Any nonfatal act of self-damage inflicted with self-destructive intention, however vague and ambiguous (Stengel, 1968). Sometimes this intention has to be inferred from the individual's behavior.

2. *Excessive use of alcohol.* The overuse of alcohol to such an extent that it interferes with the drinker's health, or interpersonal relations or economic functioning (Keller, 1960).

3. *Drug misuse.* The self-administration of chemicals to such an extent that it interferes with the misuser's health, or interpersonal relations, or economic functioning (Keller, 1960; Sapira and McDonald, 1970).

B. *Suicidal thoughts or feelings.*

C. *Physiological problems,* especially of a psychosomatic nature, e.g., spastic or ulcerative colitis, asthma, rheumatoid arthritis.

Stone (1972) in his research study found that suicide survivors are plagued with physical ailments much more than the nonsuicide survivors.

    D. *Lack of social interaction,* e.g., not dating, loss of friends, etc.
    E. *Depressive state with obvious clinical clues,* such as weight loss, appetite loss, and sleep disturbance.
    F. *Hospitalization for "psychiatric disorders."*
    G. *Taking of psychotherapeutic drugs.*

Finally, the effectiveness of a program would be ascertained at the end of a predetermined followup period by comparing the experimental and comparison groups with regard to the presence or absence of the previously mentioned evaluative criteria. Then, with the positive or negative empirical evidence collected, we would have a firmer base to initiate the special followup program on a nationwide basis or to reject it as ineffective.

Conclusion

We have stressed the importance of providing the survivor-victim of a suicide with followup intervention. A special program was designed to provide followup and continuity of care and an evaluation component was incorporated into the program to ascertain its effectiveness.

    Only by beginning now to set up and evaluate pilot followup programs for the survivor-victims of a suicide will we be able to successfully launch a systematic alleviation of the sufferings of a too-long-forgotten population.

REFERENCES

Cain, A. C., ed. 1972. *Survivors of Suicide.* Springfield, Illinois: Charles C. Thomas.

Keller, M. 1960. "Definition of Alcoholism." *Quarterly Journal of Studies on Alcohol* 21, no. 1, pp. 125–134.

Kutscher, A. H., ed. 1969. *Death and Bereavement.* Springfield, Illinois: Charles C. Thomas.

Lindemann, E. 1944. "Symptomatology and Management of Acute Grief." *American Journal of Psychiatry* 101:141 ff.

Sapira, J. D. and R. H. McDonald. 1970. "Abuse—1970." *Disease-a-Month,* November.

Shneidman, E. S. 1973. *Deaths of Man*. New York: Quadrangle/The New York Times Book Co.

Silverman, P. R. 1969. "The Widow-to-Widow Program: An Experiment in Preventive Intervention," *Mental Hygiene* 53:333 ff.

Stengel, E. 1968. "Attempted Suicides." In *Suicidal Behaviors: Diagnosis and Management*, ed. H. L. P. Resnik. Boston: Little, Brown and Co.

Stone, H. W. 1972. *Suicide and Grief*. Philadelphia: Fortress Press.

Wechsler, J. A. 1972. *In a Darkness*. New York: W. W. Norton and Co.

Welu, T. C. 1972. "Broadening the Focus of Suicide Prevention Activities Utilizing the Public Health Model." *American Journal of Public Health* 62, no. 12.

Welu, T. C., and K. M. Picard. 1973. "Evaluating the Effectiveness of a Special Follow-up Program for Suicide Attempters: A Two Year Study." Presented at the Seventh International Congress for Suicide Prevention, Amsterdam, August 27–30.

13

Bereavement and the Widows of Slain Police Officers

Bruce L. Danto

Vignette

Before she fell asleep, she snuggled up to her husband's pillow, recalling how warm his body would feel next to hers when he returned home from the precinct at 4 A.M. She then fell asleep. Soon the ring of the doorbell registered in her ears. Its ringing was accompanied by soft, rapid knocks. Through the window, she could see red and blue flashing lights, which rhythmically cast colored shadows against the wall. She thought, "That's a police car. What's it doing here? Jack will wake up the whole neighborhood." The knocking persisted, and the ringing doorbell convinced her that the noise and clamor would end only when she left her bed and answered the door.

Once she undid the lock and opened the door, she saw them. The two police officers were somber-faced, blowing vapors of cold breath, with cheeks that turned blue and then red from the light reflected from the blinking flasher of the police car. "Janice, Jack's been hurt. We gotta take you to the hospital."

"Is he hurt badly? How did it happen?"

The same face said, "We gotta take you to the hospital. We don't know more than that."

The author wishes to thank and acknowledge the cooperation of John Nichols, Commissioner, Detroit Police Department. This study could not have been conducted had it not been for his interest and the cooperation of his administrative staff, Inspector Sylvester Lingeman, and the now retired District Inspector, Delore Ricard. Rosemary Zukowski of the DPOA was most helpful in supplying a list of known widows as well as calling them personally to encourage their participation in the study. Finally, the author wishes to acknowledge the importance of the police officer as a valuable member of our society and the need to protect the officers and their families from the dangers to which they are exposed daily in the performance of their duty.

Janice quickly threw her winter coat over her nightgown. Automatically, she walked toward the police car, each officer gently holding an elbow. The set facial expressions and flasher lights continued to function without change all the way to the hospital. Once there, Janice tuned out the noise and furtive movements of the staff. She was concentrating on what could have happened to the man about whom she had had such loving thoughts when she fell asleep. A doctor with a tired and frightened face approached her and said, "I'm really sorry to have to tell you this, Ma'am. Your husband was shot very badly. He died an hour ago on the operating table. We did our best to save him, but he was shot four times and couldn't have made it. The head wounds were very bad." Stunned, she asked to see her husband. The doctor looked more pained. The still somber faces said, "Janice, we really think you'd better not see him. He was shot up pretty bad. We know that you don't want to remember him that way."

She insisted on seeing her husband. A lieutenant whom she hadn't seen before appeared and told her firmly that he could not permit her to do that. He had experienced many situations like this and hoped she would trust his judgment. He said, "We're really doing it for your own good. Would you like the doctor to give you something for your nerves?"

In countless cities throughout the United States, whenever a married police officer is slain, a similar scene can occur. An attempt to offer some insight into the bereavement patterns and problems of the widows of these slain police officers was the focus of this study.

The study was conducted among widows of slain officers of the Detroit Police Department. Ten widows, chosen more because of their willingness to cooperate than by random sampling, were interviewed. Many other widows could not be reached because they had moved, remarried or broken contact with the Detroit Police Officers' Women's Auxiliary and friends and colleagues of living members of the department.

Introductory Concepts

The types of reaction to death and the bereavement process with which this study is concerned are examples of those related to what has been called "unexpected death" (Glaser and Strauss, 1965) or "sudden death" or "shocking death." Although wives of police officers have not been included in previous studies, other groups exposed to unexpected deaths, such as nurses, have been. Glaser and Strauss (1965) found that nurses cannot develop a strategy for dealing with death if they have no death expectation, have radically changing concepts, or possess inaccurate concepts. If surprise at the death of another does occur, reduced control over emotional reactions and inability to maintain composure may be observed. It would appear that expectation of death is important for the wife of a police officer, since she is aware of the danger inherent in her husband's work, may nurse various kinds of injuries sustained by him in the line of duty, and is a member of the police family in the sense that she associates with other wives of officers and shares experiences, loneliness, and doubt. It might be assumed that until these danger clues are present, the police officer's wife will deal with the prospect of injury and death through denial. She may unconsciously block the fears initiated by her knowledge of his dangerous tasks and the risks he must take. Therefore, she may feel that injury or death are the fate of others.

Hinton (1967) has described the universality of bereavement reactions in those who have suffered the loss of a loved one. A grieving individual may experience feelings of misery, despair, sorrow, and emptiness. Apathy may inhibit any effort, work is left undone, and movements are slow; waves of yearning for the lost loved one may be very intense. Bereavement expresses itself somatically; tight breathing, weight loss, constipation, diarrhea, and headaches are common symptoms. Restlessness, particularly at night, is frequently seen as an effect of grief. Among other effects are self-doubt, questioning of whether one had done enough for the deceased and whether or not decisions were as wise or fair as they appeared when they were made (Marcovitz, 1973).

Feelings of guilt may take the survivors down suicidal paths; they may seek death as punishment or death as a reward, in which reunion with the lost loved one takes place. For most who grieve, life becomes lonely and bleak. Some bereaved feel and express anger toward the dead. There may be resentful thoughts toward the deceased because he did not take better care of himself, and the widow may regard this as lack of consideration for her and their children. Such reactions may in themselves precipitate intense feelings of guilt which, in turn, lead to pathologic grief or bereavement (Marcovitz, 1973). Grief may be tempered with feelings of relief, particularly if the deceased had suffered for a long period or if the marriage had been an unhappy one. As she sees it, death may offer the survivor a chance at a happier marriage.

Overreactions to denied anger may also lead to prolonged or pathological grief (Hinton, 1967; Marcovitz, 1973). Although one cannot designate a "normal" period or length of time for bereavement, most researchers agree that the acute phase ends after a few weeks and a lesser intensity of grief persists for about one year. Marris (1958) found that grief continued for a longer period of time for the widows in his study. Pathological bereavement is that type which persists for years and has an almost invasive quality, permeating every aspect of the survivor's life.

For many individuals the usual symptoms of the bereavement period may not be in evidence. A type of "numbness" may occur within a few hours or weeks of loss. These bereaved may function well and fail to show signs of sorrow for days, weeks, months, or even years. This phenomenon has been described among concentration camp survivors (Krystal, 1968) and under war combat circumstances. Sorrow may erupt suddenly at an anniversary, important holidays, or at the loss of a pet.

Children appear to adapt to bereavement with more difficulty than adults, but the effects of bereavement may be slow in appearing. Normal personality development may follow the loss, but not infrequently these children later become difficult for the surviving parent to manage, displaying a sociopathic personality or a history of depression accompanied by suicide attempts. Neurotic reactions with obsessive concerns may be present. Abnormal or unreasonable fears of events or conditions once viewed with confidence may occur.

Following bereavement there is a period of restitution, a phenomenon that reflects the resiliency of people. Despite the "coming together again," however, there may be permanent scars. The bereaved may not be able to replace the affection they felt for the lost loved one despite remarriage or its prospect. This seems to be the result of the small-family-unit concept that makes up our society. Living in small groups promotes deep relationships and feelings of attachment. Each member of that small unit plays a role and the loss of a person and his function may be keenly felt.

In an effort to achieve restitution, many widows remarry out of convenience. Their children frequently resent the stepparent who, according to Marris, have themselves often been married previously. Social values in regard to the special significance of monogamous marriage promote certain inhibitions about remarriage in the widow and her children. Relatives also may fail to support her plans or wishes to remarry. Without a husband, raising children will be very difficult, and the lack of adult companionship may result in a kind of loneliness that is too great for the average widow to bear.

In addition to the emotional loss and the need to deal with the broken bonds of affection, the widow can be confronted by financial problems as well. A decrease in the family income will force the widow to adjust to a lower standard of living than she or her children were accustomed to. Community organizational assistance may be required, and relatives may help by giving children spending money. Many widows find that as time passes the visits from friends and relatives decrease and they are left to their own minimal resources.

Society permits the widow to flounder. Rarely do social clubs or organizations come to assist her, even in terms of the financial problems she will have. In certain instances, the church will provide consolation in the form of religious faith and beliefs but relatively little substantive aid.

Within the context of the above general discussion about bereavement, a pilot study of widows of police officers was initiated. Information was gathered about their bereavement experiences, the problems they had to deal with, and resources for assistance made available to them. Some effort was made to elicit suggestions from them concerning the kinds of help they felt police organizations and the community could offer.

Methodology

Through the executive office of the Detroit Police Department, I was referred to the Detroit Police Officers' Association (DPOA). Staff personnel there supplied a list of slain police officers' widows to the executive office. I wrote a letter to these women in which I identified myself, outlined the aims of the project, gave my credentials, and asked for their cooperation. The letter was written under the signature of the Commissioner of Police. Calls to me were slow in coming because many of the widows were frightened by the fact that I was the Director of the Suicide Prevention and Drug Information Center. For reasons that may reflect much unconscious unrest within the widow group, these women were reluctant to cooperate, as they feared the main thrust of interest was in the area of suicidology rather than widowhood. I made followup telephone calls in an effort to present a personal explanation of the project and assure the women of anonymity.

Because of such resistance or fear the study, involving ten widows, took four months to complete. Surprisingly, the list of available names was small for the DPOA. Many factors accounted for this: certain widows lose touch with the police department, some remarry, others move out of the community; and many or most discontinue contact as an expression of their wish to remove themselves from painful memories or feelings, or even from possible bitterness over the failure of the police department and city to protect their husbands as well as themselves from such tragedy.

Since no parallel studies concerning the bereavement problems and process for widows of slain police officers could be found, these women were approached with an open-ended interview style. Demographic characteristics were obtained. Intimate details of information were either deleted or classified in such broad categories that the identification of a particular widow or her deceased husband would not be possible. This policy applied as well to the death setting, for some of the stories had been given broad press coverage and certain details had to be disguised. Each participant was assured that her name would not be recorded on the interview note sheet and that the records of the interviews would be destroyed once data were assembled into tables.

Demographic Characteristics of the Widows

Of the ten women interviewed, eight were white and two black. The youngest was 19 at widowhood and the oldest 46. Five had been born locally, four were from other areas of the United States, and one was born in Europe. Six of the women were born and reared in communities with populations of at least one million, and none of the women came from towns with a population of less than 500. One woman had not completed high school, five were high school graduates, and four had some college education. All of the women had worked for at least two years, mostly as typists, salesclerks, office clerks, secretaries, and office machine operators. One of the women had been employed as a waitress.

Questions about family background revealed that only one widow was the daughter of a police officer. Four of the widows had come from homes with parents who had been happily married, three had parents who had been divorced before their widowhood. Only one had a mother who had been widowed before her own widowhood. This mother had been unhappily married. None of the women were only children. They came from families in which the sibship ran from a low of one to a high of seven, with the average between four and five. Eight of the ten women felt close to their siblings.

Only one of the widows had been married previously. Nine felt that they had been very happily married to the deceased. Eight had courted actively with their husbands for over 14 months and four of them from two to three years. Only two had courted six months, and they were the younger widows. Only two of the ten widows had experienced earlier grief experiences due to the loss of a significant other person—a father in one case and a close grandmother in the other. All had known distant relatives or people who had died but they had not experienced grief of any intensity before their widowhood.

Four of the couples had been active in their religious faith and practice (three Catholic and one Baptist). The rest were inactive members of Christian denominations—Presbyterian, Lutheran, Baptist; there was intermarriage of a Protestant and a Catholic. All had enjoyed some level of social function and activities in their life. Their usual entertainment included visiting with friends, sports activities like bowling or dancing, and outdoor activities like camping and fishing. The costs for these recreational activities were modest, and the circles of friends were small and intimate, most frequently involving people from the "police family." All of the couples had at least one child, nine couples had from two to six children, and the average was about three children (2.8).

Demographic Characteristics of the Deceased Officers

Eight of the men were white and two black. Their age at death ranged from 22 years to 47 years, the average being 33.5 years. Five of the officers had been born in the Detroit area; the rest with one exception were born in areas in the United States with populations in excess of 500,000. Four of the men had graduated from high school; the rest had had up to three years of college. None had graduated from college but might have if they had not been killed. Only four of the men had worked at some job before becoming police officers, e.g., industrial work, stock checker, printer, and soldier. All of the men had experienced military service; three served two years, six up to a maximum of four years, and one had been in the reserves. The average time of military service was 3.3 years. Two of the ten men had experienced military combat.

In regard to their own families, five had deceased fathers. Their parents had been happily married. Another three had living parents who also had been happily married. One came from a relationship in which the parents had not been married and he had been raised by grandparents. The tenth man came from a home in which the parents were not happily married. Among the men there were three who were only children and the remaining seven had siblings numbering from one to four, the average being 2.4. Eight of the men had been close to their parents and four of the seven who had siblings were close to them. None of their fathers had been a police officer.

One of the men had been previously married. In regard to their marriage to the widows, they had been married from a minimum of four months to a maximum of 22 years, the average length of marriage for nine officers (excepting the one married four months) being 11.1 years. All of the widows had felt favorably about their husbands' either being or becoming police officers. The men had been with the police department no less than one year and no more than 22 years, the average length of service being 10.3 years. In terms of combat experience involving shooting or firing a service revolver at a suspect, seven of the men had experienced combat.

Three of the officers had verbalized fears about being killed, two of them having done so within a few days of the event. Six of the men had attended a funeral of one or more fellow officers, but only two of the widows had attended such funerals before the deaths of their own husbands.

Death and Bereavement Data

Nine of the officers had died as a result of being shot: five in the process of making an arrest and four during a criminal investigation. The tenth officer was killed while driving to the scene of a crime in progress. His car was struck by a civilian's car. Three were admitted DOA to a local hospital and the remaining seven officers lived from two to nine hours after hospital admission. Only two of the ten widows had seen their husbands before they died, but eight saw them after. These figures were affected by the usual practice and policy of officers who feel that badly shot or injured officers (or civilians for that matter) should not be viewed by surviving family members.

Of the ten widows, three have remarried, five others are dating on some kind of regular basis, and three of the nonmarried widows felt they would remarry a policeman if the opportunity arose. Of those remarried, none believed that the second marriage was as happy as the first one, yet all felt they had good husbands, two of whom are policemen. Aside from the two who have married police officers, the remaining eight widows have had minimal contact with official members of the police department. Occasionally, they maintain contact with the Detroit Police Officers' Wives' Auxiliary (DPOWA), but few had seen any former partners or officials of the department. In one case, a detective who investigated the death of an officer arranged to visit a widow and arrived drunk. All of the widows have kept some memento of their husbands (like clothing) and six have kept firearms belonging to their husbands. Of these latter, only three know how to use the weapons.

When questioned about their children, the widows revealed that in five families the children had been suffering significant bereavement problems even up to the time of this study. In four cases, the death had caused disciplinary problems among the children. These problems could not be categorized as bereavement symptoms; rather, an authoritarian type parent was missing and unable to share the responsibility of raising his children.

Seven widows recalled crying actively for at least six months during the bereavement period while one did not cry at all. Six of the widows reported talking to their husband as if he were alive for at least two weeks following his death. Seven of the widows dreamed a great deal about their husband for the first year and five still do to some degree. For all ten of the widows, reminiscences were frequent during the first two years after the death. Nine of the widows experienced feelings of waiting for their husbands to return at times when it had been customary for them to arrive home from duty. These feelings persisted for as long as one year.

Only four of the widows experienced any gastrointestinal symptoms—e.g., nausea, vomiting, diarrhea, or constipation. All of the widows experienced sleep disturbances for at least six months following the death of their husbands. Of those who smoked, six reported an increase in their smoking, which has persisted to the present time. Only two reported some short-term drinking following the death of their husbands and six had taken tranquilizers for three weeks or less, compared to one who had taken them for a longer period of time. Most had taken a sedative at bedtime for a short period of time (a few weeks) and eventually replaced it with the habit of reading themselves to sleep. Six of the widows had lost ten pounds following the death of their husbands, one had lost 15 pounds, two had lost 20 pounds, and one had lost 30 pounds. Seven of the ten widows have regained the lost weight. Four of the widows lost interest in their personal appearance and four lost interest in routine homemaking chores. Such loss of interest lasted about three to six months.

Eight of the widows reported suicidal fantasies involving reunion with their husbands shortly after the death (for less than one month). All the widows denied any suicide attempts. Three of the widows acknowledged feelings of anger toward their husbands, who they felt had abandoned them by dying or had been unfair to have worked at such an unusually dangerous job. These feelings were immediate and lasted no more than one month. Four of the widows reported wearing articles of their husband's clothing—a jacket or sweater—and this practice has persisted, even in some cases of remarriage. All the widows visited their husbands' graves from at least once every two weeks to at most twice a week. After the first or second year the cemetery visits dropped to a high of once every six weeks and a low of twice per year for the seven widows who had not remarried. Five of the women have moved to new homes, but three of them have done so because of remarriage. Two of the women sold the marital bed and another placed it in another bedroom.

Each of the ten widows reported favorable feelings about help offered them by the DPOWA, which had sent women members to care for the children and home during the funeral and had provided some social outlets after the death. All were delighted with The Hundred Club, which is a group of businessmen who pay off the home, car, trailer, and other major bills of widows of police officers. Further, each Christmas this group sent bonds to the children and offered assistance in their education. Seven of the widows felt bitter with the Police Pension Bureau for staff who displayed a cold and bureaucratically indifferent attitude toward them. They all felt resentment toward the City of Detroit for the funeral cost allotment of only $750.00 and the fact that it took many months for them to receive that money.

In six cases, the family or in-laws of the widows were very helpful and supportive during the bereavement period. In two cases they were not. And in two other cases there was no available family.

Social and Political Implications

Of the alleged killers, including the one associated with the automobile fatality, five were convicted and five were acquitted. Of those convicted, one received probation and four were sentenced to prison. Of those acquitted, one was sent to a hospital for the criminally insane. All of the alleged killers were black and six of the widows, all white, acknowledged anti-black feelings as a consequence. One of the black widows revealed she would have felt anti-white if the killer of her husband had been white.

Nine of the ten widows felt a deep sense of anger toward the community. Seven felt resentment over community apathy toward the police and their problems. Nine resented community criticism of the police, believing it unfair. The same number resented the community's failure to cooperate with the police. All ten widows were critical of the courts as being too easy on criminals and favoring the rights of criminals over law-abiding citizens.

Only five out of ten widows favored some form of gun control. However, all ten felt that it was impractical and would not work. They felt that the criminals would get guns regardless of the law. They also felt that the spirit of the times is such that people do not want gun control. All agreed that violence, not availability of firearms, is the chief problem. Eight of ten widows expressed the feeling that tougher court sentencing would be a more practical solution to violence than anything else. Adding more fuel to their argument, as they saw it, was the fact that many of the accused killers, those convicted as well as acquitted, had long records of violence and convictions, with relatively short sentences for such convictions.

Suggestions by Widows for Improving Widowhood and Bereavement for Widows of Slain Police Officers

As previously noted, all the widows favored the supportive efforts of the DPOWA and The Hundred Club. They agreed with my suggestion about having free counseling available from the onset of widowhood for themselves as well as for their children. They felt it would have been helpful to have been able to talk to a psychiatrist, psychologist, or social worker in order to work through their feelings of loss and resentment as well as their bewilderment about the future. Six of the widows favored police-department-sponsored singles clubs and dating programs, one was undecided, and three were opposed. The three widows who opposed such activities were all young and physically attractive; it was apparent that they didn't need any help meeting men. The older widows had a tougher time in this regard because there were fewer men available and few community resources to provide such contact.

All ten widows, even those without an apparent need, favored a Big Brother type of police department activity. Such a program would have young police officers spending time with the fatherless boys, especially in such "man-to-man" type activities as woodworking, fishing, and camping. They felt these areas were important notwithstanding the available scouting programs. All ten favored a vocational training program for those widows who seek work but have not been prepared for skilled jobs.

The ten widows felt that the police department should have a training program for them coinciding with the beginning of their husbands' careers. They felt that they should have been assisted with information about insurance programs, wills, educational funds for children, and management of property matters. They felt that the department should urge police officers and wives to keep up with new benefits and policies regarding death benefits. They also recognized the need for the department to encourage its men to share responsibilities with their wives in terms of the business aspects of marriage and family living so that they could be better prepared to survive if widowhood should occur. One of the widows was required to post a bond because she was foreign-born and probate wanted to insure against possible misuse of the children's estate. She felt the bond requirement was grossly unfair and insulting, as her foreign birth should not have had anything to do with her demonstrated responsibility as a parent. Many of the women resented the requirement of keeping records and receipts for Probate Court. Understandably, these bureaucratic policies made them feel like criminals rather than mothers who cared about their children.

Conclusions

The widow of a slain police officer finds herself the victim of a death circumstance whose anticipation she has denied despite the obvious danger to which her husband has been subjected during his police service. She rationalizes that such is the lot of a policeman's wife and family. From a financial standpoint, the police widow fared pretty well as compared to widows of men in many other occupations. These widows were very grateful for the benefits in these areas, but they were candid and clear about the areas of need: psychological counseling during bereavement, Big Brothers for their children (especially the boys), dating opportunities, social outlets, estate-planning programs sponsored by the police department, and vocational training for those widows in need. They found themselves saddled with anti-black feelings, and this bothered them since they had positive feelings about the value of black police officers. Many felt openly guilty about the existence of racial feelings of this type. They all felt the large funeral was an appropriate tribute to their husband for his heroism and loyalty to the community, but they felt that it did nothing for them in terms of emotional support. They were not impressed by the carnival aspects of the ceremony and the ride in the mayor's car.

The widows' feelings of abandonment because the police department offers so little meaningful contact after its employee is killed are significant. There were few warm feelings among these widows for officials or officers at the precinct level who they felt should check with them from time to time to show that the police department cares and feels for their problems. The widows had felt they belonged to a police family, only to learn that they were without such a family once their policeman husband was dead.

Adding to their feelings of bitterness were feelings about an insensitive community. They felt the community expects a great deal from the police officer but fights his efforts to maintain law and order all the way down the line, from citizen cooperation to the courts, which are too easy on criminals and too harsh and critical of policemen.

In summary it might be said that this small group of ten women have made it possible to stimulate our thinking about the style and problems of being a police officer's wife as well as surviving as a widow. They displayed clinical features of bereavement much like those seen among widows in other social settings. The differences would appear to involve more financial security, painful anti-black and possibly anti-white feelings, resentment toward the community, and to a lesser extent toward the police department itself for such total abandonment. Many of these problems can be corrected or lessened by measures already discussed in this article. Counseling and social contact would do much to assist in bringing about relief of the more distressing personal bereavement problems.

It should be apparent that findings based on interviews with ten widows or ten of any group represent only an opportunity to raise preliminary observations and questions that require greater and more significant searches. I hope I have stimulated more research about the widows of slain officers. It is apparent that the police department has developed some promising measures to bring about relief for the families of slain members of their department, and I hope that the suggestions offered here will influence and encourage more programming in this area.

REFERENCES

Glaser, B. G., and A. L. Strauss 1965. *Awareness of Dying*. Chicago: Aldine, pp. 250–55.

Hinton, J. 1967. *Dying*. Baltimore: Penguin Books, pp. 183–93.

Krystal, H., ed. 1968. *Massive Psychic Trauma*. New York: International Universities Press, pp. 8–40.

Marcovitz, E. 1973. "What Is the Meaning of Death to the Dying Person and His Survivors?" *Omega*. 4 (Spring):13–26.

Marris, P. 1958. *Widows and Their Families*. London: Routledge & Kegan Paul.

14

Sexual and Age Factors in Childhood Bereavement

Margot Tallmer

The empirical evidence and recent research in the area of childhood bereavement that has surfaced in the last three decades has been fairly extensive and indicates that loss of a parent in childhood augurs poorly for adult adjustment. Despite the vast majority of people who emerge well, we have become so accustomed to accepting the possibility of future disturbed development that early articles, i.e., those before 1940, seem surprisingly simplistic. Such reports typically dealt with semantic differentials between death-connoting items (Barry, 1936; Becker, 1930), ghosts (Becker, 1932), or even monarchs (Barry, 1936) to illustrate derived psychopathology. Premature death of a parent was often considered too inconsequential to be included in a psychiatric report. In the research literature, "broken homes" included death, separation, divorce, and the like under one rubric.

Present data do causally link parental loss in childhood to psychological trauma, either immediately or less specifically in later psychiatric illness, although there have been suggestions that psychiatry is overemphasizing the effects of bereavement and possibly thus ignoring other pertinent variables. For example, there exists, in bewildering contrast, a documentation of spontaneous remission of schizophrenic psychoses *after* a mother's death (Cohen and Lipton, 1950) in three cases. However, a negative consequence seems hardly unexpected when considered in the light of adult reactions to object loss; patently, the child's undeveloped ego, psychic equilibrium, and immature resources are far less capable of maintaining prior well-being than an older person. Indeed, childhood bereavement has been correlated with forms of infantile psychosis (Mahler, 1961), anaclitic depression (Forrest et al., 1965), suicide (Palmer, 1941; Teicher, 1947; Greer, 1964), somatic diseases (Brewster, 1952), delinquency (Bowlby, 1961; Tuckman and Youngman, 1964) and indirectly with psychoneuroses (Brewster, 1952; Barry and Lindemann, 1960). Infantile psychosis and depression have been studied observationally, in situ, by Bowlby, Mahler, Spitz, Freud and Burlingham. Adult disorders manifesting derivatives of childhood bereavement have been considered retrospectively and thus, by definition, are not so carefully controlled—anamnestic data are limited in reliability. Manifestations occur at various times in the life cycle, with expected differences due to age, stage development, ego formation, cognitive functioning and other variables. The younger the bereaved child (with the exception of early infancy, before formation of close affective bonds) the greater the expected negative outcome. Although differing conceptual frameworks lead one to different assessments of the child's ability to mourn, capacity and derivation of anxiety, and recourse to depression, acknowledgment is given to records of parental deaths in statistically significant numbers in mentally ill adults; in addition we witness grief and mourning in children empirically. Robertson (1956) describes the child from 8 to 12 months as follows.

If a child is taken from his mother's care at this age, when he is so possessively and passionately attached to her, it is indeed as if his world has been shattered. His intense need of her is unsatisfied, and the frustration and longing may send him frantic with grief. It takes an exercise of imagination to sense the intensity of this distress.

Furthermore, Deutsch (1937) postulates that the inability to complete the burden of mourning—in a child's case due to weakness of the ego—is detrimental and only provides a temporary surcease for a beleaguered psychic apparatus. The indifference noted in children is an adaptive, self-protective device to protect an unarmored ego that must later deal with the unexpressed affect.

We should like to delineate here the term ''children'' more specifically, and discuss age and sex as separate considerations in childhood bereavement. Researchers differ in regard to the most vulnerable time in respect to neurosis; age three is considered a peak period by some. Most theorists concentrate on the early latency phase—i.e., five to eight (Alexander, Colley, and Adlerstein, 1957; Barry and Lindemann, 1960). Infantile psychosis would of course result from much earlier deprivation—the second year of life (Mahler, 1961). The essential criterion in psychoneurotic conditions seems to be whether the child can comprehend the death in fact and experience the resulting affect (McDonald, 1964). Several studies have indicated that the nine-year-old is able to understand death accurately (Tallmer et al., 1973).

Age and sex are manifestly not the sole concerns, and future speculation could profitably include such variables as family constellation, amount of help available, and socioeconomic status. We shall limit our concentration here to the death of the mother, which clearly has the potential for greater psychopathological impact than death of the father (Barry, 1939; Barry and Lindemann, 1960). The basic mother-child relationship is a central force of the infant's life, and the immediate home environment is more clearly and powerfully affected by the absence of the maternal figure. It is conceivable that women's liberation may alter the mother-child equilibrium, and the father may feel more free to exhibit so-called mothering qualities of nurturance and care, in addition to sharing functional household duties.

For now, the mothering figure is generally a woman and her death during early childhood is causally linked with later neuroses and precedes that neurosis more often in women than in men. This is also shown for female schizophrenics (Barry and Lindemann, 1960; Hilgard and Newman, 1963) and female delinquents (Barry, 1936). Because of the general—albeit not absolute—disregard for sex differences in the literature, we shall use psychosociological findings that add to knowledge of child-rearing practices in order to examine the variations dependent upon the sex of the bereaved. (It is interesting to note implicit assumptions in the literature that concern the woman. For example, Lindemann switches quite unexpectedly to the female pronoun when referring to anticipatory grief.) The scarcity of direct examination of sexual differences is mystifying, as females outnumber males in psychiatric populations.

Although Freud was aware of the role of childhood mourning in pathology, he did not consider it directly and only late in his career dealt with separation anxiety. Yet he clearly underscored the importance of the early years and thus of the mother-child unit. His stage development theory of object relations would lend itself to significantly different predictive outcomes for male and female children who experience the loss of a mother in early childhood. Furman (1964) has stated "further maturations of the mental apparatus must have transpired, foremost among them being the achievement of a phallic level of object relationships." This statement then assumes that the ambivalence of the anal-sadistic phase has been resolved—an ambivalence that is often more crucially linked to mourning than is the strength of positive bonds. The period is also coincident with a lowering of the intensity of the child's attachment to the mother. The male child, having resolved some Oedipal battles or in the throes of the struggle, will have an easier experience than the female, who is deprived of reality reinforcement to assist her in ending the battle and must also deal with rage of the narcissistic blow dealt by the mother in depriving her of the penis.

Piaget's enlightenment on the presence of magical thinking and omnipotence plus the relatively stronger superego functioning, with greater concern for retaliation, in the female throws further light on potential cognitive and affectional responses that may initiate and exacerbate guilt. The boy child is assisted in his main task of severing affectional bonds by identification with a grieving father whose defenses may consist of active responses to bereavement. The girl, however, in addition to cutting emotional ties, may be bequeathed a legacy she does not wish—identification, based on incomplete introjects, with an early-dying female. Additionally, Oedipal clashes, with death wishes toward the mother, are not fully resolved for her until maturity—via marriage and child-bearing—when the revived childhood traumas centered about the maternal death may add to or account for many of the later-life disturbances that occur in women. In the case of the father's remarriage, a Scylla and Charybdis effect can be expected. If she is permitted to replace the mother, she is embarked on an unrewarding course. If she is not allowed to do so because he has selected another female, she has been twice rejected, because of the transitional period during which she played the role of the lost mother.

The process of identification needs further consideration. In general, boys must shift from initial identification with the mother and select from a variety of models a culturally acceptable masculine identification (Lynn, 1966), while girls identify directly in a personal situation with an ever-present, consistent, living Gestalt, same-sex role model. They thus have little experience in abstracting principles that would define an appropriate gender identification except through direct imitation and reward. The learning problem is consequently different for each sex, and Lynn hypothesizes that this fact may account for greater abstracting abilities in boys, who have had to define a goal, restructure the field, and abstract an opposite-sex identification. The girl is poorly equipped by early training to develop alternative modes of identification; additionally she has lost the readily available ego-ideal. The phenomenon of delaying the painful decathexis of the lost object may be extended longer for the female or even lead to an intensified cathexis of the lost object, as well as the unconscious expectation of its return. She may feel forced to accept the caring of those in her immediate environment, without seeking out and transferring libido to new object relationships. (This hypothesis is lent some support by the recent brain research indicating that lateralization of the brain occurs sooner in female children than male. The left hemisphere's earlier development may be at the expense of the right hemisphere, and may account for the female's lesser flexibility, creativity, and ability for abstraction.)

Research based on social interaction theory gives rise to speculation that Erikson's stage of autonomy versus self doubt may be more difficult for the female to traverse. After the first six months of infant life, mothers display more proximal behavior toward females, encouraging dependency, passivity, and fear. Reports are fairly conclusive that boys are permitted considerably more aggression than girls. There are many possible explanations for the mother's early attention to the male, including the greater diversity of behavior in boys (their genetic blueprint is less rigidly prescribed; therefore, male behavior is less predictable and stable), possible increased prestige for producing a male offspring, or foreseeing a need to liberate the son earlier with increased immediate attention and pleasure. It has also been shown that mothers verbally respond to and demand more from daughters than sons—an observation correlating with the greater verbal fluency and earlier left-hemisphere dominance of girls. Such increased interaction between mother and daughter may have several consequences—the girl child will be more affected by the loss, she may perceive the symptoms of the terminal ailment much sooner than the son and react accordingly, and she may be expected to assist her mother in household duties and even care for younger children. The oft-enforced dependency may augment feelings of helplessness and anger, adding to the ambivalent core and restricting ego development, thus contributing further to the burden of successful mourning procedures, for the ability to express the anger is a basic part of the mourning experience. (Even the tempo of reaction to loss may cause difficulties for the female, whose rate may be much closer to the lost object than to the remaining father.) Bowlby (1960) clearly states that

one of the main characteristics of pathological mourning is nothing less than an inability to express overtly those urges to recover and scold the lost object, with all the yearning for and anger with the deserting object that they entail. Instead of its overt expression, which though stormy and fruitless leads on to a healthy outcome, the urges to recover and reproach with all their ambivalence of feeling have become split off and repressed. Thenceforward, they have continued as active systems within the personality but, unable to find overt and direct expression, have come to influence feeling and behavior in strange and distorted ways; hence, many forms of character disturbance and neurotic illness.

Societal denial of the anger is often denied the female, thus complicating expressions of bereavement.

There are patently many possibilities and psychological avenues to explore in the sector of childhood bereavement and subsequent adjustment difficulties. We have suggested that females may be afflicted more by the loss of the maternal figure than males, bearing in mind that the great majority of people appear to avoid serious pathology. States of drive, ego development, and social roles and expectations contribute to the greater impact and derivation of anxiety, depression, and other malignant effects. We have considered a large factor—the sex of the bereaved—and have hypothesized certain differences experienced by the girl and boy child. It is an obvious area for educational and psychological recommendations and positive procedural changes. Some of the innovations may be evoked by continuously altering sexual conceptualizations in our current society; others may be brought about by direct, deliberate intervention of the family, school, and community resources, for separation tolerance involves general attitudes of all of these toward dependency, aggression, and autonomy.

REFERENCES

Alexander, J. E., R. S. Colley and A. M. Adlerstein. 1957. "Is Death a Matter of Indifference?" *Journal of Psychology* 43:277–83.

Barry, H., Jr. 1936. "Orphaned as a Factor in Psychosis." *Journal of Abnormal and Social Psychology* 29–30:134–35.

—— 1939. "A Study of Bereavement: An Approach to Problems in Mental Disease." *American Journal of Orthopsychiatry* 9:355–59.

Barry, H. and W. A. Bousfield. 1937. "Incidence of Orphanhood among Fifteen Hundred Psychotic Patients." *Journal of Genetic Psychology* 50:198–202.

Barry, H., Jr. and Lindemann, E. 1960. "Critical Ages for Maternal Bereavement in Psychoneuroses." *Psychosomatic Medicine* 22:166–81.

Becker, H. 1930. "Some Forms of Sympathy: A Phenomenological Analysis." *Journal of Abnormal and Social Psychology* 25:58–68.

—— 1932. "The Sorrow of Bereavement." *Journal of Abnormal and Social Psychology* 27:391–410.

Bowlby, J. 1960. "Separation Anxiety: A Critical Review of the Literature." *Child Psychology and Psychiatry* 1:251–69.

—— 1961. "Childhood Mourning and Its Implications for Psychiatry." *American Journal of Psychiatry,* December, pp. 481–98.

Brewster, H. 1952. "Separation Reaction in Psychosomatic Disease and Neurosis." *Psychosomatic Medicine* 14:154–60.

Cohen, M. and L. Lipton. 1950. "Spontaneous Remission of Schizophrenic Psychoses Following Maternal Death." *Psychiatric Quarterly* 24:716–25.

Deutsch, H. 1937. "Absence of Grief." *Psychoanalytic Quarterly* 6:12–22.

Forrest, A. D., H. Fraser and R. G. Priest. 1965. "Environmental Factors in Depressive Illness." *Journal of Psychiatry* 11:243–53.

Furman, R. 1964a. "Death and the Young Child." *Psychoanalytic Study of the Child* 19:321–33.

—— 1964b. "Death of a Six-Year Old's Mother During His Analysis." *Psychoanalytic Study of the Child* 19:377–97.

Greer, S. 1964. "The Relationship Between Parental Loss and Attempted Suicide: A Control Study." *British Journal of Psychiatry* 110:698–755.

Hilgard, J. and M. Newman. 1963. "Parental Loss by Death in Childhood as an Etiological Factor Among Schizophrenic and Alcoholic Patients Compared with a Non-Patient Community Sample." *Journal of Nervous and Mental Disease* 136:14–27.

Lynn, D. 1966. "The Process of Learning Parental and Sex-Role Identification." *Journal of Marriage and the Family* 18:466–70.

McDonald, M. 1964. "A Study of the Reactions of Nursery School Children to the Death of A Child's Mother." *Psychoanalytic Study of the Child* 19:358–76.

Mahler, M. S. 1961. "On Sadness and Grief in Infancy and Childhood." *Psychoanalytic Study of the Child* 16:332–51.

Palmer, D. M. 1941. "Factors in Suicidal Attempts: A Review of 25 Consecutive Cases." *Journal of Nervous and Mental Disease* 93:421–42.

Robertson, J. 1956. "Some Responses of Young Children to Loss of Maternal Care." *Child-Family Digest* 15, pp. 7–22.

Tallmer, M., R. Formanek and J. Tallmer. 1973. "Cross Cultural Factors in Children's Concept of Death." *American Psychological Association Proceedings* 1973.

Teicher, J. D. 1947. "A Study in Attempted Suicide." *Journal of Nervous and Mental Disease* 105:283–98.

Tuckman, M. and W. F. Youngman. 1964. "Attempted Suicide and Family Disorganization." *Journal of Genetic Psychology* 105:187–93.

Parent Death and Child Bereavement

John E. Schowalter

Presented here is an overview of the extant research on bereavement reactions of children to the death of a parent. There is much disagreement among authors writing in this field, so differences of approach and of findings will be obvious. An attempt will be made to clarify these differences.

A definition of bereavement at the outset is crucial, because a lack of agreement about definition understandably leads to different interpretations and conclusions. I shall consider bereavement and grief as the subjective state and observable reactions of an individual who has suffered the loss of a person with whom there has been a significant loving relationship; I shall consider mourning as the intrapsychic response to such a loss. The work of mourning was classically defined by Sigmund Freud (1917) as an adaptive function whereby there is a withdrawal of feelings by the survivor from the mental image of the lost loved one.

The initial discussion will be of the child's reaction to parental death, and then evidence will be presented to support the theory that parental death during childhood can cause delayed bereavement reactions in adulthood.

Children's Response to Parental Death

MOURNING

In a controversial paper, Bowlby (1960) postulated that from the age of approximately six months, infants are capable of mourning. He believed the

Supported by the Maternal and Child Health Division of the Health Services and Mental Health Administration of the U.S. Department of Health, Education and Welfare, the Connecticut Department of Health, and U.S.P.H.S. Grant No. 5T1 MH–5442–20.

responses to great loss observed in young children differ in no major respect from those observed in adults.

In 1940 Klein had contended that all later mourning was based on a proto-type experienced in an infant's first year, although this separation was theorized on an intrapsychic separation conjured in the child's mind rather than on physical separation of child and mother. At this young age and with the absence of object constancy, all separations represent the "death" of the mother to the child.

In a discussion of Bowlby's paper, Anna Freud (1960) stated she did not believe that very young children had the psychological apparatus capable of forming and loosening complex mental representations necessary for true mourning. She suggested that the reactions seen during the first years of life were simpler, were based on the pleasure-pain principle, and were due to the child's realization that he was separated from his usual caretaker.

Furman (1964) believes that a four-year-old has the capacity to mourn. Wolfenstein (1966) and Nagera (1970) believe that true mourning is possible only following the resolution of adolescence. Their conclusions are based on the findings that before this age many children respond to a death with inten-sified and glorified rather than with diminishing feelings for the dead person and an overt or covert denial of the irrevocability of the loss. These authors liken adolescence to a child's trial mourning for his parents and an initiation necessary for later, true mourning. Piaget's studies (Inhelder and Piaget, 1958) have suggested that only in adolescence does a child become capable of comprehending the finality of death. Furman (1973) most recently coun-tered that he believes Wolfenstein, Nagera, and others have mistakenly as-sumed that the absence of an externally visible grief reaction is evidence of a lack of the intrapsychic ability to mourn. He believes this assumption is no more accurate than the assumption that children's apparent sexual innocence is evidence of a lack of sexual awareness or interest.

Furman, however, is now in the distinct minority among psychoanalytic writers on this subject, as shown by Miller's review (1971) of the literature. Even Bowlby (1963) has retreated and now considers mourning in child-hood, when it occurs, to resemble the pathologic more than the normal mourning of adults. This is because of the child's immaturity and inability to grasp realistically the meaning of the death. Although there is consensus that by the age of two years most children are able to form and maintain a stable internal representation of the parental figure (object constancy) (Fraiberg,

1969), loss of that figure is so painful for preadolescent children that in addition to their cognitive limitations in accepting the reality of the loss, they must idealize, identify with, and cling to the image of the dead caretaker rather than face the intrapsychic separations inherent in the work of mourning.

My own view is that mourning is not an all or none phenomenon that suddenly clicks in at a certain time of life. Rather, it is an evolving psychic function for which the child has a varying capacity. Certainly the resolution of the Oedipal conflict, as well as adolescence, is a potent initiation to mourning. Because of the latency or the preadolescent child's environmental dependency and immature cognitive development, what one observes are the defenses against the pain of mourning. This does not mean there is no mourning. However, only later in life is complete mourning possible.

HOW DOES A CHILD RESPOND TO THE DEATH OF A PARENT?

Besides age, a few more variables must be considered in answering this question. A mother's death, when she is the child's primary caretaker, will generally have a more immediate and profound effect than the death of a father. The cause of death may influence the form of bereavement; for example, illness may foster phobias, while suicide may heighten feelings of guilt. If a parent commits suicide the effect on the child may be especially serious. When the lost parent is replaced, the blow of separation may be softened in very young children (Robertson and Robertson, 1972). Experience suggests that replacement can also facilitate bereavement; this may even be true when, as often happens, the bereaved child idealizes the deceased and splits the negative feelings onto the replacement. When this splitting occurs, the aggression is at least turned outward, thus circumventing turning-against-the-self, which Freud (1915) labeled one of the ego's earliest and most primitive defense mechanisms.

Our studies show that to the age of six months, the infant appears not to recognize one specific caretaker, and reaction to death of the mother is based on how well her need-fulfilling functions are replaced. After the first six months of life, the child becomes increasingly aware of specific people— mother usually first and then father or siblings.

The older child who loses a parent is often briefly sad and forlorn, and sleep and feeding problems may occur. But more surprising than the presence of these understandable signs of grief are their absence. This phenomenon was first noted by Deutsch in 1937. During World War II, Anna Freud and Burlingham (1944) wrote of orphaned children's denial of their parents' death and of their expectation of parental rebirth. Children's belief in parental omnipotence and omnipresence seems almost impossible to abandon. Feelings of ambivalence toward parents are powerful in every child and often give rise to guilt, which may mask grief, trigger frenetic, inappropriate excitation, or even foster delinquency as a means to obtain punishment (Bonnard, 1961).

Adults' reactions to death influence the response of their children. Death has been rightly recognized as a taboo topic (Feifel, 1963), and adults usually encourage children's denial. Ignorance obviates understanding, and keeping the facts of death a mystery makes effective grief less possible. This situation is all the more confusing if the surviving parent then rebukes the child for his "lack of feelings." Usually when a parent dies, the child really loses both parents—one to death and the other to mourning.

The increasing ability to understand the concepts of time and future allow the adolescent to grasp the permanence and universality of death. The psychological tasks in the Oedipal period and in adolescence to alter one's attachment and to separate emotionally from parents seems, as noted before, to act as a primer for how to mourn. Phenomenologically, the bereavement of adolescents becomes with age increasingly more like that of adults.

HOW CAN A CHILD BE HELPED
TO WORK THROUGH BEREAVEMENT?

First, the fact of death should not be hidden. Preschool children find dead animals and hear of humans' deaths. Adults should not avoid such incidents, but as with sex, divorce, and other difficult concepts use experiences that occur naturally as opportunities for broadening the child's base of knowledge. If the death of someone close to a child is expected, the child should be told. The younger the child the simpler the explanation should be and the closer it should be made to the time of death. If possible, a terminally ill parent should explain that he or she has no control over death, but is receiving the best possible care and will remain alive as long as possible. Being able to think and talk about the approaching separation often facilitates the child's ability to cope with his or her reactions to its occurrence. When the death occurs, the child should be told quickly and in a straightforward manner. This approach was found best even for severely burned children whose parents had perished in the same fire (Morse, 1971). Following a death, caretaking should be maintained as much as possible. Emotions, especially of anger at feeling abandoned, should be recognized and allowed. Kliman (1968) has found that psychotherapy can be very useful in facilitating bereavement, and at times therapy is necessary.

Delayed Bereavement Reactions to Parental Death

Hilgard (1953, 1959) was among the earliest investigators to correlate adult psychological reactions with parental death during childhood. She first used the term ''anniversary reaction.'' Since then, there have been many attempts to prove or disprove that childhood bereavement is the base-cause of specific psychopathology in adulthood. The methodologic difficulties of such research are, of course, tremendous. It is almost impossible to control a study rigorously for age of child at time of parent's death, sex of child and of deceased parent, replacement and amount of emotional support available, speed of death, cause of death, and the prolonged period of time with all of its experiences between childhood and adulthood. Hill (1972) has commented on the pitfalls facing researchers in this field.

Birtchnell (1970a) in England compared a general psychiatric hospital population with a general medical practice group. The patients were matched for age and sex. The incidence of parent death before the age of ten was significantly higher in the psychiatric patient group, and Birtchnell found most difference between populations when the deaths occurred before the age of four.

Rochlin (1965) has emphasized that early loss of a parent is often responded to as though a satisfying image of the self must be given up, and that damaged self-esteem often accompanies the child throughout life. A number of statistical studies detail findings which purport that adult depressive illness is excessively common in people who lost a parent as children. Dennehy (1966) published a study reporting that depressed adults were more likely than other psychiatric patients to have lost the parent of the opposite sex when the depressed patient was between the ages of ten and fifteen. Munro and Griffiths (1969) found that mothers of inpatient but not outpatient depressive patients were significantly ($p < .05$) more likely to have died before the patients' fifteenth year than were control population mothers. These authors found no correlation between fathers' deaths and adult depression or between childhood bereavement and adult anxiety or schizophrenia. Birtchnell (1970b) divided depressed hospitalized patients matched for age into groups with severe and with moderate symptoms. The incidence of parent deaths, especially mothers' deaths, before the age of 20 was significantly higher in the severely depressed group. In summary, these reports suggest a greater likelihood of severe adult depressive illness in individuals whose parent, especially the mother, died while the patient was under 20. Further research, however, is certainly necessary to pinpoint more directly the relationship between childhood bereavement and adult depression.

A final and more specific correlation between the childhood loss of a parent and adult psychopathology is found in suicide. Zilboorg (1937) was the first to call attention to this phenomenon. He reported the case of a young woman who committed suicide on the fourteenth anniversary of her mother's death, and he explained that suicide-proneness is found in persons who as children lost their parents and is based on the patient's identification with the dead parent. Bender and Schilder (1937) quoted the search for ''reunion with a dead love object'' as one reason for childhood suicide. More recently, Dorpat et al. (1965) found that of the subjects they studied, half who committed suicide and 64 percent who attempted it came from broken homes. The most common cause of the broken homes in the attempted suicide group was divorce, while the most common cause in the successful suicide group was death. These authors hypothesize that unresolved object loss in childhood leads to an inability to sustain object losses in later life which in turn leads to depressive reactions culminating in suicidal behavior. Hill (1969) published an English study that showed suicide attempts to be significantly more common in depressed patients who had lost a parent. He found sex and age differences to the effect that women were more suicide-prone if they were age 10 to 14 when their fathers died, and that both sexes were more prone to suicide if they were less than 10 years old when their mothers died.

As with the other statistical studies, I have emphasized the trend in the literature to find correlations between child bereavement and adult psychopathology. There are, however, in addition occasional papers, like that of Stanley and Barter (1970), which report no correlation between parent loss and suicide behavior.

In conclusion, although the statistical surveys of delayed bereavement reactions to parental death are not methodologically perfect and are sometimes at variance with one another, it seems clear that childhood bereavement can have delayed as well as immediate effects. These findings suggest strongly that bereaved children deserve priority attention from pediatricians, child psychiatrists, clergy, and others. They also suggest that these children should continue to be considered vulnerable and that prospective studies be made to give a clearer picture of the percentage of and reasons for later psychological breakdowns.

REFERENCES

Bender, L., and P. Schilder. 1937. "Suicidal Preoccupations and Attempts in Children." *American Journal of Orthopsychiatry* 7:225 ff.

Birtchnell, J. 1970a. "Early Parent Death and Mental Illness." *British Journal of Psychiatry* 116:281 ff.

—— 1970b. "Depression in Relation to Early and Recent Parent Death." *British Journal of Psychiatry* 116:299 ff.

Bonnard, A. 1961. "Truancy and Pilfering Associated with Bereavement." In *Adolescents,* eds. S. Lorand and H. I. Schneer, New York: Hoeber.

Bowlby, J. 1960. "Grief and Mourning in Infancy and Early Childhood." *The Psychoanalytic Study of the Child* 15:9 ff. New York: International Universities Press.

—— 1963. "Pathological Mourning and Childhood Mourning." *Journal of the American Psychoanalytic Association* 11:500 ff.

Dennehy, C. M. 1966. "Childhood Bereavement and Psychiatric Illness." *British Journal of Psychiatry* 112:1049 ff.

Deutsch, H. 1937. "Absence of Grief." *Psychoanalytic Quarterly* 6:12 ff.

Dorpat, T. L., J. K. Jackson, and H. S. Ripley. 1965. "Broken Homes and Attempted and Completed Suicide." *Archives of General Psychiatry* 12:213 ff.

Feifel, H. 1963. "Death." In *Taboo Topics,* ed. N. L. Farberow. New York: Atherton Press.

Fraiberg, S. 1969. "Libidinal Object Constancy and Mental Representation." *The Psychoanalytic Study of the Child* 24:9 ff. New York: International Universities Press.

Freud, A. 1960. "Discussion of Dr. John Bowlby's Paper." *The Psychoanalytic Study of the Child* 15:53. New York: International Universities Press.

Freud, A., and D. Burlingham. 1944. *Infants Without Families.* New York: International Universities Press.

Freud, S. 1915. 1957. "Repression." In *The Standard Edition of the Complete Psychological Works of Sigmund Freud,* ed. J. Strachey. Vol. 14. London: Hogarth Press, 1957.

—— 1917. "Mourning and Melancholia." *Ibid.*

Furman, R. 1973. "A Child's Capacity for Mourning." *The Child in His Family,* eds. E. J. Anthony and C. Koupernik. New York: John Wiley and Sons, 1973.

Hilgard, J. R. 1953. "Anniversary Reactions in Parents Precipitated by Children." *Psychiatry* 16:73 ff.

Hilgard, J. R., and M. F. Newman. 1959. "Anniversaries in Mental Illness." *Psychiatry* 22:113 ff.

Hill, O. W. 1969. "The Association of Childhood Bereavement with Suicide Attempt in Depressive Illness." *British Journal of Psychiatry* 115:301 ff.

—— 1972. "Child Bereavement and Adult Psychiatric Disturbance." *Journal of Psychosomatic Research* 16:357 ff.

Inhelder, B., and J. Piaget. 1958. *The Growth of Logical Thinking.* New York: Basic Books.

Klein, M. 1940. "Mourning and Its Relation to Manic-Depressive States." In *Contributions to Psycho-Analysis, 1921–1945.* London: Hogarth Press, 1948.

Kliman, G. 1968. *Psychological Emergencies of Childhood.* New York: Grune and Stratton.

Miller, J. B. M. 1971. "Children's Reactions to the Death of a Parent: A Review of the Psychoanalytic Literature." *Journal of the American Psychoanalytic Association* 19:697 ff.

Morse, J. S. 1971. "On Talking to Bereaved Burned Children." *Journal of Trauma* 11:894 ff.

Munro, A., and A. B. Griffiths. 1969. "Some Psychiatric Non-Sequelae of Childhood Bereavement." *British Journal of Psychiatry* 115:305 ff.

Nagera, H. 1970. "Children's Reactions to the Death of Important Objects." *The Psychoanalytic Study of the Child* 25:360 ff. New York: International Universities Press.

Robertson, J., and Robertson, J. 1972. "Young Children in Brief Separation." *The Psychoanalytic Study of the Child* 26:264 ff. New York: International Universities Press.

Rochlin, G. 1965. *Griefs and Discontents.* Boston: Little, Brown.

Stanley, E. J., and J. T. Barter. 1970. "Adolescent Suicidal Behavior." *American Journal of Orthopsychiatry* 40:87 ff.

Wolfenstein, M. 1966. "How Is Mourning Possible?" *The Psychoanalytic Study of the Child,* 21:93. New York: International Universities Press.

Zilboorg, G. 1937. "Considerations on Suicide with Particular Reference to That of the Young." *American Journal of Orthopsychiatry* 7:15 ff.

A Time to Speak

Rose Wolfson

Vercors's imaginative and provocative book, *Sylva,* which is more a fable than a novel, traces the development of a beautiful girl—wild, unaware, and without language—inexplicably transformed from a fox. Like most fables, *Sylva* is more concerned with truths than with facts, and in two especially insightful episodes Vercors presents Sylva's realization of self and of her mortality. The latter is poignantly moving as Sylva queries, comprehends, and, terrified, dashes into the forest, the place of her origin and nonconsciousness. But Sylva's perceptive, affectionate instructor has done his work too well for her to escape into her earlier infantile state. She returns—to develop into an adult.

No One Dies in the United States

Our children, unfortunately, have not fared so well—perhaps that is the message that Vercors, tongue-in-cheek, intends. But there is no mistaking the message in Jessica Mitford's *The American Way of Death.* Though Ms. Mitford comes down most heavily on the practices of undertakers, the reader can only conclude that an entire nation conspires to maintain the illusion of immortality. Some of us have lived through semantic and other changes: few people die, they "pass away," "go to their eternal rest," or (for the benefit of children) the beloved one "is asleep" or "in heaven." Coffins, if the bereaved can stand the cost, are more like satin couches or cozy beds; and to maintain an appearance of life, the dead are coiffured, made up, and sartorially faultless.

Science, by prolonging man's life, has tended to lend substance to this illusion of immortality. Thus, people are less likely to experience in childhood the impact of the death of someone meaningful to them and, unconsciously, are the more prone to initiate or to follow procedures that support the original, unaware belief in a deathless life. Our burial practices, often despite stern religious tradition, reflect all too clearly the infantile denial, guilt, and fear we carry into adulthood with respect to death, and which we pass on to our children. It seems sadly ironic that many children sense the death of a loved one for what it is: an irretrievable loss. But the questions and terror that rise in their young minds are seldom voiced in the face of unhappy adults whose versions of death evade the crucial point: the permanent end of all life and activities in the lost one. For most young children it is easier to "forget" the loss, and accordingly accept adult explanations. Thus, in place of "God is watching you," it may be "mother is watching you," or both. In this way, the sorry hoax begins and reverberates through our lives.

Few Escape the Illusion

So pervasive and infectious is our attitude toward death that with few exceptions it overrides educational, economic, and cultural distinctions. Even children into whose homes science does not reach to prolong life—the underprivileged and economically deprived who experience loss through death early and relatively often—encounter similar flights from mortality by solicitous adults. Thus, mama had left "to find a nicer place," "aunty is in heaven, feelin' fine now," "Daddy is sleepin'." The content of the explanation may be different, but this theme, continuing life, remains the same. Naturally, as with all children, age and circumstances of death may shape what a child makes of the adult's explanation.

Josie and David, Instances of Many

Josie, aged 5, a light skinned black child, with a beautiful oval face, was brought to the residential home at 1 A.M. by a police officer. Josie's mother, in an attempted self-abortion, had mortally injured herself and hemorrhaged fatally. Josie had last seen her mother being carried in a chair down the tenement stairs by ambulance attendants. Her father—white, unmarried, but devoted to the mother—had telephoned the hospital and Josie's grandmother. After the mother's removal, he fled, terrified of discovery and close to collapse. Since the grandmother worked during the day, she could not take care of Josie.

Left with the counselor, Josie was rigid, silent, and watchful though compliant. However, when the counselor put her to bed, Josie clung to her, babbling unintelligibly of "mama . . . blood . . . fire . . . rats. . . ." The counselor soothed and rocked her until she slept. The next day Josie joined the other children but was sulky, obstinate, and uncommunicative. With the exception of her first outburst, for over two weeks—which included a visit from her grandmother—Josie made no mention of mother or home. At that point, it seemed advisable to assess her emotional state.

She sat at a low nursery table, watching as I adjusted the window blind and prepared paper and pencil, meeting her gaze but saying nothing. Suddenly, her expression apprehensive, she said: "I have a big brother" (actually a half-brother, aged 14, who lived elsewhere but frequently visited his mother). Asked where he was, she said, "At home," and waited. Why wasn't she at home? Because her mother had "died." What did she mean? Silence. Urged to say what "died" meant, Josie responded with a seemingly disconnected account of her mother's illness and bleeding: "blood was all over mommy's bed, mommy was blooding; a policeman put mommy in a chair, mommy was in a hole and burned and the doctor didn't help mommy" and she, Josie, had a cold and was sick; "mommy was 10 and she was 9." She pursued her account, sometimes exchanging the policeman for a fireman. Asked how she knew about mommy, she indicated that grandma had told her mommy was in a hole and "got burned." Josie saw her father cry when mommy went in the car (which now and then she called "a box"). Did Josie cry? No! Why? Because mommy said "Don't cry," and "she be mad." Josie then referred to the policeman and a fire, with "jail" a new consideration. After a while, her account could be pieced together; what is relevant here is that Josie imagined her mother put into a hole alive and burned because she was bad, "and after she be in jail."

Discussion with Josie's grandmother revealed an angry, unhappy woman, torn by outrage at her daughter's conduct, and genuine compassion for her and her child. She had described the burial and mother's *everlasting* punishment, "fire," to show Josie what happens "when you're bad." To Josie's question, was that why the policeman was there, the grandmother had said, "Yes." Would mommy come to see her? No, mommy was in a kind of jail where they don't let anyone go home." Thus, the grandmother opened the way for Josie's denial of mother's death, which ultimately had to be faced more realistically. It is interesting that despite considerable gain in this direction, when Josie became quite ill, she revived "the fire," "a hole," "mommy," and "jail," obviously afraid she, too, would die—that is, in a hole like her mother—or go to jail.

It may be argued that the unusual terrifying circumstances of the mother's death outweighed all other considerations, and so invalidate it as an example of the insidiousness of denial of death in American life. Nevertheless, the fact remains that, in the grandmother's thinking, her daughter had suffered and was still suffering for her sins. The grandmother's concept of death was only superficially tinged by her religious beliefs; more meaningfully, her daughter continued to suffer in ways familiar to the mother, and her communication to Josie pictured an imprisoned but living mother.

If Josie's loss was characterized by unusual, frightening events for her, David's was sad but quietly inevitable.

David, a blond boy of 6, was brought to the juvenile home by his father, a mail carrier, who heartily promised his son he would return in a few days. Out of David's sight, the father grieved for his wife, who had been hospitalized that morning for a cancerous condition. When talking about her, he fluctuated between hope and fright: "You never can tell . . . she could be the one that gets better," then "I can't believe it—she never even got a cold. She can't be that sick. What'll I do if she . . . dies?" In David's presence, he was always cheerful and reassuring: "Mama is fine, just fine. What did you do today?" etc. However, shortly after his admission, David's mother asked to see him. The staff tried to prepare David and guide his father, and from all accounts the visit went off smoothly. David volunteered that mama couldn't walk or talk loud but soon she would be home, and so would he. She died shortly after, and his father faced the problem of his telling David. Shocked and overwhelmed by his loss, the father refused "to make David feel bad. . . . He wouldn't understand." In the end, he told David that his mother had to go to another hospital, far away, for other medicine, and "she would be away a long, long time." In the meanwhile, David could come home weekends. The father told the staff that nothing in the apartment was changed—even his wife's clothes remained in the closet, and "David would see that his mother was only away."

Such instances of denial regardless of social and cultural differences can be multiplied: the four-year-old who agrees to stay at the home until her (dead) "mommy feels better," as her aunt put it; the three siblings—aged 6, 5, and 3, a boy and two girls respectively—who wait for their (dead) sister to be found so they can go home. "She got lost in the park," and so on again and again. In talking with the bereaved, one ultimately sees that the wish to protect the child from the pain of an irreversible loss contains as well the adult's reluctance to confront a shattered illusion.

Contemporary Media Compound the Problem

Wahl (1958) has stated that just as adults in the past were certain that children have no sexual feelings, and that problems related to childhood sexuality therefore could not exist, adults persist in believing that children have little awareness of death. Further, to open up this area to children would do irreparable harm. Just so, generations ago, critics of removing the sexual taboo would have been certain that "lust and depravity would have inevitably resulted." Whether one agrees or disagrees with Wahl concerning the results of removal of the sexual taboo, it is important to recognize that the problem of death—for child development—has an urgency based on contemporary influences relatively unknown to the sexual taboo.

Much of our mass media, particularly television and radio, tend to feed into the child's infantile ideas about death. On television, soldiers in combat march across the screen; planes crash in flames; a man called "the president" is shot; buildings burn. Yet, at a later time, a familiar voice, stilled by death, will sing or talk again on a magic disc and on the television, confirming the child's belief in the immediate restoration of life.

The following incident has bearing on this discussion: Shortly after Joseph, 7, and his mother entered a bank, it was held up, and the guard shot. For a moment, the boy gazed from gunman to bleeding guard, then said excitedly, "Just like in TV."

Unfortunately, there was no way of ascertaining whether or not Joseph expected the guard to get up after the "show" was over. Certainly, Joseph may have been reacting defensively to deny the real meaning of what had happened, and the implicit danger to his own life. Nevertheless, the means he took, denial, is to the point, though violence may have been a factor too. However, in this regard, during the settlement of this country when people often died violently, children understood early at least the biological finality of death, they participated in the simple, often grim funerals. Little if anything about a death was secret, and children absorbed similar attitudes, which they in turn gave their children. It would seem, then, that the attitudes toward death determine the importance the fatal violence has. It is outside the province of this article to trace the development in this country from a levelheaded acknowledgment of death to its present fear-ridden denial, but it is not without significance that when men had to turn their energies and initiative from rural to urban conquests, interest in youth, productivity, and power became an obsession.

To return to the part mass media play in the child's belief in deathlessness: we obviously cannot outlaw our mass media (though less television watching might result in surprising changes in our children), nor should we deprive our children of an early natural phase of development when in play they hate and kill at will: "You crook! Dr-r-r, you're dead," and bestow life immediately after: "Come on, you're alive." Such play is often the means by which a child siphons off anger, hate, resentment, or death wishes, in relation to the adult world. And the magical restoration of life tends to lighten the guilt and fear involved in such "bad" feelings. Hence when children aged approximately 4 to 6 see John Wayne die a heroic death on television, they equably see his resurrection the same or the following day on another program, not because they know it's not real—as so many of us mistakenly assume about our children—but because it fits their experience and magical wishes. The only thing that puzzles them is "how he got in the box." In the many times I've had a child put this question, it has always held a double meaning: the child's intuition of our end, and the natural puzzlement of a young, liberal mind.

Admittedly, my interpretation is subjective, but there are few of us in close contact with many young children who can long remain unaware of their subjectivity and objections when a familiar character or program goes off the air. Many of us can recall the great interest shown by children in the stately, sorrowful ceremony of President Kennedy's burial. There was interest as well, in the weeks that followed, in programs portraying a smiling, animated Kennedy. With very few exceptions, the children believed that they were watching a succession of events and resisted efforts by adults to introduce a more realistic view. One child, when Kennedy no longer appeared on television, accused me of not letting him come to her home! To prove me wrong, she insisted I listen to a record of him speaking (actually an excellent takeoff of Kennedy, recorded shortly after his inauguration).

A Time to Speak

Such fidelity to fantasies of a deathless life, sustained inadvertently by our mass media, can be countered only by a greater fidelity to reality—in this instance to our mortality, which few of us want to believe and most of us deny in one form or another. So we ask, defensively, why nurture knowledge in our children of the final fact of life? But indeed "the child is father of the man," and if we insist that the child be sheltered from the true meaning of death, we have only to look at adult attitudes toward the old and the aged—relegated to homes removed from the current stream of social life—to comprehend, at least in part, where the cruelty and indifference our fear of dying can unwittingly lead us. And so sensitive have we seemingly become to the feelings of the old, that we now have not old people, but "senior citizens."

Children raised on a ruse of such magnitude must learn to walk a tightrope between their inner fearful perceptions and the adults' half-truths or pretenses when death occurs. As has often been noted, nature abhors a vacuum, and if we, as adults, fail to help our young children understand the void caused by death, they will provide answers for themselves of the kind we have already seen: magic, denial, and a secret lonely fear that they have brought about a dreadful catastrophe. The vaguer the facts, the greater the fear.

Donald, 6, returned to the therapy playroom at the end of an apparently happy summer. After two quiet sessions, unlike his more usual spirited ones, he fingered a small plastic baby doll, then let it slip through his fingers to the floor. He immediately repeated the performance but, this time whispering to himself, caught the doll before it hit the floor. Smiling, he said, "He's swimming down far," then suddenly pushed the doll aside. Questioned, he said "The boy got tired."

"Has the boy a name?"

He hesitated before answering, "Donald."

"How come Donald is tired?"

He disregarded the question but resumed his play with the doll, alternating between allowing it to walk on the bottom of "the ocean" and swimming expertly to the surface. Though Donald was usually concerned with swimming, his play with the doll was new, and his attitude gruff and angry when I wondered aloud about Donald, the baby. Shortly after, I asked Donald's mother if anything unusual had happened during the summer. No. I mentioned swimming. Oh yes, she had forgotten to tell me: a neighbor's child of 3 had fallen into the pool next door and drowned. Donald was told by their neighbors that the child, also named Donald, was tired and had "gone to sleep in the pool." She was not certain but thought Donald might have seen the child drown. After a few days of brooding silence, Donald had told her, "If I could swim better, I could have saved Donald." She tried to reassure him that he was in no way to blame, assuming from Donald's statement that he understood what had happened to the drowned child. After this first statement, he made no other references to the drowning. His mother, however, uneasy at his seeming dismissal and disregard of the tragic event, alluded to it whenever an opportunity arose. At first, Donald pretended he didn't know of whom she was talking; then he remembered: "Oh, yeah, that's the baby next door." His mother persisted, and soon he recalled that "something bad had happened to Donald."

Worried about Donald's self-blame, she stressed that no one was to blame. "Donny was too little to know what would happen," which Donald finally seemed to accept. His mother was surprised that the accident had come up in the playroom, since the drowning had occurred in early summer.

Without concerning ourselves with why someone as instinctively wise and observant as this mother forgot to relate such a shocking event, we can see that Donald either rejected the death or conceived of it as a change in residence. In view of the similarity of names, Donald's confusion and fright made rejection of the death almost mandatory—if he was to live. Later sessions confirmed the anxious identification with his namesake, and a continuing life for little Donny, who had a house under the water. With infallible children's logic, if Donny wasn't at the bottom of the pool, he lived in the ocean where Donald hoped to visit him!

A year later, I had to cancel Donald's session because of a personal loss. On his return, I explained I'd gone to a funeral. Did he know what that meant? He nodded, his eyes earnestly searching my face, "Somebody died."

"Do you know what 'died' means?"

Again he nodded, still looking at me, "Like you can't feel anything . . . you can't breathe . . . you can't move, you can't see anyone . . . you're dead . . . like you can't do things *I* . . . *we* can."

I agreed: "That's what's happened to a friend I loved very much." He put his hand briefly in mine, then quickly went for his auto model.

A Time to Build Up

Donald's sudden shift from the impersonal (I hope) "you" to "I," then swiftly to "we" suggests the fear that thoughts of death aroused in him and the need to proclaim his being alive. But this fear is realistic. Like Sylva, Donald is approaching a realization of his ultimate end, which hopefully, in place of distortion, will impel questions openly related to death: Will I die? Why? When? How? And though it may at first seem that we are only exchanging one set of questions for another—harder ones at that—this is the nature of learning and maturing! Wahl, Ross, and others point out the infantile, or often unfeeling, adults we produce in regard to the treatment of and the confrontation with death. Children are hoodwinked, presumably to spare them pain. What, however, of the misery, depression, and loneliness of the child who does not know what has happened to his vanished mommy, daddy, or whoever, yet knows that what he has been told is not so? Some of their strategies to keep going have already been suggested; there are innumerable others, few of which are conducive to growth.

To be fair, we must recognize that there are adults—parents, teachers, and other key people—who want the child to know the truth when death occurs, but do not know how to tell him so that he will understand. However, the basic problem with respect to death as a reality resides in society's attitude toward it. If our children are to outgrow the belief in magical restoration, with its dehumanizing results, we must first convince the parents who suffer the same illusion that the problem exists. That is, before we can get into the schools we must get into the homes. We have only to bear in mind the civil war over sex education to appreciate the task that faces us. Perhaps we shall have an easier time of it. If we are now permitted to learn how we are born, we may find less resistance to teaching that we shall die.

There are encouraging signs of greater recognition that a critical societal problem exists. Though some articles and books on the subject appeared in the 1940s and a trickle has continued, research, professional and nonprofessional publications, lectures, conferences, and workshops on the dying patient (child and adult), on the bereaved, and on professional attitudes toward the terminal patient and his family are being held more frequently.

Even the government has contributed with an important bibliography on death and the dying (Vernick, 1970).

Ironically, at a time when human life appears to have little value to many and death has become a haphazard commonplace, there are those making increasing attempts to sensitize us to the poignancy and inherent dignity of an individual death. Or are these two seemingly contrary phenomena related? Whatever the answer, there is yet hope that our children will grow and live and die as mature adults.

REFERENCES

Mitford, J. 1969. *The American Way of Death.* New York: Simon and Schuster.

Vercors, J. 1964. *Sylva.* New York: Macmillan.

Wahl, C. W. 1958. "The Fear of Death." *Bulletin of the Menninger Clinic* 22:214 ff.

FOR FURTHER READING

Eissler, R. R., 1955. *The Psychiatrist and the Dying Patient.* New York: International Universities Press.

Furman, R. A. 1964a. "Death and the Young Child: Some Preliminary Considerations." In *Psychoanalytic Study of the Child.* 19:321–33 New York: International Universities Press.

—— 1964b. *Death of a Six Year Old's Mother During His Analysis.* New York: International Universities Press.

Kübler-Ross, E. 1969. *On Death and Dying.* New York: The Macmillan Co.

McDonald, M. 1964. "A Study of the Reactions of Nursery School Children to the Death of a Child's Mother." In *Psychoanalytic Study of the Child* 19:358–76. New York: International Universities Press.

Schoenberg, B., A. C. Carr, D. Peretz, and A. H. Kutscher, eds. 1970. *Loss and Grief: Psychological Management in Medical Practice.* New York and London: Columbia University Press.

Vernick, J. J. 1970. *Selected Bibliography on Death and Dying*. Bethesda, Maryland: Information Office, National Institute of Child Health and Human Development, 20014.

Wainwright, L. 1969. "A Profound Lesson for the Living." *Life* Nov. 21, pp. 36–43.

Wolfson, R. 1958. *Death and a Five Year Old*. Unpublished paper, presented at a meeting of The Cathedral Forum on Religion and Psychology, St. John the Divine, July.

17

The Maternal Orphan: Paternal Perceptions of Mother Loss

John W. Bedell

The Sample

THE RESEARCH PROBLEM

Much family research has focused on the incomplete families that result from divorce or the death of the father-husband. A review of the literature shows that nothing is really known about the widower and his lifestyle; I have therefore chosen to examine it here. The research problem is as follows: Is the death of the wife-mother defined as a crisis by her surviving spouse? If so, what happens? and why? The organizing theoretical perspective is the crisis framework as formulated, for example, by Hill (1949) and Parad (1965).

The family roles, especially those of the adults, are usually constituted so that every participant has some degree of emotional soothing to do for each member of his or her nuclear family, in addition to normal tasks. However, the mother's role is considered the basic organizer for daily living. Therefore, there is a need to understand the impact of her death on the family.

Someone must perform childcare duties and take care of the home after the death of the wife-mother *if* the family is to stay together. Indeed, family budgets may be strained because of the necessity to pay for mother-substi-

This research was partially funded by a National Science Foundation Predoctoral Fellowship.

tutes. Administrators of assistance programs at all levels must know who is brought in to assume the feminine role, if anyone, and the consequences of these various substitutes for the mental and social health of those in fractured families. The adjustment patterns and problems of the widowers have to be investigated in nonfamilial settings.

RESEARCH DESIGN

Much is known about some forms of personal and social disorganization. A given type of event (e.g., death or divorce) is not ipso facto a "crisis" for everyone. What we do not know, however, is whether or not the loss of a wife causes personal or social (i.e., familial) disorganization. Since the literature offers little insight into the lifestyle of the widower, this research is basically exploratory. Accordingly, the interview schedule contained many open-ended items. It should be added that many of the schedule's items were taken from other studies dealing with family dismemberment. Although exploratory in design, this study therefore reflects the growing body of survey sociology in that it also analyzes assumptions of previous research.

METHODOLOGY

In the spring of 1969, death certificates were analyzed at the Bureau of Vital Statistics in Cleveland City Hall. Only those certificates for 1966 and 1967 were checked. I was interested only in female deaths during these years. The deceased must have been no older than 45 and married at the time of death. All causes of death were acceptable and all races were included for consideration. Those certificates meeting the sex, ages, and marital status criteria were copied. In this manner, the cause of death, the physician's name and address, and the identity of the next of kin were obtained. This information was placed on index cards, which were serially numbered. The first card was the first death in January 1966, and the last card was the last death in December 1966. Another set of cards was similarly numbered for 1967. The following table shows that there were 278 relevant deaths in 1966 and 273 in 1967:

A table of random numbers was then used to select the study sample. Two hundred cards were drawn for each year. Information recorded from the death certificates was used to ascertain the name or the location of residence of the widower. The informant on the death certificate was frequently the husband, but this was not always the case, especially for blacks. When the husband's name did not appear on the death certificate, the informant listed was contacted in order to find the widower. This was usually a fruitless exercise. The names of only six widowers were obtained as a result, and all but two had moved out of Ohio. Those widowers who had left the state since their wives' deaths were not considered eligible for inclusion in the sample, since the costs of finding them were prohibitive. The remaining two were later interviewed. Both were black.

TABLE 17.1. RELEVANT DEATHS BY YEAR AND RACE

	1966	1967	Total
Blacks	98	100	198
Whites	180	172	352
Orientals	0	1	1
Total	278	273	551

After the 400 cards were drawn, various attempts were made to locate the surviving spouses. Old and new telephone directories were first used. Letters were immediately sent to those spouses whose addresses in the phone book coincided with the death certificate information. This was the basic source of finding eligible respondents. Many letters were returned from the post office; 27 for "no such person," and 33 for "moved, left no forwarding address." Three days after these initial letters were sent, phone calls were made to each potential respondent; 55 widowers were reached this way, of whom 34 refused to cooperate. Over 20 calls were made to each widower. There were 33 widowers whose informant status, phone number, and location coincided and whose inquiry letters were not returned who could not be reached to set up an interview appointment.

In the fall of 1969, a short questionnaire was sent to a group ($N = 16$) randomly selected from those who could be reached by phone and also to a similarly selected group ($N = 22$) of those who were originally unwilling to cooperate. Not one of the widowers in this latter group returned it, four of the former filled it out, and none were returned from the Post Office. Table 17.2 gives a summary of the various procedures used to enlist the cooperation of the respondents:

TABLE 17.2. SUMMARY OF LOCATION PROCEDURES

Procedure	Potential R	Contacted	Cooperated
City Directory	14	0	0
Letters	200	55	39
Post Cards	32	2	0
Death Certificate			
Information (other)	8	2	2
Mailed Questionnaire	38	38	4

Out of a possible 400 widowers, 41 were interviewed. Table 17.3 shows the sample composition according to race and year of death:

TABLE 17.3. SAMPLE COMPOSITION ACCORDING TO RACE AND YEAR OF DEATH

	1966	1967	Total
Black	6	5	11
White	13	17	30
Total	19	22	41

Systematic but unsuccessful efforts were made to contact the others. The overwhelming majority of men contacted were also listed as the informants on the death certificates and had not moved since their wives' deaths.

It is evident from the problems encountered while trying to locate sample members that many widowers get "lost"; therefore, generalizations can only be made in terms of a stable sample of what appears to be a very unstable population. I was more interested in the sample for ideas than for some expression of population values. I began sample selection by using a form of probability sampling, but it soon became evident that self-selection was operating. Although this was discouraging, it was felt that the widowers who cooperated gave at least some clues and ideas that will be developed for another study.

SUMMARY OF THE SAMPLE

In summary, the sample is described by the following distributions of several social characteristics not necessarily occurring simultaneously: almost four-fifths of the widowers were at least 41 years old; they were residentially stable; over one-half had been married to the deceased for at least 16 years;

less than one-third had attended college; three-fifths were employed at manual occupations; almost one-half were Catholic; approximately three-fifths knew that their wives were going to die; cancer and heart disease accounted for over three-fifths of the deaths; less than one-third were black; over one-half earned $10,000 or less annually; finally, three-fourths claimed that they thought of the deceased often.

The Literature

A large body of family literature has concerned itself with the lifestyles of husbands and wives. Sirjamski (1948) noted that there is a cultural configuration that requires a sexual division of labor, with the male being slightly superior. This would mean that he has the final say, hence greater power. In her classic study of the married life of blue-collar workers, Komarovsky (1967) found that the lower the educational level of the respondent, the greater the probability of a rigid sex role division of labor between mates. Men did "men's work" and that was just about all. A high school education was associated with greater flexibility in assignment of chores. Poorly educated males as well as those who were less successful were more likely to be authoritarian and offered their wives little, if any, help in the performance of "their" duties. Rainwater (1960) obtained similar findings in his studies of lower class households. Less education and lower occupational status were associated with separate spheres of activity determined by sex. Men only helped with household tasks in the case of emergencies. Women were "tied" to the house and rarely held jobs. These people share very little of themselves.

In a theoretical discussion of the concept of crisis, Rapoport (1962) noted that death *is* a crisis for all. However, crises generally have positive potential because their resolutions can enhance personality as well as reestablish some form of societal equilibrium. Like Hill and Parad, Rapoport noted that: "in a state of crisis, by definition, it is postulated that the habitual problem-solving activities are not adequate and do not lead rapidly to the previously achieved balanced state." This quote raises the question of whether we have the constitution of a new or old equilibrium. This question plagues modern sociological theory and we shall make an attempt to analyze the equilibrium, if any, that the widowers reestablish or develop.

The normal grief reactions are (Rapoport, 1962) "When the bereaved (1) starts to emancipate himself from the bondage to the deceased, (2) makes a readjustment in the environment in which the deceased is missing, (3) forms new relationships or patterns of interaction that bring rewards and satisfactions." After the loss of a loved one, the "normal" survivor does not forever disengage himself from his social and physical surroundings. We shall see to what extent this study's sample is "normal," if at all. Like the other theorists, Rapoport claims that crises have peaks, often involve tension and anxiety, and perhaps confusion. Given this potential for anomie, Rapoport (1962) feels that "the person or family in crisis becomes more susceptible to the influence of 'significant others' in the environment."

In a recent work dealing with how families react to crises, the Glassers (1970) present a series of articles dealing with disorganization, poverty, illness, and disability. Basically, the theoretical orientations of these articles are similar to, and refinements of, Hill and also Parad and Caplan. The editors note that:

The presence of stress means that some internal difficulty or strain is experienced by the group. Family stress sometimes is accompanied by psychological stress but this need not always be so. Family demoralization frequently is a sign that stress is present. For stress to be relieved the present method of family functioning must be changed; alterations in group structures and processes are needed to handle the difficulty.

This quote is significant in terms of this study's objectives. The Glassers note that the effects of an event are not universal, that stress results from an internal change, and that role reallocation is necessary to solve these problems. This quote also reflects the negative connotations surrounding crises events in the literature. An event can "destroy" an individual member without "destroying" the whole family. In addition, we note the presence of the often "hidden assumption" of a new equilibrium evolving from personal and social reorganization after the crisis event. Reorganization implies creativity, yet crises are to be shunned, if possible. The Glassers observe, "unless family members are adequately prepared, family developmental changes may result in crises."

Blauner (1966) notes that families are more adversely affected when they lose a middle-aged member—one who performs a key role. Society and the family experience disequilibrium since "they die with UNFINISHED BUSINESS." Our society protects us from the sick and the dead by "putting them away." After they are gone, we have to face task reallocation and loneliness. The abnormality of death in the middle years is potentially disruptive. This disruption is an empirical question that needs to be studied.

The Socioemotional Adjustment of Maternal Orphans

The study of children in fractured families is not new. Hill (1949) described a variety of reactions experienced by children whose fathers go away to war. Nye (1957) studied another form of family disruption and found that children from happy broken homes are better adjusted than those living in intact unhappy homes. It was found that family disruption is not an automatic guarantee of personal or social disharmony among children.

The respondents were asked several questions about their children. Five of the black widowers had children whereas all of the whites were fathers. Generalizations will not be made, yet certain trends in the data can be identified. Because we are dealing with the father's perspective of his children's social and personal adjustments while the mother was alive as well as after her death, we are once again limited by his perceptions and awareness of what his children are feeling and doing. Some widowers responded "don't know" to a few of the items. Of the respondents, 34 had children and the total number of offspring was 99, or an average of three children per family. No one mentioned that any of the offspring were abnormal either mentally or physically. Seven of the children had been adopted.

The following is a discussion of a few variables relevant to childhood adjustment. Many American families delegate certain chores and responsibilities to their children. Now that a strategic family member is gone, there is a role gap. Do the children perform their chores as well as they did when their mothers were alive? To answer this question, the interviewees were asked if their children avoided responsibility. Table 17.4 shows that such problems were not unusual.

TABLE 17.4. CHILDREN AVOID RESPONSIBILITY BEFORE AND AFTER
MOTHER'S DEATH

	After		
	Yes	*No*	*Total*
Before			
yes	10	3	13
no	6	15	21
total	16	18	34

Over one-sixth of the fathers now have this problem with at least one of
their children (10 girls, 9 boys) and did not have it while the mothers were
alive. Less than one-tenth report that these difficulties declined over time
and over two-fifths claimed that their children (23 girls, 19 boys) met their
responsibilities during both time periods. One professional man commented:
"Now that my wife is gone, the kids have more to do but seem to do less
than they ever did. Maybe it's just that I expect more now and they have far-
ther to fall. I doubt this, however. Their teachers all told me that they are
lazy in school now, too. Especially my daughters." Several fathers commented that their daughters, especially if they were in their teens, were a
particular disappointment in this area.

Less than one-third of the fathers reported that their children (8 boys, 4
girls) had poor school grades before the mothers died. From Table 17.5 it
can be seen that school grades were often worse after these deaths.

TABLE 17.5. CHILDREN HAVE POOR SCHOOL GRADES BEFORE AND
AFTER MOTHER'S DEATH

	After		
	Yes	*No*	*Total*
Before			
yes	8	1	9
no	7	15	22
total	15	16	31 [a]

[a] *N* is 31 because some of the respondents did
not have children who were still in school.

Almost one-fourth of the interviewees did not have children who were
receiving poor grades while their mothers were alive but now report that

their offspring (12 boys, 10 girls) are not doing so well academically. Black fathers were less likely to report these problems existed before their wives died, but were more likely to perceive them as widowers. The following comment made by a black father is illustrative: "The children don't get as much help with their homework now. I don't have the time and I don't really understand what I'm doing. This is another reason why I want to get married again." Several fathers said that when their wives got ill the children had to do more around the house and that their studies consequently suffered. A few of the other fathers also mentioned that perhaps the children's grades had been bad in the past, but that they had not known about them then. Now, however, the report cards come home to the father. A related problem is the teacher-child relationship. There was a very slight increase over time in the number of fathers who reported difficulties in this relationship. In essence, several fathers perceived an overall decline in their children's school adjustment after their mothers died.

In order to obtain some idea of familial solidarity, the respondents were asked if their children were argumentative, both in the parent-child relationship and in child-child relationships. Table 17.6 shows that over one-

TABLE 17.6. CHILDREN ARGUMENTATIVE BEFORE AND
AFTER MOTHER'S DEATH

	After		
	Yes	No	Total
Before			
yes	5	3	8
no	7	18	25
total	12	21	33

half of the respondents never experienced these verbal hostilities in their homes during either time period. Over twice as many reported an increase in these verbal "encounters" as reported a decrease (8 boys, 5 girls). Parsons told us that the mother soothes, calms, and refortifies. Apparently this is true for many families. Her death means the loss of a mediator and referee. The following statement made by an engineer refers to this point: "My wife cooled off everyone. The kids let her settle their fights. Now it's one argument after another. I really miss adult conversation."

It is evident that more fathers perceive their children's arguments after the mother's death. There are many possible interpretations of this increase but many widowers mentioned that after they lost their wives, they had to "break up the kids' battles."

Hitting children may be interpreted as a possible reaction to frustration or it may reflect a show of power. The child "often works off his irritation on those he can command, but who are quite innocent" (Sandstrom, 1966). Brown and Elliot (1965) claim that children often engage in aggressive behavior because it brings a reward—i.e., attention. To obtain some measure of this aggression among the respondents' offspring, the interviewees were asked if their children hit each other. Of primary concern were many differences before and after the mother's death. Five fathers reported that their children (7 boys) engaged in this activity before they lost their mothers and six claimed that their children (8 boys, 2 girls) now hit each other. This latter group was composed entirely of the five from the first time period plus an additional father. Evidently hitting runs in families. The mother's death is not associated with an incidence or an increase in this type of behavior. A blue-collar worker made this point when he stated: "My children have always hit each other. I let them settle their fights their own ways. My wife let them do the same thing. It's their fight. It's their business. I keep out." In essence, therefore, for both time periods, less than one-fifth of the respondents observed this behavior among their children.

Our culture puts a great deal of emphasis on appropriate sex-role behavior. Wolfenstein (1968) noted that very young children play games that reinforce sex-roles and become upset if their gender is mistakenly identified. Henry (1965) noted that adolescents experience conflicts about their sex-role behavior. Boys are athletic because that is what males are supposed to do and girls are passive following the cultural dictum of femininity. Apparently sex-role problems are pervasive in our culture during all stages of the life-cycle.

We were curious to know if the respondents observed any sex-role problems in their children. They were asked if any of their children behaved like the opposite sex. None reported such behavior after the mother's death. Only one white respondent felt that his preschool son had acted feminine before he lost his mother. This same respondent claimed that this son now acted "normally." It has been noted that children perform many of the tasks previously done by the mother. Apparently, according to the fathers, the performance of these "feminine" tasks left no "female residues" on their sons. No father of either race saw any of the daughters behaving in ways defined as masculine during either time period.

According to Sandstrom (1966), "Stammering is a disorder of speech often accompanied by emotional distress." This problem often reflects parental anxiety, which produces the stress. Apparently this anxiety is caused by extreme parental concern about the child's inability to speak correctly. Stuttering generally appears in the research as a male problem that begins around three or four years of age. Despert (1970) claims that stuttering is "normal" at three or four because the child thinks faster than he can talk. Despert noted that "child psychiatrists are also familiar with the temporary speech regressions which are associated with psychic traumata in early childhood." It is assumed that stuttering beyond this developmental period is abnormal and indicates inordinate stress in the child's life or an organic speech pathology.

The widowers were asked if their children stuttered. Three reported this speech difficulty while the children's (5 boys) mothers were alive and only one of the three said this speech problem persisted after the child lost his mother. It should be noted that sons—not daughters—were reported as the stutterers, and these boys were between five and fifteen. In addition, no black father reported this problem for either time period.

The fathers were asked if their children had bad dreams. Nightmares are often associated with personal and social insecurity, and unusual and frightening life changes are also correlated with these sleep disturbances. Table 17.7 shows that some of the respondents do not know if their children had nightmares.

TABLE 17.7. CHILDREN HAVE BAD DREAMS BEFORE AND AFTER MOTHER'S DEATH

	After		
	Yes	No	Total
Before			
yes	5	2	7
no	4	18	22
total	9	20	29 [a]

[a] N is 29 because five (5) fathers did not know whether or not their offspring had these dreams.

The number who reported these dreams after the death but not before (7 girls, 2 boys) is twice the number who reported the decline of these dreams over time (3 girls, 2 boys). Clearly over one-third reported these nightmares during one of the time periods. The increase after the deaths, however, is very slight. Children may "grow out" of these experiences, as the following gentleman noted: "My children have always had bad dreams. I did not notice an increase after my wife died. They occurred at about the same rate [once a week per child]. Yet, now all have pretty much gotten over them."

Table 17.7 conceals some variation over time, which is revealed when children's bad dreams are analyzed according to race. There was a decrease in the number reporting bad dreams for black children after their mothers died and a small increase for whites. All of the interviewees who responded "do not know" to the inquiries about their children's dreams were white. No blacks reported bad dreams among their children after the deaths and only one black person respondent mentioned that they had occurred while the mother was still alive.

Evidently children express their anxiety in a variety of ways. Spock (1968) notes that "Nail biting is a sign of tenseness. It is more common in relatively high-strung, worrisome children. They start to bite when they are anxious." He adds that "It isn't necessarily a serious sign in a generally happy, successful child, but it is always worth thinking over." In order to obtain another indicator of child anxiety, the respondents were asked if their children bit their nails during either time period. The following table shows that fewer report this activity among children (10 girls, 6 boys) after they lose their mothers than before (11 girls, 10 boys). It is interesting that there is almost a 50 percent increase in the number of male children engaging in this activity.

TABLE 17.8.CHILDREN BITE THEIR NAILS BEFORE AND AFTER MOTHER'S DEATH

	After		
	Yes	No	Total
Before			
yes	6	7	13
no	3	18	21
total	9	25	34

The respondents were asked about their children's appetites. Table 17.9 shows that less than one-third of the fathers report that their offspring (19 girls, 17 boys) had this problem before their mothers died and slightly more than one-third report these difficulties after the deaths (25 girls, 9 boys):

TABLE 17.9. CHILDREN HAD APPETITE PROBLEMS BEFORE AND AFTER MOTHER'S DEATH

	After		
	Yes	*No*	*Total*
Before			
yes	8	2	10
no	5	19	24
total	13	21	34

More than twice as many respondents had these problems emerge after they lost the wife-mothers than had them decline. The following comment offered by a physician is illustrative: "My children were and still are picky eaters. My wife was an excellent cook and I'm not. Consequently, much of what I serve or what the housekeeper prepares is of little interest to my daughters. Hence, even though they are in their teens, their eating habits now are worse than when they were toddlers." His comment makes a point that often came up during the interviews. Mother was and is still revered by many children. All efforts to approximate her "excellence" (by mother substitute) almost always fail. According to the data, the mother's loss is associated with a large increase in the number of girl children with appetite problems and a large decrease in the number of boys with these difficulties.

Toilet training and bladder control are a central focus for many parents of young children. Our culture puts a great deal of emphasis on early and successful training in these areas (Sears et al., 1957). Research has shown that many adult behavior problems have their origins in the manner and rigor the parents taught control of these bodily functions (Freud, in Rogus, ed. 1969). Bowel and/or urinary accidents are often interpreted as aggression and symbolic of hostility and discontent (Huschka, 1943). These children are defined as immature and if their problems become public knowledge they are often ostracized and humiliated. Some literature notes that children may wet the bed in reaction to unhappy and tense situations. Family disorganization is seen as a possible cause of enuresis, especially among older children (Wolff, 1970).

Table 17.10 shows that less than one-fifth of the respondents had children who had bed-wetting problems. In addition, the number of interviewees reporting the emergence (4 boys, 1 girl) of these problems is the same as that reporting their disappearance (3 boys, 1 girl) over time. (White fathers were more likely to report this problem than were blacks.)

TABLE 17.10. CHILDREN WET THE BED BEFORE AND AFTER
MOTHER'S DEATH

	After		
	Yes	*No*	*Total*
Before			
yes	2	2	4
no	2	28	30
total	4	30	34

A related difficulty would be bowel movement problems. As was previously mentioned, children may withhold or release their bowel movement as acts of aggression and hostility. The respondents were asked if their children had these problems during the time periods in question. Table 17.11 shows that less than one-fifth report such problems (4 boys, 6 girls) before mother died.

TABLE 17.11. CHILDREN HAD BOWEL MOVEMENT PROBLEMS BEFORE AND
AFTER MOTHER'S DEATH

	After		
	Yes	*No*	*Total*
Before			
yes	4	2	6
no	3	25	28
total	7	27	34

Approximately one-fifth of the respondents reported these difficulties are experienced after the mother's death, at least occasionally, by their children (11 boys, 5 girls). It is interesting that what "seems" to be a female child problem during the first time period clearly emerges over time as a male child difficulty.

A recently remarried gentleman made the following comment: "My son and daughter both never had bowel movement problems until they lost their mother. Then I became so busy keeping the house and cooking that I guess they resented my ignoring them. I feel that they withheld their 'bms' in order to get my attention."

Generally, however—as has been the case with other disorders—mother's death is not associated with any massive changes in the elimination habits of the interviewees' offspring.

Summary

I have analyzed paternal perception of the socioemotional adjustments of offspring before and after the latter lost their mothers through death. As was the case with the vast majority of the respondents themselves, few changes were reported in the children's mental and physical well-being. Of course, the ideal situation would have been to interview the children themselves. Time and financial considerations made this impossible. Several of the variables mentioned in the literature emerged as irrelevant, at least according to paternal perceptions. Two good examples are masturbation and sex-role reversals. Fathers simply did not "see" their children as having these "difficulties." A few methodological problems warrant consideration. Even though the same number of fathers may have reported a particular problem among their children during both time periods, it is obvious from the data that the number of children thereby affected could, and did, vary. Another procedural problem, even mentioned by a few of the widowers themselves, was the fact that now since *they* are raising the children, they are more aware of problems experienced or caused by the offspring. Consequently, any increase in the number reporting said difficulty, or in the number of children experiencing it, may simply reflect heightened paternal participation in the youth's lives. However, given the decrease in the incidence of some problems over time, the selectivity of paternal perception is perhaps being overemphasized. Further, it should be added that some of the variables analyzed—e.g., bed-wetting—may disappear over time because of maturation. Since no efforts could be made to control for children's age, the effects of maturation, if any, will have to be studied in another project.

Given the above-mentioned limitations in the data, two basic trends should be noted: (1) children may tend to have a cluster of difficulties, e.g., the child who bites his nails very probably wets the bed and gets poor school grades; (2) mother's death may have a differential effect upon the children according to *their* sex. Generally, however, what was a "boy problem" before mother's death remained one after her demise. This is just as true for "girl problems," the only exception being bowel movement difficulties. These went from being a "girl problem" to a "male problem" over time. In conclusion, however, rarely did more than 20 percent of the children have any of the problems that were studied. Either the fathers suffered from functional blindness and deafness, or their offspring were healthy both physically and mentally.

REFERENCES

Blauner, R. 1966, "Death and Social Structure," *Psychiatry, Journal for the Study of Interpersonal Processes,* 29 (November: 378–94. Also in *Middle Age and Aging,* ed. B. L. Neugarten Chicago: The University of Chicago Press, 1968

Brown, P., and R. Elliott. 1965. "Control of Aggression in a Nursery School Class." *Journal of Experimental Child Psychology* 2:103 ff.

Despert, J. L. 1970. *The Emotionally Disturbed Child.* New York: Anchor Books.

Freud, S., "Character and Anal Eroticism." In *Issues in Child Psychology,* ed. D. Rogus. Belmont, California: Brooks/Cole Publishing Company, 1969.

Glasser, P. H., and L. N. Glasser (eds.). 1970. *Families in Crisis.* New York: Harper and Row.

Henry, J. 1965. *Culture Against Man.* New York: Vintage.

Hill, R. 1949. *Families Under Stress.* New York: Harper.

Huschka, M. 1943. "A Study of Training in Voluntary Control of Urination in a Group of Problem Children." *Psychosomatic Medicine* 5: 254 ff.

Komarovsky, M. 1967. *Blue-Collar Marriage.* New York: Vintage Books.

Nye, I. 1957. "Child Adjustment in Broken and in Unhappy Unbroken Homes." *Marriage and Family Living* 19: 356 ff.

Parad, H. J. 1965. *Crisis Intervention: Selected Readings.* New York: Family Service Association of America.

Rainwater, L., and K. K. Weinstein. 1960. *And the Poor Get Children*. Chicago: Quadrangle Books.

Rapoport, L. 1962. "The State of Crisis: Some Theoretical Considerations," *The Social Service Review*, 36,, no. 2 (1962): Also *Crisis Intervention: Selected Readings*, ed. H. J. Parad. New York: Family Service Association of America, 1965.

Sandstrom, C. I. 1966. *The Psychology of Childhood and Adolescence*. Middlesex, England: Penguin Books.

Sears, R., E. E. Maccoby, and H. Levin. 1957. *Patterns of Child Rearing*. New York: Harper and Row.

Sirjamaki, J. 1948. "Cultural Configurations in the American Family." *American Journal of Sociology* 53: 464 ff.

Spock, B. 1968. *Baby and Child Care*, 3rd ed. New York: Meredith.

Wolfenstein, M. 1968. "Children's Humor: Sex, Names and Double Meanings." In *The World of the Child*, ed. T. Talbot. New York; Anchor Books.

Wolff, S. 1970. "Behavior and Pathology of Parents of Disturbed Children." In *The Child in His Family*, eds. E. J. Anthony and C. Koupernik. New York: Wiley-Interscience.

18

Withdrawal in Bereaved Children

Phyllis R. Silverman and Sam M. Silverman

Very little is known about what happens to children who are bereaved through the loss of a parent. Most studies have been retrospective in nature and have involved the examination of adult populations in psychiatric treatment to determine what factors in their childhood may have led to their current disability. The death of a parent during childhood is found to be significantly correlated with their adult problems. The few prospective studies of children's reaction to a parent's death are of case studies of individuals in psychiatric treatment, and thus deal with an extreme situation, in which no adequate accommodation to this severe stress was made. We shall deal with one of the possible responses to the death of a father, that of withdrawal, and in which a more normal response, not resulting in breakdown, has occurred.

In two recent articles (P. R. Silverman and Englander, 1975; S. M. Silverman, 1974), we have dealt with the effects of parental loss on adolescents and on the formation of the scientific personality. Some of the data and concepts used here are dealt with more fully in those articles. Here we use the data from P. R. Silverman and Englander to illustrate the process of withdrawal that was focused on for scientists by S. M. Silverman.

A number of studies have been made of adult psychiatric disabilities correlated with retrospective childhood experiences, especially including parental deprivation. A review of these studies is included in the paper by P. R. Silverman and S. Englander (1975), and summaries with critical comments on methodology in papers by Gregory (1965) and Markusen and Fulton (1971). Despite the methodological problems there appears to be a consensus that the bereaved child has a higher-than-chance probability of developing serious disorders as an adult.

In a few of these studies the age of the child at bereavement is found to be a factor. The evidence for a distinction between effects of maternal and paternal deprivation is unclear, and it would appear that more precise definitions of outcomes might be of help here. In some cases a definite relationship is found. Thus, Newman and Denman (1971) showed that white males who had lost their fathers before they reached 18 are more likely to be involved in felonious behavior.

To understand the child's reactions many factors have to be understood, such as the death's impact on the family structure, the availability to the parent and the child of various "substitutes," and the developmental level of the child at the time of the death—this latter to include not only psychosexual development, but also ego development with particular emphasis on his cognitive capacity to understand death.

The studies of the effects of deprivation in childhood in scientists (Woodward, 1974) note that a larger number of physical scientists experienced the loss of a parent than is true of the general population, though this may not be statistically significant. S. M. Silverman added that the data point to the fact that the age at which the loss occurs is important. He suggests that the effect of the absence of the father is the impairment of the son's ability to deal with the less intimate interpersonal relationships; and given a certain intelligence level and type, the withdrawal option chosen may be that of a search for certainty in natural law.

Hetherington (1972) found the daughters of widows to be rigid and inhibited around males, and to display greater restraint, even avoidance, than did the daughters of divorced mothers or girls from intact families. She discussed these results in terms of sex role identifications. They can also be seen, however, in terms of the father's role in the family and the meaning of his absence on the growing child. If we accept the fact that mothers and fathers play different roles in a family, then we may hypothesize that the father's primary role is to teach the child how to interact with people outside the family, and that paternal deprivation leads to an inability to deal with and a fear of such interactions. Thus, all the sequelae may not be pathological in the psychiatric sense; the death of a parent can have deleterious effects on the growing child. Since there is so little data on how a child copes with death, the Widow-to-Widow Program has provided us with an attractive and rich source of data on what happens to a child as he deals with the death of his father.

The Widow-to-Widow Program was an experiment in preventive intervention in which every newly widowed woman under the age of 60, in a lower middle-class community of 250,000, was contacted by another widow for the purpose of providing her with friendship and help during this critical period after the death of her husband. These contacts were often sustained for a period of several years and, in some instances, led to lasting friendships. In two and one-half years, 430 women were reached. Two-thirds of those chose to involve themselves in the program, if not soon after the death, then within the year. Of those who accepted, 52 had children under the age of 16 at home, and of those who refused 12 had children in this age group.

The data for this paper are drawn from the followup interviews, three years after the mother became widowed, with the widow evaluating the effect of the widow-to-widow service or discussing her reasons for refusing. In addition, limited process records were kept of the intervention, where the widow talked about her children and what was happening now that their father was dead. The data have many limitations, in particular that the children were not the focus of the intervention or the research, and therefore were not interviewed.

The characteristics of the group reflected those of the community. The majority were white, working-class Catholics; there were a number of black families, and one Jewish woman. The youngest widow, with two small children, was 23, and the oldest, with a 12-year-old son at home, was in her late 50s. Death had come suddenly in most of these families. In some the men had suffered extended illnesses, which had kept them at home more and had thus to some extent brought them closer to their children.

One group of children responded to loss by becoming rebellious, withdrawing socially, and allowing their school work to fall off. It was this group who caused their mothers the most concern. These women were at a loss to understand or to know how to respond to those children. These were primarily boys, and usually from 9 to 14 years of age. This group of five children from five families includes one adolescent girl who initially withdrew completely from school and then from all activities outside of the house. About her brothers, the mother said: "They had a rough time. One was his father's alter-ego. They had a sense of responsibility and kept going. My daughter just stopped living."

These were all youngest or middle children with older sisters. All these children had enjoyed a special relationship to their father. One went so far as to say to his mother, "why couldn't it have been you instead of Daddy?" The girl did tell her mother that she was "closer to Daddy than you are." She had spent a good deal of time caring for her father (after school and on weekends) during his terminal illness, when he was at home and the mother worked. In another situation, in which the withdrawal occurred immediately after the death and was a transitory symptom, this mother saw her boy's problem as: "He's the only man in the house. He must feel picked on. His father used to protect him from me. I was the firm disciplinarian."

Several of these women talked about the boys' need for discipline, that a boy needs a father. "If his father was alive he would have made him work; he was more scared of his father." They saw the role of the father as partly involving a police function to some extent, but mostly as in getting the boys to perform properly. "He just comes home from school and watches TV. He doesn't do his homework or go out with friends. His father would have seen to it that he studied." The mother did not understand that her boy could be reacting to his father's death: that this was his way of grieving.

The children's problems seemed to be in terms of how they saw their role in the family in relation to the mother. These women had a special relationship to their other children, and they closed out the boys. The boy in a sense lost both parents. He seemed unable to get close to his mother and looked to his father to help him break away from the dependency relationship with his mother, to show him how to link himself to the outside world, to be a separate individual. At his father's death he felt helpless to know how to complete these tasks. His solution was to withdraw from the world into the family and to thereby involve his mother in a more extensive caregiving role than she would normally have played or than would be appropriate for his age.

Some of these women talked about these boys as wanting to assume the role of the father. (This can be seen as one way of maintaining the father's presence.) One, an only son, had been told directly, by relatives, that this was expected of him. Another boy, who had been his father's favorite, was told by his mother that he knew he was just like the rest. He talked about assuming his father's place, which involved giving orders and being waited on by the woman in the family. He gave this up when he realized that his mother would not allow him to behave this way. The problem disappeared when a widowed mother realized what was happening and made it clear that the boys were not to assume this responsibility—it was inappropriate to their age and role in the family. The problem seemed to continue when a mother had no idea what was going on, was receiving support from the other children, and was in fact encouraging her son to be like his father. The child who was giving her trouble didn't seem able to do this successfully. As one woman put it:

My oldest boy takes on more responsibility. He has absorbed his father's goodness. He is always asking me if I am all right and if I am happy.

She enjoyed a similar mutuality with her daughters, who took care of her while her youngest son kept talking about his father:

He idealizes him. He still talks about the way his father punished him as better than the ways his friends' fathers treat their children now. He really worries me. I think some of his answering back is adolescence, but he is becoming a loner; he won't go to scouts anymore, he's withdrawn and talks about wanting to be an artist.

This woman allowed her boys to get some fathering from a male relative, but negated this by belittling his ability, since he did not have her husband's intellectual scope. She was concerned about this particular boy's withdrawal.

Another woman who saw herself protected by her children from her grief talked about her youngest child and only son, who, like his mother, never talked about his feelings:

He is very emotional. He drives and every once in a while he goes to visit his father's grave. He talks a lot about his father. I keep saying to him, "You'd better grow up and be like your father" and he says "I will, Ma." . . .

He's not like his father though. My husband was so quiet, but in sports they were alike. But his grades have gone down. He's stopped paying attention. He seems to live in a world of his own.

With one exception the deceased had all been very much involved with their families. Some were considered gentle, leaving discipline and the like to their wives, while others were the disciplinarians and pacesetters for the family. Their relationship to their wives seemed to be good as well. The exception was a man who had gambled compulsively, and whose wife had threatened divorce. His older daughter was relieved by his death, since he had a repressive attitude toward women; his son tried to develop a similar privileged position, but the mother would not allow this to happen. This child did not withdraw.

The data do not permit further elaboration of this pattern at this point. The withdrawal and becoming ineffectual seems to be related to the child's position in the family, usually the only surviving male, and to the way his mother does her mothering, at least when she is bereaved. At this point she sees the children as giving her purpose and meaning, and helping her to keep going, and is not sensitive to any special attention that they may need now that their father is gone. The child we are focusing on now seems to have had unfinished business with his father, who would have helped him move away from his mother, and learn how to function independently outside the home. The child's behavior indicates a sense of helplessness, a sense of ineffectuality in the face of the conflict he is experiencing, and so he gives up. His mother's behavior does seem to make a difference in what happens in the long run. As she becomes aware and is able to respond to his special needs he seems to do better.

The data presented here indicate that withdrawal, in this limited sample (as shown by school problems, for example), takes place for children in any age range from 9 to 14, who have had a special relationship with their father, and who are in the middle sibling rank. The nature of the withdrawals, as well as the comments of the mothers, shows that withdrawal is inward from activities external to the home. For scientists the withdrawal is even more drastic, to the internal world of mind and the analysis of nature. The scientist deals with ineffectuality by limiting the world with which he interacts and by trying to find laws which govern his environment. The data presented here do not show to what the withdrawal has gone.[1] The age range here is completely consistent with the age range, roughly 5 to 15, in the

---

[1] It has been noted that more people who have experienced parental death in childhood commit suicide as adults. S. M. Silverman in a review of the Japanese novel *Kokoro* noted the suicide as described by the novel "is passive and afraid to take action. He is distrustful of others, particularly of his close relations and of women. He feels incapable of coping with human relationship and restricts them."

larger (but still limited) sample of scientists with paternal deprivation. The children here are in the middle rank. This factor was not examined in the sample of scientists. In general, however, scientists tend more often to be eldest children.

We have emphasized one aspect of the effects of bereavement; more work needs to be done to clarify both the various options available to the child as well as a further exploration of some of the factors brought out here. We noted that when we interpreted the child's dilemma for his mother, she seemed able to act to involve him more and give direction to his life. However, it may be necessary to introduce others into the child's life to help him move away from mother and learn to deal with others outside his family. Only as we identify the details of the problem can programs of intervention be developed for maximum usefulness.

REFERENCES

Gregory, I. 1965. "Anterospective Data Following Childhood Loss of a Parent." *Archives of General Psychiatry* 13: 99–120.

Hetherington, E. M. 1972. "Effects of Father Absence on Personality Development in Adolescent Daughters." *Developmental Psychology* 7:313–26.

Markusen, E., and R. Fulton. 1971. "Childhood Bereavement and Behavior Disorders: A Critical Review." *Omega* 2:107–117.

Newman, G., and S. B. Denman. 1971. "Felony and Paternal Deprivation: A Socio-psychiatric View." *International Journal of Social Psychiatry* 17:65–71.

Silverman, P. R., and S. Englander. 1973. "The Widow's View of Her Dependent Children." Mimeo. Laboratory of Community Psychiatry, Harvard Medical School.

Silverman, S. M. 1974. "Parental Loss and Scientists." *Science Studies* 4:259–64.

Woodward, W. R. 1974. "Scientific Genius and the Loss of a Parent." *Science Studies* 4:265–77.

Part Four

The Health Professional

19

The Health Professional

Melvin J. Krant

Our observations of and our approaches to our patients and their families are based on studies and the resulting data. It might be helpful to discuss some personal anecdotes that illustrate the work we have done, why we have done this work in a particular way, some of the errors we have made and, finally, what we are trying to achieve in understanding how one goes about being an effective helper.

We all love being helpers. I became aware of my own urgent need to help years ago as I observed in our hospital's wards and clinics the confusion and disorganization surrounding the approach to families of cancer patients, particularly terminally ill cancer patients. Even as we tried to work at assembling a solid body of data or evidence that would guide us in giving effective help, our experiences revealed confusion, disorganization, and uncertainty. I thought that the consequences of such a lack of direction must surface eventually, probably after the death of the patient, in the price that people pay as they experience the loss of a loved one.

I began to hear anecdotes that proved that family disorganization did in fact take place following many cancer-caused deaths. Contact with bereaved family members in the months and years that followed their bereavement indicated that many of them indeed seemed to be in very serious trouble. I suggested to the National Cancer Institute that one of the ramifications of cancer is that it causes an existential crisis: everybody around the patient— the medical and nursing staff, the social service worker, the chaplain, the medical and nursing students and, above all, the family—goes through the dying experience with the patient. It was time, I thought, to begin to learn how to help families going through such crises, and I proposed a demonstration project.

The members of the National Cancer Institute felt that their rather short supply of money could be better spent on other projects, such as methods of cancer prevention and early detection. Trying another approach, I suggested that, regardless of whether cancer is caused by viruses or various kinds of chemicals, there might be something in the personality of people that predisposed them to the development of a malignancy. Could not a substantial alteration in the immunologic responsiveness of people, caused by previous experiences, actually initiate the process of cancer?

Although this approach did not arouse great enthusiasm at the Institute, they continued to listen, came to visit with us, and eventually decided to initiate a research program to study the effect of terminal cancer on the families of patients. To our great surprise, we received a rather substantial grant from the National Cancer Institute to fund the studies of interest to us.

We have now organized a study group that consists of psychiatrists, psychologists, social workers, research assistants, and computer experts. It has been a joy to work with people of such different outlooks and training, all of whom approach the problem in such disparate ways. Together we are trying to synthesize an understanding of what our task is. For example, one of our psychiatrists is deeply committed to the belief that childhood and adolescent experiences play an important part in an adult's coping behavior during the loss of a loved one. The history of antecedent losses, the actual mechanics of the growing period, the process of entering into marriage, how one deals with marital difficulties, how one handles the rearing of children—all these may affect how one deals with the experience of a dying spouse or other loved one and how well or poorly one may recover from such an experience. Belief in the validity of this concept means that we must train ourselves to investigate and understand people's backgrounds as completely as we can.

Another of our psychiatrists has been much more concerned with the whole concept of the crisis model: just what is crisis? Is crisis something one has to perceive before one recognizes that one is in trouble? Is it something that *we* as caregivers perceive and then tell the person that he or she *ought* to be in trouble? Or is the "crisis" a textbook definition that indicates everybody is in trouble? We do not know, except that we have found ourselves with a feeling of being in crisis because we cannot fit ourselves into every definition of the term.

Two especially difficult problems have confronted us. The research design constructed stated that we were interested in finding out how people dealt with terminality, and how they recovered from the experience during the period we called the "bereavement time." To find this out meant that we actually had to look at people who were in the process of losing a loved one. We had to knock on their doors and say, "Listen, we are people who are interested in you. Will you help us help you?" And we found, to our amazement, that despite everything that is written in textbooks about how vulnerable people in crisis are, and how eager they are to be helped, and how important that help is to the resolution of their problems, about 50 percent of those we approached (by letter and telephone) responded by saying, "Go away, we don't want you. We can do this by ourselves."

Such a response in itself would be perfectly acceptable were it not for the fact that the social workers and research assistants who went out into the field and made personal contact with these families came back convinced that they were in very deep trouble. Something in the "don't come near our door" attitude indicated that they could not tolerate any observer or any intervention because they were so deeply involved in trying to make sense out of what was happening.

Another part of our research design required our revisiting six months later, usually after a death had occurred, to find out what did happen to those people who had turned us away. Although it is much too early to present data, we have found that some of these people are now hungry to have us come back. We are not sure of the cause of this hunger, but if you knock on someone's door six months after your first visit and after the death has occurred, the same person who told you to go away while he or she was trying to cope with the dying loved one will sometimes welcome you back.

We have identified one subset of people who seem to be particularly disorganized toward the end of the loved one's terminal period, who could not tolerate any intervention at that time, but who now, several months later, seem rather eager for some help. The obvious lesson here is that if the late stages of the dying process are important to the reconstruction of the life of the bereaved, then we must pay particular attention to the final terminal period. So we ask those physicians who work with us to give us a prognosis of the life expectancy of their patients. We first began our program with the idea of working with families approximately three months before an expected death; now we try to begin our work from six months to a year before the anticipated death. A longer leeway period is most definitely necessary.

Another problem concerns our social workers. Their training, their instincts, their total approach has been to actually *help* people in need. And yet, ironically, because of our attempts to satisfy a research protocol and set up a control population, they have found themselves in the position of entering into someone's personal agony and then having to walk away, in effect saying, "We don't really have any help to give you. You're helping us in telling us what you are going through, but we will come back periodically to see you." Rather than giving, the social workers felt that they were taking.

One day at staff meeting, we discussed a 16-year-old girl who was threatening suicide because of her mother's illness. The father had deserted the family long before and the child was attending a private school away from home. Our problem was what should we do about her now that we had "found" her? If we were to follow the guidelines of our research protocol, we would do nothing. This is what research is all about. But how could that be tolerated? How could one stand there with knowledge about something that is critically important to someone else's life and just leave it at that?

A similar dilemma arises after we conduct a complete assessment of each family and then place them at random into intervention and nonintervention categories. The needs of the families who are placed in the nonintervention group, who will not receive the attention that we had designed into our research, are so great that it is difficult to simply walk out of their lives. We should, of course, be able to say, "but our hospital system is so able to deal with family needs that our failure to intervene won't mean anything." Unfortunately, this raises a very interesting observation about the function of the modern hospital. It is very clear that today the primary contract is the patient-physician relationship. Most of the attention is paid to the patient. If the family receives any assistance, it is basically built around the idea that such assistance will help the family to face the patient. One could say that hospitals are not organized to help families face the particular crises they are facing within themselves as they experience the loss of a loved one. It is not that the social service workers and hospital administrators and medical staff are not kind and generous people. It is simply that within the format of their operation, they see their primary task as to take care of the needs of the patient—not the needs of the family.

If there is any doubt about this, there is no doubt whatsoever that the "contract" states that when a death occurs, the family should go home. They can come back a couple of days later to find out the results of the autopsy if one was performed, and they can certainly drop in whenever they are in the neighborhood to speak to anybody to whom they might wish to speak; but in essence the message is "go home."

Who, then, picks up and goes on with bereaved families afterward? Our very sensitive hospital social workers are often aware that there is a tremendous need for them to continue their association with bereaved families, but they are in no situation to do so. They are not committed to routinely visiting a bereaved family one month later. The hospital system is what it is—a primary contractual relationship with the patient.

Many of the psychological and psychiatric problems seen emerging in disorganized families as a result of the terminal period of a loved one and the approach to such an experience are very difficult to handle appropriately. We sometimes find that what is really necessary is some kind of "psychiatric penicillin"—something that we could inject into somebody very quickly, not a tranquilizing drug and not an antidepressant, but something that could reconstruct the past in a moment, clarify it and reorder it, and enable the family to work through the exigencies of the dying process in total peace and harmony. This ideal seldom occurs.

We are trying to bring about a resolution of preexisting conflicts, but this is very difficult when a family is in chaos. We are also trying to arrange something called the "final goodbye"—a time when family members can come together to say their farewells. This sounds as though it should be easy, but yet it often is impossible. We recently studied a situation in which at the very moment of death the wife was blaming the social workers and the medical staff for her husband's terminal condition. If they had not brought up the fact that he was dying, she said, he wouldn't be dying. The way that the members of this family were dealing with crisis actually prevented us from helping them to say an appropriate goodbye.

We think that we would like to individuate particular patients and family members and enable them to recognize that their particular needs must be met. Even this can be impossible. For example, how do you tell a woman who is experiencing vaginal bleeding that she really ought to go in for an operation when her husband is dying of lung cancer? It seems as though we ought to be able to manage something like that, yet this woman is much too busy or much too involved in doing what she feels is correct and necessary. In reality, she is simply keeping herself madly busy in order to overwhelm the anxiety of her relationship with her dying husband. Nevertheless, getting her at that point to discontinue those efforts and go off and take care of herself because she too may soon be sick seldom works.

We also think we are doing something about "gaining permission." That is, we think we can help families work out the problems that arise when the dying individual orders precisely what the family members should do in the future—not simply where he or she is to be buried but what to do with the children, and so forth. We think we sometimes succeed in this. But when we don't succeed, we find ourselves very upset and wonder why it is that we are unable to bring about a better resolution.

We are continuing to work with families even after death has occurred. Our social workers try to go to all of the wakes. In doing so, we have been forced to recognize that the families in our area do not share the negative reaction of many contemporary authors concerning the attempt of the funeral industry to "beautify" the corpse. Over and over again, we have heard bereaved spouses say, "doesn't he look peaceful and beautiful now?" In fact, they and we have taken the position of "Thank God" for all the embalming and other techniques because the final image is quite beautiful to remember. These families wouldn't want it any other way; and they wouldn't want a cheap funeral either. To them, an elaborate funeral is a proper funeral. They have the feeling that they are making restitution or doing something for the loved one that they were not able to do during the process of losing him or her. Therefore, to criticize the funeral industry for being barbaric does not reflect what so many of our families seem to say is important for them.

Occasionally, we do see bizarre behavior at wakes, which we are unable to understand and which causes great concern about the vulnerability of certain family members. We have observed a young boy laughing at his mother's wake. The family had already lost the father; this boy was the oldest boy, with siblings ranging from 24 to 16. When our social worker called several days after the wake to request a visit, she was told, "We're doing fine. We don't want you to visit at the present time. We'll call you." And despite several more telephone calls and even pleading that "we think you need some help," the answer was a very solid, "stay away." And so, we are left to meet together in conference, feeling that the boy is probably in serious trouble, knowing that he has a history of ulcerative colitis, knowing that he is probably reactivating certain medical needs, and yet, we are completely unable to help him.

The problems are endless but my intent is not to dwell on them, but simply to state that we are trying to meet them and understand them so that we shall learn what we can do about the issues of the dying patient as they relate to how his survivors will function. We are trying to do this in a controlled, clinical fashion, in which a certain number of patients are involved in our therapeutic model and a certain number are not—the choice having been made by random selection. We hope to understand eventually what successful intervention is, and we are learning a great deal; but it is a slow and difficult learning process.

We are recognizing that there is much we cannot do. We are also recognizing that people have many protective mechanisms to keep us away and that we don't understand yet what these mechanisms are. We are discovering that those who say "no" when we first approach them are quite apt to welcome us back after a period of time has elapsed. We think that one reason for this is that we are able to say that we were there *before* the loved one died, which seems to have some meaning for the survivors. On returning, we have occasionally found frozen lifestyles—rooms in which not a piece of furniture has been moved, not a curtain has been opened, for six months or more after death has occurred; homes in which everything is conducted as if the life of the survivor had ended with the death of the loved one. And nothing is going to budge that survivor into changing anything.

We are also finding out that some of our impressions (and these, it should be stressed again, are only anecdotal) about the very nature of people who are vulnerable to getting cancer are not unsubstantiated. We now have many anecdotes that relate to the appearance of a symptomatology of cancer during or shortly after the loss of a critical object. Some of these anecdotes are shockingly traumatic. We have worked with a family whose six children were totally disorganized, a family in which the ways of dealing with the stresses of life were cruel indeed. There was adolescent alcoholism, thievery, and school misbehavior. About four years ago, one of the sons had unsuccessfully tried to burn down the family home. Help was sought from various child and family guidance agencies, but apparently there was such difficulty in dealing with the family that none could be provided.

A second fire produced tragedy, for the father and an older son died in that blaze. Some 18 months later, the mother developed a complicated course with a breast malignancy. According to her physician, after the cancer was diagnosed and was progressing rapidly, she told him that she was "burning up," just as the house had been burning up. In the several months before her death, she exhibited no anger, no hostility, no sense of dismay at what life had given to her—only this constant "burning up" with the cancer. A totally disorganized family survived her: one daughter broke her long engagement immediately after the death and married a man she hardly knew; another daughter moved back home to take care of the 80-year-old grandmother, kept two huge dogs for protection, and let no one into the house; the younger children began to get into trouble again on the streets, although they were still apparently behaving in school; and the boy who had tried to burn the house down, living in a halfway house several miles away, almost caused the death of the grandmother on his last trip home because of his violent behavior toward her. The fact that the mother of such a family developed cancer of the breast is not an unfamiliar situation to clinicians who have tried repeatedly to determine the framework and makeup of cancer victims.

Before our twentieth-century mechanistic and biologic attitudes toward standard biology and behavior had developed, medical practitioners really looked at their patients. There was not much else that they could do, so they looked. As the surgeons operated, physicians stood by and wrote. And what they wrote, of course, was that there was a kind of atmosphere, a kind of attitude, a kind of personality, that seemed to be very vulnerable to the development of carcinoma. They wrote about the depressed personality, the grieving person who is very apt to develop cancer. In fact, there were even articles which stated that happiness and cancer are impossible to find together. I cannot say that I think this is true, but my own particular viewpoints and the work that we are doing are really aimed at understanding the effects of existential crises; and one question is whether or not people sometimes resolve their difficulties by using illness creatively, if that is the word, to move out of a situation that they cannot tolerate. If this is so, can we as helpers do anything about it?

Finally, we ask, is there any way to consider the problem of loss that will help us want to be helpers and make us truly able to help? I think we are far from certain that we do know how to help people, particularly in this area, a fact that should certainly help absolve our constant dilemma: ''Why don't those who need our help let us help them?''

Professional Roles in Thanatology

Alan Lyall and Mary Vachon

We should like to share some reflections regarding professional roles in the field of thanatology. Perhaps it is only fair to mention some of the experience upon which these comments are based. During the past two years we, a psychiatric nurse/community worker and a psychiatrist, have been consultants to a cancer hospital. Our mandate was to train and support the nursing staff. In addition to our initial work with the total nursing staff through case-focused groups, we are presently giving an intensive course to a dozen selected nurses to train them as nursing consultants. We have presented at grand rounds to the medical staff on several occasions and have initiated two research projects at the hospital. Ongoing groups at the lodge where out-of-town patients stay have also been initiated by one of us (M.V.).

Beyond the cancer hospital, we have organized a loosely knit group of professionals, representing eleven hospitals and four universities, who meet to discuss various developments and problems in the care of the dying and their families. Also, we have participated in and promoted a number of presentations to nursing and multidisciplinary groups.

In all our endeavors in this field, the degree of responsiveness has been gratifying and encouraging and is seen as a very positive sign for a healthier social and professional attitude toward thanatology. It is hoped that we can raise various concerns in this area without in any way dampening the enthusiasm of the many people who have taken an active interest.

These comments will undertake to focus particularly on some of the trends in altered professional roles in the care of the dying and on some of the problems involved in professional cooperation in this field.

One concern is that we may at times choose to become the main support of a patient when it would be more appropriate to provide indirect help through his family and friends. In grappling at a personal level with how much one should do in the emotional support of the dying patient, it has become apparent that some of the very needs that make help-giving professionals useful in their field also at times open the potential for overaction and intrusive intervention. Most of us seek out helping professions, at least partly, to meet such needs of our own as wanting to feel useful and important to others and to prove to ourselves that we can understand and cope with emotions, especially our own. As many of us come to terms with our own fears—particularly those related to death and dying—and feel that we have overcome them, we may be so eager to put our accomplishments to the test that we rush in without being truly needed as primary support givers.

We tend to respect and emulate leaders in our fields of endeavor. In the field of thanatology, Dr. Kubler-Ross stands as a much admired example of courageous dedication and insight. However, for many of us, to follow her example too far or too often may be to put ourselves at risk of exceeding our capacity to give and of ignoring other useful approaches to helping both our patients and their families. It is true that very often there is no one else to meet these needs of the dying, and in these situations professionals who are willing to undertake part or all of the task are answering our highest calling. However, at other times, the natural social supports of the patient are there and are willing to either partially or totally meet the patient's needs. It would be sad to see professionals "professionalizing" the care of the dying to such an extent that the natural members of the patient's social milieu were made to feel inadequate or unimportant. If this should happen, one drawback is that it could easily lead to a situation of helpful professionals inadvertently making things worse by alienating the naturally occurring support of family and friends. If the time ever comes that a professionally trained person is needed almost always instead of occasionally, we shall find that there is a much greater demand for this kind of help than any number of available professionals could ever meet.

There are several distinct advantages to the professional playing the roles of *identifier of needs* and *mobilizer of community resources*.

First of all, anyone trying to help someone he has met fairly recently probably has to be very careful about the attitudinal and philosophical gaps that may have to be bridged. For example, it is not uncommon to hear of well-intentioned help being perceived as intrusive simply because one party speaks in a religious framework and the other does not. Helpers from within the patient's social milieu would be much more likely to approach the patient with an accurate knowledge of his background and beliefs.

Also, because there is such anxiety and concern about the dying person himself, the emphasis is shifted from others who very badly need help at this time—those who love the patient. Anything that the professional can do to help friends and family feel important and helpful is likely to decrease the present stress and facilitate the eventual bereavement. We hear stories of the spouse who feels useless and at loose ends at the bedside while she watches others provide care and counsel that she could very well provide if the attitudes of those around her were amenable to it. To be a passive bystander at a time of crisis is an extremely taxing experience. This is particularly so the more emotionally involved one is with the dying person. Therefore, it seems that if there must be a choice as to who shall experience the anxiety of being relatively inactive in this situation, it should be the professional who hopefully is somewhat better equipped to deal with his own anxiety and who also has other obligations.

Above and beyond helping meet the needs of others, this approach offers the professional a genuinely useful role to play when he cannot undertake to be the primary support person without undue stress to himself. Perhaps no other field forces us so quickly to face and acknowledge our own limitations. Such an acknowledgment is often personally traumatic and is made even more difficult by the fact that in some professions it is against tradition to admit "unprofessional" reactions to death and dying. However, our limitations do exist and are ignored at our peril. Even Dr. Kubler-Ross acknowledges the need for limiting her involvement in direct contact with dying patients and of focusing upon other aspects of her work, although many people seem to be unaware of this aspect of her approach.

As society becomes more open regarding death and a mammoth degree of denial is swept away, there is a danger that the pendulum may swing too far, so that professionals attempt too much on their own, overextending themselves to the point of not being able to cope. Then, we could come full circle to once again having to deny the needs all around us. Therefore, we see a great advantage in sharing the load as widely as possible. The use of groups, family meetings, and volunteers are all important to this end.

In terms of sharing the load, perhaps nothing is more important than good, interdisciplinary cooperation. Perhaps no goal is so easy to subscribe to and so difficult to attain. In the face of death, we all are so terribly vulnerable and in need of support that it seems tragic if professional misconceptions, mistrust, and misunderstanding block person-to-person contact that we all need. No other topic so quickly makes equal nonexperts of us all. With that realization generally comes anxiety, usually resulting in a variety of defenses. For many, the obvious defense is to fall back on what expertise one does have, and perhaps even to flaunt it. Thus, just at a time that cries for some sharing of human experience, it is possible to see people becoming ultraprofessional and ultrajealous of their territorial preserve.

Certainly, most professionals are trained in a way that gives some sense of place in a hierarchical pecking order. This is not easily broken down or overcome even when it is recognized. Thus, although we have a stated goal—working together as equals in trying to understand our feelings and our ways of intervening in the care of the dying—a stated goal does not necessarily mean an easily attainable goal.

For example, we see doctors being ruffled at nurses' suggestions about the patient's needs and nurses hesitant to make the kinds of observations and suggestions that they are well-equipped to make by their training and continuing proximity to the patient. We hear discussion about whether providing emotional support is the function of the social worker or the nurse. Often the clergy are perplexed; they are available and willing, yet may be ignored or barely tolerated by other professions. At a time when two-way communication makes more sense than ever, it is often diminished. And often an attempt to create a more open flow of information is misinterpreted as an attempt to usurp a role. The kind of clear-cut role definition that characterizes professions can easily become role rigidity and extremely nonfunctional in providing emotional support for the dying patient. It therefore becomes imperative that we learn to identify this type of situation and work actively to alter it.

One of the common reactions, however, is to affix blame. How often do we hear, "If it weren't for 'them' [fill in your favorite scapegoat group], we wouldn't have this problem''? In the face of our own sense of impotence in confronting death, it is not surprising that we seek scapegoats and generalize in terms of professional groups. It is also not very helpful. No problem ever got solved by deciding whom to blame. It would be more useful to realize that behind each professional label is a person, probably a scared person. In this regard, it seems that the doctor often has the most expected of him, is least often seen as a person, and is therefore the most often blamed.

There are several possible approaches to improving this situation by increasing interprofessional understanding. One is the leaderless group type of format, in which people come together to try to share their ideas and where their perceptions and feelings as human beings are paramount and their professional training fades into the background. However, except for very exceptional people, this is often a traumatic and very difficult type of group to evolve and survive in. One other possibility is to use as a group leader a resource person who has no vested interest whatsoever in the working of the particular institution. In this regard, the authors have found that the role of the outside consultant is very useful, since the efforts of a group can be facilitated without a real threat being posed to anyone in terms of actual work.

Besides the types of professional prejudice that may stand in the way of cooperation, there is a difficulty that seems to cut across professions. This could be described as an attitudinal dichotomy in how people handle their feelings regarding death. Various observations made by the authors, including audience response at public speaking engagements, have shown clearly that any given attitude often makes one group of people present very uncomfortable while at the same time it reassures another group. For instance, phrases such as the goal of being fearless in the face of death, attaining a "beautiful death," and so on, are reassuring and comforting to some, while others feel restless, dissatisfied, and somewhat put down because their obvious fears make it almost impossible to envision goals of this type. On the other hand, if one begins to focus upon the kinds of fears that many people have and bring them out into the open for discussion and examination, another part of the audience becomes restless, threatened, and anxious. It is therefore important to recognize that there are various ways of thinking about this topic and of handling one's own feelings. It means that at any given moment something that may be making someone more comfortable may very well be making somebody else less comfortable. We feel that it is not necessary to separate people who do differ in this way, but that it is crucial to recognize the dichotomy and that talking about it openly can help us all to learn to be more fully understanding of people who are not entirely like-minded.

While applauding the recent burgeoning interest in the field of thanatology, we have voiced concerns about possible difficulties regarding the relationship between professionals and the friends and family of patients, and among professional groups. We are assured by many that these concerns are needless. We hope they are right.

The Helping Process
with Bereaved Families

Phyllis Caroff and Rose Dobrof

Our vantage points for this discussion reflect some differences in our profession and between us based on our own individual careers as social work educators.

We have found it essential to use the word bereavement in a precise and mutually understood way. For many of the words we use—grief, loss, bereavement, for example—are part of the everyday language of our society although we may give them a particular meaning when we use them professionally.

Finding that there were subtle differences of shadings and emphasis between the two of us in our use of the word bereavement, we began our work with an exercise in etymology. The word's origins are in the Old English language: *bereafian* meant literally *rob away,* so that the early use of the verb *to bereave* was to rob or to deprive ruthlessly or to remove by violence. From this came the later definition *to leave desolate*. The dictionary we consulted gave as an example of current usage the sentence "Bereaved of their mother at an early age, the children learned to take care of themselves."

The words *bereaved* and *bereft* were, in original usage, synonyms. Now we are cautioned that they are not ordinarily interchangeable; *bereaved* is to be used chiefly when the loss is that of a beloved person; *bereft* is correct in all other situations, as for example, *bereft* of hope.

The words *grieve* and *grief* are of Latin and Old French derivation: the Latin verb *gravare* meant *to burden,* and in ordinary usage the verb *to grieve* may be intransitive, meaning *to sorrow deeply*, or it may be transitive, *to make very sad*. Similarly the noun *grief* can be used to describe the *deep sadness* caused by trouble or loss, or to denote the *cause or subject of sorrow* as in the proverb "a foolish son is a grief to his father."

As we reviewed the literature of our own and allied professions, it did seem to us that the words bereavement, grief, and loss were at times being used interchangeably and not always with the precision and clarity that a truly scientific enterprise requires. We emphasize this, for as we talk of the helping process with bereaved families, we are talking about a universal and awesome experience: that is, the confrontation of individuals and families with the deaths of loved ones; and because of its universality and awesomeness, it is an experience around which time-honored rituals, folklore, and experiential wisdom have developed. We shall summarize here what we perceive to be the major themes for a discussion of the "helping process with bereaved families."

From our reading, in sequential fashion, of the books published under the imprimatur of the Foundation of Thanatology, it seemed to us that this interest in the impact of the process of dying on the family of the dying person was, at first, a somewhat tangential theme. The focus seemed largely on the terminally ill person; with rare exceptions, the family was mentioned only in passing, and usually with attention to the impact—for good or for ill—of the family members' behavior on the patient.

Acknowledgment must be paid to Kubler-Ross, Cecily Saunders, Avery Weisman and Robert Kastenbaum, Anselm Strauss, Barney Glaser, Jeanne Quint Benoliel, and Herman Feifel among others for their insistence that the social and psychological, as well as the medical needs of the terminally ill patient must be recognized and attended. We have come so far in so brief a time that it is sometimes easy to forget that today people are still confronting death—surrounded by people, perhaps, and with the best medical care— alone because of "the conspiracy of silence" in which the process of dying remains imbedded.

The emphasis on the social and psychological needs of the terminally ill person has been necessary and salutory, but it has also had the consequences of sometimes obscuring both the reality of the familial context of the dying process and the equal need of family members for help. The social work profession in hospitals and other medical settings has always taken responsibility for work with families, and the records of social workers in these settings testify to their early recognition of the impact of terminal illness and death on the family as a unit and the individual members within it.

It is clear, however, that studies in which the interest in the family is tangential, viewing the family as an instrument in the treatment of the patient, or accumulating work records done by hospital social workers with bereaved families are all insufficient in themselves for our task. The work accomplished, however, permits us now to suggest an approach that provides a set of theoretical notions from which can be derived principles that may inform our work.

The Family as the Unit of Service

As we have indicated elsewhere (Caroff and Dobrof, 1974), we believe that the unit of service must be defined as the patient's family, so that each member may play his or her role during the process of bereavement and grieving—in order that the family as a system and the individual actors within it may emerge from this process depleted and with a changed configuration, but intact. (Intact meaning here a family in which the dead member now occupies his rightful place in the annals of his family's history and in the memories of those still living, and with each survivor able, in Erikson's words, "to accept the historical inevitability of what has happened, including the life, the dying, and the death which has occurred." Depleted is used in the *sociological* [Shanas et al., 1968], rather than the psychodynamic sense—to describe the family depleted by the deaths of its members.) That these are lofty goals we admit, but in the words of Browning's Andrea del Sarto, "A man's reach should exceed his grasp."

In addition, our emphasis on the family as a unit permits us to direct attention to the situation of the family, which is part of the context of the illness, the dying process, the death, and the grieving.

In the literature there is considerable emphasis on the psychological dimension—individually focused, on the meaning of loss and the bereaved state in intrapsychic terms—and on the interpersonal level, focused on the kind of relationship that existed between the bereaved and the lost loved or valued person. As previously noted, the family has been referred to in general terms as one among a variety of "social forces" that may support processes enabling successful grief work.

We have only begun to understand that the family as a system—with its complex intrafamilial transactions and its transactions with other systems—can affect the bereavement process. One explanation for this imbalance between the emphasis on the individual and the emphasis on the family as a system may be that we are rich in individual personality theory as well as systems of intervention with individuals. We know more about dyads, about how to give help in a one-to-one relational system. We continue to struggle with how to translate the social sciences' contributions to the study of the family into a workable theory, and how to build the theoretical bridges between our knowledge about individual psychology and family transactions.

This emphasis on work with bereaved families becomes even more important as we examine the "Demographic Revolution" that is part of the context of bereavement in the United States of the 1970s. For the first time in the recorded history of mankind, the demographers tell us, the population of the United States—in common with most of the other industrialized nations of the world—is characterized by a low birth rate and a low death rate. The social policy implications of this demographic trend are clearly profound.

For our purposes, we must narrow the focus to the American family as it experiences the events of the life cycle. Demographic facts translated into experiential terms mean that many contemporary American families experience the events of births and deaths less frequently than did those of the past. This relative lack of familiarity with the experience—the relative lack of opportunity to watch how significant others respond to loss, to be part of a bereaved family—means that in many families there are fewer guides to how to behave and how to cope. We reported elsewhere the experience of one of us in a home for the aged: for many of the middle-aged children of the residents of this home, the death of this parent was the first death in their families in many years, and more importantly, the first for whose management they had to take primary responsibility (Caroff and Dobrof, 1974).

Also of importance is the locus of the dying process; the handling of illness and death is increasingly a responsibility shared among formal organizations—the hospitals, the long-term care facilities, the funeral homes—and the family. In addition, it is argued that changes in the social structure have fostered changes in the ceremonial observances that surround the dead.

Pine and Phillips (1970) have indicated that mourning dress in many socio-cultural groups in our society is rare; formal cancellation of social arrangements for a predetermined period has diminished; visits to the house of mourning and viewing of the body have declined.

Although the responsibility is shared between formal organizations and the family, the family as the supporting institution for its members shoulders a greater emotional burden than in the past. Moreover, the diminution of the sacred in favor of a secular outlook means that there is for many families no longer the comfort available in the certainty of an "afterlife" and a reunion with the lost loved one.

Despite all these changes in the social order, one thing has remained the same: though the events may come later in our own life cycle and in clusters in our middle and older years, most of us will inevitably experience death as we lose our parents, a spouse, siblings, a child, our friends. Blauner (1966) expresses well the meaning of these losses to the bereaved individual. "He experiences grief less frequently, but more intensively, since his emotional involvements are not diffused over an entire community, but are usually concentrated on one or a few people" (p. 390).

It is for just these reasons that we emphasize the family as a unit. This will force us to understand the bereaved state of each of its individual members. Also, with this focus we can begin to study systematically how family values and goals, role patterning, communication, and need-response patterns affect the family's responsibility to buffer for its members and its ability to assume this task.

In addition, as social workers, our approach to the subject of bereavement embodies an interdisciplinary and interprofessional perspective. The mandate derived from our professional position demands the accumulation of knowledge for action—for the rendering of direct services to individuals and families. Moreover, we view our mandate as requiring informed participation in the designing of these services so that the manpower available for helping will reach the maximum number of individuals and families with the minimum of input necessary to maintain and enhance their functioning. Thus, the professional quest requires that as social workers we emphasize the "doing" while at the same time remaining accountable through the continuing evaluation of our effect and effectiveness.

The "Family-at-Risk"

Given our emphasis on the family as the unit of service, we suggest that, in addition to families in which death of a member is sudden and unexpected, families in which a member is chronically and seriously ill should at the point of diagnosis be defined as "a family-at-risk."

Clinical and research observations provide evidence that a diagnosis of a life-threatening illness for any member of a family unit is experienced both as a personal tragedy and as an assault on the integrity of the family system itself, and that large numbers of families fail to cope successfully (Benger et al., 1969; Caroff and Dobrof, 1974; Kaplan et al., 1973) with either the tragedy or the threat to family stability. Thus, the definition of the family-at-risk accurately describes the reality within which the bereaved family will be living and will cope more or less adequately with the impact of the death.

Individuals as family members do not work out problems of stress independently, nor are they free from the impact of stress being experienced by another family member. The family has evidenced the most significant capability for mediation of stress. However, with its responsibility to protect its members from problemful situations, in those instances where stress is severe, such as bereavement, the ability of the family to buffer for its members may be seriously impaired, even destroyed.

The evidence regarding the cost to the social-health functioning of the family is compelling. We refer for example to the work of Ruth Abrams (1972) in her study of the incidence of morbidity and mortality among surviving family members in the time period immediately following a death in the family and the work of Markusen and Fulton (1971) in studying maladaptive behavior in adults who had experienced bereavement in childhood.

While there is need for more work, we have learned much that is important for identifying particular points of vulnerability for bereaved families. There is, for example, an association between the reaction to the death of a significant person and the already established patterns of coping with danger and loss (Carr, 1969). We also know that, within this generalization, the family's management of bereavement varies significantly with the role, age, and position of the deceased member.

In addition to other variables, the degree to which hopes and values for all members are threatened and the number of required alterations in the life-style will have implications for both the intensity of the grief reaction and the ability to manage the tasks of mourning. The Fultons (1971) have added clarity to our understanding of the differences observed, for example, in the family's grief reactions at the death of an elderly parent or relative and those at the sudden, unexpected death of a more vital member. Their concept of a "high grief potential" death and a "low grief potential" death demonstrates that the degree or intensity of one's grief at the time of death is a function of the kind of death experienced.

Studies under the rubric of "Crisis Intervention" based upon Lindemann's work (1944) have familiarized us with the intense reactions characterized as "normal grief" following the sudden and unexpected death of a significant member of one's family. His concept of "grief work" has become a household word for those of us working in thanatology.

The phase-specific tasks in grief work have become a paradigm for much of the research in crisis intervention. Work in the area of anticipatory grief has begun to add to our understanding of the reactions of patients and families in situations where the process of dying is protracted and the circumstances of dying appear to steer behaviors in a direction contrary to what we define as most functional for the dying patient, the family, and the institutional caregivers (Caroff and Dobrof, 1974).

Tentative findings from the work being done at Fort Logan Mental Health Center (Williams et al., 1972) in crisis intervention in sudden and accidental death suggest two important trends. First, where the role of the decedent has been that of "scapegoat" for the family, then painful and extensive role reallocation is needed after death. If this is unsuccessful, the family system tends to collapse. "That is, the reorganization of the family as an ongoing social system following the death of one of its members, is primarily a function of the role that the decedent had assumed within the family" (p. 69). Also, the healthier the roles of family members before the death of a member, the greater the likelihood that the family will have resources or support systems from which to get help. A more maladjusted family tends to deny the reality of death, cannot show or discuss emotional reactions, is more isolated, and is unable to use available support systems.

The second finding suggests that where the decedent had been a generator of conflict, survivors reported improvements in closeness, emotional tone, decision-making, and social adjustment within the family.

All the findings from research efforts to illuminate this process identified in common parlance as "bereavement" have offered us guidelines for both assessment and intervention. To all must be added the warning that these findings alert us to the danger points that may potentially interfere with the mastery of the mourning process. However, each family and all individuals within it will have their idiosyncratic means of expressing and managing the grief. What has been reinforced repeatedly is that successful management appears to be associated initially with the ability of individuals within the family to experience emotionally the reality of the loss and to find some means of expressing the feelings engendered.

SHALL BEREAVEMENT BE VIEWED AS ILLNESS?

At this point we are confronted with the conceptual dilemma posed by the definitions found in the literature that suggest that the state of bereavement and its concomitant grief reaction may be viewed as an illness. The grounds for this view are the departure from the bereaved's usual ways of thinking, feeling, and behaving and the not-infrequent association of bereavement with some physical and emotional disturbances.

At the same time, bereavement is defined as a necessary and normal response to loss of a loved one; hence, it is difficult to sustain a conceptual approach that includes in it both the notions of bereavement as illness and of bereavement as normal and natural. The bind has been beautifully expressed in the following words of a knowledgeable participant in a Symposium on Catastrophic Illness. "Basically and finally, *grief and bereavement should be treated as an illness*, as an ongoing dynamic thing, in different stages. We *should honor grief as a faith value. It is normal and healthy*" (Cancer Care 1970, page 110, emphasis added).

We believe that our conceptualization of the bereaved family as "a family-at-risk" permits us to honor grief and recognize its normality; yet it also alerts us to the potential for dysfunction if the process itself is subverted through the demands on self, the demands of others, or the demands of institutions. We therefore escape the paradox of bereavement as both health and illness, and we are provided a building block for programmatic designs to enhance human potential for dealing with this crisis.

The definition of the family as the unit to be served and the bereaved family as one at risk can then carry with it a guarantee of continuity of care. This guarantee provides the organizational mandate that the care and concern hospitals and their staffs have shown do not stop with the death of the patient; that the system and the professionals who staff it should continue to provide help and services to the family for as long as necessary. On the experiential level, the survivors of patients who have died in a hospital tell us of their feelings of being left alone and without help just at the point that they feel most helpless—about their feelings of anger at the institutions and professionals who have been so important a part of their lives during the patient's illness, but who now seem to move on to the next patient and family without regard for the feelings of the bereaved family or concern about its fate.

For many families, the death of the patient increases their vulnerability just at the point when their psychic, social, and financial resources are most depleted and their capability to sustain themselves is most limited. After the patient is buried and the period of initial mourning is over, neighbors, friends, and relatives who have rallied to the side of the bereaved family understandably return to their own tasks and routines, and the family is denied the sustained support it needs. Often its members are expected "to pick up the pieces" and get on with the task of living, and they may even be subject to well-meaning criticism if grief seems excessive or the duration of mourning unduly prolonged.

Our emphasis on the family and continuity of care means, we believe, that "social aftercare" should be defined as part of the hospital or long-term care facility, social agency, or church's task; that outreach programs to bereaved families should be built into the network of services these institutions provide; that availability of and access to these services should be articulated in the way they are organized, located, and delivered; and that the professional in charge should be held accountable for the provision of services.

Dr. John Knowles (1973) talks about the necessary increase in the complexity of hospital organization and warns that "efficiency falters, costs increase and the atomized, fragmented machine approach to the patient

dehumanizes what should be an intensely personal and human encounter''
(p. 132). Clearly an encounter between institution and family that abruptly
ends when the patient dies cannot be intensely personal and human, for how
can human beings turn away from families at what may be their most trying
time?

Essentially what we are suggesting is that in talking about work with
bereaved families, we use a public-health orientation embodying concepts of
primary prevention. This enables us to formulate broad-based programs that
will support the normal process of grieving and provide for easy identification of those conditions which may require a regimen of both medical and
social services. Crisis intervention has provided us with the conceptual
model. Our task is to lend our collective professional expertise to designing
such programs to implement this model.

REFERENCES

Abrams, R. 1972. "The Responsibility of Social Work in Terminal Cancer." In *Psychosocial Aspects of Terminal Care,* eds. B. Schoenberg, et al., pp. 173–82. New York: Columbia University Press.

Benger, C. M. et al. 1969. "Childhood Leukemia: Emotional Impact on Patient and Family." *New England Journal of Medicine,* February 20.

Blauner, R. 1966. "Death and Social Structure." *Psychiatry* 29:378.

Cancer Care, Inc. 1970. *Catastrophic Illness in the Seventies: Critical Issues and Complex Decisions.* New York: Cancer Care.

Caroff, P., and R. Dobrof. 1974. "Social Work: Its Institutional Role" In *Anticipatory Grief,* eds. B. Schoenberg, et al., pp. 251–63. New York: Columbia University Press.

Carr, A. C. 1969. "A Lifetime of Preparation for Bereavement." In *But Not To Lose,* ed A. H. Kutscher, pp. 132–37. New York: Frederick Fell.

Fulton, R., and J. Fulton. 1971. "A Psychosocial Aspect of Terminal Care: Anticipatory Grief." *Omega* 2, no. 2 (May): 91–101.

Kaplan, D. M., et al. 1973. "Family Mediation of Stress." *Social Work* 18, no. 4 (July): 60–70.

Knowles, J. H. 1973. "The Hospital." *Scientific American* 229, no. 3 (September).

Kubler-Ross, E. 1969. *On Death and Dying.* New York; Macmillan.

Lindemann, E. 1944. ''Symptomatology and Management of Acute Grief.'' *American Journal of Psychiatry* 101 (September).

Markusen, E., and R. Fulton. 1971. ''Childhood Bereavement and Behavior Disorder: A Critical Review.'' *Omega* 2, no. 2 (May):107–118.

Pine, V. R. and D. Phillips. 1970. ''The Cost of Dying: A Sociological Analysis of Funeral Expenditure.'' Social Problems 17:405–417.

Shanas, E. P., et al. 1968. *Old People in Three Industrial Societies*. New York: Atherton Press.

Williams, W., P. Pollak, and R. Vollman. 1972. ''Crisis Intervention in Acute Grief.'' *Omega* 3, no. 1 (February): 67–70.

Social Work and the Bereaved

Marta Ochoa, Elizabeth R. Prichard, and Ellen L. Shwartzer

Does a hospital have a responsibility to the bereaved, or should this responsibility be delegated to a community agency? What are the identifiable conditions that indicate intervention by a helping person is needed? Is there any particular point at which intervention is more effective and the receptivity to such help greater? What is the attitude of society toward the bereaved and how has this influenced the attitudes of the helping professions? What is the responsibility of social work? These questions form the basis for a discussion of what social work can and should do within a hospital setting.

Purpose and function must be attuned to a knowledge base. Many recent studies (Parkes, 1964; Rees and Lutkins, 1967; Carr and Schoenberg, 1970), have demonstrated that there is a high incidence of morbidity and mortality following the death of a spouse, that the necessary adaptive process for the individual and family can result in severe stress, and that there can be maladaptive reactions (Krupp, 1972). It is also recognized that the extended family group provides more supportive aid then does the nuclear family and that the latter, more prevalent today, poses particular problems (Krupp, 1972). We know also that the process of readjustment to living without the deceased—with its reorganization and the formation of new relationships and attachments—can be a very slow one. It has also been demonstrated that the emotional and physical drain of management by a bereaved parent can be overwhelming (Wargotz, 1969). Also, social workers are sensitive to the emotional and economic drains on a family when a death has been preceded by a protracted illness. Surely the process of a family's emotional reordering after a death can well be staggering; there must be a recovery process (*New York Times*, 1973).

Studies are in progress to identify high-risk individuals, to develop a means by which to identify early those likely to become ill during the bereavement period, and to determine when intervention by a social worker is indicated. However, even on the basis of the knowledge already available, preparation for the bereavement process and grief work is not an integrated part of helping the families of the dying, nor has society by and large sufficiently recognized the need to establish structured, organized support for the bereaved. In addition, while social workers have always planned for the care of children, particularly when a parent is dying, only recently have they sufficiently recognized the significance of the role of social work. Now it can be seen that the behavioral and maladjustment problems of children and adults who have lost a parent or parents constitute such a large proportion of the caseloads in family agencies, the courts, schools, adoption and public agencies as to be commonplace.

When the bereaved are abandoned, it is because society as a whole has felt little or no obligation for them, perhaps as a result of its inability to handle feelings in regard to death. Also, a society that carries the guilt of wars must, in some way, deny the destruction of human lives. (Possibly the knowledge gained from further studies of bereavement will provoke sufficient anxiety to stop wars!) Although society through rituals, funerals, condolence visits, and various expressions of sympathy has found simple means of showing concern for its members, these are limited in scope and by factors of time and do not indicate a complete awareness of the long, hard road ahead for many families. Responsibility for the bereaved has been assigned to clergy and other caring individuals.

In the United States, until the early part of this century, the general welfare and problems of indigent widows, widowers, and children were considered the responsibility of religious or philanthropic organizations. The effect on children of separation from one or both parents and their placement in an orphanage was later recognized by social workers as deleterious. The practice of foster home placement was therefore instituted.

New York and Illinois were the first states to establish pensions for widows with children through legislative action, but not without long and bitter battles. The Aid to Dependent Children Program under the Social Security Act, passed in 1936 and put into effect in 1939, recognized the need for maintaining a home and hopefully some stability after the loss of a parent, yet today the intent of that program appears to have been forgotten. Are the attempts to adjust to the loss of a parent and to handle grief met more effectively on an empty stomach? Is a mother, drained emotionally by her loss of a husband and love object, better equipped to help her grieving children when she is anxious not only for the future, but over day-to-day concerns about feeding and clothing them? And if she is willing and able to work, is there a day care center available for her young children?

In a review of the book *Motherless Families,* a study based on interviews with fathers who were raising their children alone, John Deakins comments on the "very brief treatment of adaptive tasks related to grief and loss" and notes that "crucial factors in family breakdown following death or loss of the mother remain unidentified" (p. 301). This study was part of a larger one commissioned by the Department of Health and Social Security (in England) before setting up of a Committee on One-Parent Families (Deakins, 1973). At least some recognition was given to the fact that the One-Parent Family has problems.

An agency committed to the care of the terminally ill and generous in providing care to children while the mother was dying for many years withdrew the housekeeper as soon as the mother died. Exactly how the saddened and bereaved father could mobilize care at that point, when he had been unable to do so before, was a question repeatedly asked of the agency. Until this policy was recently relaxed, this agency was unable to gear its thinking and thus its function beyond caring for the dying patient. Bereavement was simply not understood.

When a child loses one or both parents and is deprived—in addition to parental care, love and affection, and an identity figure—of economic stability, will he or she be able to move out of the first stages of bereavement, those of anger and denial? What kind of a future life will the child have, and will this result in antisocial behavior?

Dr. Douglas Damrosch (1972) stated, "If the initial investigation of increased mortality and physical and mental illness among the bereaved is substantiated, should we not consider a preventive health program during the first year of bereavement?'' (p. viii). Certainly the Widow-to-Widow program in Boston (Silverman, 1970) attests to this need, as do the studies of Helen Wargotz (1969).

Krant and Sheldon (1971) feel that the physician has a strong responsibility to the family of the bereaved, and do not see this as a social service role. Although they praise the ancillary services established in the Boston area, they feel the programs that operate away from the hospital physician cannot be so directly supportive as a physician-based program. Further, they recommend that physicians be educated to understand grief and bereavement. There is validity in this point of view, particularly since it offers an opportunity for early recognition of physical and emotional pathologies, and the identification of high-risk individuals. However, the complexities of adjustment within the family, transferences of roles, the redistribution of tasks, and the steps to be taken toward normal living do, in many situations, require intervention by those trained to help families with the problems of daily life. And in light of recent knowledge—as to morbidity and mortality, the effects of family breakdown which affect children's preparation for adulthood, the problems of parent-child relationships, and problems of maladjustment—there is ample evidence to support the fact that the social worker also has a well-defined responsibility.

Abrams (1972) stresses the social worker's responsibility to the bereaved, poses the challenge to the profession of social work, and gives thought-provoking data, which, to support our position, must be reported here. In referring to the Conjugal Bereavement Study, Laboratory of Community Psychiatry, Harvard Medical School, she notes that 26 of the 69 primary subjects had died of cancer. Since these were not sudden deaths, there had been time for preparation. Further, Abrams points out that a little more than a year later "less than one-half of the widows and widowers had made a relatively good adjustment" (p. 180). Of particular interest and concern is that only four of the 26 survivors had been known to social service during their spouses' illness, although these patients had died in hospitals with social service departments.

Reference is also made to a general observation of social workers in medical settings, that the bereaved rarely return for help to the setting where the patient has died. Abrams relates that she had accepted this as a factual conclusion, but feels now "that care of the bereaved by the social worker was discontinued not because the latter did not reach out with appropriate empathy and support but because the bereaved tended to assume that he was no longer significant once the patient had died'' (p. 181). While we do feel this is a valid point, we are of the opinion—based on our experiences—that all are sound observations and that whether one observation or belief has more validity than another is based on a range of factors, with much depending on the relationship of the survivor with the deceased, the level of the grief reaction, psychic organization, readiness and receptivity and, no less significantly, the family's relationship with the social worker. It is our impression that the length of time and depth of the relationship and meaning to the survivor or survivors before the death of the patient are the factors that determine the continuation of a relationship after the death. In one situation known to us, preparation had started years before the mother died and a relationship continued for several years wherein help was given to the father of one of the children, to the stepfather of the other, and to the two children as they grew to adulthood. These children were followed at the hospital for medical reasons, but even when these were of a nonserious nature, they turned to the social worker with the assorted problems of growing up and their vocational plans. The daughter is now a nurse. It is of interest to point out that over the years in which these children utilized our availability to them, several social workers were involved.

Individuals and families are followed for varying periods of time. This is of particular importance when they also have medical problems. To what extent these continuing relationships may have prevented emotional disturbances cannot be known but can be surmised. In many cases, the parents of children who have died in Babies Hospital are being followed by social workers. The social workers are very active in advising families whose children have an irreversible illness, and these social workers are also well equipped to handle the crisis of death. These crises, often with many family members involved, occur more frequently than on the adult services. A mother who has had a long and close relationship with the social worker attributes her ability to keep on living to the support she has received. If one wants to question the role of the social worker within the hospital in this regard, it must be recognized that there is no suitable community agency to carry on this responsibility.

We agree with Mrs. Abrams that planning a program for the bereaved should be explored. At present we do not have documentation to support our impressions. We strongly recommend that every terminal patient's family be referred to a social worker, and if this is not possible, that the physician, social worker, and nurse be alert to possible problems and that each situation be reviewed to evaluate whether or not intervention is indicated.

Planning for the terminally ill at Columbia-Presbyterian Medical Center, including all of the voluntary hospitals that constitute Presbyterian Hospital (Babies Hospital, Eye Institute, New York Orthopedic Hospital, Neurological Institute, Sloane Hospital for Women), is listed by the Social Work Department among the ten major social patient care situations for which it has responsibility. But the Social Service Department, in its list of major responsibilities, does not include the bereaved. It is assumed that there will be follow-through because of a commitment to the family, but it is significant to report that by its omission from a list, it is viewed neither as a hospital responsibility, nor a defined social work responsibility.

Case Reports

A 15-year-old boy brought his dying widowed mother into the emergency clinic one Saturday afternoon; she died shortly thereafter. On Monday, the nursing department indicated to the social service department that this was an example of why a social worker should be on duty in that clinic at all times. A physician's wife, waiting for her husband in the clinic at that time, commented later that the nurses were very solicitous of the boy, untiring in their efforts to locate an uncle, and had comforted the boy while he waited. Further discussion with the nursing staff revealed that they felt that they hadn't done enough and that a social worker could have handled the situation more effectively.

A 13-year-old boy, a serious behavior problem on the ward and ready for discharge, had no home to go to. Following his mother's death three years earlier, there had been no room in his father's life for him. His father, living first with one woman and then another and hopeful that one would become interested in the boy, was concerned but too troubled by his own problems to deal adequately with those of his son. The boy's anger was often frightening to staff and patients; psychiatric intervention was arranged. When the social worker confronted a small group of hospital personnel gathered together in the hall discussing the boy, one of the group, a woman, said, "he's a bad boy." When the social worker replied, "he's a troubled boy, he has no mother, she is dead," a look of compassion came over the woman's face. The looks on the rest of the group softened and they all quietly and slowly moved away.

A 32-year-old woman being treated for anemia struggled alone to raise five children, ages two to eleven, after the father's prolonged death from a brain tumor. It had been a happy marriage. The struggle was made the harder because of poverty; the family had to eat in shifts because there were not enough plates and utensils to go around. Each night after the children went to bed, the mother cried. Fragile and worn, she hoped desperately to keep the family together. Despite her heavy heart and grief, she attempted to keep the children and the house clean and neat although it meant washing their limited supply of clothes every night. Most upsetting to her was a note from a teacher wishing to confer with her about her oldest boy's inattentiveness in class and his ''dirty underwear.'' When the social worker explained to the teacher that the boy's father had died only a few weeks before and that his underwear was gray from age and not dirt, the teacher replied that it was the social worker's job to teach people how to adjust. The social worker persevered in her attempts to interpret the hardships of this particular family and for bereaved children and families generally to the teacher and finally was able to penetrate the insensitivity of the woman.

In general, there is response to what is visible; unfortunately, many of the problems resulting from bereavement can persist in a latent state. Only when a crisis occurs are they visible to those who are willing to provide therapy. When problems related to bereavement are not detected early and remain untreated, they can be compounded and result in physical and serious emotional problems, which adversely affect the lives of others. The following case illustrates this.

Mrs. Z. first became known to the hospital in 1970 and was seen in various clinics for a variety of complaints. Although she was not seriously ill, her symptoms required medical investigation. Contacts were intermittent. In 1972, the patient was seen in a chest clinic. She had complained of shortness of breath and related symptoms. A physician noted her depression, elicited from her threats of suicide and referred her to psychiatry.

The patient attributed her depression to problems with her 18-year-old daughter's desire for independence and to marry a young man whom the mother knew well (he had lived in their home for a while) but whom she did not consider a suitable husband for her daughter.

The daughter stated that her mother's depression had started seven years before, when she had lost her parents within three days, and shortly thereafter her husband. Her husband, to whom she had been married for sixteen years, had been shot in a holdup in his store and had died two days later.

Mrs. Z. was one of four children of a formerly affluent South American family. The family had lost a fortune when their property was destroyed by a hurricane. She had lived a sheltered life, and when it became necessary to earn money she gave music lessons. She had come to this country, with her parents and a brother, at the age of 38. Her father, suffering from a heart condition, came here for treatment. It was in this country that the patient met her husband, a European, described as the "black sheep" of a wealthy family. After his death, the patient related that she felt hysterical and depressed, wished to kill herself, and lived only for her daughter. She eventually took a job as a sales clerk.

In the intervening years she had many dreams of returning to her native country and becoming a lady once again; in particular, she held to the fantasy that her daughter would return with her and eventually marry a wealthy man. She hoped to return to her sheltered life and to achieve through her daughter what she had given up for herself. There also continued a fantasy that her husband was still alive, and many of the decisions were based on what she believed her husband would have thought best for both herself and her daughter.

When the patient definitely decided that she would return to her native land, the daughter, who was attending college and very much wanted to finish and also marry, informed her mother that she had no intention of returning with her and that she wanted to be independent. This was the first time that the daughter had ever opposed her mother. The discussion took place on Mother's Day. Shortly thereafter, the patient became more depressed and had physical symptoms that took her back to the hospital.

After the psychiatrist saw the patient, he referred her to a Spanish-speaking social worker in the psychiatric clinic. She was followed by the social worker for some time, and although she did not always keep regular appointments—at first preferring to be seen when she wanted to—she would always respond to a telephone call from the social worker. The daughter was also seen by the social worker, and one visit was arranged for both of them to be seen together.

Focus was placed on helping the patient understand herself better; encouraging her to pursue the interests and hobbies she enjoyed (she had found needlepoint to be very satisfying); encouraging contacts with others to prevent further social isolation and, in particular, visits with a sister-in-law of whom she was very fond and wished to emulate; interpreting the needs of a growing daughter, with emphasis on cultural differences in this country; and a general preparation of the patient for separation. It was decided to help the patient make decisions for a satisfying life of her own, whether it would be to remain in this country and continue in the job, which she liked, or to return to her native country, which did appear to be more a fantasy. In general, the aim was to utilize her strengths to move her out of the stage of anger and into a reorganization of her life, and to give her support in developing appropriate coping measures.

Obviously, the patient was and had been in "mourning" for several years. Despite some ability to cope with life and obtain a job, she had remained essentially at the stage of anger and denial, which had evolved into a depression. The loss of three important people in her life within a very short period of time was understandably a great shock, and the patient could have used help at that time. While still in a state of anger and mourning, several years later, she was confronted by the fact that her daughter would leave her. The problems became overwhelming, and she developed physical symptoms that resulted in her seeking medical care, but this time the depression was very visible and she was referred to the psychiatrist.

Let us look at another situation in which the relationship with social service was started early and was a sustaining force to the patient and the husband.

Mrs. A. had been referred to social service by her physician when she had been admitted as a private patient for a radical mastectomy. The social worker's role at that time was to arrange home care for the patient. The patient was optimistic about the future and thought that she would recover quickly from the surgical procedure. A sister living in another city had died shortly before from cancer, and there was a high incidence of cancer on her mother's side of the family.

Some months later the patient was readmitted to a different section of the hospital for further surgery. The social worker assigned to the service noticed in the chart that patient was "nervous" and went to see her. The patient was neither responsive to nor did she reject the social worker's interest. It was apparent that denial was very much her way of coping. The social worker made no demands on her but did visit with her each day. The visits, very short at first, gradually became longer as the patient seemed to look for the social worker. They talked of her job as a teacher, her interest in music, and the novel she had been writing. Gradually, she began to bring forth the anger inside of her, particularly against the doctors because she feared that she would not be able to return to teaching or continue to play the violin. She persisted in denying that she had cancer although the physicians had told her the truth. However, they had given her hope that she would live for years. The relationship between the patient and the social worker deepened; the social worker elicited her concerns about not being a wife to her husband, the effect on her appearance of male hormone therapy, and her general feelings of despair. The social worker brought her some lip bleach and encouraged her to look attractive. Later she became preoccupied with the fact that she had cancer, attempted to keep this from her mother, but finally told her on the first anniversary of the sister's death.

The patient became very fearful about losing her independence; the social worker helped her in facing this and in obtaining some satisfaction from attention from others. She also encouraged her to take up needlepoint, and this was most satisfying. Some months later she was sent home and received help from the local Cancer Society. Her mother, an overpowering woman, moved in to help, but this was very upsetting to the patient and her husband, and with the help of the social worker, they were able to convince the mother to return to her own home.

When the physician had referred the husband to the social worker to discuss plans for this patient's care, a relationship was begun. At this time the husband's concern was mainly to carry out what was best for the patient. He did not respond initially to attempts to elicit his feelings. However, shortly before the patient left the hospital, the husband went to see the social worker and appeared very troubled. He became tearful and stated that he didn't know what he would do when his wife died, and that when his own mother had died he became depressed, couldn't work, kept to himself, and wouldn't eat. He said that his wife had helped him through this period. He was afraid that his wife's death would be too much for him to cope with. Further discussions indicated increasing worry. The social worker tried to sustain him as much as possible as the wife's condition deteriorated and recommended that he seek psychiatric help. In view of his unpleasant associations with the hospital, he did this in his home community.

The social worker kept in touch daily with the patient via a telephone call after she returned home and continued to do so after the patient was admitted to a hospital near her home. The social worker at that hospital was alerted and the situation was discussed with her. However, the patient could not relate to her, and the social worker there stated that she did not really feel that she could help a dying patient. At the patient's request and out of a feeling of commitment to the patient, the first social worker went to visit her. She was able to talk about dying, had come to some terms with it, and discussed how her family would remember her. The following day she died.

The husband has been in contact with the social worker from time to time, has continued the psychotherapy, and seems to be able to cope.

This couple had had a very dependent relationship with each other; the wife was the stronger of the two. It was the meaning of the relationship the patient had with the social worker that helped him also turn to the social worker, and readily accept and follow through on her recommendations. The social worker recognized that the patient's anger at the hospital and the doctors because they couldn't cure her influenced the husband in this attitude, and that help would therefore have to come from another source. Also, the fact that the husband had become severely depressed after the death of his mother was a signal that he would need help as soon as possible, and that it was particularly important both for the patient and for him that this be started during the patient's terminal state. It was recognized that their sons— now in late adolescence and young adulthood—would have adjustments to work through and feelings of loss and grief, but the patient's preoccupation with her anxieties and the father's depressed state would not give recognition to the children's feelings. It was decided that the best means of helping them was by encouraging the husband to get psychiatric help and thus, hopefully, sustain him as a parental figure and one with added responsibilities.

Conclusion

We have demonstrated the function of social work and the role of the social worker. There is a ready response and more perceptible awareness on the part of many persons within the hospital that help can and should be given. While bereavement itself has not been included officially as a definite cause for intervention, neither has there been a negation of it when need has had to be met. In reporting on the contribution of social service at the Michael Reese Hospital at the time of the Chicago train wreck in 1972, Leona Grossman stated that they had reached out and offered help to the families of the deceased, and although the families appreciated this, they "sought the intimacy of family or the comfort of religion and seemed to have no immediate wish for contact with strangers" (Grossman, 1973). The key work word here is *strangers*.

Certainly the families of patients who die in the hospital should not be strangers. Too often they are. Even when they are not, there is a tendency to believe that our function in helping them ends when the patient has died. Often out of sympathy our feelings direct us to stay with the family until the funeral director arrives, to call the family a few days or a week later, or to send a note—but that is that. These acts may be all that is necessary, for although a social worker is always available, often the case is closed.

All high-risk situations should be known to a social worker, inherent problems identified, and help given during the anticipatory grief period. This is a crucial period and group therapy at this time—particularly for parents— is most effective. When a relationship is established, a commitment is made. The commitment to the family or individual, the previously delineated problems, the assessment of the coping abilities of the individual or family, and the receptivity will determine the future of the working relationship. A decision has to be made as to whether further help is needed, at what point, and whether this may be more appropriately or effectively handled by another agency; or whether merely keeping the door open is the most suitable solution. It is not unusual for many families to feel that the social worker in the hospital is the only person who understands what they are going through. It might be healthier for some families and spouses to be able to move out of the realm of the hospital for help in coping during their period of bereavement as they strive to form new relationships and return to normality, but society has not given sufficient recognition to this aspect of care. The community is not likely to, nor is the hospital in a well-defined manner. It is another important and urgent facet in emphasizing the importance of life and living and the building of productive, satisfying lives for all allied health-science professionals to become involved in a concerted effort to communicate the problems of the bereaved and to understand that inattention to their problems of adjustment can affect the future lives of individuals and the society in which they are trying to function.

REFERENCES

Abrams, R. 1972. "The Responsibility of Social Work in Terminal Cancer." *In Psychosocial Aspects of Terminal Care,* eds. B. Schoenberg, et al., pp. 173–82. New York: Columbia University Press.

Carr, A. C., and B. Schoenberg. 1970. "Object Loss and Somatic Symptom Formation." In *Loss and Grief: Psychological Management in Medical Practice,* eds. B. Schoenberg, et al., pp. 36–48. New York: Columbia University Press, 1970.

Damrosch, D. S. 1972. Foreword to *Psychosocial Aspects of Terminal Care,* eds. B. Schoenberg, et al., pp. vi–viii. New York: Columbia University Press.

Deakins, J. 1973. Review of *Motherless Families,* Victor George and Paul Wilding (London: Routledge and Kegan, 1972). In *Social Service Review* 47 (June).

Grossman, L. 1973. "Train Crash: Social Work and Disaster Services." *Journal of National Association of Social Workers* 18 (September):38.

Krant, M. 1972. "In the Context of Dying." In *Psychosocial Aspects of Terminal Care,* eds. B. Schoenberg, et al., pp. 201–9. New York: Columbia University Press.

Krant, M., and A. Sheldon. 1971. "The Dying Patient: Medicine's Responsibility." *Journal of Thanatology,* January–February.

Krupp, G. 1972. "Maladaptive Reactions to the Death of a Family Member." *Social Casework,* July.

New York Times. 1973. "Impact, Costs and Consequences of Catastrophic Illness on Patients and Families." Study by Cancer Care and National Cancer Foundation, 1973. As reported on August 15.

Parkes, C. M. 1964. "Effects of Bereavement on Physical and Mental Health: Study of Medical Records of Widows." *British Medical Journal* 2:274–79.

Rees, W. D., and S. G. Lutkins. 1967. "Mortality of Bereavement." *British Medical Journal* 4:13–16.

Silverman, P. R. 1970. "The Widow-to-Widow Program." *Archives of the Foundation of Thanatology* 2:3 ff.

Wargotz, H. 1969. "Widowers with Teen Age Children." In *Death and Bereavement,* ed. A. H. Kutscher. Springfield: Charles C. Thomas.

The Role of the Nurse
in the Maintenance
and Restoration of Hope

Clara L. Adams and Joseph R. Proulx

"Where there is life there is hope." How often have we heard, and indeed heeded, this maxim? Perhaps other central questions we should ask ourselves are what *is* hope? what is the relationship of hope and the hoping process to bereavement? And finally, a poignant question for the nursing profession would be how can nurses assist the bereaved in maintaining hope and, if the bereaved reaches a state of hopelessness, how can nurses assist in the restoration of hope?

Hope is such an integral part of everyday speech that little if any attention is paid to its underlying complexities and various meanings. "Hope has become a word that is often used but rarely with the same meaning. This is due partly to the lack of descriptive analyses of hope and implications relating to those persons who would most likely apply the analyses to conditions of life" (Butler, 1962). We believe that professional nurses, and persons in the bereaved state (clients or family members) would benefit from a detailed analysis of hope. The phenomenon does not lend itself to an objective, definitive analysis; yet hope would seem to be a fundamental part of every man's being.

Hope has been described as an expectation, an illusion, a virtue, an emotion, a disposition. However, most social scientists refer to hope as an emotion. But when the phenomenon is subjected to stringent analysis, hope rarely meets the necessary criteria commonly used to describe the generic term "emotion." However, if hope is considered to be an emotion, it clearly concerns a subject (the person who is hoping) and an object (the particular thing the person hopes for). In addition, hope has a desire component and a probability element, and the entire affective state is based on thought (Day, 1969).

Psychiatric literature offers some salient, albeit tendentious, commentary on the subject of hope. It is seen as a guide to a plan of action that results in goal-oriented, integrated behavior; it is also viewed as but part of one large, unconscious wish (French, 1952, 1958). In any case, the phenomenon is considered crucial to the individual's well-being and health. Although hope may be thought of as internal to the subject, it requires and depends upon external help to become truly effective. This idea of exteriority highlights the role of the nurse.

The genesis and development of hope are also seen in a number of ways. Psychosocially speaking, it is the earliest of virtues to be developed and arises out of a trusting relationship based on material infallibility (Erikson, 1961). Others have viewed the concept as part of the developmental process of ego-autonomy, particularly in terms of sexual identification (Schmale, 1964).

The French philosopher Gabriel Marcel has written extensively on hope and the hoping process (1962). For Marcel, hope arises out of a time of trial, a period of suffering, a state of captivity. It is only in a situation in which one is tempted to despair that hope has its true beginnings. The state of captivity is envisioned as an integral part of one's very being, thereby necessitating the hoping process.

According to Marcel, hope is subject to and dependent upon a firm intersubjective relationship, referred to as an "I-Thou" or "us" relationship. In terms of death and dying, then, it is suggested that the hoping process may come to fruition in the interpersonal context between the bereaved and the nurse as a caring professional.

One of our central assumptions here is that there is a relationship between health and hope. The hoping process plays an important part in the physical and emotional well-being of man and animals. This fact has been demonstrated in conjunction with studies of animal behavior, hospitalized patients, terminally ill persons, cancer victims, concentration-camp survivors, and theoretical works in psychology. In even more specific terms a relationship seems to exist between separation and depression (defined here as a psychic pattern of unsuccessful resolution of object loss) and the onset of medical disease. For example, one investigator reported that "the relatively short period of time between the final findings of helplessness and hopelessness and the onset of medical disease suggests that there are changes in biological activities related to these psychic reactions to unresolved loss" (Schmale, 1964).

The incidence of physical and mental illness and even death in the bereaved has frequently been documented. It would seem, then, that what is needed—among other things—in working with the bereaved is a better understanding of the phenomenon of hope. Jourard (1964) has spoken of the general hope syndrome, which is usually a gradually rising titer of spirit which in turn decreases the entropic level of the body system; that is, "it mediates higher level wellness." However, too often in health care the phenomenon of hope is relegated to an unscientific, poetic, or even fanciful category. This probably occurs because the phenomenon is not so objective as a blood sample, an X-ray film, or an observable aberrant behavior associated with a psychotic break. Nonetheless, we suggest that hope is an appropriate area of study for truly concerned and caring individuals, particularly in working with the bereaved.

Our central themes are, first, that hope is a distinct, albeit nonspecific force, which is related to health and illness. Secondly, the understanding, maintenance, or restoration of hope in relating to the bereaved is essential to their improved well-being. In effect, we may now paraphrase our opening statement: "Where there is dying there is also hope."

We shall define the bereaved as one who is being—or has been—deprived of the association with another person because of the death or the impending death of a significant other. Further, the dying person may also be the bereaved, because he is being stripped of his own life. Within the framework of this operational definition, one can readily discern that loss and grief are very closely associated with bereavement. Those who are bereft have usually entered the early stages of grieving over a loss that has occurred or a loss that is pending.

A series of very different emotional reactions or behaviors may be observed in the bereaved depending upon whether he or she is the dying person or the survivor. For example, if the bereaved is the one to die, he or she may be in the acceptance stage of emotional awareness, while the survivor has not yet completed denying the impending loss.

In a contrasting situation, a bereaved survivor may go through the grief process before the loved one dies, turn to new relationships, and abandon the dying one. The latter may then become angry and hostile, and another emotional crisis is precipitated (Neale, 1973).

We have been viewing hope and bereavement generally as separate entities. Now we shall ask are they compatible? Is it possible for hope and bereavement to coexist in the process of dying?

When one enters the bereaved state one is so overwhelmed by feelings of powerlessness and hopelessness that all of one's emotional horizons are severely clouded. Consequently, the state of bereavement is frequently viewed as being devoid of hope. It is our contention that while feelings of helplessness and hopelessness may initially predominate in the bereaved person, with assistance this situation can change.

Weisman (1973) has stated that

people without hope see no end to their suffering, whether or not they are suffering from a fatal illness. Hope, however, is not dependent upon survival alone; survival can be the "no exit" reason for losing hope, not for preserving it. Hope means that we have confidence in the desirability of survival . . . [hope] arises from a desirable self-image, healthy self-esteem, and a belief in our ability to exert a degree of influence on the world surrounding us. . . . the key issue is between survival and significant survival.

In essence, Weisman is saying that hope and bereavement may coexist in the dying process when persons are able to accept themselves and their experiences rather than clinging to objects or unrealistic goals and aspirations.

The inference is clear that change is dynamic in the dying process and the degree of acceptance is dependent upon the willingness of the bereaved to deal with the changes as they occur. Hope, then, is part of an ongoing process, which changes as the reality of the situation changes.

Two final questions are, how can the nurse assist in maintaining hope in the bereaved? and, if the bereaved reaches a state of hopelessness, how can the nurse assist in the restoration of hope?

Professional nurses will be able to participate more actively in the hoping process and the bereavement state by alerting themselves to the possibilities that are open to them. However, it is difficult to relate hope and bereavement to the practice of nursing, because both the phenomemon of hope and the nurse's role are ill-defined. Nonetheless, nurses, in the activation of hope, may demonstrate awareness, sharing, orientation and redefinition, and creativity.

"Awareness is a unitary process, a passive state of openness, a sensitivity to things, nature, people, and ideas" (Sarosi, 1968). Before becoming fully aware of the hoping process in bereavement, the nurse must become self-aware, both as a person and as a professional. This awareness is not easy to come by, because it necessitates a self-disclosure that may not always be favorable or pleasant. Awareness also implies that the nurse possesses distinct human qualities—strengths or weaknesses. Further, one must be accepting of what such introspection reveals.

The nurse's self-awareness as a individual and as a professional tends to influence understanding and identification of hope and the hoping process in bereavement. As an individual, the nurse must be aware of the presence or absence of hope in oneself. For many, hope is viewed myopically—i.e., only as possible to the person actually immersed in the captive situation. However, others may also be cognizant of the dying patient's captive state, and these others—nurses for example—may trigger the hoping process by experiencing and transmitting hope themselves. In manner both the ideal of the nurse's commitment and the essence of hope are embraced in relationship with the bereaved. With awareness both the bereaved and the nurse are able to evaluate objectively the realities of situations as they occur. Awareness is an integral part of maintaining and restoring hope.

Sharing is another factor. Essentially hoping is sharing. To hope means to involve oneself in a relationship with another human being. The self is transcended and a partnership is formed. A spirit of communion underlies the trials and sufferings of the captive state. "I" becomes "we" and together an end to the time of hardship and trial is hoped for.

Sharing implies a give and take and the formation of a bond between two people that unites individual strengths and weaknesses. The basis of this sharing is an interpersonal relationship. Hoping, by necessity, includes an interpersonal interaction and entails being and feeling with another.

Many nurses are in favorable positions to form meaningful relationships with patients. Unfortunately, the availability of the nurse—who is always seen as being at the bedside in opposition to other health professionals who make periodic visits to clients—does not signify that a viable relationship is being, or will be, formed. Too often the reverse is true: nurses tend to ignore the human aspects of their practice and focus on the work at hand, perhaps because of feelings of discomfort experienced in forming meaningful relationships. Some of these feelings are loneliness, agony, suffering, and fears of death and dying.

It is most difficult, however, for the nurse who must relate to the bereaved to circumvent the fact that when one enters into this sharing relationship, one must invest a certain amount of time and energy. This professional, like no other, must understand and accept the discomforts and rewards with equal vitality. The bereaved need someone—a significant someone—who willingly enters a relationship with them, in a situation that may be viewed as inescapable, to instill hope in their suffering. Nurses are in an ideal position to engage in this meaningful interaction.

Hope and the hoping process are responses to the state of captivity. The expression of hope, however, may vary from person to person as the process is influenced by the individual's own perception of the captive state.

Before hope can take root and flourish, the bereaved person must become aware of the situation in which he or she is enmeshed and accept this predicament. In effect, a reality-orientation seems to be a precursor to the authentic hoping process.

Wright and Shontz (1968) have spoken of this orientation in terms of reality grounding, and have suggested that hopes must have a realistic base if they are to come true.

Once again, the professional nurse is an ideal candidate to assist in this reality-orientation. By virtue of intimate involvement with the patient over an extended period of time, the nurse is able to appraise both patient and environment as well as the former's responses to the captive situation. "The patient is understood to have extensive strengths and capacities in latent and unrecognized form. It then becomes the function of the helping person to help the patient identify and actualize this potential and develop the unique propensities of his being" (Otto, 1965).

Closely related to the reality of the captive situation is the concept of the object of hope. Hope is a fluid phenomenon, which undergoes constant modification in terms of the individual's perception and experience of reality. Many patients verbalize hope by speaking of their physical or mental limitations and the possibility of recovery. These concerns are personal and pragmatic, and are often difficult to distinguish from such similar notions as wishing and desiring. The nurse must be attentive to and accepting of these communications.

Ideally speaking, the role of the nurse is that of a listener. The nurse does not personally select the bereaved person's hope, but rather will help him or her to redefine the object of hoping in terms of the reality of the state of captivity. The nurse becomes a sounding-board against which the patient can test his hopes. In an active and authentic hoping process the bereaved person will modify and redefine his or her own hopes along the lines of the real possibilities left open.

Since reality is often difficult to accept, especially when death is imminent, the nurse must guard against offering invalid objects of hope to the bereaved. Reassurance for which there is no sound basis may be easier than facing the realities of the situation. However, such an approach leads only to false hoping which is detrimental and frustrating to the patient and demoralizing to the professional staff.

Reality-orientation and redefinition imply new horizons. In the sharing relationship with the professional helper, the bereaved may extend the boundaries of the possible and overcome limitations that heretofore seemed insurmountable. Hope is an active element in the creation and pursuit of other possibilities. By participation in the hoping process, the bereaved's being rather than his or her existence is enhanced.

Creativity is not only the ultimate possibility in terms of hope and the hoping process in bereavement, it is also a summation of the three previously mentioned possibilities open to the nurse. By becoming increasingly aware of the personal dimension of the self and the therapeutic effects the self may exert on another, the nurse grows—and growth is a part of creativity. Likewise, if the nurse becomes aware of the dignities and values inherent in the bereaved, and communicates this awareness in sharing relationship, the latter also begins to show evidence of personal growth.

Then, too, growth and creativity are vividly portrayed in reality-orientation and redefinition because the nurse-client relationship forms the nucleus of hoping activity as professional and the bereaved expand the boundaries of the possible or confront the realities of the impossible.

Creativity and hope are intertwined. As the persons in the hoping process become more attuned to the potentialities present in the interpersonal matrix of the captive situation, the hoping process itself becomes stronger and exerts greater force. Hoping necessitates creativity and vice versa.

What creativity and hope lack in objective explication they more than make up in personal terms. "One sees clearly the strength and dignity of human beings, the deep altruism, the positive qualities that exist at all levels of personality. Working with people who are under the hammer of fate greatly increases one's respect for them and makes one proud of being a human being" (LeShan, 1964). Working with bereaved persons is a creative experience; it is hoping in the truest and most helpful sense.

REFERENCES

Butler, N. L. 1962. "A Theory of Hope Based upon Gabriel Marcel with Implications for the Psychiatrist and the Minister." (Ph.D. dissertation, Boston University).

Day, J. P. 1969. "Hope." *American Philosophical Quarterly* 6:90 ff.

Erikson, E. H. 1961. "The Roots of Virtue," *The Humanist Frame,* J. Huxley, ed., New York: Harper.

French, T. M. 1952, 1958. *The Integration of Behavior.* Vol. 1: *Basic Postulates* and Vol. 3: *The Reintegrative Process in a Psychoanalytic Treatment.* Chicago: University of Chicago Press.

Jourard, S. M. 1964. *The Transparent Self.* Princeton: D. Van Nostrand Company.

LeShan, L. L. 1964. "Some Observations on the Problem of Mobilizing the Patient's Will to Live," in *Psychosomatic Aspects of Neoplastic Disease,* D. M. Kissen and L. L. LeShan, eds. London: Pitman Medical Publishing Company.

Marcel, G. 1962. *Homo Viator: Introduction to a Metaphysic of Hope.* New York: Harper and Row.

Neale, R. E. 1973. *The Art of Dying.* New York: Harper and Row.

Otto, H. A. 1965. "The Human Potentialities of Nurses and Patients." *Nursing Outlook* 13:33 ff.

Sarosi, G. M. 1968. ''A Critical Theory: The Nurse as a Fully Human Person,'' *Nursing Forum* 7:360 ff.

Schmale, A. H. Jr. 1964. ''A Genetic View of Affects: With Special References to the Genesis of Helplessness and Hopelessness.'' *The Psychoanalytic Study of the Child* 19:299 ff. New York: International Universities Press.

Weisman, A. D. 1973. *On Dying and Denying*. New York: Behavioral Publications, Inc.

Wright, B. A., and F. C. Shontz. 1968. ''Process and Tasks in Hoping,'' *Rehabilitation Literature* 29:32 ff.

Bereavement and the Nursing Student

Elsa Poslusny and Margaret Kelley Arroyo

By far the most difficult task for teachers is to educate the student to care for the dying patient and his or her family (or significant others, if they exist). Schoenberg and Carr (1972) report that the "task of managing the dying patient is sufficiently formidable as to require that it be a shared responsibility" (p. 12). Strauss (1969) offers suggestions for improving the care dying patients receive in institutions, especially hospitals. J. Quint Benoliel (1972) discusses the existing care practices, which focus more on technical procedures than on the experience of dying patients and the bereavement of others. She recommends also that nursing students should be provided group teaching-learning experiences throughout their education (Quint, 1967). Through such experiences the teachers can provide the student with the needed support to work through the anxiety-provoking experience of dying and bereavement.

Description of Program

Teaching of psychosocial aspects of patient care including death and dying is integrated in the Behavioral Science course series at the School of Nurs-

The Psychosocial Aspects of Patient Care course series offered at the School of Nursing, Faculty of Medicine, Columbia University, were, in part, supported by the Psychiatric Nursing Training Branch, The National Institute of Mental Health, Grant No. MHO6397. The authors are indebted to nursing students and to the multidisciplinary faculty—nurses, psychiatrists, and behavioral scientists who participated in these psychosocial group teaching-learning experiences.

ing, Faculty of Medicine, Columbia University. The multidisciplinary faculty teams—nurses, psychiatrists, and behavioral scientists—teaching in this program believe that psychosocial needs and problems should be a concern in the care of all patients. The multidisciplinary group teaching is offered in the junior and senior year of the nursing major. The program has sought to equip nurses to give better care to the mentally ill, as well as to recognize and deal with actual and potential problems of a psychosocial nature in general nursing practice. Each multidisciplinary teaching team—consisting of a nurse, psychiatrist, behavioral scientist, and clinical resource person—meets with a group of 20 to 25 nursing students two hours weekly through the two years of their nursing major. Concurrently, students are enrolled in clinical nursing courses and have experiences with patients in medical, surgical, maternity and pediatric, psychiatric, and community health nursing care situations in a large metropolitan medical center and in the community (Poslusny, 1968).

The Nursing Student

It might be helpful to examine some of the expectations of the beginning nursing students. As adolescents they are idealistic, altruistic, and eager to help people. They anticipate feeling like a nurse once they don a student uniform and are in the clinical area. They expect to feel competent and self-assured, and have most of the answers to their patients' problems. They do not, for the most part, expect to have to study behavioral dimensions of nursing care. In their opinion, the fact that they are concerned about the patient and have interacted with people all their lives should provide them with the competence in this area of nursing. Furthermore, they expect that their gratification will come from the patient rather than learning in the classroom. They anticipate being successful in every helping endeavor that they undertake on behalf of "their" patients. Moreover, they usually presume that their patients will have attitudes and values similar to their own. Thus, students are often unprepared for the different value systems and lifestyles that they find on the hospital wards or in the community. Consequently, they encounter difficulties in being helpful with patients and with the health and medical staff. Students seem unprepared for extremes on the health-illness continuum—especially the experience of dying and bereavement.

Some of the students' expectations in relation to their nursing faculty and physicians should be mentioned. The nursing instructor is expected to be kind and fair. She helps the students live up to their own self-image of a nurse. The doctor may be looked upon as an omnipotent healer, concerned for the patient, kindly, and helpful to students. The approval of the instructor and doctor is important. Students have little or no concept of the health team and its purpose.

In view of these expectations, it is essential that the nursing faculty face the challenge of assisting the nursing students to recognize their own feelings and those of others. Moreover, by examining anxiety-ridden situations faced by students and their patients, the teachers can encourage a more realistic, problem-solving approach, thus aiding in the professional growth of the nursing students. To achieve this, in the education for the care of dying and bereaved-to-be, is the most difficult task facing the teacher.

Dying and Bereavement

What is bereavement—how do the nursing students experience bereavement in relationships with their patients? Peretz (1970) describes bereavement as "A state of thought, feeling and activity which is the consequence of loss of a loved or valued object" (p. 20). Do the nursing students experience the death of their patients as a loss of a valued object? The answer is a complex one and depends upon a multiplicity of factors, such as how well they knew the patient, whether they related to the patient over a period of time, whether there is some cathexis to the patient. Furthermore, experiencing the death of another reminds one of one's own mortality. As Freud and others have said, no one can experience his own death. Peretz states further: "Death is represented in the imagination as a separation from those who love and nurture. It is not oblivion but the pain of being alone" (p. 21). Throughout their nursing education, students are confronted with the experience of dying and bereavement. On one level nursing students see a patient die; this may or may not be experienced as the loss of a valued object, depending on the nature of the relationship. On a deeper level students can be reminded of their own mortality and can experience the symbolic loss of "the nurturing one," connectedness with living.

Cultural Perspectives

The nursing students are a product of the larger American culture that characteristically denies man's mortality by glorifying youth, placing aged people away, and focusing on specialization—i.e. placing those who are dying in the realm of the uninvolved (Jackson, 1969). The American culture safeguards the young and others from the reality of death. As the students move into the hospital subculture they are no longer shielded from the reality of death. However, the hospital system has its own protective mechanisms to manage the care of the dying and bereaved, for example, task orientation and isolation from intimate contact with the dying (Schoenberg, 1971). The rituals, regulations, roles and organizational structures are highly complex (Leininger, 1970) and serve many functions, one of which is protecting the staff from "difficult situations." The nursing students who enter this subculture are taught by the nursing faculty to formulate their goals with the patient, emphasizing a one-to-one therapeutic nurse-patient relationship, and in a broader sense the mutuality of all human interaction. In light of the realities of the hospital care system, and in view of the values of the American culture, how do the nursing students cope with the experience of death and bereavement? The following excerpt illustrates how others expect the nurse to function in caring for the dying, the dead, and the bereaved.

The nurse is often the first to learn of the patient's death and she must prepare the family for the news. Because death can be legally established only by a physician, the nurse must maintain the illusion that life remains until the physician arrives and tells the family of the death. In the accompanying shock and grief, the physician comforts the family, may secure permission for an autopsy, and then hurries to other duties, leaving the nurse to help the family with any technical details of hospital discharge and with any questions about the disposition of the body. When the family leaves, the nurse must wrap the body securely, identify it, and arrange for removal to the morgue. Then she must fill out the necessary papers. Her last official duty is to inform the new nursing shift of the death. All of the above duties are unpleasant, if not painful (Rabin and Rabin, 1972).

Students' Experiences With Death, Dying and Bereavement

CASE 1

The students are confronted with death as soon as they are introduced to the school. As a part of the anatomy laboratory experience they come in contact with cadavers. And in the psychsoc seminars they initiate these beginning questions: "Where did they get the bodies from?" "If I touch the cadaver I have to block out that the cadaver was a person, I have to look at it merely as an anatomical figure." This is a very painful experience for the students and they immediately become angry. Why do "they" have to do research? It is extremely difficult in those beginning days for the student to look at a dead body, to look at a dead person, and the person is *not* all that removed from themselves. In addition to coping with these discomforting feelings they are also required to know the muscles, nerves, and other anatomical structures. Students feel conflict because they have to learn all these facts intellectually, and yet emotionally they are reacting to the dead person. It is most comfortable for them to focus on the intellectual task in this situation and deny, displace, and repress their feelings.

CASE 2

During initial experiences on the medical-surgical wards, the students will not be assigned to caring for a dying patient. But there will be patients around them who will be in various stages of terminal illness. The following is an illustration of what beginning students may encounter as they take care of patients during their initial clinical experience:

Student appeared nervous, anxious and somewhat angry in her psychsoc group when she was asked to share her clinical experience. She reported that she was on the ward this morning and attending to her patient, when suddenly, everyone on the open 12-bed ward started running to one bed, and the curtains were drawn around the bed. Over ten people, staff members, ran in and out over a period of an hour. Then, suddenly, all activity ceased. The curtains remained drawn. The student became increasingly anxious, suspecting but not wanting to know what had happened. Her patient was also curious and asked what had occurred. The student went to a staff member and was told that the patient had died. She returned to her patient's bedside, and shared this information. The patient began to cry; so did the student. The student was upset at her own loss of control and the additional stress she caused her patient. In the future, she feels she will withhold such information from her patients and she will control her reactions concerning death.

This is an example of a sudden, unplanned encounter with death. Realistically, all situations cannot be monitored, but some questions can be raised at this point: what kind of emotional support can be provided for the nursing student? Is it realistic to expect the beginning student not to be shocked at witnessing the death of a patient—even though she is not responsible for that patient? This is a very critical point for the clinical instructor to provide support that will help the student identify and bring into awareness some of these early reactions concerning death. The psychosocial group experience provided another opportunity, a reflective experience, for the student to discuss and validate her feelings with her fellow students. The multidisciplinary faculty explored crying as the initial feeling of helplessness one experiences when faced with death.

CASE 3

At this early time in the nursing education students identify with their patients. They feel keenly the experiences their patients are undergoing: the pain, the suffering, the helplessness in the face of death. A student related the following clinical situation while having a surgical nursing experience: A 30-year-old woman, who spoke only Spanish, was a patient for six weeks on a gynecological ward, where she was undergoing radiotherapy. Her diagnosis was metastatic carcinoma of the cervix. She experienced pain, nausea, debilitation, and was bedridden. To relieve her pain and discomfort Demerol injections were given as needed. The patient was a mother of three children, ages six months to four years. Her husband had been told by the attending physician of her condition and of her poor prognosis. However, the patient had been told neither the prognosis nor diagnosis.

Several students were caring for this patient over a period of time and this interpersonal experience created many problems. Initially, a translator was needed to communicate basic information. The students felt frustrated and angry at not being able to communicate directly with the patient. The students' anger reached the point of rage, as they discussed the patient's prognosis and age—"Why must a 30 year-old woman die? She has everything to live for, husband and family." To control their emotions the students selected the nursing instructor as the target for their anger. Throughout the semester and at the end of the term the student group was unanimous in their criticism of the instructor, especially regarding final evaluations. The instructor acknowledged the feeling content of student communication. Talking helped the students identify some of the difficulties they were facing. They proceeded to describe that they were coping with their anger and impatience by displacing feelings of anger and impotence on their instructor. The instructor, in turn, was the same age as the patient. She had to sort out her own feelings in terms of identification with this terminally ill patient.

Some of the following questions were further explored in the psychsoc group seminar: What were the students angry about? Were they angry in terms of their lack of control over the destiny of the patient, lack of authorities to assist, to intervene, to interrupt the disease process? Were they angry that at their age, prematurely, they had to face people who were dying, while they were in the process of struggling with their definition and affirmation of life? How did the students cope in this painful situation? Identification, displacement, projection, and prevailing mood of anger were the behaviors the students displayed.

CASE 4

Another encounter with death and bereavement was described by a student in maternity nursing. This experience was related to the psychsoc group that ran concurrently with Maternity and Pediatric nursing courses. A student was assigned to the labor room and was with "her young mother," who was having regular contractions. As she looked at the labor room board, she noticed that there was no fetal heart rate recorded, whereas dilation of the cervix was progressing. Delivery was imminent. The student stated, "My stomach dropped"; she felt paralyzed when she read "no fetal heart rate"; the baby was dead. The mother told her that there had been no felt fetal heart beat for a period of several hours. The student asked no more questions, and the mother offered no more elaboration. The student assisted with the delivery of a stillborn.

There was difficulty initiating any discussion in the psychsoc group after this clinical incident was reported. The student expressed her feeling of helplessness and uselessness while nursing the mother through all of this pain. Neither the faculty nor the student group asked questions about the mother's reaction, the physician's reaction, or the management of the bereaved mother and expectant father—whether the husband was waiting, whether the mother wanted or didn't want a child, whether there were other children in the family. Obviously, the answers to some of these questions would indicate how the bereaved woman could be assisted in coping with the loss of her baby.

The overriding feeling in the group was one of helplessness. It can be related to the students' close identification with the young mother. The student is in the process of negotiating her professional and sexual identity. Womanhood—and motherhood, with its wish for and fear of pregnancy and its possible disastrous outcomes—is experienced by the young female student. The nursing instructors, being mostly women, may be coping with similar issues, while they are helping the student identify feelings of guilt, insecurity, and poor self-image that can be precipitated by the birth of a stillborn.

In this situation there was no one to strike out at, no one toward whom direct anger and frustration could be directed. There was no physician ordering that the patient should not be told the truth, there were no hospital regulations restraining the student's therapeutic intervention with the patient. The birth of a stillborn child was a natural process against which the whole group felt helpless. The overwhelming feeling of helplessness was such that the group remained on the affective level of experiencing and could not move into the area of cognitive conceptualization during most of the class. During subsequent classes, the group was able to move from the level of feeling to the level of cognition.

The faculty team initiated the conceptualization of this experience for and with the student; they identified the prevailing mood of the group, related this mood to the students' identification with the patient, as well as to each student's working through of her own psychosocial tasks of late adolescence.

CASE 5

As the nursing students proceed into their senior year, they are expected to care for multiproblem patients and families. One of the overriding difficulties the students face are their unrealistic expectations of themselves. They now move more closely toward identification with the nurse. They expect to be able to cope with their own feelings. They now feel responsible, as nurses, to intervene effectively with and on behalf of the patient and his or her family. In reality, these expectations are greater on their part than on the part of others. The following clinical experiences illustrate how the student copes when encountering a dying patient.

The senior student related her experience, which occurred in the receiving emergency during the evening hours. As she arrived in the receiving area, ambulance drivers carried a young male on a stretcher into the receiving emergency area. The patient was black, apparently in his early twenties, unconscious, bleeding on the side of the head and neck, and immobile. Medical and nursing personnel assigned to the acute emergency hurriedly started to work on the patient, cutting and stripping his clothing, attempting open heart massage. Soon more health team members descended on the scene; at the same time, police arrived and three policemen demanded the identification of the apparently dying or dead person. There were no immediate relatives. Two apparent buddies, who had accompanied the patient, did not appear eager to get involved with the police. The student felt, and apparently she was correct, that the patient had been "DOA." However, the cardiac arrest procedure was put into effect. She believed it was unnecessary; it was more for the staff's benefit than the patient's. Furthermore, she was revolted by the intrusion of the police officers on the scene. These outsiders assumed the authority to ask questions regarding this patient during those critical moments when lifesaving procedures were attempted. In addition to the above dilemma, she was placed in the position of observing the function of the health team and police, but could do nothing.

The behavior the student evidenced when describing this situation was one of being revolted and frustrated. She dealt with these discomforting feelings by questioning the heroic efforts of the medical and nursing staff, and the inappropriateness of the policemen's intrusion on the scene. She functioned in the situation as an observer. Her expectation to perform as a nurse was frustrated—she could do nothing.

In the psychsoc group discussion her level of expectation was questioned by her peers. "You are not legally responsible for the patient, you are only a student." The student took this remark as a "put down" and also a "cop out." The multidisciplinary teaching team used this provocative statement to begin analyzing this clinical incident on a cognitive level through the problem-solving approach.

They explored the expectations connected with the role of a "student" and that of a "nurse." The role of student implies the right and responsibility to ask questions, to clarify ambiguous issues with those legally responsible for patient care, whereas the role of a "nurse" implies responsibility to perform, to act on behalf of the patient or with other medical and nursing staff. The teaching team attempted to clarify the conflicts the student experiences at this level. The emergency receiving experience thrusts one directly in contact with violence, and death due to violence. And these are very threatening experiences for both the student and the nurse.

CASE 6

"Attempted" or "successful" suicide by a psychiatric patient is another threatening experience for the student. A "successful" suicide was reported by a senior student in a psychsoc group: the student had clinical experience in an adult unit of a psychiatric hospital. She was assigned to an adult, male, white patient with ground privileges. One day the patient went out and did not return. The next morning the patient's body was brought back to the psychiatric hospital. The student could not relate the specifics—how the suicide was committed, where the body was found, or how it was brought back to the hospital. She was overwhelmed with guilt in relation to this violent and premature death. As a nurse she felt responsible: "I should have intervened." On another level she experienced overwhelming anxiety—the meaning of which she related as, "Here but for the Grace of God go I; I too may lose control." "I have the power to kill myself."

The multidisciplinary faculty focused on the high level of anxiety experienced by the group as this incident was reported. The self-destructive nature of this man's death precipitated the awareness that each individual has the power to destroy himself. Varying degrees of loss can be felt with each death experience. Suicide evokes feelings of loss and rejection on the part of the helping professional. Taking one's own life is condemned by most social institutions in the culture at large. This moral taboo against suicide was explored in relation to the student's belief system. The guilt felt by the student was explored in terms of the expectations she has of herself as a professional person.

CASE 7

In contrast to these experiences with sudden, violent death, the student also encounters more protracted experiences with death and dying. A student was having her community nursing field experience and related the following incident in her psychsoc group. The student made a home visit to a 70-year-old, white, retired male, as part of her community health field experience. The patient had been hospitalized for exploratory abdominal surgery and the student was sent to his home to change his dressing. Medically, he had a diffuse pain at this time and was taking an oral pain medication. The exploratory surgery uncovered inoperable metastatic bowel carcinoma with poor prognosis. The patient was apparently not aware of this prognosis. The hospital referral stated that the patient was not to be advised of his prognosis. The patient had retired on Social Security and had to apply for welfare in order to supplement his meager income.

During her initial visit the student changed the dressing, obtained the necessary information for the agency record, but experienced difficulty communicating with the patient. The patient was deaf and appeared dissheveled. The apartment was dirty. The patient was a widower and lived alone in a fifth floor walk-up tenement, which had been burglarized several times. The last time this happened his TV set had been stolen. The patient told the student that his brother and son visited occasionally; he had a home health aide who visited and did the shopping weekly. The patient felt weak, was unable to climb the stairs at this point, and was therefore housebound.

The student reported that the patient appeared bitter, resentful, and lethargic during her visit. She felt that he did even less for himself than he was able. As she spoke, she seemed frustrated and dejected. Hesitantly, she raised the question, "Wouldn't it be best to close the case? Really there is nothing more I can do."

The student's behavior reflected frustration with, and a wish to withdraw from, this disheartening and depressing situation. She was rendered helpless to influence either the patient's current state of being or his bleak future. This home visit brought the student face to face with the realities of isolation, alienation, poverty, and progressive physical debilitation of the aging person. The student was also confronted with a person who was terminally ill, who had given up living, and was medically and psychosocially in the process of dying.

The student was coping by focusing on specific nursing tasks: the dressing change, the need for more activity, the pain medication—to name a few. She evaluated this situation, "everything that can be done is being done. The case can be closed." The teaching team and the student group provided a supportive climate in which these painful realities of aging and dying were explored.

Summary and Recommendations

The vast majority of clinical difficulties encountered in the care of the dying and the bereaved cannot be met without considering the concomitant psychosocial aspects, which have been well accepted by nursing professionals and the related educational and service agencies. But the problem of formulating these into effective techniques of nursing education and nursing practice constitutes a challenging task for the nursing teacher and administrator.

Students who enter a nursing major expect to live up to their idealized image of a nurse. Initially, students identify with "their" patients. Students' identification shifts from the patient to the graduate nurse as they become socialized into the nursing role. When they are unable to live up to these expectations in the clinical situations, they experience varying degrees of anxiety and feelings of frustration, anger, helplessness, passivity, a lower level of performance and anger at the school and instructors.

The clinical incidents reported in this paper portray the nature and the scope of students' encounters with death and bereavement. The nursing instructor, the multidisciplinary teaching team, and the group seminar provide crucial support for nursing students as they progress through the junior and senior years of nursing major. Through the individual, team, and group interactive processes, the faculty help students develop greater awareness of the necessity, as well as the competence, to intervene in relation to the psychosocial needs of dying patients and their families.

As the student who had the kind of educational experience described in this paper graduates, she could be expected to provide for psychosocial aspects of nursing care with continued support in the service agency. Quint (1967) recommends that in order to provide for this kind of nursing care the provisions for psychosocial accountability need to be built into the institutional and nursing policies and procedures. Any reorganization of services requires coordinated efforts among nursing, medical, social service, and other professionals. The economics and politics of medical treatment must be considered.

But "here and now," the in-service and the continuing education in nursing service agencies are providing a vital link between the existing knowledge in care of the dying and the bereaved and nursing care. The clinical nurse specialists and nurse educators can contribute further in this area of knowledge through clinical investigation and research. The question is being raised as to who shall be prepared as a specialist in thanatology. Should there be a subspecialty of thanatology within the education of health care professionals? Collaborative efforts among all health care professionals and interested community organizations can contribute toward realization of dying as the final human living experience.

REFERENCES

Benoliel, J. Q. 1972. "Nursing Care for the Terminal Patient: A Psychosocial Approach." In *Psychosocial Aspects of Terminal Care,* eds. B. Schoenberg et al., pp. 145–61. New York: Columbia University Press.

Jackson, E. 1969. "Attitudes Toward Death in Our Culture." In *Death and Bereavement,* ed. A. H. Kutscher, pp. 212–18. Springfield, Illinois: Charles C. Thomas.

Leininger, M. 1970. *Nursing and Anthropology: Two Worlds to Blend.* New York: John Wiley & Sons, Inc.

Peretz, D. 1970. "Reaction to Loss." In *Loss and Grief: Psychological Management in Clinical Practice,* eds. B. Schoenberg et al., pp. 20–35. New York: Columbia University Press.

Poslusny, E. 1968. "Leadership: Preparation for Innovation." In *Teaching Psychosocial Aspects of Patient Care,* eds. B. Schoenberg, H. Pettit, and A. C. Carr, pp. 297–313. New York: Columbia University Press.

Quint, J. 1967. *The Nurse and the Dying Patient.* New York: Macmillan.

Rabin, D. L., and L. H. Rabin. 1972. "Consequences of Death for Physicians, Nurses, and Hospitals." In *The Dying Patient,* eds. O. G. Brim et al. New York: Russell Sage Foundation.

Schoenberg, B. 1971. "The Nurse's Education for Death." In *For the Bereaved,* eds. A. H. Kutscher and L. Kutscher, pp. 77–79. New York: Frederick Fell.

Schoenberg, B., and A. C. Carr. 1972. "Educating the Health Professional in the Psychosocial Care of the Terminally Ill." In *Psychosocial Aspects of Terminal Care,* eds. B. Schoenberg et al., pp. 3–15. New York: Columbia University Press.

Strauss, A. 1969. "Reforms Needed in Providing Terminal Care in Hospitals." *Archives of the Foundation of Thanatology* 1:21.

Part Five

Therapeutic Intervention

Approaches to Intervention with Dying Patients and Their Families: A Case Discussion

Gerald Adler, Morton Beiser, Rosanne Cole, Lee Johnston, and Melvin J. Krant

Since September 1972, we have been on a project designed to investigate the bereavement process in families of cancer patients. This work has been based on several major observations and assumptions.

1. The loss of a loved person can have a long-enduring pathogenic influence. The dislocation in the functioning of families and individuals can be severe, leading to a variety of psychiatric disorders—particularly serious depressions not infrequently requiring psychiatric hospitalization. Families may break down when the loss is expressed through disturbances in interpersonal relationships that further unbalance the family equilibrium. Some of the responses one sees among family members as a result of unsuccessful grieving are alcoholism, drug abuse, antisocial behavior, and lower levels of performance in school and work activities (Maddison and Viola, 1968; Hilgard and Newman, 1963; Parkes, 1964a). The physical health of individuals may also be adversely affected, psychosomatic symptoms and illnesses

This is the first paper in a series being generated by the Bereavement Study Unit under the terms of U.S.P.H.S. Grant NIH–Ca–14121, Interventive Therapy in Dying and Bereavement. Study is based at New England Medical Center Hospitals, Boston, Massachusetts.

may increase, and preexisting medical problems may be exacerbated (Parkes, 1964b).

2. Symptoms related to bereavement may not appear until some time after the death. Modern society is less responsive to the needs of the bereaved. Many of the institutions and practices that in earlier times may have been effective in facilitating mourning and easing the passage through the critical periods surrounding a death are no longer viable. Modern technology and medical practices have made effective mourning more difficult.

3. The course of bereavement not only is affected by the nature of the relationship to the deceased, and the strengths and weaknesses of the survivor and his or her social support system, but also is intimately tied to what transpires in the critical period of dying.

4. Our most important assumption is that the ultimate outcome of bereavement can be favorably influenced by therapeutic intervention with families begun before and continuing after the death of a family member.

We shall test the hypothesis that a short-term intervention program, begun three to four months before death and continued for six months after, can significantly decrease disturbance in families following bereavement.

In addition, we shall observe, record, and understand the patterns of response and interaction of family members during the terminal stage of a cancer patient's illness, and relate these observations to the family's responses to bereavement over time. We are also interested in testing and refining intervention techniques in both the pre- and post-death phases of bereavement.

Our unit of study is the family. In each family studied, one member is dying of cancer. When the research is completed, we shall have examined 160 families in three different hospitals. All families receive an initial research evaluation consisting of a series of clinical research interviews, questionnaires, and brief psychological tests. The families are randomly assigned either to a treatment group, where they are offered intervention by the project social workers, or to a control group. Six months post-death, and every six months after that, both the intervention and control families are reevaluated.

The purpose of this panel-type reporting is not so much to focus on our formal research as to share some of our feelings, insights, and experiences regarding the nature of intervention with bereaved families both before and after death.

Case History

(reported by Rosanne Cole, Project Social Worker)

Mr. P. was a 59-year-old Catholic who worked as a compositor at a printing plant; in addition, for the 11 years before his death, he also had a job at the Post Office. He was a tall, thin, handsome man with a friendly, easy-going manner. He was married, with three children. His wife described him as very helpful, generous, and considerate of others.

Mr. P. was admitted to the hospital in June 1971, for evaluation of a pain in the left buttock. The diagnosis of carcinoma of the prostate with metastasis to the left sacroiliac joint was made. Surgery was performed. During the early course of his illness, he received radiotherapy. Later he was placed on a special chemotherapy protocol.

Mr. P. stated that he assumed he was cured after his operation, since the doctors didn't tell him otherwise. Some months later, when the cancer spread to his hip, Mrs. P. talked with his sisters, and they decided that he should be told. When Mrs. P. told her husband, he wouldn't believe it at first; he said that the doctor would have told him if the cancer had spread.

During the course of Mr. P.'s illness, he was an inpatient eight times. The presenting problem with each admission was acute pain, which cleared up spontaneously upon admission. His final admission was for 72 days. It was during this final admission that my first contact with the family took place.

Mrs. P. is an attractive, neatly dressed 48-year-old woman, who gives the impression of being precise, efficient, and capable. Mrs. P. is the oldest of three daughters and was overprotected and dominated by her parents. They dictated where she would live and the kind of work she would do. After her marriage, Mrs. P. did not work outside her home until shortly after her husband became ill. Two years before he died, she began work in a department store.

Sarah is 22. She is married and had her first baby about one month before her father's death. Whenever I met Sarah at the hospital during her father's last weeks of life, she seemed quite aloof.

Peter is 18 and still lives at home. He had a close relationship with his father. His father gave in to his son on everything the boy wanted. Peter dropped out of high school in the middle of 11th grade, after his father became ill. He began drifting from job to job.

Linda is 11. She is active, outgoing, and talkative. Since her father worked two jobs from the time of her birth, she saw him only on weekends. During the last year of her father's illness, she began doing poorly in school, especially math. She appears to have a close and easy relationship with her mother.

Mr. P.'s long illness had caused many conflicts for the patient and for the family members. Mr. P. was a very accepting, cooperative, and understanding man who was in extreme pain during the second (and last) year of his illness; he wanted his wife to leave her job and devote her time to caring for him. Mrs. P. was not able to play this role; her needs did not coincide with her husband's. She felt a great personal need to keep working in order to maintain her own mental health, and could not face taking care of her ill husband. She explained that she did not have the constitution to give close physical care; she felt this to be the function of doctors and nurses.

Mrs. P. had many concerns about her ability to care adequately for her husband, particularly in an emergency situation, which certain experiences had reinforced. She was extremely frightened by his occasional seizures; and when he had begun to hemorrhage at home, she had experienced difficulty in having him readmitted to the hospital, owing to the fact that different doctors were on duty at night. Mrs. P. watched as her husband hemorrhaged into a wastebasket. In addition to Mrs. P.'s fright, from that time on Linda refused to be left alone in the house with her father.

Mrs. P., discussing her problems with me, stated that she realized what her husband's diagnosis meant, and that she had felt a need to prepare herself by talking things over with him. Since he had always made the decisions, she wanted to talk over her concerns about the children, financial matters, and about her own future. Mr. P. was totally unable to do this.

Mr. P. was depressed over his wife's inability to quit work and care for him. Because of this, Mrs. P. became estranged from his brothers and sisters, as well as from the hospital staff. The sicker her husband became, the more she pulled away from him.

Mr. P.'s extreme pain became a major factor. After he had been admitted to the hospital several times, the medical staff began to feel that the pain was an indication of deeper problems within the family. Since he was unable to express any verbal anger at his wife, he seemed to communicate it in physical ways. Although the pain would be acute while he was at home, once he was in the hospital, with little or no change in medication, the pain became bearable.

Communications between Mr. and Mrs. P. became increasingly strained. Mrs. P. continued to come to the hospital each night, but began spending more time talking with the nurses and other patients. When she did visit with him, she would stand at the foot of his bed—so there was always physical distance. One of the nurses said that she thought they were a strange family. She said that the oldest daughter rarely came to see her father; when she did come she spoke with her mother, not her father.

One day Mr. P. told the doctors a very convincing story to the effect that his wife had divorced him and married a man she had met at work. Because of the obvious lack of communication between Mr. and Mrs. P., the doctors had no difficulty believing the story. The nurses on the floor had heard the story and some were angry at Mrs. P. for "playing around on the side." Mr. P. also told a cousin who visited him that his wife had remarried. The cousin relayed this to his family. His sisters and Mrs. P. told him it wasn't true. Mrs. P. said she had flirted with a man at work but that she would never be unfaithful to her husband. Both the patient and his wife attributed this "hallucination" to the fact that he was on methadone for pain.

Mrs. P. felt pressure from all sides—her husband wanted to go home and have her there to care for him, his family felt that she was deserting him and even wrote her a "nasty" letter about it, and the doctors said that he could be cared for at home. It was difficult to get her to see that I was there to help her and not to judge her or urge her to take her husband home. Before I could accomplish this, I had to examine and work through my own feelings about Mrs. P., as I also tended to feel negatively toward her.

The first time I called, Mrs. P. said she was too busy because of the Christmas season. After the New Year, I called her again, and she hung up on me. At this point Dr. Krant spoke with her and suggested it might be helpful for her to see me. She agreed.

I began seeing Mrs. P. in January, about two months before her husband's death. Since Mrs. P. visited her hospitalized husband in the evenings, I would stop by at that time. I tried to build an alliance with her by accepting her and listening to her ventilate her feelings and tensions. She clearly felt a great need to be in control of her own life. I tried to respect this in our contacts by asking how I could be of help, rather than by trying to be directive.

In the past, Mrs. P. had experienced two serious depressions. The first time was before she had met Mr. P. During World War II, she had been engaged to a pre-med student who was in the paratroopers. One day, he parachuted from a plane, but his chute did not open. He lived for three days. Mrs. P. said: "I was shattered. I guess I became antisocial and didn't want to do anything or go anywhere. A year later I met Jim. He was so good to me and really helped me. He wouldn't let me dwell on it or talk about it. He more than made up for it."

She had also experienced a severe postpartum depression following the birth of her son. She voiced concern about how she would function after Mr. P.'s death. During his long hospitalization, meaningful communication was made more difficult by his reluctance to talk directly to her about his anger at her for not taking care of him at home. This was apparently part of a life long cycle of avoidance of problems, unpleasantness, and conflict. He was unavailable to talk with her about problems she was facing at home, such as their son's dropping out of school and the daughter doing badly in school. Mrs. P. wanted to talk with him about how she would live after his death, and wanted to seek his permission to remarry. If there was any problem to be discussed, she had to force him to listen.

During the last weeks of Mr. P.'s illness, I began talking with her regarding her fears about how she would function without her husband. Mr. P. had always made the decisions and so she was becoming increasingly concerned with the fact that following his death these would become her responsibility, and felt incapable of facing this. Emphasis was placed on the immediate decisions she would have to make. I became someone with whom she could work out her ideas, and hopefully give her some confidence in her own ability—e.g., making arrangements for his funeral. She told me that at one time she felt guilty about not taking her husband home. Now she no longer did, for she knew she couldn't give him the care he needed. She said she thought her husband really understood the difficulties but that his medication made him act and talk strangely.

Toward the end of his illness, Mr. P. became extremely weak and talking was almost impossible. Mrs. P. spoke further of her own conflicts, as she watched her husband linger on.

After his death, I went to the wake. The family was both surprised and pleased that someone from the hospital had come. Mrs. P. introduced me to several people. I told her I'd like to keep in touch with her. She said "Oh yes. I have your phone number, but if I don't call you please call me."

It was easy after Mr. P.'s death to set up regular appointments with Mrs. P. She needed to have someone with whom she could talk over her concerns, and took advantage of our meetings to do this in a constructive manner.

A continuing area of concern was decision making. Mrs. P. needed to feel more separate from Mr. P. and gain confidence in her own ability. At the same time, she needed help to understand that it was normal to think about how he would have done something. For example, she told me about how during a discussion with her son regarding his buying a car, the towel on the rack near the oven went up in flames. She said that when her husband was about ten years old, he had almost burned the house down. He was chastised and never forgot it. She regarded the towel incident as a warning from her husband not to help Peter buy a car.

She had to be assured several times that thinking she heard Mr. P. coming in, feeling his presence, crying at night, and not being able to concentrate on the newspapers or television were normal.

Mrs. P.'s second area of concern was her relationship with her son. She felt very strongly that she had the total responsibility for him. She was able to look at how her concern with his living his life exactly the way she wanted might drive him away from her. She was able to try to give him some leeway to make some of his own decisions. He wasn't able to hold down a steady job, but he did decide to return to night school.

Her third area of concern is for herself and her relationship with men. I tried to help her live with her loneliness and pointed out that loneliness is hard, but may not be the worse thing possible, especially if in desperation she may get involved in a relationship that will be more painful than her present loneliness.

She finds herself being very uncomfortable with men. She feels that other women look on her differently now—more or less as competition—and when she is with men she can't think of anything to talk about. She has a general feeling that people treat you differently when you are eligible. For example, she told me that a man came to her door and wanted to put vinyl on the exterior of her house. She agreed. His reply was "you'll be seeing a lot of me from now on." She wondered what he meant by that and if he would have made the same remark if her husband was living. She cited several other examples of how she felt men were more or less making advances. I tried to help her see her need for companionship. She was afraid and not quite capable of moving into social situations. We talked about how she could come in contact with more people.

Six months after the death, she was able to recognize her vulnerabilities in this area to some extent and was trying to look at constructive ways of coping with this need, as she began to feel more ready to move out a bit. Clearly, the role shift from married woman to widow was most traumatic on the social level. She commented that, in many ways, she felt somewhat like a teenager just beginning to date. Shortly before I stopped seeing her she told me of a dream she had about her husband. She said they were at a party and Jim was introducing her around as he always had when all of a sudden he disappeared and she woke up. She felt he was saying he wanted her to get out and meet people.

In many ways Mrs. P. has so far made a much better adjustment than I would have predicted before Mr. P.'s death (because of her history of depression, and her conflict about taking care of her husband). Apparently Mrs. P. has been able to defend herself against any guilt feelings by blaming her husband's behavior on the medication and telling herself that he really understood her position. Also, her work was a source of strength, and she was able to plan to get training for a better job.

She was also able to talk with me in a constructive way about her son and her feelings toward men. She seemed to feel that during the first six months she was very preoccupied with gaining confidence in her decision-making ability, and now that she feels at ease in that area, she will have to face and cope with her loneliness, particularly on a social level.

Diagnostic Assessment of the Family Facing Bereavement

(reported by Gerald Adler, M.D., Project Investigator)
The careful diagnostic assessment of the family facing a loss is crucial for

optimal work with them before and after the bereavement. We feel that this evaluation can offer data to help predict difficulties for the family and its individual members and to formulate an intervention plan that can assist family members as well as the personnel in a hospital, outpatient, or home setting.

The detailed story of the family members' lives and their interaction during the assessment can provide the cornerstone of the evaluation. The Philips family illustrates how much a worker can learn about a family within a short time. Mrs. P.'s past history revealed the loss of a fiancé in a parachuting accident before she met Mr. P. She withdrew after her fiancé's death and seemed to "recover" when she met her husband. As she described it, Mr. P. not only did not permit her to think about her fiancé but also became a substitute for him. In addition we learned that Mrs. P. had a serious depression after the birth of her son. We also learned that, throughout her life, Mrs. P.'s parents overprotected her. She was the first of three daughters, and Mr. P. seemed to have assumed a parental role in their marriage.

Our assessment of Mrs. P.'s past history led us to the conclusion that she had a significant vulnerability to loss. At the time her fiancé died, she could not grieve adequately, and tended to withdraw and avoid turning to a substitute to fill the void in her life. Her postpartum depression after the birth of her son could have been a recrudescence of this earlier loss of a male figure. In addition, Mrs. P.'s life history revealed a dependent relationship with her parents, and evidence that she had never worked out a complete separation from them and had expected her husband to fulfill the parental role.

Our concerns centered around the worsening relationship between Mr. and Mrs. P. As Mr. P.'s death approached, Mrs. P. retreated to her avoidance defenses of distancing herself and working hard in order to stay in control. In spite of the serious strain in their relationship, we had evidence that much of their marriage had been happy, with many fond memories. We also had the important data of Mrs. P.'s ultimate ability to form a useful positive relationship with our social worker. This observation was in contrast to patients with poor prognosis described by Maddison who experienced no source of support regardless of the help offered (Maddison and Walker, 1967). Mrs. P.'s ability to work, though partially a defense, was also a source of strength, and implied a capacity to remain in control when under stress, and to get relief and a sense of self-esteem through constructive activity. Yet Mrs. P.'s inability to say good-bye to her husband appropriately concerned our team. Mr. P.'s problems with pain at home, and his conviction that his wife had remarried, represented in part the breakdown of their relationship.

Mr. P.'s illness had a significant impact on his children. Peter's decision to leave high school and Linda's poor school grades appear to be related to the family's knowledge that Mr. P. had cancer. In addition, Linda became afraid to be alone with her father (paralleling her mother's feelings) after his serious hemorrhage at home. The family's inability to discuss Mr. P.'s inability to continue as the decision-maker resulted in a serious increase in tension and conflict in their home.

The evaluator's evolving relationship with the family is also an important diagnostic tool. Recent tentative data lead us to believe that the family that rejects an evaluation may be particularly vulnerable to the loss. Mrs. P.'s initial rejection of all contacts with us seemed consistent with her avoidance defenses. The intervention of a staff physician appears to have reestablished a sense of strong parental control for her and allowed her to cooperate in the study. Her relationship with the worker then evolved in a fashion that permitted Mrs. P. to share her grief and gradually begin to talk over realistic plans for her future and the problems she and her children would face. This ability to make use of the worker led to our sense of greater optimism about the outcome than we had anticipated earlier.

The diagnostic assessment can help us to formulate the answers to such intervention questions as (1) Who are the most vulnerable family members; how can we help them? (2) How much grief can the family bear; how can we best support their capacity to bear grief? (3) How can we facilitate realistic family planning? (4) How can we help the family members communicate better and be more supportive? (5) How can we support other personnel to work with the family?

Though we feel that a careful diagnostic assessment of the family is important in planning intervention and predicting outcome, we recognize that grief is not resolved in months or even a year or two. Our work is still in an early stage compared with the many years required to study the natural history of a death within a family and the impact of short-term intervention on that natural history.

Approaches to Intervention

(reported by Morton Beiser, M.D., Project Investigator)

Interest in intervention around the time of a death and bereavement is increasing. It has seemed to us, however, that descriptions of the goals and techniques of such intervention have not been stated clearly enough in the literature. I shall place my emphasis on the goals of intervention and the techniques for implementing them, with the P. family.

This was a family in need of help. While not all bereaved families are needy, and while there is great variability among those who are, some themes are common enough that they may in time be formulated as general principles of intervention. While the following are specific goals derived from work with this family, we feel some at least can be generalized.

1. *Timing and Intervention:* Initial contact with families occurs at least three months before the anticipated death. Even though most of the literature on bereavement focuses on the post-death period, we have come to believe that the establishment of a therapeutic alliance earlier, in cases such as this where death can be anticipated, has certain advantages.

Many families and patients must learn how to perceive the role of the intervention worker and to begin to understand how this relationship may be helpful to and supportive of them. Once established, the relationship carries over into the bereavement period, when the needs and concerns of survivors sometimes shift quite dramatically. In this case, the intervention worker served as buffer against the tremendous hostility displayed toward Mrs. P. by practically everyone. Following her husband's death, when instead of being the center of a great deal of hostile attention she found herself faced with practically no attention at all, the consistent presence of the social worker was, according to Mrs. P., most helpful.

Mrs. P. was also comforted by the fact that the worker had known her husband before his death. For Mrs. P., as well as many other people in our series, this added an important dimension to the therapeutic work during the bereavement period.

2. *Support as Intervention:* Another factor of undoubted importance is the attitude conveyed by the worker. While everyone else was highly critical of Mrs. P.'s behavior, the social worker, without judging her, helped her to

look at the reasons for her decisions and to place them in perspective.

Mrs. P.'s decision to look for full-time employment was doubtless a defensive maneuver in part. Taking a long-range point of view, one might also say that it was a productive defense and helped her to adapt as successfully as she seems to have done during the bereavement period.

One aspect of this situation was not successfully dealt with, despite our best attempts. We feel it is important that people be able to separate their own feelings and needs from those of others who are also involved in this critical transition period. While Mrs. P. was able to acknowledge her own need to defend herself against feelings of abandonment by trying to create a new life for herself before her husband's death, she was unable to deal with his feelings of guilt.

3. *Role Rehearsal:* Death often means a drastic shifting of roles; such a change may be catastrophic or it may present new opportunities for personal growth and satisfaction. For Mrs. P., the changes involved assuming new responsibilities for decision-making.

Evidence is accumulating that when there is opportunity for rehearsal before the assumption of new roles, the chances for positive outcome may be increased. Such role rehearsal occurs both in action and in fantasy, and is actively encouraged.

Sometimes this may be accomplished by encouraging survivors to take on the elements of a new role even before the dying person has vacated the role. Mr. P., however, blocked his wife's hesitant attempts to assume a new decision-making stance while he was still alive.

After her husband's death, it became apparent that Mrs. P. had incorporated some elements of her husband's role as head of the family, but she needed help in playing it comfortably. When her son badgered her about giving him money to buy a car, she was reluctant but felt powerless to say no. When the towel hanging near the stove caught fire, Mrs. P. interpreted this as a direct sign from her husband that she not accede, and that ended the matter. While it would be presumptuous indeed to challenge such a belief, it was possible to help her look at the entire process as one in which her own desire had been transferred into a concrete action. She felt the need for a sign from her husband to finally catalyze her action, but there was also evidence that she was gaining confidence in her ability to play the role of family head.

4. *Understanding Loneliness:* The bereavement period is a lonely time, and widows are often very vulnerable during it. While the visit of the vinyl siding salesman may have been pure happenstance, we have been struck by the fact that salesmen of various kinds do visit recently bereaved widows in numbers that exceed chance. One is forced to conclude that our society, as so many others, has its predators.

One aspect of our work with Mrs. P. was to help her discuss loneliness and its pain. In so doing, we also helped her to test reality by simply asking her whether "you'll be seeing a lot of me from now on" was a romantic promise or something she might be prone to interpret as such because of her need for comfort and companionship.

From a clinical standpoint, the intervention with the P. family is neither the most nor the least successful in our series. In some cases, for example, it is possible to involve many more people in various family and community systems. In this case, attention was centered on one isolated, vulnerable, abused, and misunderstood woman who required a great deal of attention, but whose progress has been a source of gratification for our entire intervention team.

REFERENCES

Hilgard, J. R., and M. F. Newman. 1963. "Parental Loss by Death in Childhood as an Etiologic Factor Among Schizophrenic and Alcoholic Patients." *Journal of Neurological and Mental Disorders* 137:14–28.

Maddison, D., and A. Viola. 1968. "The Health of Widows in the Year Following Bereavement." *Journal of Psychosomatic Research* 12:297–306.

Maddison, D., and W. L. Walker, 1967. "Factors Affecting the Outcome of Conjugal Bereavement." *British Journal of Psychiatry* 113:157 ff.

Parkes, C. M. 1964a. "Recent Bereavement as a Cause of Mental Illness." *British Journal of Psychiatry* 110:198–204.

—— 1964b. The Effects of Bereavement on Physical and Mental Health—A Study of the Medical Records of Widows." *British Medical Journal* 2:274–79.

Coping and Vulnerability Among the Aged Bereaved

Delia Battin, Arthur M. Arkin, Irwin Gerber, and Alfred Wiener

The literature to date has given evidence through retrospective studies that the first year of bereavement can bring about psychological, social, and physical problems (Maddison, 1968; Engel, 1961). No controlled prospective longitudinal study was available to verify these data. To fill the gap, we designed such a study. We followed for a minimum of three years a group of individuals, members of the Montefiore Medical Group, who had lost a close relative from either cancer or cardiovascular disease; part of this group, 58 individuals randomly assigned, was offered psychotherapeutic help through a period of six months after the loss, while the others received no treatment. Another group of individuals, who had experienced no loss for three years before the project began, was matched to the two bereaved groups by age, sex and number, and age of offspring; it was studied through the same time period.

This project was geared to investigating the process and effects of bereavement, the effect of brief therapeutic intervention on the bereaved, and the possibility of discovering a vulnerable group among the bereaved who would require therapeutic intervention to prevent future morbidity and maladjustment.

We shall examine observed coping mechanisms among the 58 treated bereaved, how these patterns relate to vulnerability to future morbidity and maladjustment, and what treatment techniques appear to be useful.

Treatment Plan

In view of the general expectation that unsolicited bereavement counseling would be viewed as a stigma (Goffman, 1961; Szasz, 1961; Scheff 1966), or as an invasion of privacy, the total study was conducted with the close cooperation of the family physician whenever possible; the key family members [1] received from the physician a condolence letter, followed by a phonecall in which he would inquire as to their well-being and offer the assistance of a professional. Regardless of whether the patient would accept or refuse this offer, the psychiatric social worker called the family and actively tried to convince the key family member to accept this service. The acceptance rate as compared to other studies (Silverman, 1971, 60.5%) has been a surprisingly high 94 percent. The key family members were seen weekly at home or in the office, individually or with all the family members who were part of the same household. Some accepted weekly telephone contacts with occasional office or home sessions. The intervention was carried out under psychiatric supervision and was not to extend beyond six months. The original plan of treatment was as follows:

1. Permitting and guiding the patient to put into words and express the affects involved in: the pain, sorrow, and finality of bereavement; a review of the relationship to the deceased; feelings of love, guilt, and hostility toward the deceased.

2. Helping the patient to acknowledge the existence of and understand alterations in his emotional reactions.

3. Helping the patient find an acceptable formulation of his future relationship to the psychic representation of the deceased.

4. Acting as a "primer and/or programmer" for some of the patient's activities and organizing among available and suitable friends or relatives a flexible, modest scheme for the same purpose.

5. Helping the patient deal with reality situations—care of children, legal problems, and the like.

6. Mediating referrals to the family physician for prescriptions of psychic

---

[1] The key family member is the surviving figure who is the chief authority and who assumes the major responsibility and leadership for keeping the family functioning as a unit.

energizers, tranquilizers, or hypnotics, if necessary, for excessive depression, anxiety, or insomnia.

7. Offering assistance in making future plans.

8. As a rule, we would try to avoid interpretation of key defenses and highly charged, warded-off, unconscious trends; and excessive solicitude and overprotection of the patient.

The basic attitude of the therapist, from which appropriate departures could be made, was to be compassionate but temperate concern, avoiding sentimentality and overidentification. The therapist would recognize the full extent of the emotional loss, but gently convey to the patient—after subsidence of the acute, initial, intense phase of grief—that it was the normal, expected course that he or she would recover and did indeed possess the required inner strength for this. This treatment plan was followed with variations to fit individual needs.

Coping Behavior Mechanisms

By coping behavior mechanisms we mean those psychological capabilities an individual uses to cope with life situations at a time of stress. From our clinical observations we developed a descriptive classification based on coping behavior mechanisms. We avoided APA and personality classification schemes because they did not seem usefully to apply to our material. (For instance, we are fully aware that a "manic-depressive" patient and one with a "character disorder" are presented in the section pertaining to the "dependent type.")

A combination of coping behavior characteristics that we include in different categories may be present in the same individual. The prevalence of specific characteristics determines which category applies to which individual. The six categories we devised and their distribution are as follows:

Category	Percent
Complainer	15.5
Manipulator	5.2
Pseudo-independent	12.0
Dependent	19.0
Independent constructive	29.3
Accepting-resigned	19.0

COMPLAINER

Characteristics.
1. Complaining about past and present situations: "life has been rotten."
2. Feeling victimized; fate is against him/her.
3. Expressing superficial wishes to die as a plea for attention: "life is not worth living."
4. Expressing feelings of anger and frustration to seek sympathy.
5. Expertise in guilt provocation.
6. Whining voice.
7. Use of frequent somatic complaints.

In treatment, it seemed helpful to allow complainers to express all their feelings of helplessness, hopelessness, anger, and frustration, while reviewing their life histories, with emphasis on past losses. Thereafter, the focus would be on how such long-suffering people deserve to find some gratification in life.

Guilt feelings were superficially touched on; the therapist barely recognized that an individual has all kinds of regrets when a relative dies and accepted whatever material this would evoke, as limited as that might be; at the same time, he gave particular support to the anger the person might express around the deceased (e.g., "faulty" behavior during the marriage or his/her "gall" for dying, i.e., abandoning the spouse). Almost no attempt was made to convince complainers that they might alienate people by their actions, or make them feel guilty for not satisfying their demands: the therapist would become another "egotistic" person, who did not care about his patients. A great deal of work had to be geared to complainers' families— allowing anyone around to express the anger and frustration that such a relative evoked, interpreting to them the real emotional suffering the patients did experience and eliciting the help of the family members in seeking inner and environmental resources for this relative. It also seemed helpful for the therapist to be aware of the feelings of annoyance and irritation he might experience in treating complainers, so as to avoid countertransference problems.

Complainers seemed to adapt relatively well: they might never admit to feeling better, but changes in appearance and description of social activity, sleeping, and eating habits could be clearly noted. It was not difficult to extract life patterns showing improvement (e.g., in the course of a conversation such patients might mention waking up at 8:30 A.M. and at the same time insist that they spend sleepless nights). Their vulnerability seemed to depend on the availability of resources in the environment (e.g., people who could put up with the complaining).

A case in point is that of Mrs. A. She perceived herself as a victim of fate in that she had a miserable childhood. The "ugly duckling" of the family, she had lost her father by age 10, had gone to work by age 14, had been married to a man who had never earned a good living and who liked to play the horses, and had now been left all alone by "everyone." Mrs. A. still had a very old mother in a nursing home, whom she resented having to visit because Mrs. A. was a complainer interested only in herself. Her three sisters also were completely self-involved. I (D.B.) happened to be there one day when a niece of hers called. It became apparent that this niece had invited her to her home in New Jersey on weekends and had called often.

Having received permission to contact the niece, I was able to support the young woman in her attempts to be close to her aunt, and I led her to encourage Mrs. A. to baby-sit for her young children. Of course Mrs. A. continued to complain about being "used" even as a baby-sitter. I then encouraged her niece to ignore the complaints and simply build on positive thinking and behavior. For example, since Mrs. A. was a good baby-sitter, maybe she could baby-sit for other people in her building and get paid for doing it. Moreover, intervention was geared to relieving the niece's guilt feelings about her occasional impatience and outbursts of anger toward her aunt.

A dramatic incident points up the importance of working with relatives. Mrs. A. once left me a message that she was going to kill herself by opening the gas range. I phoned her niece and told her to call up her aunt and make believe she knew nothing of this note; at the same time, I explained that her message to me was just a plea for attention. The niece did call Mrs. A., and a half-hour later I phoned Mrs. A. She told me how her niece had called her just when she was so desperate, whereas I had waited so long to phone her back (guilt-provoking). I agreed with Mrs. A. that her niece cared a lot about her and wanted to have her around for a long time. By the end of six months, Mrs. A. looked rather peppy and well-dressed in comparison to the beginning; she was on a diet, had two baby-sitting jobs . . . and was still complaining.

MANIPULATOR

Characteristics. Manipulation of interaction and situations:

1. Excessive praise of therapist and other people for their help, with concomitant inability to describe in what way he/she is being helped.
2. Veiled passing criticism of people ("the doctor was so marvelous, I do understand the fact that he could not always be available to talk to me at crucial times").
3. Obvious attempts to get involved in friends' and relatives' plans by offering help with such plans.
4. Expression of feelings of helplessness combined with evidence of resourcefulness.
5. Absence of whining.
6. Guilt provocation and excessive demands at work, although less tangibly than in the case of the complainer.

In working with manipulators—keeping in mind the six-month treatment limitation—it seemed helpful to encourage them to verbalize how much they were missing the deceased, their right to feelings of anger they might be experiencing about having to suffer, as well as their anger toward doctors, God, and other people who in their opinion had not been doing enough. In other words, the therapist had to help them grieve, but could at the same time gently allude to the mixed feelings the patient experienced toward relatives, friends, and the therapist by verbalizing the experience for them. When relatives and friends reacted with open or veiled hostility to their manipulative attempts, it seemed possible to help them become aware that they were contributing to these attitudes. It is not uncommon to get a shy, giggly reaction, like that of a kid who has been found out. Again, it helped the therapist to be aware of the anger he/she might experience at being "used" by this type of individual so as to avoid countertransference problems.

The adaptation and the vulnerability are very much like the complainer's. Mr. B., a 62-year-old professional whose wife had died of a heart attack began treatment by expressing gratitude galore. He talked at great length about his wonderful wife, whose occasional nagging was constructive and whose bequeathing her pension and jewelry to their children was right, except for the fact that the son was refusing to share his bequest with the father because of his own needs. It seemed natural for the therapist to tell this man that he obviously felt hurt by his dead wife as well as by his children and that it seemed difficult for him to openly express the rage any man would feel in his place. Yes, his wife had been a bitch, and her children took after her. Additional exploration also brought to the fore overwhelming guilt toward the deceased. The patient's wife had suffered the heart attack while they were having intercourse; he felt he had killed her. Before then he had done many other things to "kill her," such as having affairs with other women, which she certainly knew of even though he had manipulated things so as to keep them from her.

In discussing these feelings of guilt and anger mixed with genuine affection toward the deceased, we also came to discuss in some detail Mr. B.'s use of manipulative tactics in dealing with people (such as his wife and the therapist). He talked about his childhood with a domineering mother and a passive father; how he discovered that he had to "talk around," i.e. charm, his mother to obtain things; how he had convinced his wife to marry him in secret without her parents' consent and so on.

Mr. B. even felt he had charmed the therapist into giving him good treatment. Discussion of this, however, did lead him to recognize that the therapist had seen through his "technique" and had sent him messages that he could continue treatment without using it. Significantly, at the end of the six months, Mr. B. asked to continue treatment with the same therapist on a private basis. Indeed, Mr. B. had admitted that he had been advised to seek help before; he had done so, but had been unable to continue on a regular basis.

PSEUDO-INDEPENDENT

Characteristics.
1. Vehement refusal of help (denial of the need for help).
2. Preoccupation with showing how "strong" one is.
3. Isolation of affect when talking about the deceased, even one or two months after the loss.
4. Emphasis on how well one is functioning in a particular area (e.g., work).

5. Extreme suspiciousness (projection).
6. Inability to express obsessive thoughts of guilt (conscious suppression).
7. Use of above pseudo-independent patterns in "normal" daily living and to an extreme in stress situations.

In treating pseudo-independents, the therapist found it mandatory to search for someone close in the environment. That person was contacted and told how vulnerable to future morbidity and maladjustment the relative or friend might be and how important professional help was at this point. Pseudo-independents might not be able to share obsessive thoughts of guilt because they might consider them too horrible to share and at times overwhelming. As time went on, the repressive mechanisms would fail and by the time the first anniversary of the death came around, such a patient might experience what is commonly called a "breakdown"; even in the area where he/she was efficient (work), the patient's concentration might fail, there might be explosions of anxiety resulting in sleeplessness, lack of appetite, feeling that the deceased was present in the room and so on.

Ideally one would elicit the cooperation of a close friend or relative and explain that grieving ought to be encouraged, and the earlier the better. One could even go into the details of the grieving process, universalizing in particular the feeling of danger one experiences in connection with feelings of guilt and hurt common to all people at a time of bereavement, and possible fears of insanity. Actually the therapist would not call guilt by this name; rather he/she would talk about the regrets that one always experiences after a person has died. People can be terribly hard on themselves and not allow for human frailty.

The therapist might not succeed in getting the pseudo-independent into treatment for some time, perhaps because the individual so desperately needs the defenses he/she is using that any interference might also result in a breakdown. This type of person might be able to use treatment one year or even two years later.

Countertransference problems might arise for the therapist in reaction to what could be interpreted as rejection of the therapist by the patient; these would require particular attention. Two case reports follow, one where we succeeded in engaging the individual in treatment, and one where the survivor continued to "resist" for one year.

Mrs. C. "resisted," leaving no opening whatsoever. She would simply hang up the phone. She had stated that she did not want to think about her horrible experience. One year later, however, she requested help. She could no longer work. She could not concentrate, kept making mistakes in her work, and was extremely fearful of losing her job. At 60, she felt she could hardly hope to find another one. She was desperate. She could neither sleep nor eat and had lost a lot of weight.

She started treatment, and began to talk about her fears for her own life. She had been operated on for cancer of the uterus two years before. She had been constantly preoccupied by the possibility that she might experience a recurrence of the disease and she would then have to face this horror all alone.

Of course, it did not help her, she would say, to think back to the horror of her husband's disease and death: his living with a respirator by his bedside, her anxiety when his phone call was a little late, her always coming home wondering if he were still alive.

In a way she had had no time to think of her own illness. During the first year following her husband's death, she could only attempt to banish all thoughts of horror. She would go to work, come home, and busy herself frantically with household chores. At the time of the unveiling, she discovered that she no longer had any control over her feelings and actions. It took over a year to help this woman "get a hold of herself" (as she liked to call her state of relative well-being) by retracing the feelings she had been unable to face in connection with her own illness, previous losses (her mother and sister had died of cancer), and husband's illness and death.

The so-called success concerns a widow, Mrs. D., who had also initially refused treatment, but who had less difficulty accepting telephone contact and then weekly sessions.

Everyone thought that Mrs. D. was a "strong," cheerful woman. She had been very efficient as a homemaker, wife, and counselor to her husband and parents. When I first spoke with her, she told me that she was a strong person and that she needed no service of any sort. She considered the fact that she did not need to cry "strong"; and she had a "good head" as evidenced by her efficiency in settling her business affairs. I accepted her statements without comment, but ended the conversation by saying I would call her the following week. When I did so, we had a similar conversation, except for the fact that I began talking about how human it is to avoid facing pain when one is badly hurt and how it seems easier to chase away those thoughts involving pain. She asked me how other patients of mine reacted. I answered that it was a very individual experience. However, most people expressed feelings of anger and pain after a while, since they needed to do so. Mrs. D. began to talk about how angry she felt toward her daughter, who was going on with her plans to get married and leave the city. The more she talked about her daughter, the more obvious it became that this only daughter had been the apple of Mr. D.'s eye. Competitive feelings between mother and daughter had been rampant; at the same time, the mother perceived her daughter's marriage and departure as an additional loss.

The next time we spoke, Mrs. D. was rather distant and cold. When I mentioned this to her, she said she felt that my phone calls were an imposition. When I observed that many people feel like running away when they think they have exposed themselves too much to a stranger, she was obviously moved but still maintained she was strong and too busy to spend time on the phone. This time I told her I was concerned about her and wanted us to meet so that she could find out for herself that she could trust me. She rather hesitantly denied the need for this. I asked her when was her next appointment with her physician. When she told me, I said that I would introduce myself at that time. She did not object. I spoke with her physician, who was also concerned because Mrs. D. was complaining about all kinds of pains for which there was no medical basis. We finally met in the physician's presence, and both the doctor and I encouraged Mrs. D. to come to my office after the medical check-up.

She followed through. I mentioned the mixture of curiosity and anger she probably felt about the meeting. She confirmed this. My attempts to explore her anger led her to explain that she was called "Sunshine" because she never expressed any overt anger to anyone. She could not tell me what she did with those feelings. I offered her a plan. She could try to explore the angry feelings she experienced toward me. A Pandora's box was indeed opened. This woman was suicidal; she had planned all the details of her suicide. There was an outpouring of feelings of anger and guilt involving the deceased and the rest of her family. She allowed herself to begin the process of grieving. Many of her problems are still there (e.g., overattachment to her father), but her functioning is adequate. She is working as a fund-raiser, has a reasonably full social life, and her relationship with her daughter has improved.

DEPENDENT

Characteristics.

1. Almost complete lack of resourcefulness if people are not available to think things through with him/her.
2. Lack of capacity to do things on his/her own.
3. Excessive fear of loneliness.
4. Suspiciousness.

Dependent people are not difficult to reach; indeed, they do not want to leave treatment. Since time was limited and crisis intervention seemed advisable, the following steps were taken. If there was a person in the environment capable of enjoying or withstanding such a patient's dependence, treatment was geared to helping the patient grieve and at the same time eliciting the "dependable" person's cooperation. If such a person was not available, there was trouble at the door—

Mrs. E., who had lost her husband from a heart attack, responded eagerly to the idea of treatment. Her life history was one of continuous dependence, first on her parents and then on her husband. She had experienced three manic-depressive episodes in 20 years. She had been helped through various types of treatment, among them sleep therapy and electroshock. All surviving relatives avoided contact with her. Supportive psychotherapy relieved her temporarily, but Mrs. E.'s depression still seemed severe. After consultation, it was decided to submit Mrs. E. to electroshock. After receiving a great deal of support in this direction, Mrs. E. did undergo electroshock, which was effective; she experienced a mood lift and was extremely grateful for the treatment. Life seemed wonderful even without her husband, who after all had made her suffer a lot.

Mrs. F. is another example. Her husband had died of a heart attack. According to the history I was given by the family physician, Mr. F. had been the decision-maker in the family. I discovered that her older son was currently very involved with her. I decided to contact him and explain the nature of the service we were providing. At first he was very suspicious, but then he responded to the idea of coming to see me with his mother. Of course, I also called Mrs. F. to make the appointment. At the first interview, the son asked me to see him first, alone. He had many questions to ask about grief, talked about his guilt feelings in connection with his father's death, and finally told me that Mrs. F. had cancer but did not know it.

He was frightened at the idea of also losing his mother. Most important from the point of view of Mrs. F.'s treatment was the fact that he was prepared to do anything for his mother's welfare. Throughout the period of treatment with Mrs. F., once a week, I kept in touch with her older son and involved her younger one as well. The goal was to help all the family members to grieve, while encouraging the sons to share the emotional and material support Mrs. F. needed. Mrs. F. felt much better by the end of the six months. She was going regularly to a beach club, visiting her sons on weekends, and other family and friends during the week. No attempt was made to change the sons' decision to keep the knowledge of her disease from their mother.

Another case was that of Mr. G., who was an alcoholic. After he lost his wife, it was difficult to find Mr. G. sober. One daughter and one aunt tried to be of help, but could not possibly spend 24 hours a day with him. The most important accomplishment in treatment consisted in relieving some of his guilt feelings toward his wife and in helping him to see a physician. Unfortunately, he saw the physician once and never went back; he argued that he preferred alcohol to tranquilizers. All efforts to direct him to organizations such as Alcoholics Anonymous also failed at that point. He categorically refused to continue treatment beyond the six months. Mr. G. developed cirrhosis of the liver, and the prognosis was guarded. However, at followup time, Mr. G. had been off alcohol for three months and had been marginally involved with Alcoholics Anonymous.

INDEPENDENT-CONSTRUCTIVE

Characteristics.
  1. Ability to express feelings freely.
  2. Gradual, steady recovery in psychosocial functioning in most areas through the six months of treatment, after the initial period of shock.

These were people who could grieve easily. They could talk about their deceased spouse, review their life together, and cry. Their healthy makeup became increasingly obvious through the six months of treatment. The depressed mood lifted steadily and the level of activity and involvement increased without special support from the environment. They still went through waves of intense sorrow mixed with denial about the loss, but the degree and intensity wore off steadily. Their vulnerability to future morbidity and maladjustment would be expected to be minimal.

Let us consider the case of Mrs. H. Her husband died of a heart attack. According to her and others, they had been a devoted couple, although naturally not free from the usual strife and disappointments. She was very depressed when I first saw her and she had suicidal thoughts. Her only son lived far away. In treatment, she was very open and outspoken about her feelings of loss, despair, guilt, and anger. She spoke openly about her powerful illusions of hearing or seeing her husband and her lowered self-esteem resulting from being widowed. Slowly but surely, Mrs. H.'s depression began to lift. She became involved again with a bridge group and started to organize theater trips. By the end of the six months she was still bereaved, but was not insensitive to the attentions of a widower, feelings I encouraged as being natural and human.

ACCEPTING-RESIGNED

Characteristics.

1. Ability to express feelings freely.
2. Gradual, steady recovery of psychosocial functioning in most areas through the six months of treatment after the initial period of shock.
3. Particular acceptance of suffering as part of life and fate.

The accepting-resigned were viewed as a variation of the independent-constructive type, their vulnerability to future morbidity and maladjustment also being minimal.

Mrs. I., for instance, was a 68-year-old Italian woman from a village in Tuscany. She had lost her husband from cancer after years of going through operations with him and nursing him. When he died, Mrs. I. admitted that she had had feelings of relief mixed with feelings of sorrow and despair at being left alone. In the past he had done the cooking and the shopping, and taken care of their little garden outside their first-floor apartment. She had to take over these functions when he became sick. She gave the impression that nothing weighed heavily on her. She had already been through taking care of her aged mother, who had died of cancer nine months before her father died of a heart attack in Tuscany. This had happened about seven years before the loss of her husband. She had an only daughter, who was single and in her late forties. This worried her, but she was resigned to it. This woman was very much in touch with her feelings and accepted the painful situations that gave rise to them. Explorations using the technique of learning how she "did it" always brought to the fore the fact that she knew that life, not death, brought hell, purgatory, and paradise; so she enjoyed what she could and suffered through the pain that life held in store for her, since she was powerless to change the situation.

Discussion

The importance of recognizing vulnerable individuals, what makes them vulnerable, and the necessity of providing professional help for them are supported by preliminary research findings in our study (e.g., the nontreated bereaved seem to show a higher rate of morbidity and maladjustment than the treated bereaved). Vulnerability being defined in terms of potential physical, social, or psychological malfunctioning, our clinical observations suggest that four of the above categories constitute vulnerable groups, depending on the environmental circumstances and psychic resources as correlated with the emotional state of the individual.

As can be seen from our descriptions, the complainers' and manipulators' vulnerability can be limited: they can usually admit to their dependency and they do have inner resources to tap (even though these are at times highly neurotic), which they can also use to mobilize people around them. With treatment, the grieving process can be facilitated and the use of inner and outer resources can be skillfully encouraged.

The dependent person can function adequately if there are one or more "dependable" persons in the immediate environment or in a professional long-term service-oriented agency.

The pseudo-independents seem to be the most prone to "vulnerability" and the most difficult to treat. The remainder of this paper will be devoted to a more detailed discussion of their problems. Pseudo-independents usually have strong dependency needs, intense narcissism, and low self-esteem; they are nevertheless unable to admit their dependency needs, which they deny by mobilizing all available defense mechanisms. Exposing these needs in a nonsensitive manner, without supporting their narcissism, could be devastating. They require highly skilled handling by a professional.

The dynamic and genetic factors involved vary considerably. The life history often points to pseudo-independent patterns of behavior as being almost identical to those observable in meaningful parental figures, which suggests identification with them. In other instances, the parent figures were perceived as being depriving, demanding, or authoritative. Early experience of object loss has also been observed in some cases. In any case efforts to overcome such strain and shock trauma lead to the use of pseudo-independent attitudes as coping devices (Jacobson, 1947). Such individuals select mates most likely to gratify their narcissistic needs.

Moreover, as Piaget, Nagy and others indicate, the above pathogenetic mechanisms seem to originate at the stage when children believe that all events, object losses included, are "willed." It follows that bereaved individuals often feel responsible for the loss—feeling enhanced by the inevitable ambivalence in the prior relationship with the deceased. Such factors partly account for the magnitude of the guilt feelings these patients experience. In addition, as Freud states, an overvaluation of the lost object takes place among most bereaved individuals, but it occurs to an extreme degree for the pseudo-independents; it does so, as Bak (1973) mentions, "to counteract or countercathect aggression"—aggression that also occurs because the survivor feels abandoned by the love object and therefore deprived of narcissistic supply, but does not find it acceptable to recognize such negative feelings toward the lost object. Finally, pseudo-independent patients do not usually have an opportunity to replace the object (one of the "natural" resolutions in the object-loss syndrome). At this advanced age, "single" women outnumber "single" men: women tend to marry older men and men die at a younger age. But even if the opportunity for a new relationship arises, both men and women in this category lack the emotional strength to build it. They are consciously or unconsciously afraid to be placed in a position in which they have to meet another person's needs—emotional or physical; they can only take an object choice that will gratify their narcissistic needs.

Individuals in the environment therefore remain vitally important for providing narcissistic supply to these patients.

Therapeutic attention can be particularly beneficial in these cases. The most efficacious techniques seem to be the following: (1) helping the patients to recognize and accept their dependency needs as natural, without loss of face; (2) encouraging fuller expression of the affect involved in grief; (3) facilitating expression of guilt and all other feelings related to grieving.

In summary, 58 treated bereaved individuals were grouped into six categories according to coping behavior personality characteristics: the objective was to help mental health professionals recognize vulnerable bereaved individuals and their need for therapy in order to prevent future morbidity and maladjustment.

REFERENCES

Bak, R. 1973. "Being in Love and Object Loss." *International Journal of Psycho-Analysis* 1:54.

Engel, G. L. 1961. "Is Grief a Disease?" *Psychosomatic Medicine* 23:18–22.

Goffman, E. 1961. *Asylums*. New York: Doubleday.

Jacobsen, E. 1947. "The Effect of Disappointment on Ego and Superego Formation in Normal and Depressive Development." *The Yearbook of Psychoanalysis* 3:109–27. New York: International Universities Press.

Maddison, D., and A. Viola. 1968. "The Health of Widows in the Year Following Bereavement." *Journal of Psychosomatic Research* 12:297–306.

Scheff, T. J. 1966. *Being Mentally Ill*. Chicago: Aldine.

Silverman, P. R. 1971. "Factors Involved in Accepting an Offer of Help." *Archives of the Foundation of Thanatology* 3:161–171.

Szasz, T. S. 1961. *The Myth of Mental Illness*. New York: Harper.

Brief Therapy to the Aged Bereaved

Irwin Gerber, Alfred Wiener, Delia Battin and Arthur M. Arkin

"A man's dying is more the survivors' affair than his own"—Thomas Mann, *The Magic Mountain*

In one form or another survivors will feel the impact of the loss of a loved one. For almost all individuals, depending upon their psychological and social environment, bereavement is the most painful of all life changes. Thomas Holmes and his colleagues (Holmes, 1967) have shown in research on their "social readjustment scale" that out of 43 life events the loss of a spouse is the most stressful. In additional research in the area of life crises by Smith (1971), Brown (1969), Paykel (1971) and Myers (1972), the same result has been observed. What is critical for students of thanatology is the relationship between the crisis of bereavement and the onset of physical, psychological, and social problems.

Although, a good portion of the data describing the consequences of a loss are based on less than desirable study designs (e.g., lack of control subjects, and retrospective data collection), there is substantial evidence to

The data for this article are from an investigation entitled, "The Aged in Crisis: A Study of Bereavement." This program was supported in part by U.S.P.H.S. Grant MH–14490 and Grant 93–P–57454/2 from the Administration on Aging, Social and Rehabilitation Service, D.H.E.W. The authors wish to thank Roslyn Rusalem, M.A., and Natalie Hannon for their dedicated work on the program and their critical suggestions during the preparation of this article. The authors would like to acknowledge that Dr. Arthur M. Arkin was responsible for the original idea and basic design of the Montefiore Bereavement Studies.

conclude that the period of bereavement presents a host of serious problems. The untoward consequences of a loss include, among others, death of survivors (Kraus, 1959; Parkes et al., 1969; Rees, 1967; Young, 1963; Cox, 1964); psychosomatic reactions such as ulcerative colitis (Lindemann, 1945) and rheumatoid arthritis (Cobb, 1939); increased rates of mental illness (Parkes, 1964; Stein, 1969); poor physical health (Parkes, 1970; Maddison, 1968); and general emotional unrest (Clayton et al., 1968; Clayton et al., 1971; Marris, 1958; Parkes, 1970).

These various maladjustments to a loss are fundamentally community health problems requiring specific preventive intervention. However, one may argue that bereavement is so deeply a private matter that individuals other than the bereaved have no right, or even responsibility, to interfere with this normal life struggle. From a public health point of view the privacy of bereavement is not a strong argument against the need for professional intervention. As indicated above, the loss of a loved one does in fact affect the normal functioning of a significant proportion of the bereaved population. Also, recent services to the bereaved indicate that survivors will utilize outside professional support (Gerber, 1969; Silverman, 1971). This demonstrates that the bereaved themselves do not consider professional support as a personal intrusion. Another reason why supportive intervention with the bereaved is indicated is that customary lay support offered by close family members and friends does not appear to be very effective in reducing morbidity and maladjustment (Maddison, 1967).

During the past decade, interest in thanatology has produced a public as well as professional awareness that the lack of specific assistance for the bereaved represents poor preventive medicine. The response in this country, and in Great Britain, has been the development of several programs of assistance and support for the bereaved. These services vary in structure from brief therapy to "helping hand" support. Some are solicited by the bereaved, while others are not. Based on the goals of each program, differences in the type of intervener are noted. Psychiatrists, psychologists, psychiatric social workers, medical social workers, and even the widowed have been used as sources of support. Through personal communication and a search of the literature, we are aware of the following crisis intervention programs specifically designed for the bereaved: The Widow-to-Widow program in Boston, the Widows Consultation Center in New York City, the newly created Interventive Family Therapy project at the New England Medical Center Hospital in Boston, the Fort Logan program in Denver, and, in England, the Cruse Club and the Society of Compassionate Friends. The diversity in type of service and type of intervener reflects to some extent uncertainty about the most effective plan for bereavement crisis intervention. We are aware that different bereaved populations need different approaches. Support for the elderly bereaved should differ, based on client needs, from assistance to younger survivors. However, we actually have limited knowledge about which type of service (individual versus group therapy), which intervention orientation (long-term versus short-term), and what type of intervener (professional versus lay support) produces the most effective result. We are unaware of any systematic attempt with proper scientific controls to evaluate the effectiveness of any of the above programs. There is a definite practical need for such evaluation, and we shall attempt to fill it here.

The data for this paper are from an ongoing longitudinal investigation, using an experimental design, of a *nonpatient* aged bereaved population. The major aims of the parent study are to evaluate the relative effects of a specific type of unsolicited crisis intervention to the aged bereaved after the loss of a spouse, and to longitudinally explore the medical, psychological, and social reactions of the aged to the bereavement crisis. This article will concentrate on the first research aim.

Setting of Study: Montefiore Hospital Medical Group

The group practice on which the research program is centered is a hospital-based medical group, in the Bronx, New York, which gives comprehensive medical care in the home, office, and hospital to approximately 25,000 people. The mode of medical payment is fee-for-service arranged around third-party insurances such as Medicare, Medicaid, Blue Shield, and Group Health Insurance. Over 42 physicians, representing the various specialties of medicine, are engaged in providing these medical services and there are in addition 80 nonmedical personnel working with them. Each family is assigned for medical care to an internist and when children are present to a pediatrician. Most families belonging to the medical group are lower-middle-class and predominantly Jewish. Although approximately one-third of the patients are over 65, they utilize 50 percent of the medical services. The setting for this study is located in a health area of New York City, in which 22 percent of the population is over 65. This is striking when compared to the national figure of 10 percent. Also, during the past decade the senior citizen population of this area has increased by 7 percent, while only a 2 percent increase has occurred nationally. These figures indicate that the parent study is in an ideal geographic location for the study of the aged bereaved.

The Service: Crisis Intervention as a Form of Brief Therapy

All bereaved families were randomly assigned either to a treatment group or to a nontreatment control group. The treatment group received support and assistance from either a psychiatric social worker or a psychiatric nurse. No attempt will be made at this time to present data differentiating between survivors who were randomly assigned to the two interveners. The service was accomplished under psychiatric supervision and was not to go beyond six months. Survivors were informed of this time limit at the outset and during the course of the intervention.

The bereavement service was unique for several reasons. It was community oriented and unsolicited by the bereaved, and was designed as a possible model distinguished by simplicity, flexibility, and low cost so that it might be duplicated in communities where psychiatrists are not readily available and where the geriatric population forms a large segment of the population at risk. In accordance with this general orientation, the psychiatric social worker and psychiatric nurse worked within the following framework of brief therapy:

1. Permitting and guiding the bereaved to put into words and express the affects involved in: the pain, sorrow and finality of bereavement; a review of the relationship to the deceased; feelings of love, guilt, and hostility toward the deceased.
2. Acquainting the bereaved with the existence or understanding of alterations in their emotional reactions.

3. Helping the bereaved find an acceptable formulation of their future relationship to the psychic representation of the deceased.
4. Acting as a "primer or programmer" of some of the activities of the bereaved and organizing among suitable friends and relatives a flexible modest scheme for the same purpose.
5. Assisting the bereaved in dealing with such situations as legal and financial matters, and household chores.
6. Offering of assistance in making future plans.
7. Avoiding interpretation of key defenses and unconscious trends, and excessive solicitude for and overprotection of the survivor.

The bereaved knew they needed professional help; the clinical acceptance rate was 94 percent. In accordance with the general design for clinical flexibility, therapeutic contacts were executed in the home, the intervener's office, or by telephone. As the prime mode of contact, telephone support was clearly the most popular (used by 53 percent of the 116-member treatment group) followed in order by home and office contacts. The service consisted of moral support through consistent concern, grief work, and environmental manipulation.

Grief work was most often emphasized by the interveners, followed by moral support, and environmental manipulation.

In practical terms, the bereavement service we were evaluating was primary crisis intervention and a form of brief therapy. This innovative service followed the general guidelines for primary crisis intervention presented by Caplan (1964). The aim of the service was to reduce, the medical, psychological, and social consequences usually associated with bereavement. The intervention plan was to "counteract harmful circumstances" before morbidity set in. As is the case for most primary crisis intervention programs, the present one was not structured to prevent a specific individual from becoming ill. It sought to reduce the risk for a whole population. The individual was seen as a representative of a population labelled "the aged bereaved." The flexible nature of the service allowed the interveners the opportunity to structure individual support not only on the basis of the individual's needs but also in relation to the community problem he or she represents. The bereavement service also contained the general characteristics of brief therapy as defined by Barton (1971, p. 8), ". . . a technique which is active, focused, goal-oriented, circumscribed, warmly supportive, action oriented, and concerned with present adaptation.''

Methods and Procedures

As was stated previously, the sample for the parent investigation was drawn from the Montefiore Hospital Medical Group. Surviving spouses of deaths due to cancer and cardiovascular diseases (these two causes of death were selected because they represented over 80 percent of all deaths at the medical group) were sampled for two years and randomly assigned on a 2-to-1 basis to a treatment group, which received the support, and a nontreatment control group. Every third bereaved spouse regardless of group assignment was matched with a nonbereaved spouse (i.e., no deaths in the immediate family for a three year period) according to age and sex, and number and age of children. Bereaved spouses were interviewed in their home approximately two months after the death and also at five, eight, and fifteen months. The original research plan was to complete the interviews slightly earlier. However, the tendency of elderly subjects to stay with close family members and relatives immediately after the loss caused a delay in the initial interview and, of course, in subsequent research contacts. The first interview for treatment subjects occurred after the intervener completed the first clinical contact. The matched nonbereaved subjects were interviewed as close as possible to the time when the bereaved were. The interview acceptance rate ranged from a high of 94 percent to a low of 75 percent. There were 228 subjects, of which 116 were treatment, 53 nontreatment and 59 nonbereaved.

The following description represents the background profile for all subjects. Seventy percent of the study population were within the geriatric age range, and within this grouping approximately 38 percent were 71 and over. Females made up 72 percent of the sample and males 28 percent; 47 percent of the subjects were Catholic and the same percentage was Jewish. The remaining six percent were Protestants, members of lesser known religions, or subjects who expressed no religious preferences. Three social class levels were identified by using a modified version of the Hollingshead Two Factor Index of Social Position (Hollingshead, 1957). This index is defined by two

7-point weighted scales of occupation and education. Of the sample, 32 percent was classified as Social Class I (the highest class level), 40 percent as Social Class II, and 28 percent as Class III. Forty percent of the bereaved lost spouses because of cancer and 60 percent through cardiovascular diseases. In regard to the "history of death-related illnesses," 72 percent were survivors of a long-term (i.e., chronic) fatal illness, while 28 percent of the bereaved survived a short-term (i.e., acute) illness death.

Although random assignment assumes equivalent research groups, we nevertheless tested the degree of similarity. The following eight background characteristics were selected: sex of main respondent, age, social class, religious preference, national background, age of deceased, cause of death, and history of death-related illness. There was only one statistically significant difference (chi-square) between the two groups of bereaved subjects. The nontreatment group had a higher representation in the first (highest) social class position than the treatment group. Comparing the nonbereaved to each bereaved group revealed the same direction of statistical differences. There were no differences between nonbereaved and nontreatment subjects, while a difference was noted between the nonbereaved and treatment bereaved. A higher percentage of nonbereaved subjects was from the first social class level than for the treatment subjects. It should be mentioned that no other variable for comparison even approached the level of significance. We can safely conclude that our randomization and matching procedures produced equivalent research groups.

Another important aspect of comparability between samples is possible differences in the composition of subjects who are interviewed and those who refuse. If differences are noted between "acceptors" and "refusers," then the findings do not represent the total sample. The acceptors and refusers were compared on the eight characteristics that were previously used and possible differences were looked for at each testing period by type of research group. No statistically significant differences were noted between acceptors and refusers at the first, second, and third interview periods. At the fourth and last testing period, refusers from the treatment group statistically differed from those who were interviewed on two characteristics. There was a higher rate of survivors of cardiovascular deaths and more Eastern-European subjects in the refuser group. In general, subjects who were not interviewed, for various reasons, at each testing period were not substantially different from those who were. The differences were small in number, and therefore the findings can be generalized to those subjects for which data were not collected.

A variety of research forms were used to document the impact of the therapeutic service on elderly survivors' medical, psychological and social adjustment. Most of the questionnaires and scales were developed by the research staff and used after extensive pretesting. Several scaled measures with good reliability were borrowed from the literature. For each of the three areas of adjustment more than one research form was used to collect appropriate and wide-ranging information. For example, medical data were received from two sources. The *General Family Medical Questionnaire* elicited information from surviving spouses, such as number of and reasons for physician contacts, use and type of prescribed and nonprescribed medications, and feeling ill without physician contact. To complete the medical history, respondents' medical charts were scrutinized and all physician contacts, diagnoses, and prescribed medications were recorded on the *Medical Chart Form*. Eight questionnaires were used at each interview, which lasted approximately an hour.

Before the program began, an important methodological decision was made regarding the form of the data to be collected—whether "hard" objective data were to be used or "soft" subjective data. The literature in thanatology has been and continues to be permeated with important but nevertheless subjective measures of bereavement adjustment. We were not entirely satisfied and did not feel comfortable with the limited generalizations that can be made when one is totally dependent upon subjective data. Our decision was to concentrate on tangible indicators of bereavement behavior. Measures that were objective, discrete, easily available, and easily countable were selected. Number of office visits to a physician, types of illnesses, and use of medications appeared to be more meaningful than asking subjects to describe their health. The macroscopic variables used in this investigation were based on the assumption "Where there is fire, there is smoke." From a public health point of view, data based on objective criteria should offer significant guidelines for the structuring of community preventive services to the bereaved.

The following is a selected specific set of predictor (i.e., independent) and outcome (i.e., dependent) variables from the many for which we have data.[1] The focus will be on objective *medical* measures of the effect of supportive intervention.

The medical outcome criteria are:

1. Office visits to a physician.
2. Major illnesses (malignant neoplasms, diabetes mellitus, circulatory diseases, emphysema, and rheumatoid arthritis).
3. Minor illnesses (benign neoplasms, varicose veins, upper respiratory infections, general gastroenteritis, sprains, burns, and lacerations).
4. Use of prescription and nonprescription medications.
5. Use of psychic medications (tranquilizers and antidepressants).
6. Use of general (nonpsychic) medications.
7. Not feeling well but no physician contact.

Most of this information was culled from the Medical Chart Form. Because of respondents' questionable ability to remember specific occasions of physician office visits and reasons for these medical contacts, we concentrated on medical chart data. However, the General Family Medical Questionnaire, completed by respondents, was used to gather such information as not feeling well but no physician contact and use of nonprescribed medications.

The major predictor variable for final outcome was type of research group—the differences between the bereaved in the treatment group and those who were assigned to the nontreatment control group. In addition, the following background predictor variables were related to the above mentioned outcome measures:

1. Sex of main respondent.
2. Age of main respondent. The age of 60 was the basis for defining our geriatric group. This decision was based on more than research expediency. The traditional use of 65 as an indicator of senior citizenship could be some-

---

[1] Data were collected for the rate of survivor deaths, hospitalizations, and accidents. During the first 15 months of bereavement only four survivors died, and an average of only five hospitalizations and three accidents were recorded at each time period. Because of these small figures, statistical cross-tabulations were inappropriate.

what unrealistic when one considers the present trend toward retirement at an earlier age than 65 and the concomitant Social Security benefits. In addition, the age of 60 has been used in previous research on the elderly (Kutner, 1956).

3. History of death related illness. For the present analysis subjects were grouped as survivors of either acute or chronic fatal illnesses. The distinction between acute and chronic illness was not contingent on a specific medical condition, but on the course or history of the illness. An *acute illness death* was defined as occurring *without* warning and prior knowledge of the condition, or a medical condition of less than two months duration with the absence of multiple attacks and hospitalizations. A *chronic illness death* was any condition (cancer or cardiovascular) of two or more months duration, clearly life-threatening by medical standards and supported by multiple attacks and hospitalizations. The medical history of the deceased spouse was reviewed and appropriately classified—74 percent were classified as acute illness deaths and 26 percent as chronic.

4. Religious preference of main respondent.

5. Social class of main respondent.

6. Prior medical history. Are the observed morbidity and maladjustment related to the state of bereavement? or are they simply a continuance of previous poor health? If maladjustment in bereavement is related to previous poor health, then it can be inferred that death of a loved one does not necessarily bring forth new medical problems, but rather aggravates previous conditions. The predictor variable of prior medical history is important for our evaluative data. The brief therapy then would not have simply to meet the challenge of reducing medical problems for all survivors, but would in particular have to aid those who have a history of poor health. Recognizing that this important area of analysis has not been systematically studied, we developed an "Index of Prior Medical History." Using one year before the death, and an equivalent time for the nonbereaved, as the period for prior medical history, we selected three medical criteria for the index. Subjects who frequently visited a physician's office, suffered major illnesses, and received much medication were categorized under "poor" prior medical history; subjects with low rates for all of the above criteria were defined as having "good" prior medical history; and respondents showing combinations of the above (such as good for major illnesses but poor for use of medications)

were grouped in the "fair" prior medical history category. Among the subjects, 28 percent had good prior medical history, 61 percent fair, and 11 percent poor. Since the present analysis is for nominal frequency data, the statistical test used was the chi-square with the Yates's correction for continuity applied when necessary.

Findings

The results of the relative effects of brief therapy to the aged bereaved will be presented for each medical outcome measure by predictor variable. The four time periods for evaluation are two, five, eight, and fifteen months from time of loss. The comparison at the eight-month period is for data collected immediately following the termination of the service. The data will be analyzed for each of the four time periods and appropriate interpretations made between treatment and nontreatment subjects. The tabled findings reflect our initial plan for statistical analysis. For each time period the chi-square statistic was used to test possible differences between the two research groups for all outcome variables. In addition, comparisons were made *within* each group for individual background predictor variables.

OFFICE VISITS

Although there was no consistent pattern of differences, observed in Table 27.1, between the aged bereaved who received the brief therapy and those survivors who did not, a statistical difference was noted at the third research period. The results for this testing period, which were for visits to a physician from slightly over five months to eight months after the loss, indicate that a smaller percentage of treatment bereaved visited their physicians than the nontreated bereaved. The potential importance of this statistically significant difference is augmented when one takes into account that during this research time period there were more therapeutic contacts than during the baseline point (*T*-1), for which no substantial differences were observed between the research groups.

Several background predictor variables differentiated between subjects *within* each study unit. These differences were either statistically significant

TABLE 27.1. FREQUENCY OF OFFICE VISITS TO PHYSICIANS BY TREATMENT AND NONTREATMENT BEREAVED BY PREDICTOR VARIABLES AT DIFFERENT TIME PERIODS [a]

	T-1 From Loss to 2 Months				T-2 Over 2 to 5 Months				T-3 Over 5 to 8 Months				T-4 Over 8 to 15 Months			
	T		NT		T		NT		T		NT		T		NT	
	%	N	%	N	%	N	%	N	%	N	%	N	%	N	%	N
Research *Group*	69.4	(50)	68.9	(31)	59.8	(64)	66.0	(33)	50.9	(55)[b]	66.7	(32)	61.9	(65)	62.2	(28)
Male	57.9	(11)	64.3	(9)[b]	46.4	(13)[b]	60.0	(9)	35.7	(10)	61.5	(8)	53.9	(14)	72.7	(9)
Female	73.5	(39)	70.9	(22)	64.6	(51)	68.5	(24)	56.2	(45)	68.5	(24)	64.6	(51)	58.8	(20)
Under 60	59.1	(13)	53.9	(7)	52.9	(18)	57.1	(8)	55.8	(19)	46.2	(6)	54.5	(18)	33.3	(4)[b]
Over 60	75.5	(37)	75.0	(24)	63.9	(46)	69.4	(25)	49.3	(36)	74.2	(26)	64.8	(46)	66.7	(24)
Illness:																
Chronic	69.6	(39)	64.5	(20)	56.6	(43)	58.3	(21)	44.7	(34)	68.5	(24)	60.8	(45)	63.7	(21)
Acute	68.7	(11)	78.5	(11)	67.7	(21)	85.6	(12)	65.0	(21)	61.5	(8)	64.5	(20)	58.3	(7)
Catholic	68.6	(24)	63.2	(12)	51.5	(17)	63.2	(12)	58.9	(20)	66.7	(12)	50.0	(17)	64.7	(11)
Jewish	79.3	(23)	70.8	(17)	80.0	(24)	68.1	(15)	63.3	(19)	66.7	(14)	73.3	(22)	57.9	(11)
Other	33.3	(2)	50.0	(1)	33.4	(2)	100.0	(2)	0.0	(0)	100.0	(2)	75.0	(3)	50.0	(1)
Social *Class:* I	72.8	(8)	62.5	(10)	70.0	(7)	66.7	(10)	50.0	(5)	80.0	(12)	40.0	(4)[b]	46.6	(7)
II	73.4	(22)	72.2	(13)	67.9	(19)	58.8	(10)	51.7	(15)	56.3	(9)	75.0	(21)	71.4	(10)
III	65.2	(15)	77.3	(7)	59.1	(13)	87.0	(7)	63.7	(14)	71.4	(5)	45.5	(10)	57.1	(4)
Prior *Medical* *History:* Good	53.9	(7)	53.9	(7)	25.0	(6)[c]	53.3	(8)	28.0	(7)[b]	46.0	(8)	37.5	(9)[b]	35.7	(5)
Fair	79.2	(38)	70.9	(17)	71.8	(51)	69.2	(8)	57.6	(41)	75.0	(18)	66.7	(46)	72.7	(16)
Poor	75.0	(3)	80.0	(4)	63.6	(7)	87.5	(7)	63.5	(7)	75.0	(6)	81.8	(9)	87.5	(7)

[a] Only affirmative responses are reflected.
[b] Chi-square significant at .05 level.
[c] Chi-square significant at .01 level.

or *approached* the level of significance. Approximately two months after the loss, which is the initial baseline period, *no* differences were observed between treatment male survivors and their female counterparts. However, after the interveners had more contact with the bereaved the service was more effective inasmuch as widowers were *less* likely to visit their physicians than female survivors. These differences were noted for the second and third testing periods (all differences approached the level of significance). During the same timespan male and female survivors without the professional support did not substantially differ for visits to their physicians.

For the present outcome variable there is some indication that bereavement support does not benefit Jewish survivors. No substantial differences were noted between Catholic and Jewish survivors in the nontreatment group. However, within the treatment group percentage differences approached the level of significance and were in the same direction at *each* testing period. The Jewish bereaved who received brief therapy were more likely to visit physicians than Catholic survivors. Any generalization of this present finding will have to wait until we look at the results for the other outcome variables.

One of the objectives of a service to the bereaved should be to hold medical problems in check for survivors with poor health before their loss and to prevent the onset of medical morbidity for those whose health has been good. Unless the intervention is heavily oriented toward preventive medical care, the above goal may be difficult to accomplish. The bereavement program presently under evaluation appears to have had some success with the aged bereaved who enjoyed comparatively good health. At the baseline testing period $(T-1)$ there were no significant or near significant differences for prior medical history within each research group. No differences between good, fair, and poor prior medical history were observed during the subsequent research periods for survivors who did not receive supportive intervention. This was not the case for the treatment bereaved. Survivors with either fair or poor medical histories prior to their loss were more likely to seek medical care than survivors who had good prior health.

We anticipated that the interveners would tend to encourage their clients to visit physicians when medical complaints were presented. For those bereaved who had legitimate medical complaints because of their general poor health the intervener would have no choice except to make such a suggestion. In order to document if this would in fact occur, the psychiatric social worker and the psychiatric nurse reported on a special form after each clinical contact if medical complaints were expressed by the bereaved and what advice, if any, was offered. It was found that for 26 percent of all medical complaints, the interveners encouraged the bereaved to see a physician. It is therefore possible that the basic thrust of the intervention was not the reason for the high rates of office visits observed for the bereaved with a poor previous medical history, but rather the concerned influence of the intervener.

MAJOR ILLNESSES AS THE REASON FOR SEEING PHYSICIANS

The findings for the second outcome measure will not be presented in a table. There were no significant or near significant differences for major illnesses between the treatment and nontreatment bereaved. The only background predictor variable that differentiated between subjects within each research group was prior medical history. The results were inclusive.

MINOR ILLNESSES AS THE REASON FOR SEEING PHYSICIANS

As was the case for major illnesses, both treatment and nontreatment survivors did not differ for minor illness complaints requiring medical attention. However, as presented in Table 27.2, there are either significant or near significant differences for treatment subjects with specific types of background characteristics. At the initial, second, and third testing periods, which represent approximately eight months of bereavement, *female* survivors in the treatment group were more likely to visit their physicians for minor illness complaints than their male counterparts. Religion was also a factor. At all testing periods, in the treatment group a larger percentage of Jewish survivors visited their physicians for minor illnesses than Catholic survivors. Age, history of death-related illness (i.e., chronic and acute fatal illnesses), social class position, and prior medical history show sporadic statistical differences; but these are too diffuse to offer a meaningful pattern for analysis.

USE OF MEDICATIONS

This present outcome variable includes psychic as well as general medications, which could have been either prescribed by physicians or purchased over the counter. As shown in Table 27.3, there were either statistically significant differences or percentage differences approaching the level of significance at the second and third testing periods. The aged bereaved who received professional support were less likely to use medications than nontreatment survivors. It should be noted that this limited positive impact of brief therapy on survivors' consumption of various types of medications

TABLE 27.2. FREQUENCY OF OFFICE VISITS TO PHYSICIANS FOR MINOR ILLNESSES BY TREATMENT AND NONTREATMENT BEREAVED BY PREDICTOR VARIABLES AT DIFFERENT TIME PERIODS [a]

	T-1 From Loss to 2 Months				T-2 Over 2 to 5 Months				T-3 Over 5 to 8 Months				T-4 Over 8 to 15 Months			
	T		NT		T		NT		T		NT		T		NT	
Research Group	%	N	%	N	%	N	%	N	%	N	%	N	%	N	%	N
	65.3	(47)	62.2	(28)	56.1	(60)	64.0	(32)	47.2	(51)	62.5	(30)	57.7	(60)	62.2	(28
Male	47.4	(9)	57.1	(8)	39.3	(11)[b]	60.0	(9)	32.1	(9)	53.8	(7)	50.0	(13)	72.7	(8
Female	71.7	(38)	64.5	(20)	62.0	(49)	65.7	(23)	52.5	(42)	65.7	(23)	60.3	(47)	58.8	(2
Under 60	54.5	(12)	53.8	(7)	50.0	(17)	50.0	(7)	55.9	(19)	46.2	(6)	50.0	(16)	33.3	(
Over 60	71.4	(35)	65.6	(21)	59.7	(43)	69.4	(25)	43.8	(32)	68.6	(24)	60.6	(43)	72.7	(2
Illness:																
Chronic	64.3	(36)	58.1	(18)	53.9	(41)	55.6	(20)[b]	40.8	(31)[b]	62.9	(22)	56.2	(41)	63.6	(2
Acute	68.7	(11)	71.4	(10)	61.3	(19)	85.7	(12)	62.5	(20)	61.5	(8)	61.3	(19)	58.3	(
Catholic	68.6	(24)[b]	47.4	(9)	45.4	(15)[b]	63.2	(12)	50.0	(17)[b]	61.1	(11)	44.1	(15)	64.7	(1
Jewish	72.4	(21)	70.8	(17)	73.3	(22)	68.2	(15)	60.0	(18)	61.9	(13)	70.0	(21)	57.9	(1
Other	16.7	(1)	100.0	(2)	33.3	(2)	100.0	(2)	00.0	(0)	100.0	(2)	66.7	(2)	50.0	(
Social Class: I	72.7	(8)	50.0	(8)	60.0	(6)	66.7	(10)	50.0	(5)	73.3	(11)	30.0	(3)[b]	46.7	(
II	66.7	(20)	72.2	(13)	64.3	(18)	58.8	(10)	41.4	(12)	50.0	(8)	70.4	(19)	71.4	(1
III	58.3	(14)	66.7	(6)	54.5	(12)	87.5	(7)	63.6	(14)	71.4	(5)	40.9	(9)	57.1	(
Prior Medical History:																
Good	53.8	(7)	53.8	(7)	25.0	(6)[c]	53.3	(8)	28.0	(7)	46.7	(7)	41.7	(10)	35.7	(
Fair	72.9	(35)	66.7	(16)	67.6	(48)	69.2	(18)	53.5	(38)	70.8	(17)	60.3	(41)	72.7	(
Poor	75.0	(3)	60.0	(3)	54.5	(6)	75.0	(6)	54.5	(6)	62.5	(5)	72.7	(8)	87.5	(

[a] Only affirmative responses are reflected.
[b] Chi-square significant at .05 level.
[c] Chi-square significant at .01 level.

occurred after approximately 50 percent of the clinical contacts were completed. Within the research groups, sex and religion again played a differentiating role. Although percentage differences for sex of survivor only approached the level of significance, a definite pattern was observed. After the first two months of clinical contact differences were noted for the bereaved who received the service, while there were no differences between nontreatment survivors. In the treatment group, a larger percentage of female survivors used medications than male survivors. The identical pattern existed for religious preference. No significant or near significant differences were observed for the nontreatment group. Within the treatment group, the Jewish bereaved were consistently more likely to use medications than the

TABLE 27.3. FREQUENCY OF USE OF MEDICATIONS BY TREATMENT AND NONTREATMENT BEREAVED BY PREDICTION VARIABLES AT DIFFERENT TIME PERIODS [a]

	T–1 From Loss to 2 Months				T–2 Over 2 to 5 Months				T–3 Over 5 to 8 Months				T–4 Over 8 to 15 Months			
	T		NT		T		NT		T		NT		T		NT	
	%	N	%	N	%	N	%	N	%	N	%	N	%	N	%	N
Research Group	80.2	(57)	80.0	(36)	35.0	(37)	42.0	(21)	29.9	(32)[c]	43.8	(21)	35.6	(16)	33.3	(15)
Male	63.2	(12)	64.3	(9)	17.9	(5)	40.0	(6)	14.3	(4)	30.8	(4)	19.2	(5)	36.3	(4)
Female	86.5	(45)	87.1	(27)	40.9	(32)	42.8	(15)	35.4	(28)	48.6	(17)	41.0	(32)	32.3	(11)
Under 60	86.4	(9)	77.0	(10)	38.2	(13)	42.8	(6)	32.3	(11)	30.8	(4)[b]	34.4	(11)	16.6	(2)
Over 60	77.1	(37)	81.3	(26)	33.8	(24)	41.6	(15)	29.2	(21)	48.6	(17)	35.2	(25)	39.4	(13)
Illness:																
Chronic	83.6	(46)	87.1	(27)	36.0	(27)	36.1	(13)	18.0	(21)	48.6	(17)	34.2	(25)	33.4	(11)
Acute	68.8	(11)	64.3	(9)	32.3	(10)	57.1	(8)	34.4	(11)	30.8	(4)	38.8	(12)	33.3	(4)
Catholic	80.0	(28)	73.7	(14)	39.4	(13)	47.4	(9)	26.5	(9)[b]	38.9	(7)	35.3	(12)	29.4	(5)
Jewish	85.7	(24)	83.3	(20)	55.1	(16)	40.9	(9)	55.1	(16)	42.8	(9)	36.7	(11)	31.6	(6)
Other	50.0	(3)	100.0	(2)	0.0	(0)	50.0	(1)	0.0	(0)	50.0	(1)	0.0	(0)	0.0	(0)
Social Class: I	81.8	(9)	81.2	(13)	50.0	(5)	33.3	(5)	40.0	(4)	26.6	(4)	20.0	(2)	20.0	(3)
II	76.7	(23)	83.3	(15)	48.1	(13)	47.0	(8)	42.8	(12)	56.2	(9)	40.7	(11)	28.5	(4)
III	82.6	(19)	77.8	(7)	40.9	(9)	50.0	(4)	27.2	(6)	42.8	(3)	27.2	(6)	28.6	(2)
Prior Medical History:																
Good	76.9	(10)	69.2	(9)	12.5	(3)	13.3	(2)[b]	8.0	(2)[c]	26.6	(4)	29.2	(7)	14.3	(2)
Fair	85.0	(40)	79.1	(19)	44.2	(31)	53.9	(14)	32.8	(23)	50.0	(12)	38.3	(26)	36.3	(8)
Poor	75.0	(3)	100.0	(5)	27.3	(3)	62.5	(5)	63.5	(7)	50.0	(4)	36.4	(4)	62.5	(15)

[a] Only affirmative responses are reflected.
[b] Chi-square significant at .05 level.
[c] Chi-square significant at .01 level.

Catholic bereaved. Brief therapy does reduce the use of various types of medications; however the impact appears to be less effective for female Jewish survivors. This finding, in conjunction with the previous results for the outcome measures of office visits to a physician and minor illnesses, suggest that aged female Jewish bereaved are almost totally unaffected by professional support.

USE OF SPECIFIC TYPES OF MEDICATIONS

The above analysis described the influence of crisis intervention on survivors' use of medication without differentiating between type of medication. Table 27.4 indicates the use of psychic medications while Table 27.5 shows the results for general medications. Brief therapy has a temporary positive influence on survivors' use of psychic medications. The results contained in Table 27.4 reveal that approximately two to five months after the loss (*T*-2) those bereaved who received the service were less likely to use tranquilizers and antidepressants than survivors without the professional support. Immediately following the termination of the service, no significant or near significant differences were noted between the treatment and nontreatment bereaved. The likelihood that during the period of bereavement, when there is no available professional support, physicians will prescribe an ex-

TABLE 27.4. FREQUENCY OF USE OF TRANQUILIZERS AND ANTIDEPRESSANTS BY TREATMENT AN NONTREATMENT BEREAVED BY PREDICTOR VARIABLES AT DIFFERENT TIME PERIODS [a]

	T–1 From Loss to 2 Months				*T–2* Over 2 to 5 Months				*T–3* Over 5 to 8 Months				*T–4* Over 8 to 15 Months			
	T		*NT*		*T*		*NT*		*T*		*NT*		*T*		*NT*	
Research	%	N	%	N	%	N	%	N	%	N	%	N	%	N	%	N
Group	41.7	(30)	35.6	(16)	9.3	(10)	22.0	(11)	7.4	(8)	10.4	(5)	10.5	(11)	13.3	((
Male	26.3	(5)	28.6	(4)	3.5	(1)	6.7	(1)	3.6	(1)	0.0	(0)	3.8	(1)	0.0	((
Female	47.2	(25)	38.7	(12)	11.4	(9)	28.6	(10)	8.8	(7)	14.3	(5)	12.7	(10)	17.6	((
Under 60	63.6	(14)[b]	30.8	(4)	5.9	(2)	35.7	(5)	5.9	(2)	7.7	(1)	6.1	(2)	0.0	((
Over 60	32.7	(16)	37.5	(12)	11.1	(8)	16.7	(6)	8.2	(6)	11.4	(4)	12.7	(9)	18.2	((
Illness:																
Chronic	42.9	(24)	35.5	(11)	9.2	(7)	16.7	(6)	6.6	(5)	11.4	(4)	10.8	(8)	12.1	(4
Acute	37.5	(6)	35.7	(5)	9.7	(3)	35.7	(5)	9.4	(3)	7.7	(1)	9.7	(3)	16.7	(2
Catholic	42.9	(15)	21.1	(4)	6.1	(2)	21.1	(4)	2.9	(1)	0.0	(0)	5.9	(2)	11.8	(2
Jewish	48.3	(14)	45.8	(11)	16.7	(5)	27.3	(6)	20.0	(6)	23.8	(5)	16.7	(5)	18.8	(3
Other	0.0	(0)	50.0	(1)	0.0	(0)	0.0	(0)	0.0	(0)	0.0	(0)	0.0	(0)	0.0	((
Social																
Class: I	45.5	(5)	25.0	(4)	20.0	(2)	20.0	(3)	20.0	(2)	13.3	(2)	10.0	(1)	13.3	(2
II	43.3	(13)	33.3	(6)	14.3	(4)	23.5	(4)	10.3	(3)	18.8	(3)	10.7	(3)	7.1	(1
III	43.5	(10)	55.6	(5)	4.5	(1)	25.0	(2)	9.1	(2)	0.0	(0)	13.6	(3)	14.3	(1
Prior Medical History:																
Good	38.5	(5)	15.4	(2)	8.3	(2)	13.3	(2)	4.0	(1)	0.0	(0)	4.2	(1)	100.0	(14
Fair	47.9	(23)	41.7	(10)	7.0	(5)	26.9	(7)	7.0	(5)	12.5	(3)	13.0	(9)	13.6	(3
Poor	25.0	(1)	40.0	(2)	27.3	(3)	25.0	(2)	18.2	(2)	25.0	(2)	9.1	(1)	37.5	(3

[a] Only affirmative responses are reflected.
[b] Chi-square significant at .05 level.

cessive amount of psychic medications is somewhat supported by the above result. After a loss, survivors will present to physicians complaints indicating emotional unrest. Difficulty in sleeping, feeling "on edge," extensive periods of crying, and constant headaches will produce a request by the bereaved for some medication. Physicians will usually honor such requests. The finding that after the intervention was terminated, treated bereaved revert to the use of tranquilizers and antidepressants indicates that supportive intervention reduces the need for these specific types of medications. A possible interpretation is that brief therapy has this effect because it acts as a substitute for psychic medications. Also, the termination of the service may represent an additional loss for the survivor. The loss of a significant other in the form of the intervener may create sufficient anxiety for the bereaved to turn to psychic medications.

The effect on the use of general medications seems to be positive. As noted in Table 27.5, for two months from the loss (T-1) and for over five to eight months after the loss (T-3), a smaller percentage of the bereaved who received the service used general medications than did those who did not. These differences were statistically significant, and the strongest differences occurred when the bereaved had maximum exposure to the intervention (T-3). Statistically significant differences in the use of general medications *within* each research group were only observed for the background predictor variable of prior medical history. The treatment bereaved with good previous medical history were less likely to use other than psychic medications than survivors with fair and poor previous health. As was the case for previous significant findings, differences were observed after the bereaved had a substantial number of clinical contacts. There were no substantial differences for previous medical history within the nontreatment group. Supportive intervention to the aged bereaved reduced the use of general (nonpsychic) medications for at least one segment of the bereaved population—those with good previous medical history—while under normal circumstances without professional support all bereaved consumed the same amount of medications regardless of their previous health.

NOT FEELING WELL WITHOUT PHYSICIAN CONTACT

Information received from medical charts reflects only medical problems that are brought to the attention of physicians. Incidents of unreported poor

TABLE 27.5. FREQUENCY OF USE OF GENERAL MEDICATIONS BY TREATMENT AND NONTREATMEN[t] BEREAVED BY PREDICTOR VARIABLES AT DIFFERENT TIME PERIODS [a]

	T–1 From Loss to 2 Months				T–2 Over 2 to 5 Months				T–3 Over 5 to 8 Months				T–4 Over 8 to 15 Months			
	T		NT		T		NT		T		NT		T		NT	
Research	%	N	%	N	%	N	%	N	%	N	%	N	%	N	%	N
Group	39.4	(28)[b]	60.0	(27)	28.3	(30)	24.0	(12)	21.3	(23)[c]	41.7	(20)	28.8	(30)	24.4	(1?
Male	36.8	(7)	42.9	(6)	14.3	(4)	26.7	(4)	10.7	(3)	30.8	(4)	15.4	(4)	27.3	(3
Female	40.4	(21)	67.7	(21)	33.3	(26)	21.6	(8)	25.0	(20)	45.7	(16)	33.3	(26)	23.5	(8
Under 60	36.4	(8)	53.8	(7)	36.4	(12)	14.3	(2)	23.5	(8)	23.1	(3)	21.9	(7)	16.7	(2
Over 60	39.6	(19)	62.5	(20)	25.0	(18)	27.8	(10)	20.5	(15)	48.6	(17)	31.0	(22)	27.3	(9
Illness:																
Chronic	41.8	(23)	67.7	(21)	28.0	(21)	22.2	(8)	19.7	(15)	45.7	(16)	27.4	(20)	24.2	(8
Acute	31.2	(5)	42.9	(6)	29.0	(9)	28.6	(4)	25.0	(8)	30.8	(4)	32.3	(10)	25.0	(3
Catholic	31.4	(11)	57.9	(11)	37.5	(12)	31.6	(6)	20.6	(7)	38.9	(7)	23.5	(8)	11.8	(2
Jewish	46.4	(13)	62.5	(15)	43.3	(13)	18.2	(4)	33.3	(10)	38.1	(8)	33.3	(10)	26.3	(5
Other	50.0	(3)	50.0	(1)	0.0	(0)	50.0	(1)	0.0	(0)	50.0	(1)	0.0	(0)	0.0	(0
Social																
Class: I	27.3	(3)	62.5	(10)	50.0	(5)	20.0	(3)	20.0	(2)	20.0	(3)	20.0	(2)	13.3	(2
II	40.0	(12)	61.1	(11)	32.1	(9)	29.4	(5)	31.0	(9)	56.3	(9)	29.6	(8)	21.4	(3
III	39.1	(9)	55.6	(5)	42.9	(9)	25.0	(2)	13.6	(3)	42.9	(3)	22.7	(5)	14.3	(1
Prior Medical History:																
Good	38.5	(5)	61.5	(8)	9.1	(2)[b]	6.7	(1)	4.0	(1)[b]	26.7	(4)	25.0	(6)	14.3	(2
Fair	40.4	(19)	58.3	(14)	38.6	(27)	30.8	(8)	23.9	(17)	45.8	(11)	30.9	(21)	22.7	(5
Poor	25.0	(1)	60.0	(3)	9.1	(1)	37.5	(3)	45.5	(5)	50.0	(4)	27.3	(3)	50.0	(4

[a] Only affirmative responses are reflected.
[b] Chi-square significant at .05 level.
[c] Chi-square significant at .01 level.

health are in effect lost medical data. Either the problem is defined as minor, or the individual uses medications that were previously prescribed for the same or a similar medical problem, or there is fear of the potential seriousness of the condition.

In order to present a complete medical picture of the relative effects of the brief therapy, respondents reported the number of times when they did not feel well but did not contact their physician. The results in Table 27.6 indicate that the bereaved without therapeutic support were more likely to feel ill without seeing a physician than survivors who had the supportive inter-

TABLE 27.6. FREQUENCY OF FEELING ILL WITHOUT PHYSICIAN CONTACT BY TREATMENT AND NONTREATMENT BEREAVED BY PREDICTOR VARIABLES AT DIFFERENT TIME PERIODS [a]

	T-1 From Loss to 2 Months				T-2 Over 2 to 5 Months				T-3 Over 5 to 8 Months				T-4 Over 8 to 15 Months			
	T		NT		T		NT		T		NT		T		NT	
Research	%	N	%	N	%	N	%	N	%	N	%	N	%	N	%	N
Group	40.3	(29)	48.9	(22)	43.6	(17)	66.7	(16)	40.5	(17)[b]	64.3	(18)	50.0	(31)	44.4	(16)
Male	21.1	(4)[b]	28.6	(4)	12.5	(1)[b]	66.7	(4)	27.3	(3)	42.9	(3)	37.5	(6)	27.3	(3)
Female	47.2	(25)	58.1	(18)	51.6	(16)	66.7	(12)	45.2	(14)	71.4	(15)	54.3	(25)	52.0	
Under 60	50.0	(11)	46.2	(6)	46.2	(6)	33.3	(3)[c]	35.7	(5)	54.5	(6)	50.0	(9)	45.5	(5)
Over 60	36.7	(18)	50.0	(16)	42.3	(11)	86.7	(13)	42.9	(12)	70.6	(12)	50.0	(22)	44.0	(11)
Illness:																
Chronic	37.5	(21)	48.4	(15)	32.3	(10)[c]	76.5	(13)	39.4	(13)	60.0	(12)	46.8	(22)	40.0	(10)
Acute	50.0	(8)	50.0	(7)	87.5	(7)	42.9	(3)	44.4	(4)	75.0	(6)	60.0	(9)	54.5	(6)
Catholic	34.3	(12)	47.4	(9)	36.8	(7)	45.5	(5)	38.1	(8)	41.7	(5)	48.4	(15)	40.0	(6)
Jewish	55.2	(16)	50.0	(12)	56.3	(9)	81.8	(9)	47.1	(8)	78.6	(11)	52.4	(11)	44.4	(8)
Other	16.7	(1)	50.0	(1)	25.0	(1)	100.0	(2)	25.0	(1)	100.0	(2)	40.0	(2)	100.0	(2)
Social																
Class: I	63.6	(7)	43.8	(7)	62.5	(5)	50.0	(3)	42.9	(3)	50.0	(6)	75.0	(6)	50.0	(6)
II	33.3	(10)	55.6	(10)	58.3	(7)	55.6	(5)	33.3	(6)	77.8	(7)	40.9	(9)	46.2	(6)
III	43.5	(10)	44.4	(4)	54.5	(6)	42.9	(4)	38.5	(5)	66.7	(4)	40.0	(8)	37.5	(3)
Prior Medical History:																
Good	30.8	(4)	53.8	(7)	57.1	(4)	50.0	(3)	37.5	(3)	50.0	(4)	61.5	(8)	41.7	(5)
Fair	45.8	(22)	50.0	(12)	42.9	(12)	66.7	(10)	44.8	(13)	62.5	(10)	46.3	(20)	47.4	(9)
Poor	25.0	(1)	40.0	(2)	0.0	(0)	100.0	(2)	0.0	(0)	100.0	(3)	50.0	(2)	25.0	(1)

[a] Only affirmative responses are reflected.
[b] Chi-square significant at .05 level.
[c] Chi-square significant at .01 level.

vention. The statistically significant differences and percentage differences approaching the level of significance were again observed after maximum contact with the interveners. For differences within the treatment and non-treatment groups only one background predictor variable was related to not feeling well without physician contact. A larger percentage of female survivors in the treatment group complained of not feeling well than their male counterparts. No substantial differences were noted for sex in the nontreatment group. The statistically significant differences observed for age and history of death-related illness are too limited in number to offer a basis for discussion.

Discussion

With the use of selected medical data, we have attempted to determine
whether appropriate brief psychotherapy administered to elderly surviving
spouses has a prophylactic effect on morbidity and maladjustment precipitated by a natural death in the family. Realizing that other data—such as
psychological and social adjustment—still remain to be analyzed, the fact
that our sample was drawn from a specific type of medical care setting and
the host of problems associated with behavioral science evaluation, we offer
a cautious positive response.

The results for 75 percent (five of the seven) of the measures of therapeutic outcome tend to suggest that the type of brief therapy we offered was to
some extent medically beneficial. The overall positive impact of the intervention was not evident at the initial stages. As the aged survivors passed
the halfway point of therapeutic contact, the reduction in medical morbidity
when compared to the nontreatment bereaved was more evident. From our
experience, it appears that a therapeutic service to the bereaved will begin to
have a positive impact approximately three months after the intervention
begins.

The finding that bereavement intervention does not benefit all types of
aged survivors was most stimulating and suggests several practical implications. It was noted for the outcome variables of office visits to physicians,
minor illnesses, and the use of medications that the aged female bereaved of
the Jewish faith were less likely to benefit from the service than other survivors. From the many possible interpretations of this finding there is one
that deserves particular attention: the results from sociological studies of the
cultural differences in illness behavior—that is, how medical symptoms are
defined and what the response is to this definition—clearly show that Jewish
respondents have a stronger traditional concern about health than members
of other cultural groups. Research by Zborowski (1952), Segal (unpublished), Suchman (1964, 1965), Linn (1967) and Scheff (1966) indicate
that Jews respond to pain emotionally, look upon any deviation from normal
behavior as a sign of illness, are oriented toward preventive medical care,
and in general consider complaining behavior as appropriate when one is ill

or under a stressful situation. This health orientation is more evident among the older Jewish population.

It is very likely that the high rates of visits to physicians, complaints about minor illness, and use of medications observed for the aged female Jewish bereaved in the treatment group reflect their cultural response to illness and stress more than the ineffectiveness of the intervention.

In addition, having available an intervener who is a representative of the health professions could have been an ideal situation for the initial presentation and verification of medical complaints before physician contacts were made. We must remember that for approximately 26 percent of all medical complaints presented to the interveners, the response was encouragement to see a physician. What all this means is that interveners working with the aged Jewish bereaved should scrutinize the expressed medical complaints in order to distinguish between those which truly call for medical assistance and those complaints which are exaggerated because of the unique cultural health orientation. In order to accomplish this task there must be a close working relationship between nonmedical interveners and family physicians.

As reported by Stern (1951) and supported by Gramlich (1968) a common manifestation of grief in the aged is somatic illness. On the basis of these observations, a major goal of a therapeutic service to the aged bereaved should be an attempt to prevent these physical manifestations of grief. The findings presented in this paper indicated that survivors who enter the bereavement crisis with comparatively good health are more favorably affected by professional intervention than the bereaved with the poor medical history. It appears that nonmedical interveners are appropriate for those aged bereaved who are less vulnerable during the period of bereavement because of good health, but medical personnel are definitely needed for the more vulnerable survivors. The family physician must play an important role in the bereavement service. There should be open communication between the intervener and the physician. Without proper feedback between these two parties, the success of the intervention will be reduced and the aged bereaved with a poor medical history will be constantly visiting their physicians.

At the outset of the paper, we expressed the opinion that we now know very little about who benefits from bereavement crisis intervention and what type of intervener is most effective. There are many questions to be answered regarding the value of crisis intervention to the bereaved. The present results have probably generated more questions than answers. However, we feel that an important pioneering step has been taken. It is our hope that the findings we have presented will assist in the structuring of future services to the aged bereaved and will stimulate scientific evaluations of such services.

REFERENCES

Barton, H. H. ed. 1971. *Brief Therapies.* New York: Behavioral Publications.

Brown, G. W., and J. L. T. Birley. 1969. "Crises and Life Changes and the Onset of Schizophrenia." *Journal of Health and Social Behavior* 9:203–14.

Caplan, G. 1964. *Principles of Preventive Psychiatry.* New York: Basic Books.

Clayton, P., et al. 1971. "The Bereavement of the Widowed." *Diseases of the Nervous System* 32:597–603.

—— 1968. "A Study of Normal Bereavement." *American Journal of Psychiatry* 125:168–78.

Cobb, S., et al. 1939. "Environment Factors in Rheumatoid Arthritis." *Journal of the American Medical Association* 113:667–72.

Cox, P. R., and J. R. Ford. 1964. "The Mortality of Widows Shortly after Widowhood." *Lancet* 1:163–64.

Gerber, I. 1969. "Bereavement and the Acceptance of Professional Service." *Community Mental Health Journal* 5:487–95.

Gramlich, E. P. 1968. "Recognition and Management of Grief in Elderly Persons." *Geriatrics* 23:87–92.

Hollingshead, A. B. 1957, 1965. "Two Factor Index of Social Position." Yale Station, New Haven.

Holmes, T. H., and R. H. Rahe. 1967. "The Social Readjustment Rating Scale." *Journal of Psychosomatic Research* 11:213–18.

Kraus, A. S., and A. M. Lilienfeld. 1959. "Some Epidemiologic Aspects of the High Mortality Rate in the Young Widowed Group." *Journal of Chronic Diseases* 10:207–17.

Kutner, B., et al. 1956. *Five Hundred over Sixty: A Community Survey on Aging.* New York: Russell Sage Foundation.

Lindemann, E. 1945. "Psychiatric Factors in the Treatment of Ulcerative Colitis." Archives of Neurology and Psychiatry 53: 322–24.

Linn, L. 1967. "Social Characteristics and Social Interaction in the Utilization of a Psychiatric Outpatient Clinic." *Journal of Health and Social Behavior* 8:3–14.

Maddison, D. C. and A. Viola. 1968. "The Health of Widows in the Year Following Bereavement." *Journal of Psychosomatic Research* 12:297–306.

—— and W. L. Walker. 1967. "Factors Affecting the Outcome of Conjugal Bereavement." *British Journal of Psychiatry* 113:1057–67.

Mann, T. 1924. *The Magic Mountain.*

Marris, P. 1958. *Widows and Their Families.* London: Routledge and Kegan Paul.

Myers, J. K. et al. 1972. "Life Events and Mental Status: A Longitudinal Study." *Journal of Health and Social Behavior* 13:398–406.

Parkes, C. M. 1964. "Recent Bereavement as a Cause of Mental Illness." *British Journal of Psychiatry* 110:198–204.

—— 1970. "The First Year of Bereavement: A Longitudinal Study of the Reaction of London Widows to the Death of Their Husbands." *Psychiatry* 33:444–67.

Parkes, C. M. et al. 1969. "Broken Heart: A Statistical Study of Increased Mortality among Widowers." *British Medical Journal* 1:740–43.

Paykel, E. S. et al. 1971. "Scaling of Life Events." *Archives of General Psychiatry* 25:340–47.

Rees, W. D., and S. G. Lutkins. 1967. "Mortality of Bereavement." *British Medical Journal* 4:13–16.

Scheff, T. 1966. "Users and Non-users of a Student Psychiatric Clinic." *Journal of Health and Human Behavior* 7:114–21.

Segal, B. n.d. "Scholars and Patients: Religion, Academic Performance, and the Use of Medical Facilities by Male Undergraduates. Dept. of Sociology, Dartmouth College.

Silverman, P. R. 1971. "Factors Involved in Accepting an Offer of Help." *Archives of the Foundation of Thanatology* 3:161–71.

Smith, W. G. 1971. "Critical Life-events and Prevention Strategies in Mental Health." *Archives of General Psychiatry* 25:103–9.

Stein, Z., and M. Susser. 1969. "Widowhood and Mental Illness." *British Journal of Preventive and Social Medicine* 23:106–10.

Stern, K. et al. 1951. "Grief Reactions in Later Life." *American Journal of Psychiatry* 108:289–94.

Suchman, E. A. 1965. "Social Patterns of Illness and Medical Care," *Journal of Health and Human Behavior* 6:2–16.

—— 1964. "Sociomedical Variations among Ethnic Groups." *American Journal of Sociology* 70:319–31.

Young, M., et al. 1963. "The Mortality of Widowers." *Lancet* 2:454–56.

Zborowski, M. 1952. "Cultural Components in Responses to Pain." *Journal of Social Issues* 8:16–30.

"Re-Grief" Therapy

Vamik D. Volkan

A technique of "re-grief work," short-term psychotherapy for established pathological mourners, was developed at the University of Virginia (Volkan, 1966, [and Showalter] 1968, 1971) as part of a general study on death and grief (Volkan, 1970, 1972a, 1972b). Re-grief therapy is designed to help the patient bring into consciousness some time after the death his memories of the one he has lost and the experiences he had with her, in order to test them against reality, to accept with affect—especially appropriate anger—what has happened, and to free himself from excessive bondage to the dead.

Who Are the Established Pathological Mourners?

Uncomplicated grief may be seen as nature's exercise in loss and restitution. It involves pain, but it is worked through and ultimately resolved, offering no drastic obstruction to the conduct of daily life after an average time of six months. In some persons, however, a death may precipitate recognizably connected mental disturbances the form of which may range from neurosis to psychosomatic distress to psychosis. *Established* pathological grief is, I believe, a clinical entity in its own right. It may be continuous, or it may appear periodically at the anniversary of the death or when a symbolic loss reminds the patient of the death. I consider this diagnosis when, six months or more after a death, I observe an attitude toward the loss indicative of intellectual acknowledgment of its occurrence accompanied by emotional denial as a reflection of a splitting mechanism. The patient has a *chronic hope* (Volkan, 1970) of the dead one's return. The hope to recover the dead is, of course, a manifestation of *initial* reactions to death following the shock, numbness, and disbelief. Thus the established pathological mourner is that person who became fixated in the initial reactions to death and is caught in the struggle of loss and restitution without coming to resolution.

Bowlby and Parkes (1969, 1970) accounted for the mourner's yearning and searching for the dead as an aspect of *attachment behavior,* the kind of clinging to closeness with the mother Bowlby (1969) described as instinctive among all mammals. Engel (1971) offered a critical evaluation of this concept.

Like Parkes (1972), we found our patients eagerly seeking reunion with the dead. However, we had further appreciation of the fear that accompanies such a search, particularly when the quest is still compelling long after the death has taken place. I found this reflection of ambivalence toward the dead person among all of my established pathological mourners; while Parkes suggests its presence as a contributory factor in the formation of pathological reactions, he sees evidence of it as less than definitive.

The preoccupation of the established pathological mourner is intense. It may increase to the point where the thread of daily life is lost. One of our patients, for example, changed his wife's place of burial three times in three years, and was about to effect a fourth change when he came into treatment. These changes, we observed, were reflections of his ambivalence toward the dead wife. She had been an invalid for more than ten years, during which time her husband's conservative code of ethics had required that he remain faithful to her.

I have written elsewhere about the typical dreams of established pathological mourners (Volkan, 1970). The manifest content of these dreams shows the patient's attempt to save or to destroy the deceased, again in a reflection of ambivalence and in a reflection of the obstruction of the grieving process. In established pathological mourners, as I have pointed out, the searching for the dead becomes habitual and specific enough to be called the patient's basic mechanism of defense, a defense mainly against the tension of ambivalence and the eruption of derivatives of those aggressive and libidinal drives originally directed toward the deceased (Volkan, 1972).

The typical established pathological mourner uses the present tense in referring to the dead, even one who has been dead a long time. He either believes in or is fascinated by the concept of reincarnation. He has "peculiar" feelings about the grave of the one he has lost, and it is usual to find that he has never visited it, as if it did not exist. He invests some objects with magical and symbolical powers that permit a link with the dead. In an earlier article (Volkan, 1972), I described how these objects represent a place external to the self in which the mourner can magically accomplish communion with the dead person. By avoiding this place he can reduce the anxiety generated by the thought of such reunion. I called these objects *linking objects*.

Differential Diagnosis

Established pathological mourning should be differentiated from three other conditions: (1) depression (because internalization processes exist in both states); (2) fetishism (because the fetishist as well as the established pathological mourner invests inanimate objects with special properties); (3) schizophrenia (because both the established pathological mourner and the schizophrenic have breaks with reality).

In depression identification with the lost one is total, and thus the conflictual relatedness to the dead is totally internalized. In established pathological mourning, outside of a transient feeling of merging with the dead one, the representation of the deceased stays as if it has a boundary and is felt as if it is buried within the bosom of the one who mourns. Its purpose is to keep contact with the dead internally. By this means the mourner can have "internal conversations" (Volkan, 1972) with the deceased resident in his chest.

The basic function of the fetish used by an adult is to deal with his castration anxiety; by taking it in visually the adult becomes sexually potent. The inanimate object (linking object) of the established pathological mourner deals with separation anxiety, and is a response to castration anxiety only secondarily and infrequently. It is adopted as a response to death, and provides an external contact with the dead.

Although in schizophrenia the break with reality is general, the mechanism of splitting protects the pathological mourner from generalized psychosis. His only breaks with reality are connected directly with the failure to accept the fact that death has taken place.

A Description of Re-Grief Therapy

Since the established pathological mourner is in a state of chronic hope (as well as dread) of reunion with the dead, we help him, during the first phase of this therapy, to make rational distinctions between what actually belongs to himself and what actually belongs to the one he has lost. We have referred to this initial phase of treatment as the "demarcation" phase (Volkan and Showalter, 1968). At this time we ask the patient to bring a picture of the dead person, and ask him to look at it and describe the appearance of its subject. As indicated, the patient is at this time in a "state of contact" with the dead individual—internally by keeping the introject of the deceased; externally through the linking object. The taking of a detailed history initiates the building of "boundaries" between the patient and the representation of the dead at these "contact"points. We conduct our history-taking in non-directive exchange, and we arrive at a formulation as to why the patient would not permit the deceased to die, seeking to understand the patient's dependency on the deceased in the sense that dependency is a general term referring to the wish from every level of psychosexual development, and that the deceased, at least in fantasy, could gratify it had she lived. We explore these areas and offer interpretations if we feel the patient can bear them. The circumstances of the death are also examined carefully. One woman in her late thirties lost her son in an automobile accident and began the course of her grieving. It became complicated, however, by the arrival in her home of a younger sister, who had left her own husband and accused the patient's husband of having an affair with her. The patient had always assumed a protective role toward her younger sister. When we saw her, two years after the loss of her son, the history of this complication led us to interpret to her the interruption that had prevented the completion of her grieving process.

We next focus on the patient's "linking objects." They are not hard to identify. We may ask, "What kind of special token of the dead person do you keep?'' Possibly the patient is aware of it only in a secretive way, but his reply usually points to some highly symbolized object. We must then formulate reasons for the choice of this object. After we know what concepts are condensed in the linking objects, we are able to loosen the points of contact between the patient's self-representation and the representation of the dead person. The linking objects are brought to the therapeutic sessions and the patient is asked to look at and touch them; in short, they are used to stimulate memories, and make the patient aware of the magical ties with the dead. The therapist should never forget that the linking objects are magical for the patient only, and that the way he interprets the patient's use of them will ultimately be of help.

Now more actively, we help the patient to review the circumstances of the death—how it occurred, the patient's reaction to the news and to viewing the body, the events of the funeral, etc. Anger usually appears at this point if the therapy is going well; it is at first diffused, then directed toward others, and finally directed toward the dead. Abreactions—what Bibring (1954) calls ''emotional reliving''—may then take place and demonstrate to the patient the actuality of his repressed impulses. Using our understanding of the psychodynamics involved in the patient's need to keep the lost one alive, we then explain and interpret the relationship that had existed between the patient and the one who died.

Throughout re-grief therapy we encourage the patient to examine his dreams and fantasies. We help him take the responsibility for the negative aspects of his ambivalence—for any death wishes he may have had toward the dead, for example. He is helped to understand the source of his guilt feelings.

We then bombard his splitting mechanism by asking at an appropriate time how he became aware that the dead person was in fact no longer alive. The question will obtain good results if the time is ripe, and if it is not posed as an intellectual exercise. The patient may show genuine surprise, and blurt out, ''I *thought* she had stopped breathing, but I didn't really look!'' We have helped him revisit the point where the splitting occurred, and to reevaluate reality.

It is characteristic of our patients' experience that the funeral rites did not go well. Our findings here suggest the importance of this kind of ritual, among others, and the benefits of full participation in it. Many of our patients had not seen the coffin lowered into the ground. When asked at the proper moment how he knew the interment had taken place, such a patient is likely to surprise himself by the realization that one part of his awareness never did believe that it had been. He is then likely to feel anger at those who stood in the way of his participation in the funeral ceremony. It has been pointed out to him that one part of himself felt and indeed knew that death had occurred, but that another part had continued to behave as though nothing had happened. Disorganization overtakes the patient in this phase, and he may be flooded with primary process thinking. Possibly he may require hospitalization at this point.

The final phase of treatment is reached when the patient sees that he wanted something from the dead, or that the dead represented part of himself. Since most of these patients have not visited the grave, they are asked to do so as part of their treatment, and then examine their feelings about the visit. When possible, the therapist may spend an hour at the grave with the patient. Since they have been denying the death, few such patients have had a tombstone set in place. The therapist encourages them to do so now. He then helps the patient direct his energies toward new objects.

Warnings

Since re-griefing is a short-term therapy, we see the patient four times a week to promote intensity. We need to help the patient avoid the development of a sticky transference neurosis, and must keep gratification of the patient's instinctual demands at a minimum. As the patient evidences a transfer of feelings and attitudes toward the therapist, they are quickly interpreted in order to prevent their ripening. This technique is contrary to the therapist's practice in long-term psychoanalytic treatment.

Obviously, each pathological mourner must be evaluated and a formulation accounting for his inability to grieve at the "normal" time must be made. His capacity to tolerate anxiety, sadness, etc., must also be assessed before introducing him to re-griefing. Since a loss by death in adult life reactivates whatever feelings and attitudes one had concerning earlier losses, special attention should be given to the patient's handling of these in the past, including actual events of loss in childhood as well as the psychic loss of separation from the mother. Established pathological mourners are usually those who have some fixation at the separation-individuation level (Mahler, 1968), and we must examine the degree of difficulty that persists from this level. Once launched on this therapy, some pathological mourners without obvious psychosis or other severe psychopathology may manifest a great degree of fixation instead of regression and/or partial fixations at the symbiotic or early separation-individual level, or narcissistic personality structure. The therapist must be prepared to treat these ''severe'' pathological mourners for a long time, or to make appropriate referrals for them elsewhere.

Re-Grief Work Applied

We have chosen two cases to illustrate the process of re-grief therapy. The first patient is a typical pathological mourner; the second was diagnosed initially as schizophrenic. Although it is possible for established pathological grief to appear on the clinical level as a discrete entity, we soon recognized that its basic symptomatology may be concealed behind the kind of neurotic and psychotic manifestations we are in the habit of attributing to other conditions. In such cases, where the covering clinical states are not highly crystallized and evidences of established pathological grief reaction manifest themselves soon after treatment is begun, we diagnose the patient as having pathological grief and being a candidate for re-grief therapy.

Case #1

One of our patients, Julia, was an educated black secretary in her early thirties who had lived with her mother, a widowed diabetic cripple to whom she had devoted herself for ten years before the older woman died. The mother had been extremely demanding, domineering, critical, and often disparaging and humiliating. As the youngest child, Julia was the only one in the family to have had this ''special'' relationship with the mother, for whose behavior the others had little tolerance. Julia accepted the role of martyr, although it required the surrender of college scholarships and what she considered "good proposals of marriage" and severely limited her social life. She had intensely ambivalent feelings toward her mother, and confessed to having wished often that she were dead. She handled these feelings by reaction formation, telephoning her mother from work three times a day, and sleeping at the foot of her bed by night, awakening from time to time to "make sure that she was still alive." In spite of what she gave up, she, rather than the neglectful brothers and sisters, was the target of her mother's hostility. One might speculate about the genetic aspect of this "special relationship," since when Julia was six months old her mother became bedridden for a year because of severe burns. In frustration the father had begun heavy drinking, and turned to other women. From the age of six to 18 months, Julia had been without an adequately functioning mother, and it is possible that this early disruption of the mother-child unit was reflected in their later relationship and the daughter's need to keep her mother alive after her death.

While Julia's history suggested severe trauma during her separation-individuation period, her siblings had provided mother substitutes. Outside of her sticky relationship with her mother she was capable of forming rather stable object relationships. Thus, we accepted her for re-grief therapy in a hospital setting.

Her initial symptoms at the time she was first seen—eight months after her mother died—included a loss of interest in others, an extreme preoccupation with the mother's image, insomnia, and disturbing dreams. Her mother, undisguised and living, appeared in these dreams, from which Julia awoke in acute anxiety state, feeling that perhaps her mother "might not be gone." Julia maintained a cheerful façade toward others in spite of her distress.

A contract was made with her for goal-limited brief psychotherapy, and 30 therapeutic sessions took place within less than a month and a half. Julia was told that she had not completed the work of grieving and that the goal of her therapy was to help her do so. The first concern was her dreams. In one of them the mother lay in her coffin but attempted to get out; the daughter then dreamed of calling the mortician to give the mother "a shot of something to calm her down." She complained, "These dreams are killing me!" and the therapist was able to interpret her conflictual feelings—torn between wanting to keep her mother alive and wanting to "kill" her.

At the time of her mother's death Julia had been "protected" by sympathetic friends and relatives from facing the reality of her loss. All of her mother's clothing, photographs, etc., had been removed from the home or "hidden" to spare her. She had not viewed the corpse, and she fainted at the funeral as she approached the coffin. She left the cemetery before the casket was lowered. All of these evasions fortified denial of her loss.

She complained of weakness in her legs and trouble in walking, recalling her mother's incapacity. Attempts at identification with the mother were interpreted. She lay in bed all day "like a corpse," and was upset over flowers placed in her hospital room. She was told to bring two pictures of her mother to her therapeutic sessions for demarcation exercises, and did so on the fifth session, but refused to view them until three more hours had been concluded. When she did look at one of them she screamed, "That's her!" and began crying. She refused to face the picture while she cried, since "Mother never cried, not even when Daddy died." She then told in some detail the circumstances of her mother's last two days of life, and her death. After three sessions of demarcation exercises Julia had a genuine abreaction and recalled the last day of her mother's life. She also talked more openly than before of the abusive treatment she had suffered, and was able to verbalize wishing from time to time that her mother were dead.

At this point Julia's dreams about her mother were primarily concerned with running away and attempting to escape the powerful, vindictive parent. Ward nurses reported that she had put aside her cheerful façade and become more overtly depressed and withdrawn. It was learned that a red robe, which Julia with rare self-indulgence had purchased for herself, had been preempted by her mother, who wore it many times throughout her last year of life. It appeared in Julia's most vivid memories of her mother and was now highly charged with symbolic meaning. A sister had hidden it after the death in order to spare Julia's feelings, but the therapist persuaded Julia to bring it to the twelfth session. She brought it in a paper bag, which she had difficulty touching because of her fear of what it contained. She was flooded with feeling when asked actually to touch the garment; when she did so she panicked, screaming, "Let me out of here! I can't stand it!" and ran out of the office. She was asked in later sessions to examine the robe, to describe it, and to verbalize all of the feelings it evoked. During these sessions she displayed further genuine abreaction and wept, giving more details about the day of her mother's death, particularly details connected with the red robe, her linking object.

Again her dreams altered. Now her mother was shrunken, small, and powerless. In one dream she floated in a tiny casket. Julia's nurses observed her getting "worse," and on the ward she seemed anxious and agitated. Therapy then focused on the funeral. Julia discussed it in detail and recalled the minister's sermon, having further abreaction as she did so. She confessed how she had wanted praise at the funeral and how she hoped that protracted mourning would inspire praise and sympathy. The minister had praised her masochistic devotion and wished her luck and happiness in her new freedom; these remarks evoked intense feelings of guilt.

In subsequent sessions she described the funeral at greater length, and reported dreaming of a cemetery in which mourners, her mother among them, looked disappointed at the absence of a grave. In another dream her mother appeared in a wheelchair and Julia pushed her off a cliff, noticing that the old woman did not seem to object.

After 20 sessions, Julia made her first attempts at directing psychic investment toward new objects. She spoke of the possibility of resuming the relationship she had enjoyed with a former suitor. Now she was able to view her mother's picture, and the photograph of the mother's grave we had asked a relative to provide, without apparent anxiety. The photographs and the robe, which had been kept until that time, were returned to her, and she and the therapist looked at advertisements for tombstones in the therapist's office. Although she had arranged for a marker for her father's grave within a month of his death, she had not been able after eight months to order her mother's. She was able now to talk much more realistically than before about the death, and was no longer intensely occupied with thoughts about her mother. She began to leave the hospital for weekends out of town, and reported enjoying herself for the first time in her life. Two sessions later she announced that she had burned the red robe and ordered a tombstone. She also spoke of a dream that reflected the rage that lay within her mourning; in it the therapist appeared with a ring through his nose and another in his ear—she was now making a monkey out of her physician. Her "transferred" anger was then interpreted.

The final step in her re-griefing was a visit to the grave. She had been afraid to return to the cemetery since the burial, and was anxious at first over the proposed visit, doubting that she would be able to go through with it. At the graveside she was encouraged by the therapist's assistant, who had accompanied her there, to associate freely and to verbalize her thoughts about the body within. She was able to talk realistically about it, and seemed quite relaxed within a few minutes. She did not shun stepping on the grave. Pleased with herself, she smiled and commented, "There's nothing to it!" Therapy was then terminated.

Followup: A three-year follow-up showed that the patient was doing well; her established pathological grief symptoms had not returned.

Case #2

Clyde, 36, married, was admitted to the psychiatric service with a diagnosis of paranoid schizophrenia. His symptoms had appeared eight months earlier, when he had become extremely suspicious of his wife. She had just started working outside the home, and he felt that she was involved with another man. He also had a number of somatic complaints and his sleep pattern had undergone significant change. Two months before we saw him the discovery of a yellow spot in the bottom of his coffee cup increased his suspicions and convinced him that his wife was trying to poison him. His family, exhausted by his delusional and physical complaints, arranged for psychiatric care in a hospital setting.

Two weeks after he was hospitalized it was discovered that the appearance of Clyde's symptoms coincided with the accidental drowning of his 15-year-old half-brother. A closer look made it clear that beneath his "schizophrenia" he had an established pathological grief.

His mother had died of melanoma after a lengthy illness when Clyde, the eldest of three children, was 13. Shortly thereafter the father remarried and had three more children. Clyde and a full sister each underwent surgery for melanoma within 11 years of their mother's death, and they lost an aunt to the same disease, so it was not surprising that he reacted to his half-brother's sudden death with great anxiety. Very early in his treatment we understood the connection of his main delusion to his complicated grief. The yellow spot in the coffee cup represented the melanoma, the sign of anxiety, and death; and the coffee stood for the muddy waters in which his half-brother had drowned while fishing.

News of his brother's accident had reached Clyde when he was home alone, putting a stack of records on his turntable. It was several hours before the body of the boy was recovered, and during this interval his brother refused to believe that death had taken place; friends encouraged his hope that all would turn out well. After the body was found and identified, Clyde still could not accept the reality of what had happened.

Since the body had been so long in the water, it was necessary to arrange for the burial quickly. Clyde, the eldest man in the family since the death of his father ten years earlier, was so occupied with funeral plans that he had no time to express his grief. He later described the funeral as a tearless, unemotional affair. He left the cemetery before the body was lowered into the grave, and did not return. Friends accepted the death as being God's will, but Clyde felt anger, which he suppressed, and was hypercritical of himself, saying that he had failed the youngster and that if he had accompanied him the drowning would not have occurred. Obsessed with the boy's image, he continued to speak of him frequently in the present tense.

Clyde's re-grief therapy took place in a hospital setting and lasted a little more than two months. At its start Clyde remembered the repetitive dreams he had had after the death. They involved his diving into muddy water to save his brother, searching unsuccessfully for him. He would awake from them with anxiety. Since the death he was concerned about teaching his children to swim lest they drown in a shallow brook on his property. Soon the therapist learned that Clyde, after his own brush with death, wanted to make sure that he could save himself, and "bargained" (Kubler-Ross, 1969) with the family threat of melanoma by becoming a "good" person—one who did not express anger and who did not question God's will as manifested in the drowning.

Encouraged by the therapist, Clyde talked about his brother during the early sessions. He insisted that he had failed his brother, and expressed strong feelings of guilt about the accident. In his attempt to keep his brother alive he signed up to study electronics with the idea of finishing a television set his brother had been putting together. Again, severe headaches led him to abandon the course.

Early in treatment the therapist tried to learn why Clyde's paranoid ideation was so greatly concerned with his wife. It came out that the brother had called Clyde's home asking for a loan on the day before he died. Clyde's wife had talked to him and refused him the money, which was to have been for the purchase of a car (the couple had previously discussed the boy's reckless driving). Displacement accounted for Clyde's anger, since he saw her as having failed the boy just before he died. An interesting feature of the relationship between husband and wife was his high degree of dependency on her, and his sensitivity to separation from her. The family history of melanoma had led to a realistic sense of caution, exemplified by his protecting his skin from sunlight. When his brother died, Clyde's anxiety about his own death was exacerbated, and the idea of separation from his wife required solution. His delusional system was, in a sense, pushing his wife into divorce, so that he was forestalling the dereliction of the woman he depended on by paradoxically initiating separation himself, on his own terms. These two interpretations of what was going on between man and wife were adhered to by the therapist throughout Clyde's griefwork, and offered for his consideration each time he reintroduced his delusional system about her faithfulness.

Clyde brought his brother's picture to the fourth session. The therapist took it from its envelope and placed it face down before his patient. This practice, customary in re-griefing, grants the patient the initiative of looking at the picture when he is ready. Clyde made no immediate move to examine the photograph. During the interview he reported an incident that helped him toward insight. On the previous day he had spilled coffee on his neck and shirt collar while talking to a medical student on the ward, and jokingly remarked that he was trying to drown himself. The therapist complimented him on the astuteness of his observation, and suggested that he felt the same way about his unexpressed emotions concerning his brother's death, fearing that their expression would end up by drowning *him*. From this point on, Clyde showed an increasing ability to express his angry feelings, and by the end of the hour he stated that his brother had been a ''fat show-off'' who had been stupid in getting himself drowned and making all kinds of complications.

While telling about a dream that had occurred at the end of the first week of re-griefing Clyde had his first abreaction. The affective storm was intense. In it Clyde had seen his eldest son, and the thought ''Kill! Kill!''

came to him. He spontaneously associated the dead brother with his son, and in so doing consciously acknowledged his feelings of aggression toward his brother. Toward the end of the hour he related another dream that he had had shortly after making the contract for re-grief therapy. In this he had been in a dark valley, riding a bicycle. He rode on a wet and slippery road, but was able to hurry along and escape an impending storm. At the end of this session the therapist complimented him on his tolerance of the emotional discharge that had taken place, warned him that the process was not yet over, but encouraged him by saying that the experience of similar feelings might not be so frightening in the future.

The next day there was another dream. Clyde had seen a small man and a tall dark one whose shoes were old and comfortable, with *wrinkles*. Clyde's association to the dream indicated that he was the little man, who had felt humble all his life and who had tried not to provoke trouble such as the melanoma sent by God's will. The tall man represented the therapist. His shoes indicated wide travel, and they had an easy fit. Clyde's shoes were uncomfortable and they fit poorly; he longed for more comfortable ones. After reporting this dream, Clyde began to tell about his first delusion after the drowning. This had led him to believe that the soles of his feet were red and itching because of a powder his wife put in his socks to poison him. Although he had not seen his brother's feet after he drowned, he had seen his hands and had observed that they looked "wrinkled" because the body had been so long in the water. After talking about his foot delusion he made his first attempt to look at the photograph, but was unable to do so. He felt cold; the interpretation of this was that his brother was cold in death. He gave "sighing responses," and declared emotionally, "I wish I could start living again!" The wish to keep contact with the dead brother through internalization of him was interpreted. He was reminded of his earlier dream of "Kill! Kill!" and he had an abreaction.

During the following session he looked for the first time at the picture and exclaimed, "He's dead, and I had nothing to do with it!" He began to cry, and talked about how handsome the brother looked and how unfortunate it was that he had died on the verge of manhood. About this time Clyde's behavior on the ward changed considerably. He gave up reporting his delusional ideas to ward personnel and other patients. He went into what he called a state of grieving, weeping violently, and suddenly becoming angry with the dead boy. During this agitated state he shouted at the introject within his breast several times, saying, ''Leave me alone! Get out! Get out!'' Clyde reported the next day to his therapist that he felt better than at any time during the year just past.

At this point, over a month in therapy, his attention was directed to his receipt of the tragic news and the funeral. He reported a dream in which he was relaxing comfortably in what might have been his own home. There was a knock on the door and a tall woman appeared. He explained to her that he was ''just relaxing—waiting for my brother.'' The tall woman was associated with a next-door neighbor whose house his children frequented. Finding himself alone at home since his brother's drowning, he had felt uneasy, rejected, and emotionally separated from his wife and from the children who so often played next door. When this association was worked out he was able to laugh and to say, ''Here I go again—sour grapes. Yes, I was very mad at my kids who left me alone by going to the neighbor's house.''

The records he was about to listen to when the news of death came had become his linking object. They were brought to the hospital and the patient and his therapist listened to them—the same ones he had not been able to bring himself to listen to or to touch since his brother's death. The experience caused a flood of emotions, and Clyde cried aloud for a long time. The next day he exhibited abortive emotional spells, saying ''Ah-Ah'' but being unable to continue. He finally described a ''weight on his chest'' that he wanted to remove. Then he voluntarily suggested that he and the therapist talk about ''that fellow''—the dead brother. He recalled how reckless the dead boy had been, and how unrealistically he had dreamed of the future. He kept asking his therapist, ''What do you do with a fellow like that? How do you advise him?'' as though his brother were still alive and the questions still in need of solution. At the height of this negative outburst the therapist asked, ''He was a big show-off, wasn't he?'' to which Clyde replied by expressing anger and explaining that it was his brother's recklessness that had led them to withhold money for the car he wanted, and that it was this recklessness that had, in the end, killed him.

Clyde then told of something that had angered him at his brother's funeral. The boy's friends had come from a distance for the funeral, and spoke of seeing the town as soon as the services were over. They rationalized this proposal by saying that the dead boy had so often spoken of a certain part of town that he had awakened their interest in seeing it for themselves. Clyde felt that these mourners were behaving like casual tourists, and that he had been pressed into service as a tour guide even before the coffin was finally put in the ground. The therapist then asked him how he knew that his brother had actually been buried, and reminded him that he was so much preoccupied with his brother's image that he had in effect buried him within his own breast rather than in a grave.

The therapist asked Clyde to get snapshots of the grave for examination at therapeutic sessions. This created a sudden interest in various aspects of the burial—the depth of the grave, the efficacy of the concrete vault, the absence of a marker—all the preoccupations typical of pathological mourning and indicative of anxiety that the dead might rise. Toward the end of the second month Clyde reported a dream in which he had found himself alone at the grave, had lowered the casket containing his brother's body into the vault, and fastened the cover. He had started shoveling dirt into the grave when a second man—probably the therapist—appeared and joined him in his work.

During this time Clyde began trying to reinvest in new objects the attachments withdrawn from the dead brother in the course of re-griefing. He was concerned about improving the relationship with his wife, returning to work, and assuming normal involvements and activities. A sportsman most of his life, he had given up sports after the drowning, but once again he expressed an interest in golf, fishing, and hunting. He reported feeling more relaxed, and his behavior during the interviews bore this out. He voluntarily brought a cup of coffee to one interview, and drank it before the therapist.

Next day he went to a funeral home, in spite of considerable anxiety, and inquired about monuments. At the end of two months of hospitalization he spent a weekend at home with his family and twice visited his half-brother's grave, which he had avoided since the funeral. He also visited his stepmother, and with her decided on a marker to be put on the grave. A few days later he was discharged from the hospital, and his re-grief therapy was at an end.

Followup: Clyde was seen three times during the first year after receiving treatment, twice during the second year, and once during the third. His "psychosis" never returned, nor was he any longer preoccupied with his brother's image. He had gone back to his previous way of life as a rather cautious man. He enjoyed playing golf. He experienced no difficulty with his work, and his relationship with his wife had undergone considerable improvement. His "cure" still holds at the end of a third year.

REFERENCES

Bibring, E. 1954. "Psychoanalysis and the Dynamic Psychotherapies." *Journal of the American Psychoanalytic Association* 2:745 ff.

Bowlby, J. 1969. *Attachment and Loss*. Vol. 1: *Attachment*. London: Hogarth Press.

Bowlby, J., and C. M. Parkes. 1970. "Separation and Loss Within the Family." In *The Child in His Family,* eds. E. J. Anthony and C. Koupirnik, vol. 1. New York: Wiley Interscience.

Engel, G. L. 1971. "Attachment Behavior, Object Relations and the Dynamic-Economic Point of View. Critical Review of Bowlby's *Attachment and Loss*." *International Journal of Psychoanalysis* 52:183 ff.

Kubler-Ross, E. 1969. *On Death and Dying*. New York: Macmillan.

Mahler, M. S. 1968. *On Human Symbiosis and the Vicissitudes of Individuation,* vol. 1. New York: International Universities Press.

Parkes, C. M. 1972. *Bereavement: Studies of Grief in Adult Life*. New York: International Universities Press.

Volkan, V. D. 1966. "Normal and Pathological Grief Reactions—A Guide for the Family Physician." *Virginia Medical Monthly* 93:651 ff.

—— 1970. "Typical Findings in Pathological Grief." *Psychiatric Quarterly* 44:231 ff.

—— 1971. "A Study of a Patient's Re-Grief Work Through Dreams, Psychological Tests and Psychoanalysis." *Psychiatric Quarterly* 45:255 ff.

—— 1972a. "The Linking Objects of Pathological Mourners," *Archives of General Psychiatry* 27:215 ff.

—— 1972b. "The Recognition and Prevention of Pathological Grief." *Virginia Medical Monthly* 99:535 ff.

Volkan, V. D., and C. R. Showalter. 1968. "Known Object Loss, Disturbance in Reality Testing, and 'Re-Grief' Work as a Method of Brief Psychotherapy." *Psychiatric Quarterly* 42:358 ff.

A Technical Device
for the Psychotherapy
of Pathological Bereavement

Arthur M. Arkin and Delia Battin

We shall describe a technique that has seemed useful in the psychotherapy of pathological bereavement. The idea it is based on arose during the course of participation in the research of the Montefiore Hospital Program for the Aged Bereaved and has been employed both in some of our research and private cases. The device might be found useful under one or more of the following conditions:

1. The patient is suffering from pathological bereavement.
2. The patient, following bereavement, is experiencing excessive difficulty in coping with the ordinary demands of living and seems unable to develop an effective psychological posture toward the future.
3. The patient has had the benefit of a reasonable amount of interpretation of and opportunities to work through the significant aspects of the psychological meanings and implications of his or her relationship to the dead person (including such factors as death wishes toward him, beliefs in magical thinking, guilt, self and other reproaches, depression, loneliness, feelings of helplessness and disorganization resulting from loss of an emotionally important and beloved figure, denial in varying

Supported by USPHS Grant #MH 14490 and Grant #93–P–57454–2–01 from the Administration on Aging, Social and Rehabilitation Service, DHEW.

degrees of grief, the fact of the death itself and similar inhibition of the affective expression of grief).

4. The patient has *not* received the above therapeutic procedures, as the therapist has been convinced by clinical experience and assessment that the patient is either unlikely to benefit from them or else undergo a negative therapeutic reaction.

5. Financial and/or time limitations render long-term therapy unfeasible, and the therapist hopes that the recommended device will expedite the treatment.

The rationale of the device will be clearer if preceded by a few considerations and illustrative case material.

It has been documented (Leuba, 1971; Choron, 1964) that beliefs in the survival of personality after death are ubiquitous and well-nigh inextinguishable, despite considerable intellectual knowledge and conviction to the contrary. In certain instances, such nonrational, wishful beliefs are accepted consciously and dwell side-by-side with cognitive systems based on scientific approaches to the problems of life. For example, Leuba reported that of a sample of physicists holding academic posts, 44 percent believed in God and 51 percent in immortality. In other instances, beliefs in post-death survival are consciously disavowed but are nevertheless strongly held unconsciously. Clinical practice provides many opportunities to observe these phenomena.

A case in point is that of a patient in his middle thirties who was compelled to seek treatment when he experienced an outbreak of sustained panic accompanied by expectations of fatal illness, fear of acute insanity, inability to carry out routine duties, and dreams of injury and bleeding to death. His father had died eight months before. Intensive psychoanalytically oriented psychotherapy was undertaken, during the course of which he recounted many memories and fantasies in relation to his father, in which fear, awe, and guilt played a potent role. Much of these were related to worries about keeping intact a large legacy bequeathed to him. Even "paper losses" in the stock market were often sufficient to plunge the patient into a panic. The father had been preoccupied with amassing a fortune and was relentless in forceful commentary that without his money the patient would be helpless, count for nothing in the world, and be valued by nobody; but that with his money, he could buy and control a commanding place in society. The patient was warned repeatedly against permitting depreciation of capital and "gold-digging" women. One gained the impression that the patient believed this uncritically and that the intact legacy was endowed with all of the magical strength and protectiveness his father seemed to have for him while alive—i.e., the legacy seemed like a magical effigy of his father.

Naturally, attempts were made to intervene psychologically in whatever manner seemed most likely to ameliorate the patient's psychopathology. These included confrontation, clarification, interpretation, and opportunities to work through psychological meanings and implications of his relation to his father as well as his self-representations, ego impairments, and so forth. What we wish to focus on here, however, is a specific intervention involving the patient's feeling of guilt toward his father, fear of his retaliation from the grave, and loss of the magical protection and love with which the intrapsychic representation of his father was endowed and incarnated partly in the intact legacy.

First, the therapist pointed out on many occasions that the patient manifestly spoke, felt, dreamed, and lived as if his father were alive somewhere else in the universe, but within striking distance of the patient and closely watchful of his every move. These comments evoked acknowledgment tinged with embarrassment, because of the incongruity between such magical beliefs and contemporary rationality. Furthermore, the wishful, needful, and defensive aspects of this belief were *pari passu* clarified and interpreted; but this work did not result in sufficient expected emotional change and the patient would still say with anxious fervor things like "my father would be furious if he knew" or "If I lost money in an investment on my own, my father would be able to say, 'you see, you *think* you know something but *actually,* you don't.' "

Although the most likely source of factors responsible for the insufficient improvement was unanalyzed transference, the therapist's assessment of the patient, for complicated reasons that cannot be set forth briefly, persuaded him that it would not be feasible to embark upon the lengthy and detailed analysis of the transference resistance that would be required for the problem at hand. Probably because the therapist could think of nothing else, he found himself saying one day, "You know, beliefs in survival of the personality after death in some manner seem ingrained in man. Some of the ablest intellects consciously believe in it, even today. The fact is, nobody knows for sure one way or the other. So let's say for the sake of discussion that your father is still alive somewhere in some manner. If *that* is indeed possible, could it not *also* be possible that, since his death, he has acquired wisdom, a mature sense of values, and charitable and kindly attitudes toward people? He could well have realized that he overvalued money and be regretful that he tormented you so about it. He might even hope that you become more relaxed about money and see it in proper perspective.''

Judging by the patient's intrigued facial expression, the therapist felt that the patient seemed to be impressed by this comment. Following repetitions on other occasions, he was able to acquire a more appropriate affective orientation toward women and became far less anxious. Furthermore, he seemed more accessible to interpretations regarding unconscious death wishes toward his father with attendant guilt and fears of punishment—i.e., he became able to talk more easily about his having wished his father dead.

With another patient, a variant of the device was used: The patient was a professional man in his late fifties, whose wife had died suddenly of a stroke while they were having sexual relations. Subsequently, the patient became troubled with anxiety, insomnia, hyperphagia, uncontrollable weeping, fear of insanity, guilt, and self-reproaches—with a conviction of having killed his wife. Important in the past history were repeated episodes of infidelity and separation—all initiated by the patient. On each such occasion, his wife would finally relent and accept him again. Despite the patient's conscious militant atheism, he came to believe that some force associated with his wife was chastising him. During treatment sessions, he would often repeatedly say, ''My wife is punishing me.'' During the course of therapy, which consisted of weekly sessions for six months, the therapist finally said, ''Suppose your wife were here with you right now, what sort of dialogue might you have?'' He thereupon recited a long list of accusations as if they had come from her, such as ''You have killed me—you've been unfaithful to me—you finally killed me through sex, just what you've been obsessed with.'' The therapist then commented to the effect that, yes, his wife was imagined to utter a long list of reproaches but that inasmuch as she had relented and softened in the past, was it not possible that she would do the same now if she were present—and maybe be even more understanding than ever before? With repetition, within three or four sessions, the patient began to improve and he finally recovered from his acute condition.

Because other events and influences operate in a patient's life, however (and also in his therapy), one is on shaky ground in believing uncritically that this intervention plays a crucially significant role. But this is an ever-present problem in clinical work. There *is* no Wasserman test to evaluate the effectiveness of an intervention in a clinical situation.

Be that as it may, this experience encouraged us to use this approach with other patients whose unresolved acute and chronic problems associated with bereavement apparently had a powerful influence and who fulfilled the criteria described above. We have not been aware of any deleterious effects, and there is usually a variable degree of amelioration as a sequel.

We have outlined an intervention that may be employed in situations that should fulfill specified criteria, where patients are burdened with painful, persistent, unresolved residua attendant upon bereavement. First, the patient's attention is drawn to his stubborn belief in the immortality of his dead relative and informed that such beliefs are ubiquitous; second, the patient is told that for the sake of discussion let us grant that the dead relative may indeed be "alive" in some manner (that nobody knows for certain); but if such a thing is possible, it may also be possible that the deceased may have undergone a personality change for the better, so that he would earnestly approve of the patient's acquisition of mature, reasonable, and benevolent attitudes toward life and toward the memory of the person who died.

This intervention is meant to *supplement,* and not replace, appropriate comments and interpretations with regard to the pain and anxiety of object loss, feelings of guilt, anger toward the dead relative, prior death wishes toward him or her, wishful and magical elements in the patient's psyche, etc.

If we are correct in our impression that the above device may be helpful, it is of interest to speculate about the reasons. First, it is possible that the fantasy of the dead relative being "alive," serene, wise, and charitable may reduce the patient's anxiety about the magical potency of his or her death wishes and may result, therefore, in diminished guilt, remorse, and fears of retaliation. It may also be perceived as permission from the therapist-parent to feel absolved, complete the mourning work in a normal manner, and to live in the present and future untrammelled by unresolved issues toward the dead relative. In addition, it may make it easier for the patient to more fully acknowledge and verbalize the content of his or her hostile attitudes toward the dead.

REFERENCES

Choron, J. 1964. *Modern Man and Immortality*. New York: Macmillan.

Leuba, J. H. 1921. *The Belief in God and Immortality*. Boston. Cited in *On Introduction to the Psychology of Religion,* R. H. Thouless. Cambridge: Cambridge University Press, 3rd ed., 1971.

The "Waiting Vulture Syndrome"

Glen W. Davidson

The Waiting Vulture Syndrome sometimes appears when relatives and staff have processed their initial sense of loss after realizing that a patient will die, but before the patient's demise. The physical symptoms of the Waiting Vulture Syndrome are drooped head, shoulders falling forward, and general exhaustion. The emotional symptoms are despondent affect along with a general sense of "there's nothing more we can do." Sometimes there is evidence of guilt: "We're ready too soon." Relatives and staff who are afflicted with the WV Syndrome appear startled by how quickly they have accepted the reality of a patient's dying and have accommodated themselves to their anticipated loss. Therapeutic intervention is needed in order to restore the patient's sense of dignity and relatives' and staff's sense of propriety.

One of the goals of thanatology is to help us learn how to help patients, relatives, and health care staff members accommodate themselves to the reality of dying and to use the resources of the grieving processes to cope with their loss. Appearance of the Waiting Vulture Syndrome is a sign of both the success and failure of our efforts. It is the sign of success because it indicates that those afflicted have begun to process their sense of loss and have converted "anticipatory grief" into "real grief." It is a sign of failure because it exposes those afflicted to the sense that they have precipitously accommodated themselves to a loss which "feels real," and therefore leads one to assume that "there is no more relationship possible with my loved one," before that loved one dies. Feelings of helplessness ("there's nothing more we can do") are coupled with feelings of guilt ("we're ready too soon").

Case Study

A typical example of Waiting Vulture Syndrome occurred during the illness of Betty, a 43-year-old mother of two. Betty was readmitted to the hospital with advanced cancer of the colon. Exploratory surgery found that her colon was totally blocked and that her cancer was rapidly and widely metastasizing. The patient, like her family, had come into the hospital with the full expectation that whatever it was that was now wrong could be corrected again by some medical procedure. Two previous surgeries had relieved her of cancer symptoms.

The patient was quiet, articulate, and fully in command of her senses. At no time from the point of admission to the hospital until she died was she without the presence of at least one member of her family. To the casual observer, to most of the staff, and to many of her relatives, she had a very strong ego. She played a very strong role in most family affairs. With her husband, however, she had a dependent personality and endured his alcoholism and promiscuity with countless rhythms of martyred feelings, forgiveness, and reconciliation.

When Betty was told that she was inoperable, she responded to the physician with the rhetorical question, "Then that means that this will be my last hospitalization, won't it?" The physician was direct but not tactless in confirming her suspicion. The patient went into shock for a brief period of time, but after a similarly brief period of catharsis, set herself to the immediate task of getting her affairs in order.

Several of the in-laws responded to her initial efforts by running errands, collecting legal papers, and making telephone calls for her. Her husband fled from the hospital upon receiving the physician's diagnosis and was found the following day in a tavern. Her children went into almost immediate shock and had difficulty functioning for more than 48 hours.

Both physicians and nurses sensed that Betty would deteriorate quickly. They conveyed this prognosis to the family and responded in positive and therapeutic ways to the patient's and family's needs. Their behavior could be summed up in the words of the Head Nurse, who said, "I believe we are doing everything possible to make her comfortable."

On the second day following diagnosis, most of the family members came out of their shock and spent their time crying or ventilating in other ways. They would not grieve in front of the patient and took turns being in her room when they were in command of their emotions. The male members of the family had begun to concern themselves with three questions by the end of that day: (1) "Are we doing all that can be done to help her suffering?" (2) "How much more time is there?" and (3) "Is it all right to begin making 'final arrangements'?" To the first question, several of the hospital's staff gave sympathetic encouragement by suggesting things the family could do to help. To the second question, the physicians and staff were noncommittal regarding the precise time that death could be expected, but noted that Betty's physical condition was continuing to deteriorate rapidly. To the third question, the staff encouraged them to "make arrangements" as soon as they felt competent.

On the third day after diagnosis, the patient began a siege of vomiting, and the staff expected her death at any time. The patient's mind remained oriented, but focused on the single concern of how to be comfortable. Between bouts of nausea, the patient from time to time concerned herself with healing ruptures in family affairs and would call estranged members of the family together at the bedside. By the end of the fourth day, the patient seemed ready to die and informed me, "I think all of my business is finished now." The family had, by and large, begun to express their grief less frequently and for shorter periods of time. They had completed legal, financial, and funeral arrangements. As for the physicians, they called several times during the day to see if she were still alive.

On the fifth day, the patient revived dramatically. She had ceased vomiting and was mentally so alert that she reported on the emotional and physical conditions of all her family with the same kind of detail she shared about herself. She was so bright in spirits that she was telling all who would listen, "I think I'll be going home again."

The relatives were physically and emotionally drained by the fifth day. They stood in the hallway and in the patient's room manifesting the physical characteristics of waiting vultures. And they became increasingly angry— first with the patient, then with the staff, and finally with themselves. They expressed their hostilities toward the patient by avoiding eye contact with her, by not responding verbally to her comments and questions, and by long absences from her room. As one of her brothers blurted out, "If she's going to die, why doesn't she go ahead and die? If she's going to live, what are we all standing around here for?'' Then he controlled himself and said, ''I don't really mean that. I want her to live, but not if she's going to be eaten up with cancer some more.'' The family also expressed feelings about how the staff had misled them into thinking Betty was going to die. The staff had even encouraged them to make ''final arrangements.'' Now what would people think of them? What would Betty think of them if she were ever to find out? What were they to think of themselves? They felt guilty and angry with themselves for precipitously acting out their sense of loss when they were told that the patient was dying.

Many of the hospital staff were very uncomfortable with the turn of events. They had expected the patient to continue going through the ''stages all terminally ill patients are supposed to do,'' as the nurses put it. ''Now she's out of synch!'' They were embarrassed by the patient's failure to conform to preconceived ideas of terminal illness and by the relatives' hostility. ''We've thought we were really doing everything we were supposed to.''

By the end of that day, the patient felt estranged, and said so. ''It's as though I've become some sort of pariah. I'm being treated like I'm an object, changed from a person into a thing by my cancer.'' The relatives seemed unable to respond. ''What more can we do, we've done everything we know how to do!'' Thinking they could best support the relatives by agreeing, the staff assured them they *had* done everything they could do.

Therapeutic Intervention

The Waiting Vulture Syndrome was broken by therapeutic intervention in three ways: (1) The patient was encouraged to release most of her relatives from staying continuously at the hospital in order to get a night's sleep. Two of the closest relatives would stay with her through the night. (2) The relatives were encouraged to consider that there were several things that would be needed from them so long as the patient lived—affection and assurance that she wouldn't be abandoned. They were encouraged to hold her hand, massage her legs and arms, brush her hair. (3) Relatives and staff were encouraged, in very small groups, to articulate their frustrations. Both members of the family and the health care staff seemed relieved by discovering that neither side was holding quite the expectations of the other that were assumed.

When the patient died on the eighth day after diagnosis, she died with a sense of ease. Several times during her final hour, she thanked those around her for their presence. She remained conscious until about 15 minutes before her death. The relatives and staff seemed genuine in their self-assessment: "We *did* do everything we could."

Advice of the Bereaved for the Bereaved

Bernard Schoenberg, Arthur C. Carr, David Peretz, Austin H. Kutscher, and Daniel J. Cherico

In the past decade, there has been increasing interest in the investigation of the attitudes and practices concerning dying, grief, mourning, and other issues related to death. Review of the accumulating literature on the topic of death may appear to challenge the idea that it is the "taboo" topic it has been labelled. Nevertheless, as part of a process previously of interest only from the physiological standpoint, the practices surrounding death and mourning require further investigation and clarification. The necessity for elucidation of the area of death and bereavement becomes highlighted by the increasing awareness of the relationship between separation (loss, grief, etc.) and disease processes.

This report represents the results of a survey related to death and mourning which are of special importance, and, hopefully, of help and guidance to those who find themselves in and undergoing bereavement. A multiple choice type of survey was constructed dealing with the following five areas: signs and symptoms of bereavement; guilt and bereavement; what the bereaved should be told by the physician; what the bereaved should be encouraged to do; advice concerning remarriage.

Groups sampled included physicians, clergy, social scientists, and widows and widowers. With the cooperation of the Parents Without Partners organization, 300 widows and widowers throughout the country were polled. Of those approached, 42 percent (125) replied, a return considered extremely favorable in view of the somewhat lengthy questionnaire involved.

Results are based on a compilation of the data obtained from the total group of widows and widowers who responded. It is hoped that the results of this survey will not only provide certain guidelines but also will accelerate recognition of the difficulties and decisions that face the bereaved in their attempts to integrate death, separation, and loss when these occur.

SIGNS AND SYMPTOMS OF BEREAVEMENT

Regarding the appearance of grief before the death of the patient, the bereaved believe that the appearance of symptoms in the bereaved-to-be appear always or frequently 48 percent of the time. Common signs of grief and depression such as loss of appetite and/or weight, sleeplessness, feelings of despair, and feelings of helplessness are described as occurring always or frequently by a substantial percentage of the group.

Approximately 90 percent of the bereaved indicated that dreams of the deceased occur at least sometimes; 39 percent reported that such dreams occur always or frequently. Illusions of the deceased occur at least sometimes, according to 51 percent of the bereaved, although 22 percent believe these illusions never occur.

Over half of the bereaved believe that angry thoughts and feelings toward the deceased never occur; 19 percent believe that guilt feelings occur always or frequently; 67 percent believe that feelings of infidelity occur rarely or never.

That the bereaved will at least sometimes have subjective symptoms similar to the deceased is the opinion of only one-third of the group of widows and widowers.

Sexual symptoms in the bereaved (diminished sexual desire, impotence, and greater inclination toward masturbation) are reported relatively rarely by the bereaved respondents. For example, only 32 percent expect impotence to occur at least sometimes; diminished sexual desire is expected by 58 percent to occur at least sometimes—but 38 percent expect that it rarely or never occurs.

GUILT AND BEREAVEMENT

Guilt is always or frequently less likely when there has been free expression of feelings between the dying person and the "bereaved-to-be," according to 69 percent of the bereaved. Approximately 60 percent expect that the bereaved will rarely or never experience guilt under the circumstances of beginning to function on his or her own, accepting the inevitability of the death and then beginning to take up old or new interests once more. When more specific questions are asked concerning putting away pictures of the deceased, having renewed interest in members of the opposite sex, and deciding to remarry, over half of the bereaved group expects there will rarely or never be such guilt feelings. They do not, however, anticipate early experiences of pleasure in the bereavement state—only 19 percent expect it within a few weeks after the death occurs.

WHAT THE BEREAVED SHOULD BE TOLD BY THE PHYSICIAN

It is always or frequently important to advise the bereaved how often the dying face death with serenity (according to 41 percent of the bereaved respondents) and 78 percent feel that such advice is at least sometimes important. One-third of the group feels that bereaved individuals should always be made aware of the patient's right to die, although 12 percent believe this should never be the case. More than 58 percent of the bereaved believe that the practitioner should always advise the bereaved in detail that everything possible was done for the deceased.

More than half of the bereaved group feel that physicians should encourage the bereaved to think that he will experience less fear of future tragedies following the current loss. Approximately three-fourths tend to feel that emphasis should be placed at least sometimes on the bereaved's being fortunate to have a child by the departed spouse, if that is the case.

WHAT THE BEREAVED SHOULD BE ENCOURAGED TO DO

On the subject of seeking care and advice, 72 percent of the bereaved feel that regular visits to the physician during the first year should be encouraged at least sometimes; there is strong agreement that the bereaved should not be

hospitalized for an elective procedure soon after or during the course of bereavement. More than two-thirds suggest that the bereaved seek advice at
least soon after the funeral; however, only 29 percent suggest that such advice should, at the least, be considerable, and more than half prefer that it be
minimal. The group of bereaved suggests turning to a clergyman (27 percent), a lawyer (25 percent), and a physician (21 percent). When the
bereaved is religiously inclined, 79 percent of the widows and widowers
suggest that at least sometimes he should be urged to attend religious services on the day(s) which have special significance with regard to the deceased. More than 74 percent agree that psychiatric advice would be of
benefit at least sometimes, and 65 percent feel that this would also be true of
vocational guidance at this time.

Over 88 percent of the bereaved feel that expression rather than repression
of feelings, and crying, should be encouraged at least sometimes. Almost
half feel that repression of distressing memories should rarely or never be
encouraged. They favor encouraging the bereaved to speak about the recent
bereavement: 87 percent agree that the bereaved should be encouraged to
talk to old friends at least sometimes; 92 percent encourage talking with
someone who has had a similar experience at least sometimes; nearly all encourage the bereaved to talk to someone about feelings related specifically to
the deceased.

Over half of the widows and widowers favor keeping the deceased's
wedding ring permanently. As to various other personal belongings of the
deceased, there seems to be general agreement: keep some, give some to
family or friends, give some to a charity. Promises made by the bereaved to
the deceased during life should be followed if practical and reasonable, but
hardly any bereaved indicated that such promises should be followed if not
practical. The bereaved should always or frequently be encouraged to relinquish excessive attachments to the deceased, according to 72 percent of the
bereaved respondents.

It was predominantly felt that at least sometimes the person in grief
should obtain a pet, seek a companion (if elderly), travel, go shopping,
change jobs if he or she had long wanted to do so, move to a new living
location, or seek vocational guidance. They are also predominantly in favor
both of continuing old hobbies and beginning new ones at this time. About
half would encourage the bereaved to resume work within a week, and

three-quarters within two weeks. Some 14 percent would encourage a return to work only when the bereaved feels up to it. More than 78 percent indicate that at least sometimes this might be a time to encourage the bereaved to change jobs, if this had been his or her long-time desire. More than 90 percent see working as frequently or always being good for the bereaved—of those, nearly two-thirds emphasized "always." Many (37 percent) suggest that the bereaved always or frequently make major decisions as early as possible.

ADVICE CONCERNING REMARRIAGE

An impressive majority of the widows and widowers—92 percent—indicated that the bereaved should be encouraged to remarry if age permits; 78 percent regard remarriage as the major problem of the young bereaved spouse. That those who have loved deeply and satisfyingly tend to remarry more quickly is the opinion of 59 percent of the bereaved. However, 63 percent feel that it is not desirable to encourage the bereaved to make the decision whether or not to remarry before a particular person is considered, and 80 percent also feel that it is not desirable to inform relatives and in-laws of a decision to remarry before a particular person is considered.

DIFFERENCES BETWEEN ADVICE RECEIVED FROM THE BEREAVED AND FROM PHYSICIANS

There appears to be general agreement between the group of widows and widowers and the physicians, who were also surveyed, concerning attitudes toward death and mourning, although some differences can be noted.

It is relevant to consider what factors may have influenced those differences which appear most consistently (namely, appearance of signs and symptoms of bereavement), since both groups represent, in a sense, "experts" who have had either personal or professional knowledge of the bereaved state. It may be that physicians' impressions are dependent upon experience with bereaved persons who have chosen to turn to a physician for help or whose reactions are so intense as to require medical assistance.

On the other hand, the differences may testify to the lack of understanding and the need for education on the part of both groups concerning what occurs during bereavement. Physicians might develop greater sensitivity as to what the bereaved expect, seek, and find acceptable to themselves in this most critical period. The lay public, which includes the bereaved and those who are involved with them, also should be educated as to what bereavement entails. More open recognition of the difficulties and decisions present, including the necessity of dealing with feelings that are difficult to tolerate at the time because they appear inconsistent with the loss, might help all individuals in their attempts to integrate death, separation, and loss when these occur. It is hoped that the results of this survey will contribute data in this direction.

Index

Compiled by Lucia Bove

Contributors

Major Clara L. Adams, R.N., M.S., Assistant Chief, Department of Nursing, Kimbrough Army Hospital, Fort Meade, Maryland

Gerald Adler, M.D., Project Investigator, New England Medical Center Hospital, Clinical Unit of Tufts-New England Medical Center, Boston, Massachusetts

Arthur M. Arkin, M.D., Adjunct Attending Psychiatrist, Psychiatry Division, Montefiore Hospital and Medical Center, Bronx, New York

Margaret Kelley Arroyo, R.N., Philadelphia, Pennsylvania

Delia Battin, M.S.W., Chief Psychiatric Social Worker, Department of Social Medicine, Montefiore Hospital and Medical Center, Bronx, New York

John W. Bedell, Ph.D., Chairman, Department of Sociology, California State University, Fullerton, California

Morton Beiser, M.D., Project Investigator, New England Medical Center Hospital, Clinical Unit of Tufts-New England Medical Center, Boston, Massachusetts

Lucia Bove, Editorial Associate, The Foundation of Thanatology, New York, New York

Phyllis Caroff, D.S.W., Associate Professor, Hunter College School of Social Work, New York, New York

Arthur C. Carr, Ph.D., Professor (Medical Psychology), Department of Psychiatry, College of Physicians and Surgeons, Columbia University, New York, New York; Member, Executive Committee, The Foundation of Thanatology

Ned H. Cassem, M.D., Associate Professor, Department of Psychiatry, Harvard Medical School; Department of Psychiatry, Massachusetts General Hospital, Boston, Massachusetts

Jean M. Chalmers, Department of Psychiatry, College of Medicine, University of Florida, Gainesville, Florida

Paula J. Clayton, M.D., Director of Training and Research, Malcolm Bliss Mental Health Center, State of Missouri Department of Mental Health, St. Louis, Missouri

Daniel J. Cherico, Ph.D., Assistant Professor, Queensborough Community College, Bayside, New York

Rosanne Cole, M.S.W., Project Social Worker, New England Medical Center Hospital, Clinical Unit of Tufts-New England Medical Center, Boston, Massachusetts

Shirley J. Conroy, Department of Psychiatry, College of Medicine, University of Florida, Gainesville, Florida

Bruce L. Danto, M.D., Director, Suicide Prevention Center, Herman Keiffer Hospital, Detroit, Michigan; Associate Professor, Department of Psychiatry, Wayne State University, Detroit, Michigan

Glen W. Davidson, Ph.D., Chief of Thanatology and Associate Professor in Psychiatry; Chairman, Department of Medical Humanities, Southern Illinois School of Medicine, Springfield, Illinois

Rose Dobrof, M.S.W., Assistant Professor, Hunter College School of Social Work, New York, New York

Patricia B. Farris, Department of Psychiatry, College of Medicine, University of Florida, Gainesville, Florida

Irwin Gerber, Ph.D., Head, Social Research Unit, Department of Social Medicine, Montefiore Hospital and Medical Center, Bronx, New York

Lee Johnston, Ph.D., Project Psychologist, New England Medical Center Hospital, Clinical Unit of the Tufts-New England Medical Center, Boston, Massachusetts

Melvin J. Krant, M.D., Director, Oncology Unit, Lemuel Shattuck Hospital, Tufts Medical Center, Boston, Massachusetts

Austin H. Kutscher, D.D.S., Associate Professor and Director, New York State Psychiatric Institute Dental Service, School of Dental and Oral

Surgery, Columbia University, New York, New York; President, The Foundation of Thanatology

Lillian G. Kutscher, Publications Editor, The Foundation of Thanatology, New York, New York

Jeffrey C. Lerner, M.A., Doctoral Candidate, Columbia University, New York, New York

Alan Lyall, M.D., Community Resource Service, Clarke Institute of Psychiatry, Toronto, Canada

David Maddison, M.D., Dean of the Faculty of Medicine, University of Newcastle, New South Wales, Australia

Robert E. Markush, M.D., Center for Epidemiological Studies, National Institute of Mental Health, Rockville, Maryland

Marta Ochoa, M.S.W., Psychiatric Social Worker, Washington Heights Inwood Mental Health Clinic, New York, New York

C. Murray Parkes, M.D., The Tavistock Institute of Human Relations; St. Christopher's Hospice, London, England

David Peretz, M.D., Assistant Clinical Professor, Department of Psychiatry, College of Physicians and Surgeons, Columbia University, New York, New York; Editor-in-Chief, *The Journal of Thanatology;* Member, Executive Committee, The Foundation of Thanatology

Elsa Poslusny, R.N., M.S., Associate Professor, Department of Nursing, Faculty of Nursing, College of Physicians and Surgeons, Columbia University, New York, New York

Elizabeth R. Prichard, M.S., Director of Social Service, The Presbyterian Hospital in the City of New York, New York

Joseph R. Proulx, Ph.D., Assistant Professor, School of Nursing, University of Maryland, Baltimore, Maryland

Beverley Raphael, M.D., Department of Psychiatry, University of Sydney, New South Wales, Australia

W. Dewi Rees, M.D., London, England

Paul C. Rosenblatt, Ph.D., Department of Family Social Science and Psychology, University of Minnesota, Minneapolis

Bernard Schoenberg, M.D., Associate Dean, College of Physicians and Surgeons, Columbia University; Professor, Department of Psychiatry, College of Physicians and Surgeons, Columbia University, New York, New York; Chairman, Executive Committee (Medical Affairs), The Foundation of Thanatology

John E. Schowalter, M.D., Professor of Psychiatry and Pediatrics, Yale Child Study Center, Yale University School of Medicine, New Haven, Connecticut

John J. Schwab, M.D., Professor and Chairman, Department of Psychiatry, University of Louisville, Louisville, Kentucky

Ellen L. Shwartzer, M.S.W., Social Worker Adult Surgical Service, The Presbyterian Hospital in the City of New York, New York

Victor W. Sidel, M.D., Chief, Department of Social Medicine, Montefiore Hospital and Medical Center, Bronx, New York

Phyllis R. Silverman, Ph.D., Lecturer, Department of Psychiatry, Harvard Medical School, Boston, Massachusetts

Sam M. Silverman, Ph.D., Lexington, Massachusetts

Joseph H. Smith, M.D., Chairman, The Forum on Psychiatry and the Humanities of the Washington School of Psychiatry; Editor, *Psychiatry and the Humanities;* Teaching Analyst, The Washington Psychoanalytic Institute; Associate Clinical Professor of Psychiatry, George Washington University, Washington, D.C.

Margot Tallmer, Ph.D., Assistant Professor, Department of Psychology, Hunter College, City University of New York, New York

Mary Vachon, B.S., M.A., Community Resource Service, Clarke Institute of Psychiatry, Toronto, Canada

Vamik D. Volkan, M.D., Professor of Psychiatry, University of Virginia Medical Center and Director of Psychiatric Inpatient Services, University of Virginia Hospital, Charlottesville, Virginia

Thomas C. Welu, M.P.H., Ph.D., Suicidologist, San Francisco, California

Alfred Wiener, M.D., Attending Psychiatrist, Psychiatry Division, Montefiore Hospital and Medical Center, Bronx, New York

Rose Wolfson, Ph.D., Coordinating Supervisor of Training (Psychology); Clinical Associate Professor of Pediatrics (Psychology), New York Medical College, New York, New York